The Unwanted Europeanness?

The Unwanted Europeanness?

—

Understanding Division and Inclusion in Contemporary Europe

Edited by
Branislav Radeljić

DE GRUYTER

ISBN 978-3-11-068415-5
e-ISBN (PDF) 978-3-11-068421-6
e-ISBN (EPUB) 978-3-11-068425-4

Library of Congress Control Number: 2020945571

Bibliographic information published by the Deutsche Nationalbibliothek
The Deutsche Nationalbibliothek lists this publication in the Deutsche Nationalbibliografie;
detailed bibliographic data are available on the internet at http://dnb.dnb.de.

© 2021 Walter de Gruyter GmbH, Berlin/Boston
Cover image: Punnarong/iStock/Getty Images Plus
Typesetting: Integra Software Services Pvt. Ltd.
Printing and binding: CPI books GmbH, Leck

www.degruyter.com

Contents

Preface and Acknowledgements

Can we be optimistic about the future of Europe? More than trying to provoke sarcasm and negative emotions, this question is an invitation to reconsider the current concerns and imagine their impact on future developments. The examination of Europe as a whole or the European Union and its relations with both European and non-European neighbors is rarely straightforward. This means that credible conclusions and accompanying decision-making depend on careful examination of both specific phenomena (such as individual crisis and policies) and a larger picture (such as longer trajectories as the result of major geopolitical shifts). Accordingly, while some of the available analyses tend to speculate and suggest what needs to be done in order to overcome problems, some others go as far as to claim that the Brussels administration and the individual European leaderships have failed to consolidate the European integrationist project, seeing its collapse as the most probable outcome. As we have witnessed, every crisis and consequent evaluations have inspired individual member states to point the finger and use the momentum to discredit one another, rightfully or not, thus contributing to the debate about fragmentation of the EU. They have expressed strong feelings and disagreements concerning Brexit, the powerful role of Germany, the alleged lack of responsiveness from the Mediterranean region, the Europeanization fatigue of the Central and Eastern European members, the (im)possible democratization and EU accession of the Western Balkans, and so on. In any case, past events have shaped present political and socioeconomic cooperation (or its deficiencies) and there is no reason to believe that present challenges will not influence future arrangements at supranational or intergovernmental level, and between the EU or its individual members and the states on the outskirts (in the case of enlargement). Whichever the period, the question of belonging and the (un)wanted Other has penetrated discussions; while the very notion of otherness has often been associated with migration and the potential threat stemming from the growing influx of immigrants, refugees, and asylum seekers, the Other has also come from within, in the form of proper states or regions, some of which often referred to as semi-periphery.

This volume brings together a diverse group of researchers interested in Europe's past, present, and future, all trying to shed light on the understanding of Europeanness and the position of those who may, at times or continuously, be viewed as the Other. It starts by reviewing some of the dominant arguments in the field, altogether suggesting that the EU has struggled with the development of a joint position, required in order to speak with a single voice and convey clear messages about crucial matters. Such a deficiency has surely affected its credibility, not only among its own member states, but also in the wider context, beyond the EU's official borders. Here, by looking at a range of challenges, the focus is on the gap between the EU elites and ordinary people or public intellectuals, as well as between the so-called core and (semi-)periphery, which in return has implied

https://doi.org/10.1515/9783110684216-202

more consideration of intergovernmental rather than supranational ways forward. While such shifts do serve certain policy agendas, they simultaneously open questions concerning the so much spoken about European unity or solidarity, and the subsequent opening to external interferences, either cultural or geopolitical. As also observed, such a context has been accompanied by the emergence of political alternatives and escalation of political polarization, with a number of political parties and elected establishments seeking to consolidate their EU-skeptic popular support through the exploitation of the Other and unwanted Europeanness.

Following the introductory reflections, the volume is broadly divided into two parts. The first part reminds us of some truly relevant evaluations. Jan Květina examines Jean Jacques Rousseau's involvement in the debate about the collapsing Polish state, which he joined with his last political work *Considerations on the Government in Poland.* While this work is often ignored when considering Rousseau's political thinking (and this is largely due to the uncertainty concerning Rousseau's interest in the Polish matters), its main controversy derives from the author's message, which is in stark contrast with the general body and arguments of his well-known political writings. In his conclusion, Rousseau urged Poles not to change their traditional yet problematic constitution, maintaining that it was its very essence that had actually shaped the Polish nation to be what it was – a preference indirectly suggesting that later Rousseau might have become an open advocate of hierarchical status quo. Going forward, Marius-Mircea Mitrache looks at the process of mental mapping of East-Central Europe and the French interest in the region in the late nineteenth and early twentieth centuries. Back then, some scholars, including several eminent geographers, maintained that the milieu goals of French foreign policy were inextricably linked to East-Central Europe. However, it was only during the First World War, in the aftermath of the collapse of Czarist Russia, that the French leadership started to perceive nations of the region as potential allies. As it happened to be the case, during the Paris Peace Conference, the junction between the scholarly expertise and the new French diplomatic ambitions came to view East-Central Europe not only as a mental map for French foreign policy milieu goals, but also as a geopolitical representation of possibilism.

Moving to a different region, Jasmin Hasanović looks at the complex relationship between Europeanization and Balkanization, and the auto-colonial narrative in Bosnia and Herzegovina. While having in mind the often pejorative (mis)perceptions of the Balkans, he shows how the negative imagination of the region formed an important spatial identity, which operates as the otherness representing the essential inferiority and alienation in the discourse of the geopolitical core. Accordingly, the progressiveness of Europeanization and the repressiveness of Balkanization are to be enlightened as inseparable ideological artefacts of the post-socialist Bosnia and Herzegovina's political and social realty, as well as in most of the (Western) Balkan countries. This theoretical insight contributes to identifying their local materialization as a form of auto-colonialism, symbolically significant for decomposing of the former Yugoslav state. By being aware of the available pluralities and of the friend-enemy line, and thus the colonial narrative that places the Balkans beyond the political consideration alone, the author seeks to draw possibilities for alternate, counter-hegemonistic, narratives arising out of the liminality of the Balkans. The dilemma about belonging or the complex relationship between Europeanization and anti-Europeanization is also featured in Kürşad Ertuğrul's debate about Turkish coming to represent the incomplete Other of the center. He argues that while Turkey's early application for the then European Community membership was seen as necessary by the ruling elites, the whole process has regularly been countered by a conservative backlash emphasizing the Ottoman heritage, the relevance of Islam, and the so-called Turkish authentic culture. Interestingly, even the modernist Turkish left was critical of the European project emphasizing its imperialist character and has supported the conservative assertion of the historical and cultural difference of Turkish society. More recently, with the Justice and Development Party in charge, Turkey has experienced different forms of authoritarianism, altogether reasserting Turkish differences and making its relationship with Europe an eternal suspense.

The first part rounds off with William Jay Risch's evaluation of the role the European Union played as a symbol in mobilizing popular protest and opposition to protest in Ukraine's Euromaidan Revolution. As argued, Euromaidan supporters at home and abroad viewed the protests as a European rebirth, as a spiritual and national awakening. Their opponents, both at home and abroad, saw Europe poisoning relations with Russia and dividing Ukraine. The uprising in Kyiv produced what seemed to be a civil war as protesters and security forces exchanged fire with each other on Independence Square (the Maidan), and in provincial cities like Lviv, crowds ransacked administrative buildings and even seized weapons (or claimed to have done so). The so-called Russian Spring, while coordinated and manipulated by Russia, was at first a spontaneous protest of the bloodshed in Kyiv, which Europe was responsible for provoking. The armed seizure of power in Crimea and the Donbas unleashed hatred and fear of pro-Russian forces, threatening to destroy Ukraine's European integration aspirations and the Ukrainian state itself. In the years that followed, seizing administrative buildings, a practice of Euromaidan protesters, became a legitimate act of political protest. Instead of upholding the rule of law and the principles of nonviolent protest, the Euromaidan Revolution thus became a national tragedy suggesting the EU's limitations in transforming the post-Soviet sphere.

The second part of the volume is concerned with a number of ongoing processes. To begin with, Lia Tsuladze examines how the idea of Europe and Georgians' Europeanness is invented and reinvented through the political, intellectual, and population's discourses. They reveal Georgians' ambivalent views regarding pragmatic considerations and identity concerns related to the country's Europeanization; both elite and popular discourses construct an EU that improves the protection of human rights in Georgia concurrently doubting that Georgians need to be taught human rights because of their natural tolerance. In addition, these discourses present the EU as Georgia's security guarantee and doubt that the EU can really safeguard the country against Russian threats. Also, both discourses assume that Georgia shares European values and are concerned that European values might threaten Georgian traditions. The question of values and complexities concerning the wanted and unwanted aspects of European integration are also at the core of Biljana Vankovska's analysis of Macedonia's EU path. From its onset, the EU accession process has been a means rather than an objective goal: troublesome states in the region (including Macedonia) were meant to be civilized and pacified after the Yugoslav imbroglio – yet not necessarily fully integrated. Up to 2019, the so-called name dispute with Greece served as a good excuse for the long drawn out process; once the Prespa Agreement was signed and Macedonia renamed to North Macedonia, Euro-optimists have come to believe that all the obstacles have disappeared. However, the October 2019 EU summit uncovered a deep-rooted lack of enthusiasm; while the Brussels elite has used different mechanisms to incentivize and legitimize the state-building process in its near neighborhood, the end result is a series of stabilitocracies that live in a geopolitical limbo.

The Albanian matters are discussed in two chapters. First, Migena Pengili questions whether or not Albania can actually Europeanize. Its recent past, including the domestic uncertainties caused by violent political developments and the incapacity of the political elite to manage the local election processes, suggests that Tirana's readiness to join the EU is a matter of serious concern. Still, given that the net advantages of EU membership are beyond question, and also given the fact that the Europeanization logic about one size fitting all does not always work, the author argues that the European stakeholders should be prepared to act as mediators, so that the Albanian state could eventually move ahead. A Europeanized Albania is a strategic necessity not only because of its location, but also its impact on the future standing of the Western Balkans and the region's subsequent impact on the EU. Second, Leandrit Mehmeti is interested in Kosovo's EU perspective. He addresses the role of governments in Kosovo and Serbia, as well as different EU institutions, in the understanding and development of EU integration and enlargement challenges. More precisely, the chapter looks at corruption and state capture as obstacles to successful democratization, the expected outcomes of the normalization process between Belgrade and Prishtina, and wider geopolitical considerations closely related to Kosovo's (in)stability. While acknowledging the cruciality of the EU in the region, the EU's approach is in need of major adjustments, largely because of the emerging geopolitical challenges; in fact, the more the Brussels leadership sticks with the current model, the higher the risk of seeing the region opt for alternative geopolitical arrangements, with potentially unfavorable consequences.

The second part ends with another chapter on Turkey, which is surely insightful when approaching other cases of EU accession. Elif Uzgören discusses how Turkey's course is analyzed in the European studies literature, as well as how the Turkish EU membership is studied in the context of crises and the rise of populism. As argued, in contrast to the dominant theoretical explanations that have rarely managed to shed light on future prospects, the critical political economy approaches are truly important since they help us to examine European trends within the structural tendencies largely defined by globalization and neoliberalism. As such, they provide us with useful tools in order to challenge the existing power relations and welcome alternative socio-economic options. In the author's view, integration and enlargement decisions are not outcomes of economic or market necessity but are determined by class struggle, and with this in mind, it is difficult to predict future developments. Moreover, EU accession is not a priority for the Turkish political establishment; while the 2000s were characterized by reforms and negotiations with the EU, since the 2010s, the overall environment has changed and the relations between Ankara and Brussels further deteriorated. In fact, Turkey is seen as moving away from the EU.

The volume finishes with Zuzana Lučkay Mihalčinová's thought-provoking reflection on the question of dignity in Europe. While stressing that the EU is definitely going through a difficult time, stretched between various political forces who wish to see it vanish and those clearly passionate about the European integrationist project and thus hoping for its survival. While creating unions of humans where sharing, communication, and mutual support seem rational and also logical, the obsession with unwanted Europeanness and its participation in a strategic coalition seems ludicrous. However, as insisted, we are still short-sighted; geographical facts, past experiences, and scientific evidence are too often ignored vis-à-vis politics and policymaking. Looking at the EU framework, this chapter argues that regaining human dignity is impossible; while according to different human right provisions, human dignity cannot be lost and it is inviolable, the problem we are confronted with is that the very concept of human dignity appears too elusive. It is an abstract notion which is either too complex for many people to grasp or considered too abstract to have practical impact, or, in fact, both. Accordingly, in her remarks, Lučkay Mihalčinová addresses the differences between human dignity and the applicable, descriptive dignity, the understanding of which is likely to clarify the conflicting nature of Europeanness.

The contributing authors deserve a major recognition by the editor, as without their ideas, hard work, and timely submissions, this volume could not have been possible. Some portions of their research and fresh conclusions have already been presented and appreciated at various international conferences and workshops. With this in mind, Emanuel Crudu and his team deserve a special mention for providing a platform where different opinions about Europe interact and for putting the editor in touch with some of the contributors. In addition, it is a pleasure to thank Stefan Giesen, senior acquisitions editor for De Gruyter, and two members of his team, Lucy Jarman and Natalie Wachsmann, for their advice and support from the very beginning to the finishing line. Also, it is important to thank the anonymous reviewers for providing valuable comments on earlier versions of the chapters and the collection as a whole.

Branislav Radeljić

1 The Threatening Other or Very Own? EU Drawbacks and the Politics of Self-Undoing

There are two ways for an intellectual to betray at present, and in both cases he betrays because he accepts a single thing – that separation between labor and culture. The first way is characteristic of bourgeois intellectuals who are willing that their privileges should be paid for by the enslavement of the workers. They often say that they are defending freedom, but they are defending first of all the privileges freedom gives to them, and to them alone. The second way is characteristic of intellectuals who think they are leftist and who, through distrust of freedom, are willing that culture, and the freedom it presupposes, should be directed, under the vain pretext of serving a future justice. In both cases the profiteers of injustice and the renegades of freedom ratify and sanction the separation of intellectual and manual labor which condemns both labor and culture to impotence.

Albert Camus, speaking at Uppsala University, after he was awarded the Nobel Prize in Literature (Camus 1957)

Back in the 1980s, Paul Kennedy assessed the then context and a number of future dilemmas; while expressing admiration for the European Community's soft and hard power achievements, he also pointed out to the obvious disunity and possible economic stagnation and eventual downturn. In his own words, "Europe remains an enigma. If the European Community can really act together, it may well improve its position in the world, both militarily and economically. If it does not – which, given human nature, is the more plausible outcome – its relative decline seems destined to continue" (Kennedy 1987, 488). In fact, when the Cold War, being the longest extent of peace in European history, came to an end, the number of questions and possible uncertainties in Europe increased. Indeed, Jacques Derrida was right to observe that "[h]ope, fear and trembling are commensurate with the signs that are coming to us from everywhere in Europe, where, precisely in the name of identity, be it cultural or nor, the worst violences, those that we recognize all too well without yet having thought them through, the crimes of xenophobia, racism, anti-Semitism, religious or nationalist fanaticism, are being unleashed, mixed up, mixed up with each other, but also, and there is nothing fortuitous in this, mixed in with the breath, with the respiration, with the very 'spirit' of the promise" (Derrida 1992, 6). With all these issues in mind, it was obvious that the signing of the Treaty of Maastricht in 1992 and consequent consolidation of the European integrationist project, would be accompanied by challenges of a political and socioeconomic nature, altogether likely to require reconsideration of policy preferences in order to ensure progress and well-being across Europe. Moreover, the failure to pursue just steps and please individual member states' leaderships and their respective publics was seen as potentially detrimental, as it could incentivize exploration of alternatives or new external penetration, clearly facilitated by global multipolarity and redefining of geopolitical aspirations.

https://doi.org/10.1515/9783110684216-001

For example, while imagining the unity and optimal performance of the post-Maastricht EU, Paul Taylor talked about "an apparent paradox: that, on the one hand, pressures toward an increasing centralization of arrangements under the heading of political and monetary union seemed to have increased . . ., whilst, on the other hand, a number of members, most obviously Spain, Portugal and Greece, even the new Germany, were obviously using the Community to develop their sense of their own identity as separate states . . . [N]o member government had shown any inclination in specific terms to abandon its sovereignty" (Taylor 1993, 80). Other scholars argued that "the EU lacks an unambiguous, clearly defined aim" (Middlemas 1995, 672), calling it "an animal in motion, whose destination . . . is not fixed;" as insisted, the EU is "a strange creature, a kind of hybrid" whose evolution "has been a paradoxical business" (McAllister 1997, 7–8). Equally, if not more, alarming was the criticism according to which the EU had "no real capacity to predict crises and no forward contingency planning for crises" (Mayhew 1998, 106). As witnessed, by the end of the decade, the Brussels authorities had already exposed their weaknesses and policy discrepancies in the case of the former Yugoslavia, both during the very outbreak of the crisis and the consequent treatment of the post-Yugoslav space. While prioritizing the recognition of Croatia and Slovenia as independent states in early 1992, they ignored the warnings that such a move would actually result in conflict intensification in the neighboring Bosnia and Herzegovina, eventually witnessing the worst atrocity in Europe since the end of the Second World War (Radeljić 2012). Moreover, although they had identified and placed the blame for the Yugoslav drama on the Serbian leader Slobodan Milošević, both Brussels and Washington kept welcoming him as their key negotiator and thus helped him to preserve his hold on power, regardless of his detrimental policies at home; it was only with the escalation of the long-disregarded Kosovo crisis in the late 1990s that the same West decided that the moment to get rid of Milošević had come (Spoerri 2015).

In the new millennium and, more relevantly, in the context of the 9/11 terrorist attack on the United States, some scholars found it appropriate to speculate about American decline and its leadership position being taken over by Europe. For example, Charles Kupchan criticized the Americans for "thinking too traditionally" and thus misinterpreting the reality: "As a result, they fail to appreciate that a collective Europe is next in line – even though it is rising before our eyes . . . America must figure out just what this new entity is – and start taking it seriously – if the country if to get right its new map of the world" (Kupchan 2003, 132). Such a perception was contradicted by some other analyses maintaining that there was no real reason for panic: "The EU is populous, but senescent. Its economy is large but sluggish . . . It is a successful but still insufficiently liberal customs union . . . And as a political entity it seems likely to remain confederal for the foreseeable future . . . [A] common foreign and security policy seems a remote and perhaps unattainable ambition" (Ferguson 2005, 256–257). This round of skepticism was additionally complemented with the referendum on the treaty aimed at the establishment of an EU constitution, with French and Dutch voters rejecting it in May and June 2005, and thus throwing the EU into a new critical situation (Best 2005; Laursen 2008). Later, the outbreak of the eurozone crisis at the end of the decade did nothing but cement the feeling of powerlessness and lack of European unity. For example, Kupchan reversed his original standpoint and began to claim that Europe was in serious trouble due to the ever-present renationalization of politics, with EU member states being concerned more about their individual position and future performance than the EU's (Kupchan 2010). Even more drastically, another American scholar talked about Europe as "a spent geopolitical force," a region "condemned to second-tier status" (Moravcsik 2010, 91). At home, the eurozone emergency and accompanying differences in standpoints between creditor countries and recipient countries (in need of bailouts but not wishing to pursue socioeconomic reforms), confirmed the dependence of EU action on economic nationalisms of its own member states (Conti et al. 2018; Dăianu et al. 2014; Galpin 2017; Glencross 2014).

More recently, but clearly inseparable from the dilemmas stemming from the eurozone challenge, the 2015 refugee crisis, the 2016 United Kingdom's EU membership referendum, and the 2019 eruption of the far-reaching coronavirus pandemic, have cast doubts upon the stability of the European project. They again scattered the EU's supranational agenda and inspired its individual member states and their publics to approach each of these occurrences as another reason for more intergovernmentalism. Some studies have rightly connected migration to the subject of solidarity and tried to warn us of a state-centric mindset when dealing with global movements of people: "While Europe's states have demonstrated their capability to renationalize asylum policy and to fortify national borders, in a globalized world these rejections of responsibility to one's neighbor provide merely local relief but no permanent solution" (Gruber 2017, 55; see also Mainwaring 2019; Trimikliniotis 2019). Migration was also at the core of Brexit vote in 2016, which consequently provided space for speculation as to whether some other EU members had a good reason to organize exit ballots, which could potentially weaken the EU and eventually lead to its fragmentation (Baciu and Doyle 2019; da Costa Cabral et al. 2017; Grimmel 2017; Martill and Staiger 2018; Oliver 2018). As stressed by one study, the EU was failing in front of its most vulnerable citizens: "It is no surprise that the losers revolt. If the EU continues with its prescription of austerity and structural reforms, revolt will spread and will take the form of attempts in further countries to exit the Union. It is time for the EU to take the side of the losers of globalization instead of pushing for policies that mainly benefit the winners" (De Grauwe 2016, 249–250). Covid-19 restated discrepancies across the EU, both in terms of intrastate dynamics (shaped by the type and competency of leadership, the readiness of the health care system to confront the pandemic, and the measures adopted in order to protect the well-being of citizens) and interstate relations (either at the bilateral level, through continuous discreditation of each other's strategies and preferences, or at the multilateral level, while expecting the EU to use its supranational powers to assist struggling member states). Yet again, by seeing Dutch and German authorities insult Italian and Spanish responses to the pandemic (as if the two Mediterranean partners wished to face socioeconomic complications and international discreditation), the issue of solidarity as a key EU value was widely scrutinized (Bertoncini 2020; Stevis-Gridneff 2020). As also admitted by European Commission President Ursula Von Der Leyen, "[w]hen Europe really needed to be there for each other, too many initially looked out for themselves. When Europe really needed an 'all for one' spirit, too many initially gave an 'only for me' response" (cited in Rios 2020).

The EU's track record of incapacity to develop a joint position and speak with a single voice about crucial matters has eroded its credibility not only among its own member states (the peripheral or disadvantaged ones) and in the wider European context (in its dealings with countries aspiring to become EU members or those in the neighborhood), but also globally. Understandably, political misconceptions, decisions purely driven by economic nationalism, and the largely unfirmed and, therefore, easily manipulated society, have put the EU to the test. All these aspects, encourage the question: Can we be optimistic about the future of the European integrationist project and, regardless of the answer, what are the responsibilities of different authorities as well as citizens in such a complex process? For so long, we have witnessed a major gap between the EU elites and ordinary people as well as between the core and (semi-)periphery, altogether encouraging discussions about democratic deficit and contributing to a greater interest in intergovernmentalism rather than supranational modus operandi. Such a shift, apart from providing EU member states with flexibility and thus more freedom to determine their own status (facilitated by the 2009-agreed Article 50, which is the only legal mechanism for a member state to leave the EU), has come to represent a threat to the EU suggesting that in contrast to the well-established narrative about external challenges (either cultural, such as Islam, or geopolitical, such as China and Russia), the actual danger can also come from the inside as the result of internal alienation and polarization, with a number of political parties and elected establishments priding themselves on their EU-skeptic, if not pessimistic, views and policy alternatives.

The Complex Path from Exclusion to Inclusion

If we consider the notion of stability, which states tend to take for granted if it goes on for too long, the immediate post-Cold War context suggested that the European project was in front of some major challenges, in terms of both greater integration (including the German unification, the 1992 signing of the Maastricht treaty, and planning of future enlargement rounds) and gradual disintegration (including the case of the former Yugoslav federation and the post-Yugoslav space, which has necessitated continuous external involvement for the sake of stabilization). In contrast to the mainly skeptical academics, policymakers seemed much more optimistic about the future of Europe. The October 1990 German reunification was seen as a great step forward that, as insisted by Helmut Kohl, Chancellor of West Germany, "did not pose any danger to the process of European integration, but on the contrary offered numerous opportunities" (cited in Jansen 1998, 90; see also Genscher 1998; Spence 1992). The official enthusiasm completely abandoned the then warnings that at one point, "Western European states will begin viewing each other with greater fear and suspicion, as they did for centuries before the onset of the Cold War. Consequently, they will worry about the imbalances in gains as well as the loss of autonomy that results from cooperation" (Mearsheimer 1990, 47). In addition, the collapse of the Warsaw Pact and the disintegration of the Soviet Union in 1991 led some of the existing or the newly established states (such as the Baltics) to look even further westward, seeking economic exchanges, political partnerships, and security cooperation. In their view, the European project was "a source of stability. It symbolized the way in which democratic states had transcended military rivalry among themselves and developed a new form of multilevel governance in Europe" (Marsh and Rees 2012, 4; see also Croft and Williams 1992; Duff et al. 1994; Lane 2007; Larivé 2014; Sarotte 1989; Surovell 1995).

With the outbreak of the Yugoslav crisis, the Brussels administration tried to be confident by stating that "the hour of Europe has come" and "if one can be solved by the Europeans, it is the Yugoslav problem. This is a European country and it is not up to the Americans. It is not up to anyone else" (Almond 1994, 32). But, as observed by Warren Zimmermann, the last American ambassador to the Yugoslav federation, "the Europeans simply couldn't believe that Yugoslavia was in serious trouble. There had been too many cries of wolf in the decade after Tito's death in 1980, when practically everybody had predicted that the country would fall apart. When it didn't, Europeans blinded themselves to the cataclysm that was now imminent . . . their approach to Yugoslavia was without any of the urgency with which they acted fourteen months later, when the breakup they said couldn't happen was upon them" (Zimmermann 1996, 65). In fact, as further documented by the journalist Viktor Meier, "[t]he Western diplomats in Belgrade, most of whom went beyond the city limits of the capital only with great reluctance . . ., seemed, practically without exception in the last two years of Yugoslavia's existence, to have misunderstood the realities of this country. In the last six months of Yugoslavia, their hostility to reality assumed grotesque dimensions . . . I had never before encountered such a colossal jumble of political error, lazy thinking, and superficiality as I encountered then among the Western diplomatic corps in Belgrade" (Meier 1999, 217). In any case, the official handling of the Yugoslav crisis throughout the 1990s as well as the treatment of the post-Yugoslav space have also been complemented with narratives about the region's otherness, if not backwardness. For example, numerous debates hosted by different EU institutions and individual member states (including their links with the Vatican), promoted the republics of Croatia and Slovenia as superior vis-à-vis the rest of the Yugoslav state, further validating the two republics' drive for independence and international recognition. As they themselves advocated, their economy and interest in liberalization, Catholic denomination and westward-oriented culture, and failed efforts to spread Western European values within the country stood out, and once they were confronted and their self-realization suppressed by the Belgrade-led state apparatus, they had to opt for a different strategy and detach themselves from the then regime. Moreover, both local secessionist forces and numerous EU representatives (including the respective non-state actors, such as the media), used to present the Yugoslav crisis as a threat to European stability and by doing so, expected the Brussel leadership to support the two republics.

Interestingly, the inauguration of the post-Maastricht EU was also complemented with discussions on European identity as an adhesive instrument of a greater European unity in the post-Cold War context. Since then, European identity has been distinguished as "a collective identity that involves not only an attachment of individual citizens to the EU itself but also as an encompassing individual self-perception of being a member of a salient social group or community – Europe – that includes multiple political and social dimensions" (Bellucci et al. 2012, 61; see also Bayley and Williams 2012; Checkel and Katzenstein 2009; Green 2015; Kaina et al. 2017). While stretched between identification with the EU's norms, which requires alteration of perceptions, and the growing heterogeneity of the EU, because of its continuous enlargement and inclusion of Central, Eastern, and Southeastern states, the very category of European identity has served to either praise and reward or punish and disqualify. Having in mind the complexity of the argument and potential conflicts, Douglas Holmes concluded that "Catholic social doctrine was widely embraced – encompassed by the principle of subsidiarity – to guide intellectually and regulate institutionally the cognitive meanings and political exigencies of a pluralist Europe" (Holmes 2009, 63). Such a framework is useful when examining the attitude and policy preferences of the Brussels administration toward the aspiring member states; as explained in the context of eastward enlargement, "Catholic/Protestant countries, countries with some previous experience with democratization, countries which had begun earlier their political and economic reforms and countries in which people who had not been officially connected with the former communist/socialist regime came into power after elections in the period 1989–91 have been viewed much more favorably by both the EU decision makers and Western public opinion as a whole" (Andreev 2003, 264). Apart from confirming that some states that at one point in the past were excluded from debates of European enlargement were able to meet certain criteria and were eventually admitted to the EU, the 2004 and 2007 enlargement rounds have also upgraded the peripheral status of some of Europe's regions to that of semi-periphery, otherwise seen as remote, underdeveloped and insufficiently civilized compared to the West. Still, in one of his studies,

Jürgen Habermas questioned whether a European identity in the new circumstances is even necessary and whether transnational civic solidarity is actually possible. In his view, the 2004 enlargement represented an immediate challenge for the EU, as it was obvious that "active political interventions will be necessary to bridge the gaps in socioeconomic development between the old and new members," suggesting that the discrepancies between the old, pre-2004 members, and new, post-2004 members "will aggravate conflicts over the distribution of the scarce resources of a comparatively small EU budget, conflicts between net contributors and net beneficiaries, core and periphery, old recipients in Southern and new recipients in Eastern Europe, small and large member states, and so forth" (Habermas 2006, 69–70).

The above dilemma about European identity is further complicated by the presence of Islam, which has in itself been a highly controversial matter. As correctly warned in the literature, "[q]uestions concerning religion are invariably associated either with the challenge of multiculturalism or with the migratory flows of the past few decades, thereby rendering the topic a politically sensitive one" (Foblets 2012, 1). In reality, following the end of the Second World War, various western European countries and later founding states of the European Coal and Steel Community decided to sign numerous bilateral agreements with countries such as Morocco, Tunisia and Turkey, who were to provide them with cheap labor to rebuild the war-torn infrastructure. In contrast to the expectations of the host countries, temporary Muslims, within a relatively short period of time, decided to stay in Europe permanently – an understandable decision, which consequently provoked endless debates and dilemmas about the compatibility of the immigrants' own, imported, identity with the identity of individual European states or even European identity (Radeljić 2014). Accordingly, as indicated elsewhere, "[t]he visibility of Muslims in public spheres concerns both self-presentation and the perception of the other," implying "another reorganization of the boundaries between the private and public domains, inside and outside, sacred and secular" (Göle 2013, 4–5). Issues evolving around the representation of Islam, be it through halal, prophets, headscarf and the position of women, or through artistic initiatives and religious institutions serving Muslim communities, have generated socio-political tensions and skepticism concerning acculturation and assimilation (often listed as the prerequisites for a successful integration) of the Other (Joppke 2009; Wallach Scott 2007). Our society is generally afraid of the unknown, an aspect that has to do a lot with misinformation we continue to absorb; as revealed by Sara Silvestri's comparative analysis of burqa debates in Europe, "much of the European public and citizenry will have 'seen' on television but never actually 'encountered' a Muslim. It is quite possible that if they ever see or meet a Muslim woman wearing even a simple headscarf, they will not see a person in front of them, but instead the totalitarian dogmatism and machismo of the Taliban and of Al-Qaida" (Silvestri 2012, 288).

Given that such questions are left with individual EU members to regulate, there has not been much European institutions and, especially, their legislative instruments could do. As a matter of fact, it was not until 1997 that the Treaty of Amsterdam provided the EU with an authority to deal with discrimination; this was done in response to the growing pressure to come up with a strategy to deal with the problems of racism and discrimination due to the rise of right-wing parties and ideologies. Consequently, the 2000 Racial Equality Directive meant that national legal standards had to be upgraded (EU Council 2000); however, as it turned out, in contrast to the initial period when the transposition of the directive was relatively successful, by 2010 it had become dominated by uncertainty, largely caused by the economic crisis and thus limited funding (Givens and Evans Case 2014, 118). Accordingly, in the absence of major supranational intervention, different European countries have continued to rely on their own specific understanding of the public–private divide, often accompanied by sharp discussions about dress codes and places of worship. Somewhat paradoxically, legal instruments can regulate the existence of groups and diversity (such as the French legal ban on the burqa and niqab in March 2011), but at the same time, they are supposed to promote anti-discrimination policies and protect multicultural aspects of present-day society. A similar discrepancy is found when analyzing the right to build and maintain places of worship in the context of human rights standards and interference of the state and non-state actors in planning permission and building regulations approval: "The right to establish and maintain places of worship is an integral component of the right to freedom of religion or belief. A denial of the former always results in the curtailment of the latter. States therefore cannot sincerely proclaim that they respect and protect religious freedom when there are violations, both direct and indirect, of the right to establish and maintain places of worship" (Villaroman 2012, 321). Finally, other challenges included the local authorities' reluctance to document discrimination complaints, the general lack of awareness, and the impression among citizens that even if they reported discrimination, nothing would really change (Givens and Evans Case 2014, 128).

Back in 2010, when assessing the state of multiculturalism, the German Chancellor Angela Merkel stated that such an approach had actually failed and, in light of future developments, encouraged reexamination of Europe's problematic relationship with its Muslim minorities (cited in Emerson 2011, 1). In response, some scholars found Merkel's assessment irrelevant since "it would be more accurate to say that multiculturalism has hardly been tried. More accurately put, it has been tried only in limited contexts and in a few countries" (Giddens 2014, 133). As even assessed in some earlier EU-sponsored initiatives, multiculturalism (and not democracy) was the main issue for the Muslim community; while seeing Islam as utterly superior, Muslims' approach toward multiculturalism is extremely biased, which leaves no room for compromise (Parekh 2005). With all this in mind, it is understandable why the question about Turkey's European future continues to penetrate EU-related debates, official meetings, and scholarly evaluations. Opinions are rather contrasting; while some claim that Turkey is ready to join the EU and that its membership would strengthen Europe's position with regard to numerous aspects (economic performance, energy security, and foreign policy matters), others think that admitting members such as Turkey (given its size, religion and democratization issues, location and geopolitical orientation, the Turkish–Armenian problem, the Cyprus and Kurdish questions, etc.) could seriously erode the existing EU institutional mechanism and overall performance (Tocci 2011, 48–76). Although Turkey was granted EU candidacy in 1999 and the accession negotiations were launched in 2005 – the process interpreted as "the opportunity to become part of Europe again, from which [Ankara] had so much feared to be excluded with the ending of the Cold War" (Terzi 2010, 5) – the EU's decision to freeze the talks in late-2006 directly eroded the position of pro-European forces. While the Turkish government refers to the constitution and thus sees their country as a democratic, secular, and social republic, there is a significant difference between the EU and Turkey when it comes to the perceptions on democracy – a discrepancy that, in the view of various nongovernmental organizations, should be addressed through an open debate on democracy in Turkey, as problems in this area can negatively affect its EU accession (Jonasson 2013, 113–180). If we add the question of religion to this (and the unavoidable discussion of uniqueness and exceptionalism), then the EU's politics of exclusion could easily keep Turkey outside for a long time: "Notwithstanding the EU's activity in the area of racism and anti-discrimination on a number of grounds, including religion, the case law of the ECtHR [European Court of Human Rights] and domestic courts regarding the public manifestation of Islam suggest that the accession of a country of more than 70 million Muslims may also be a determining factor among the political elite" (Hughes 2011, 8). In fact, as the result of the general EU's negative attitude toward Turkey, the Ankara leadership has invested additional efforts in exploration of possible alternatives, including greater links with countries in the Balkans, the Black Sea, and the Middle East.

Thus, with numerous political and socioeconomic challenges as part of the European integrationist project, the notions of multiculturalism and European identity have served to restate Europe's diversities and expose inconsistencies with regard to the treatment of the Other. As already discussed elsewhere, apart from the impression that the multicultural environment can hardly generate identity balance at the EU level (as obvious from the question of Muslim headscarves in Europe, which reconfirms that culture is part of identity and thus it is capable of affecting identity harmonization), every new round of EU enlargement (as already experienced in 2004 and 2007, when the EU welcomed some countries from Central and Eastern Europe), adds new layers to identity formation and complicates the work that is already in progress (Radeljić 2014). Back in his 1992 study, Anthony Smith suggested that, in order to overcome future confrontational feelings, it would be much wiser to approach Europe as "a family of cultures" – given the differences among the Europeans themselves as well as between the Europeans and non-Europeans, in terms of traditions (legal and political) and heritages (cultural and religious). He recommended not being too preoccupied with multiculturalism and European identity, especially given the past experiences which had managed to bring distant parties together and ensure collaboration and peaceful coexistence (Smith 1992, 70). Indeed, such an approach seemed to have partially characterized the 2007 Berlin Declaration, which marked the fiftieth anniversary of the signature of the Treaties of Rome; while proudly defending the EU's ambition to preserve "the identities and diverse traditions of its member states," the participants also kept stressing that Europeans were facing "major challenges which do not stop at national borders" (European Union 2007). By saying so, they sent a message that individual states, many of which are signatories to the 1985 Schengen Agreement, leading most of the European countries toward removal of controls at their national borders, could come to see cross-border crossing in need of greater regulation in order to restrict the movement of both the Other and the EU's very self. Accordingly, as witnessed during the euro, refugee, and Covid-19 crises, the repositioning of the Brussels authorities and polarization of European citizens, and the consequent fortification of intra-European divisions with some obvious separatist or disintegrationist tendencies, have altogether managed to prevent the so much spoken of consolidation of the EU, often evoking the warnings presented at the end of the Cold War about future risks and potential responses.

A Troubled Relationship between Elites and Citizens

In the debate about the European integrations project, the very role of citizens has often come across as marginal, even though it is difficult to picture the EU progress with its agenda without securing the commitment of its citizens regardless of their level of cosmopolitanism. According to one study, in order to measure citizenship and engagement, we could consider six basic factors – identity, institutional confidence, political efficacy, preferred geographical scope, and current and future policy scope preferences – that can be analyzed individually or combined, given that each of them covers a set of different attitude items (Sanders et al. 2012, 27). In any case, the involvement of citizens largely depends on the EU's institutions that are responsible for providing space for the genuine citizen participation in public life. Here, Habermas insists on the relevance of building mutual trust and, as he puts it, "increasing trust is not only a *result* but also a *presupposition* of a shared process of political opinion- and will-formation" and, therefore, "the path to a democratic deepening of the union and to the requisite mutual networking of national public spheres can only proceed via such an already accumulated capital of trust" (Habermas 2006, 81). This explains Richard Rose's provocative evaluations concluding that citizens' response to Europeanization "reflects individual circumstances" and, in fact, "European citizens may be more interested in how well their favorite football team represents them in

UEFA competitions than how well their prime minister represents them in Brussels" (Rose 2013, 61). Such an attitude also explains why many citizens are still much more interested in national elections than the European Parliament ones, which are characterized by low turnouts; their attitude toward European elections is a reflection of "a high degree of indifference toward what the European Parliament does," which eventually "gives MEPs substantial leeway in what they do" (Rose 2013, 109–110). Even more problematically, Rose sees the citizens' position as actually quite weak, one of the reasons being that interest groups do not necessarily act on their behalf: "Instead of linking Europe's citizens at the bottom level of the pyramidal structure of Europe's political system, interest groups often represent intermediate 'meso-level' organizations whose members are other organizations rather than individual citizens" (Rose 2013, 74).

Thinking about the question of participation, the year 2008 was earmarked as the European Year of Intercultural Dialogue, with EU representatives having agreed that "a fundamental step is promoting the participation of each citizen, men and women on an equal footing, of each member state and of European society as a whole in an intercultural dialogue, in particular through the structured cooperation with civil society" (EU Council 2006). Moreover, with regard to the question of European identity, as clarified by the White Paper on Intercultural Dialogue, its realization would require recognition of "shared fundamental values, respect for common heritage and cultural diversity, as well as respect for the equal dignity of every individual" (Council of Europe 2008). Even the more recent initiatives, including the Citizens' Dialogues and Citizens' Consultations, have communicated that "many participants express concerns about rising inequalities," which is even more alarming when combined with their perception of the European institutions "as too remote" that should instead "be more efficient and transparent" (European Commission 2019; see also ECNL 2016; Russack 2018; Valmorbida 2014). Although being acknowledged as key in discussions about European polity, the low visibility of citizens and civil society in the public sphere points to a major discrepancy between the official rhetoric and accompanying documents, on the one hand, and policies embraced by both the EU and individual member states, on the other. For example, the public in Central and Eastern Europe, although in favor of EU membership (largely framed around democratic reform, economic benefits and the reunification of Europe discourse), have developed ambiguous feelings in the post-accession period. More precisely, the EU's reputation and, therefore, its relevance has decreased since the public has believed that their voices regarding democratic legitimacy and political irregularities do not really matter (Stefanova 2018). Here, Habermas's observation about human dignity is of the utmost importance; as noted, "the concept of human dignity transfers the content of a morality of equal respect for everyone to the status order of citizens who derive their self-respect from being recognized by all other citizens as subjects of equal actionable rights" (Habermas 2012, 87). Thus, the more people are puzzled about the scope of the European project and the more they perceive their own status as inferior to somebody else's, the more they are likely to ignore the

EU's supranational ambitions and turn toward national governments and, in particular, their anti-EU representatives. Even more so, if the EU's own citizens feel alienated and grossly betrayed by the EU's misleading promises of inclusion and better living conditions, than it is difficult for the unwanted Other to expect a significantly different practice.

The three key impediments to EU legitimation – transparency, balanced inclusion, and sound representation – are altogether associated with the top-down Europeanization trend (Guasti 2013). In this arrangement, the role of national governments is crucial; still, while expected to act as a link between their own polities and the EU, they tend to preserve their own influence and manipulative power by carefully selecting the type and volume of information to be shared. In their role, they can act as drivers of Euroscepticism. For example, in the Czech Republic, the former President Václav Klaus, who openly criticized the EU and opposed further integration, provoked negative views of the EU among local political parties and civic organizations – a trend that changed only after the Klaus presidency and his reduced presence in the media (Havlík and Mocek 2018). Looking closely at the contractual relationship between national governments and their respective citizens, who are expected to take part in European elections, some scholars have rightly concluded that "political elites like to invoke citizens when justifying their positions on European integration, and they tend to blame them when explaining crises in the integration process" (Díez Medrano 2009, 105–106), and that "actual levels of trust in EU institutions have more to do with levels of trust in (or political disaffection with) all institutions at the national level than with a real evaluation of the functioning and performance of EU institutions" (Torcal et al. 2012, 110). This way, national governments shape their citizens' perception of the EU, either in a positive or negative way, largely depending on their own standing among the Brussels bureaucrats and capacity to agree and respond to the EU's supranational or individual member states' demands. However, the problem is that the politicians, even though aware of the issues, do not seem ready to lay the cards because of their own fear that if they start encouraging greater supranational solidarity, especially in the time of crisis, such an attempt could be seen as a threat to state sovereignty and thus their own careers (Habermas 2012). Accordingly, if national governments are struggling with the accommodation of the Other, signals coming from the Brussels administration and requests to alter policies in place are more likely to provoke tensions and resistance, further contributing to anti-EU sentiment. Here, given that the widely uninformed citizens are likely to believe that the solution to their problem is with their own governments and not the Brussels authorities, the European identity factor, which implies strong attachment to Europe and readiness to upgrade the state of mind in a way that it is not only national identity that matters but also some other, supranational one, comes across as insignificant.

Referendums, while combining the aspects of representative and direct democracy, provide citizens with an opportunity to have a say in some processes. The research concerning the question as to who really wants referendums shows that elites do not and citizens actually do (Rose 2013, 94–95). Still, they do not happen often, and when they do, the outcome can be disappointing, as in the case of the 2005 vote on EU constitution and the 2016 United Kingdom's EU membership referendum, both generating post-referenda uncertainty concerning the future direction of the EU. In both cases, the respective publics expressed their strong disapproval of the state of EU affairs and gave priority to their national (and possibly subnational) identity. Still, even between the countries which rejected EU constitution there were some obvious differences concerning the treatment of electorates and rationale for their ultimate preference; as noted, "[w]hile in the Netherlands the most often mentioned reasons are 'lack of information' and 'loss of national sovereignty;' these items only play a very minor role in France – unsurprisingly given the intense debates preceding the referendum there" (Gattig and Blings 2013, 73). This confirms the relevance of both state and non-state actors in such processes, with the latter depending on the former and the behavior of the former depending on its relationship with the Brussels administration. Citizens are left without or, in contrast, provided with crucial information because their national governments and media outlets, as the most powerful (non-)state actor decide to do so. The media and news agencies are responsible for the production of elite discourses; in Habermas's words, "[t]he kind of media-based mass communication with which we are familiar from national public spheres is not subject to any standards of discursive quality, or even representativeness" (Habermas 2009, 154). Moreover, the social media and invasion of troll armies have provided governments worldwide with an opportunity to spread propagandistic, yet convincing, explanations for their decisions, making the monitoring of policy processes, from proposal to implementation, extremely complicated (Eberwein et al. 2019). So, if the agenda is to present an immigrant (as during the refugee crisis), an accession of another country to the EU (as in discussions concerning the Western Balkan region), or an existing EU member state (as in the case of the eurozone crisis) as a threat to the stability of the EU as a whole or that of individual member states, national governments are likely to identify strategies that will serve their own advocacy of accountability and transparency, as well as help them to preserve office and benefits.

In the case of Brexit, the voters were presented with two Others, one being in the form of a threatening individual (immigrant) and the other in the form of a threatening system (the very EU). With the Brexit campaign, the question of arrival and settlement of immigrants, which has traditionally been viewed less negatively in the United Kingdom than in some other European states often suffering from immigration-related moral panic (Morley and Taylor 2012), was stirred and, in order to matter more than ever before, connected to the debate about British sovereignty, democratic principles, and economic prosperity. As such, immigration was presented as capable of triggering identity erosion and social fragmentation through alteration of demographic layout and, therefore, Brexit was a wakeup call for the

British to protect their island and Britishness (lifestyle and social norms) and ensure lower level of external, EU interference. As explained elsewhere, "[t]he 'we' that was dominant within public debate on Brexit was a 'we' that was believed to be historically constituted in national terms, and it was this history of being located within the nation that was seen to determine who should or should not have rights" (Bhambra 2017, 92). Once the image of immigrants as a bold threat had sufficiently consolidated, it was important to discredit the relevance of EU membership by insisting that the arrangement in place did not safeguard British interests and, therefore, the UK would be better off by investing efforts into intergovernmental cooperation, instead of supranational governance (Adam 2020; Cap 2019; Ridge-Newman et al. 2018). This was not difficult given the continuity of British reservedness vis-à-vis European integration; as Margaret Thatcher, to cite just one example, used to put it: "We have not successfully rolled back the frontiers of the state in Britain, only to see them reimposed at a European level, with a European super-state exercising a new dominance from Brussels" (Thatcher 1988; see also Gifford 2014; Wall 2019). Thus, for many British citizens, even those with a limited knowledge, if any at all, about EU affairs and their country's position therein, it was a combination of two negatives, one at home and the other one in Brussels, that were enough to make up their mind and opt for Brexit.

As different evaluations of the problem of social exclusion have suggested, the Brexit referendum represented an opportunity for the working-class people – for too long labelled as racist and ignorant, and, even more relevantly, for too long suffering the detrimental consequences of neoliberal reorganization – to have their say and hopefully generate change that would reform their condition (Mckenzie 2017a; see also Hobolt 2016; Lees 2020; Mckenzie 2017b; Shipman 2017). In the aftermath of the referendum, which left the liberal spectrum disappointed (largely because of its middle-class status and misunderstanding of the precarious livelihoods of the Brexiteers), arguments and street protests calling the government to revoke Article 50 and stage another referendum emerged. They suggested that the voters had been misled and, if they had been properly lectured about the negative impact of Brexit, many of them would have voted otherwise – an attempt ignored by the government whose leadership went on to claim that the original outcome represented the will of the people. However, the claim that the voters were insufficiently briefed, and their decision was not levelheaded is less significant: "When you have almost nothing to lose, when you can see nothing positive on the horizon, and when you're convinced that you have been betrayed and cast aside, 'logic' and 'rationality' cannot remain dominant. For many of those struggling on low incomes after decades of EU membership and liberalism's promises, it was 'logical' to do the only thing that stood even a remote chance of substantively improving their immediate circumstances" (Winlow et al. 2017, 201). So, while concerned about their survival and threats coming from the two Others, the British citizens' Brexit vote sent a clear message to other Europeans about the citizens' power to punish the system. They

also sent a message to different European establishments that could eventually decide to limit citizens involvement in policymaking, even though such an approach
would be in contrast with the EU's rhetoric concerning the role of citizens and calls
for their great participation in decision making processes. Understandably, Brexit
has prompted many debates concerning the right to vote in similar referendums
elsewhere, based on the fact that the UK intends to leave the EU after a fractious
process of campaigning which stoked nationalist sentiments and was not always
based on evidence and convivial debate. With this in mind, both the periods before
and after Brexit must be taken into consideration when discussing the European
integrationist project and the citizens' role in the disintegration of the EU because
of their dissatisfaction with national governments. Accordingly, Brexit represents a
valid case study and potentially a valuable lesson learned.

Finally, in addition to everything mentioned above, it is important to reflect
upon the role of public intellectuals in the debates addressing the position of the
Other or, more generally, the future of Europe. Despite the perception of intellectuals as capable of offering inside-out evaluations of specific phenomena and,
therefore, capable of distinguishing between truth and big lies (and anything in between), their participation has become limited. The status of intellectuals – and
preference to serve as sidelined commentators or passive bystanders, rather than
key figures in the awakening and transformation of the society – is a matter of both
the institutional willingness to provide space for their engagement and their own
willingness to play an active role (individually or by joining other like-minded comrades) in certain processes. In any case, as Noam Chomsky has stressed, "[w]hen
we consider the responsibility of intellectuals, our basic concern must be their role
in the creation and analysis of ideology" and "[s]ince power tends to prevail, intellectuals who serve their governments are considered the responsible ones"
(Chomsky 2017, 57, 96; see also Bourdieu 1990; Etzioni and Bowditch 2006; Fleck
et al. 2009; Kauppi 2018; Said 1994). What this really means is that not all intellectuals share the same mission and, therefore, we should be very careful with regard
to their agendas, since some are also likely to act on behalf and accept compensa-
tion from dishonest portions of the establishment, including both state and non-
state structures, and push forward agendas that do not necessarily reflect their
training in the field of ethical principles. Rather than trying to persuade and tell
people what they should do, intellectuals are expected to use their ability to provide
constructive examination of complex issues and make them accessible, so that the
ones who listen to them can hopefully understand the impact of specific policy preferences and minimize their own losses in the increasingly competitive environment.
Accordingly, the exclusion of intellectuals – either in the form of self-censorship or
somebody else's decision to limit their access and interaction with the public – suggests that something should be covered up, the exposure of which could represent
a danger. While some regimes tend to be more inclined toward a genuine inclusion
of intellectuals in decision making processes, others tend to show reluctance,

treating them as nuisance or even promoting anti-intellectualism. Anyway, the bigger the isolation of intellectuals, the stronger the ground for speculation pointing in the direction of uncertainty or wrongdoing with potentially detrimental outcome, is likely to be. Science and technology have additionally complicated the position of intellectuals; while providing new tools to pursue discreditation or promotion of intellectual thought, they have also contributed to the overall confusion by linking the success of those battles to financial capacities, as in the case of government-sponsored internet propaganda through the use of troll armies for the sake of cyber populism.

The Brussels administration as well as the EU's individual members have only occasionally welcomed public intellectuals to the debates about the future of the European integrationist project. Generally, based on Henry Kissinger's experience, "the intellectual is rarely found at the level where decisions are made . . . It is the executive who determines in the first place whether he needs advice . . . [I]n short, all too often what the policymaker wants from the intellectual is not ideas but endorsement" (cited in Draper 2006, 210). This goes hand in hand with the growing gap between democratization and elitism in the EU, suggesting that the approaches different leaderships have decided to embrace are far from democratic, even though their public appearances seem to send a different message (Cotta 2012; Haller 2008; Lacroix and Nicolaïdis 2010). For example, the eurozone crisis has managed to stress the differences existing within the EU and individual member states, when it comes to representation and electoral support (for example, in Germany and Greece). According to Rose, "European Union policies cannot be agreed simply on the basis of national interests, for that would produce an endless sequence of national vetoes. Its policies are meant to express a European interest that is unlikely to match exactly the interest of all 27 member states" (Rose 2013, 70). Economic crises are particularly painful because their causes are hard to detect in real time and the complex linkages within an economic system make it difficult to establish causal relationships. Consequently, they are vulnerable to erroneous diagnosis, harmful simplifications, and spread of disinformation or the so-called fake facts. This is why the role of impartial intellectuals is crucial, so that they can provide a realistic status check and a sound roadmap of necessary steps to overcome a crisis (Gerba 2018). Yet, as during the eurozone crisis, only voices offering simplistic views or with particular political agendas were favored, since they offered easy reading and solutions. This assured that the systemic status quo is maintained and that the established structures or perspectives are not put into jeopardy – an approach apparent in our modern capitalist system, where the role of nonpartisan intellectuals is reduced to negligible with the pretext that they are not productive or profitable enough.

Later, the refugee crisis, which exposed stark contrasts among EU members, managed to polarize the intellectual community, dividing it into those who seek to defend the so-called universal values and those who subscribe to radical parochialism and the exclusion of the Other, both camps encouraging questions about European solidarity and tolerance. In one of his pieces, Nick Riemer examined the assessments provided by Habermas, Peter Singer, and Slavoj Žižek, and concluded that their intellectual engagement did not really abandon the common discourse about the crisis the Western public had already got used to: "As [their] interventions demonstrate, intellectual authority can easily barricade the real strongholds of power and mystify its operations. For anyone who wants to put analysis to the service of fundamental social change, diagnosing and preventing this transformation of critique into intellectualism should be among the many responsibilities of 'intellectuals' today" (Riemer 2015). Furthermore, intellectuals failed to predict Brexit. While often coming from privileged, middle-class, backgrounds, many of them seemed no to have fully grasped the precarious position and living conditions of the Brexiteers: "Rarely can university intellectuals have been so uncritical of the unquestioning adherence by such elites to the status quo. Throughout the Brexit debate, the belief that the future of the UK lay within the EU received little challenge and much support in universities" (Salter 2018, 468). So, whenever they appeared in the media, the occurrence of which was highly limited (let alone debates hosting both Brexiteers and Remainers), they kept praising European integration and listing the reasons (mainly economic) as to why the UK was better off as a member of the EU. Finally, the outbreak of Covid-19 and consequent response by international organizations and different governments inspired many intellectuals to comment on the state of the affairs. While some of them have rightly argued that the handling of the pandemic exposed "another colossal failure of the neoliberal version of capitalism" (Chomsky cited in Magdaleno 2020), and that "[m]ore than open barbarism [they] fear barbarism with a human face – ruthless survivalist measures enforced with regret and even sympathy, but legitimized by expert opinions" (Žižek 2020), some others went on to warn the audiences that the measures put in place (for example, in Italy) were "irrational and entirely unfounded," used by governments to paralyze countries and limit our freedom "in the name of a desire for safety that was created by the same governments that are now intervening to satisfy it" (Agamben 2020a; see also Agamben 2020b). However, whichever the level of expertise or whomever the target of public intellectuals, the governments seem to have remained unaffected by them – in the pursuit of their agendas, they have relied on their own hand-picked advisors, instead.

Conclusion

The European integrationist project is in trouble, since concerns evolving around the environment, natural resources, laws and human rights, euro and economic development, and stability and securitization of borders, pose a serious challenge for the Brussels authorities. While none of these issues is a novelty per se, the fact that some of their key features remain insufficiently tackled or even completely disregarded, even though they are capable of leading to further disappointment and fragmentation of the EU, does come as a surprise. Having experienced a number of major crises in the post-Cold War context, the Brussels administration and the individual and ever-competitive member states' governments have sought to exploit supranational and intergovernmental approaches for the sake of economic advancement. Understandably, not all of them have been equally successful; as one study has put it, "Germany seems to have achieved by pacific means what it was unable to bring about through military conquest – the domination of Europe" and, therefore, given the disproportionality, "it is essential that some powers be returned to nations, regions and localities" (Giddens 2014, 9, 35; see also Fouskas and Gökay 2019). With this in mind, Brexit should be treated as a lesson learnt, regardless of how unsuccessful and unpopular the very notion of learnt lessons within politics and international relations has actually been. Moreover, attempts such as Catalonia's bid for independence, apart from being a hard blow to the mother state, capable of inspiring secessionist movements in other EU states to exploit similar avenues, are also a major challenge for the EU system, especially when durable solutions have not been achieved and such cases cannot be described as sui generis anymore (Closa 2017). Thinking about future levels of interdependence, Rose has rightly warned that "[c]ooperation outside EU institutions does not deny interdependence; it encourages the development of an ever-looser union. The greater the extent of interdependence, the sooner events outside the control of Brussels are likely to disrupt the ties that maintain a policy equilibrium in place" (Rose 2013, 143).

In addition to the internal Other (as in the case of the so-called disobedient or confrontational EU states, such as Viktor Orbán's Hungary), the EU has continuously struggled with the dilemma about the external Other, either the one who is already inside (as in the case of immigrants) or the one hoping for an EU accession (as in the case of the Western Balkan region). However, in contrast to the 1950s and 1960s, when the idea of a united Europe did not take immigration into consideration and European support and tolerance of cultural diversity seemed genuine, the subsequent decades were accompanied by a growing polarization of both official and non-official rhetoric in which the Other has repeatedly appeared as a potential threat and an agent incentivizing doubts as to whether Europe can be the same with different people in it (Caldwell 2009). For many observers, the numerous EU-sponsored initiatives, altogether determined to present the EU as inclusive and showcase its occasional baby-steps improvements in terms of treatment of the Other, cannot be taken seriously in the absence of a greater participation of citizens in the decision-making processes and proper accountability of the ruling elites, regulated through additional legal provisions and a more binding nature of inter-governmental arrangements (Habermas 2012, 130–131). More recently, and mostly in the context of the eurozone and refugee crises, the rise of right-wing populist discourse and discord among EU member states concerning the suitability of adopted measures have additionally promoted the different Others as a threat to the EU. This is also relevant for future enlargement rounds; given that each call implies all sorts of adjustments acceding countries are expected to go through, new entrants, both territorially and demographically, are unavoidably subject to various procedures clearly making them aware of their otherness. Simultaneously, and very problematically when considering the much-advertised European values, the Brussels administration has openly supported semi-authoritarian regimes in the Western Balkans (Radeljić 2019). By doing so, it has sent a clear message that for as long as the regional leaders respond to the EU's demands (mainly through accommodation of its economic dealings), the quality of institutions, political pluralism, and journalism and media reporting, among others, are less relevant. Accordingly, whichever the level of support for the EU in the region, its involvement has revealed hypocrisy, leaving many members of the public, who firmly advocated EU accession in the past, disenchanted with the EU's lack of reaction to the elites' alleged undermining of democratic principles. By option for such an approach and by knowing that the ultimate decision concerning enlargement will rest with the EU's member states and not the Western Balkan ones, the EU has preserved for itself an option to use the rise of authoritarianism as a valid reason to block their accession or to start promoting regime change.

The most recent Covid-19 crisis has accentuated the lack and importance of solidarity across the whole of Europe, with states accusing the EU or one another of delayed and mismanaged policies. In fact, as one earlier study explained the trend in times of crisis, states sometimes "employ the EU as an excuse for action or inaction within the domestic arena and, sometimes they even refer to the EU as a scapegoat, thus fueling nationalism and reinforcing national identity" – an approach that is even better explained if we take European identity as a "non-emotional identity, in contrast with the powerful and emotionally charged national identities of our time" (Guibernau 2009, 287). With all the crises the EU has gone through, both the Brussels authorities and European citizens have realized that achieving a common European identity is much more complicated than creating a political or economic union. Moreover, every crisis has managed to further erode the notion of common (or even shared) and to restate the power of national borders and preference for intergovernmental model of cooperation, as well as for a greater freedom in relation to new partnerships and policy alternatives. Such an approach has been welcomed by citizens and different EU member states that have often felt marginal and threatened by the decisions taken in Brussels. In one way or another, citizens do find ways to punish their leaderships and the individual member states do find ways to obstruct the EU's supranational agenda. Indeed, and somewhat paradoxically, in addition to the existing Others (internal and those on the EU's doorstep), every crisis has had the potential of attracting new state and non-state actors, thus additional Others, to exploit the momentum for the advancement of their own multidimensional objectives, which could eventually accelerate the undoing of the European integrationist project.

References

Adam, Rudolf G. 2020. *Brexit: Causes and Consequences*. Cham: Springer.

Agamben, Giorgio. 2020a. "L'invenzione di un'epidemia." *Quodlibet*, 26 February, https://www. quodlibet.it/giorgio-agamben-l-invenzione-di-un-epidemia.

Agamben, Giorgio. 2020b. "Chiarimenti." *Quodlibet*, 17 March, https://www.quodlibet.it/ giorgio-agamben-chiarimenti.

Almond, Mark. 1994. *Europe's Backyard War: The War in the Balkans*. London: William Heinemann.

Andreev, Svetlozar A. 2003. "Path dependence and external shocks: The dynamics of the EU enlargement eastwards." In *Comparative Regional Integration: Theoretical Perspectives*, edited by Finn Laursen, 251–270. London: Ashgate.

Baciu, Cornelia-Adriana, and John Doyle, eds. 2019. *Peace, Security and Defence Cooperation in Post-Brexit Europe: Risks and Opportunities*. Cham: Springer.

Bayley, Paul, and Geoffrey Williams, eds. 2012. *European Identity: What the Media Say*. Oxford: Oxford University Press.

Bellucci, Paolo, David Sanders, and Fabio Serricchio. 2012. "Explaining European identity." In *The Europeanization of National Polities? Citizenship and Support in a Post-Enlargement Union*, edited by David Sanders, Paolo Bellucci, Gábor Tóka, and Mariano Torcal, 61–90. Oxford: Oxford University Press.

Bertoncini, Yves. 2020. "European solidarity in times of crisis: A legacy to be deepened in the face of Covid-19." *Fondation Robert Schuman European Issues*, 20 April, https://www.robert-schuman.eu/en/european-issues/0555-european-solidarity-in-times-of-crisis-a-legacy-to-be-deepened-in-the-face-of-covid-19.

Best, Edward. 2005. "The European Union's constitutional crisis: Causes and consequences." *Intereconomics* 40(4): 180–200.

Bhambra, Gurminder K. 2017. "Locating Brexit in the pragmatics of race, citizenship and empire." In *Brexit: Sociological Responses*, edited by William Outhwaite, 91–99. London: Anthem Press.

Bourdieu, Pierre. 1990. *In Other Words: Essays Towards a Reflexive Sociology*. Stanford, CA: Stanford University Press.

Caldwell, Christopher. 2009. *Reflections on the Revolution in Europe: Immigration, Islam and the West*. London: Penguin Books.

Camus, Albert. 1957 (2018). "Create dangerously." Speech delivered at Uppsala University after being awarded the Nobel Prize in Literature. London: Penguin Books.

Cap, Piotr. 2019. "'Britain is full to bursting point!' Immigration themes in the Brexit discourse of the UK Independence Party." In *Discourses of Brexit*, edited by Veronika Koller, Susanne Kopf, and Marlene Miglbauer, 69–85. Oxon: Routledge.

Checkel, Jeffrey T., and Peter J. Katzenstein, eds. 2009. *European Identity*. Cambridge: Cambridge University Press.

Chomsky, Noam. 2017. *The Responsibility of Intellectuals*. New York: The New Press.

Closa, Carlos, ed. 2017. *Secession from a Member State and Withdrawal from the European Union: Troubled Membership*. Cambridge: Cambridge University Press.

Conti, Nicolò, Borbála Göncz, and José Real-Dato, eds. 2018. *National Political Elites, European Integration, and the Eurozone Crisis*. London: Routledge.

Cotta, Maurizio. 2012. "Political elites and a polity in the making: The case of the EU." *Historical Social Research* 37(1): 167–192.

Council of Europe. 2008. "White paper on intercultural dialogue: Living together as equals in dignity." 2 May, http://www.coe.int/t/dg4/intercultural/Source/White%20Paper%20final% 20EN%20020508.pdf.

Croft, Stuart, and Phil Williams, eds. 1992. *European Security without the Soviet Union*. London: Frank Cass.

da Costa Cabral, Nazaré, José Renato Gonçalves, and Nuno Cunha Rodrigues, eds. 2017. *After Brexit: Consequences for the European Union*. Cham: Palgrave Macmillan.

Dăianu, Daniel, Giorgio Basevi, Carlo D'Adda, and Rajeesh Kumar, eds. 2014. *The Eurozone Crisis and the Future of Europe: The Political Economy of Further Integration and Governance*. Basingstoke: Palgrave Macmillan.

De Grauwe, Paul. 2016. "What future for the EU after Brexit?" *Intereconomics* 51(5): 249–251.

Derrida, Jacques. 1992. *The Other Heading: Reflections on Today's Europe*. Bloomington, IN: Indiana University Press.

Díez Medrano, Juan. 2009. "The public sphere and the European Union's political identity." In *European Identity*, edited by Jeffrey T. Checkel and Peter J. Katzenstein, 81–107. Cambridge: Cambridge University Press.

Draper, Theodore. 2006. "Intellectuals in politics." In *Public Intellectuals: An Endangered Species?* edited by Amitai Etzioni and Alyssa Bowditch, 201–226. Lanham, MD: Rowman & Littlefield Publishers.

Duff, Andrew, John Pinder, and Roy Pryce, eds. 1994. *Maastricht and Beyond: Building the European Union*. London: Routledge.

Eberwein, Tobias, Susanne Fengler, and Matthias Karmasin, eds. 2019. *Media Accountability in the Era of Post-Truth Politics: European Challenges and Perspectives*. Oxon: Routledge.

ECNL [European Center for Non-for-Profit Law]. 2016. "Civil participation in decision-making processes." https://rm.coe.int/civil-participation-in-decision-making-processes-an-overview-of-standa/1680701801.

Emerson, Michael. 2011. "Summary and conclusions." In *Interculturalism: Europe and Its Muslims in Search of Sound Societal Models*, edited by Michael Emerson, 1–16. Brussels: Centre for European Policy Studies.

Etzioni, Amitai, and Alyssa Bowditch, eds. 2006. *Public Intellectuals: An Endangered Species?* Lanham, MD: Rowman & Littlefield Publishers.

EU Council. 2000. "Council Directive 2000/43/EC of 29 June 2000 implementing the principle of equal treatment between persons irrespective of racial or ethnic origin." *Official Journal of the European Communities*, 19 July, https://eur-lex.europa.eu/legal-content/EN/TXT/PDF/?uri=CELEX:32000L0043&from=en.

EU Council. 2006. "Decision No. 1983/2006/EC of the European Parliament and of the Council of 18 December 2006 concerning the European Year of Intercultural Dialogue (2008)." *Official Journal of the European Union*, 30 December, L 412/45.

European Commission. 2019. Citizens' dialogues and citizens' consultations: Key conclusions." 30 April, https://ec.europa.eu/commission/sites/beta-political/files/euco-sibiu-citizensdialogues_en.pdf.

European Union. 2007. "Declaration on the occasion of the Fiftieth Anniversary of the Signature of the Treaties of Rome." http://www.eu2007.de/en/About_the_EU/Constitutional_Treaty/BerlinerErklaerung.html.

Ferguson, Niall. 2005. *Colossus: The Rise and Fall of the American Empire*. London: Penguin Books.

Fleck, Christian, Andreas Hess, and E. Stina Lyon, eds. 2009. *Intellectuals and their Publics: Perspectives from the Social Sciences*. Farnham: Ashgate.

Foblets, Marie-Claire. 2012. "Religion and rethinking of the public-private divide: Introduction." In *Religion in Public Spaces: A European Perspective*, edited by Silvio Ferrari and Sabrina Pastorelli, 1–21. Farnham: Ashgate.

Fouskas, Vassilis, and Bülent Gökay. 2019. *The Disintegration of Euro-Atlanticism and New Authoritarianism: Global Power-Shift*. Cham: Palgrave Macmillan.

Galpin, Charlotte. 2017. *The Euro Crisis and European Identities: Political and Media Discourse in Germany, Ireland, and Poland*. Cham: Palgrave Macmillan.

Gattig, Alexander, and Steffen Blings. 2013. "Disaffected citizens? Why people vote in national referendums about EU Treaty reform?" In *Democratising the EU from Below? Citizenship, Civil Society and the Public Sphere*, edited by Ulrike Liebert, Alexander Gattig, and Tatjana Evas, 61–82. Farnham: Ashgate.

Genscher, Hans-Dietrich. 1998. *Rebuilding a House Divided: A Memoir by the Architect of Germany's Reunification*. New York: Broadway Books.

Gerba, Eddie. 2018. "Mission impossible: Calculating the economic costs of Brexit." *LSE Blog*, 19 June, https://blogs.lse.ac.uk/brexit/2018/06/19/mission-impossible-calculating-the-economic-costs-of-brexit/.

Giddens, Anthony. 2014. *Turbulent and Mighty Continent: What Future for Europe?* Cambridge: Polity Press.

Gifford, Chris. 2014. *The Making of Eurosceptic Britain: Identity and Economy in a Post-Imperial State*. Farnham: Ashgate.

Givens, Terri E., and Rhonda Evans Case. 2014. *Legislating Equality: The Politics of Antidiscrimination Policy in Europe*. Oxford: Oxford University Press.

Glencross, Andrew. 2014. *Politics of European Integration: Political Union or a House Divided?* Chichester: Wiley-Blackwell.

Göle, Nilüfer. 2013. "Introduction: Islamic controversies in the Making of European Public Spaces." In *Islam and Public Controversy in Europe*, edited by Nilüfer Göle, 3–20. Farnham: Ashgate.

Green, Stephen. 2015. *The European Identity: Historical and Cultural Realities*. London: Haus Publishing.

Grimell, Andreas, ed. 2017. *The Crisis of the European Union: Challenges, Analyses, Solutions*. Oxon: Routledge.

Gruber, Oliver. 2017. "'Refugees (no longer) welcome:' Asylum discourse and policy in Austria in the wake of the 2015 refugee crisis." In *The Migrant Crisis: European Perspectives and National Discourses*, edited by Melani Barlai, Birte Fähnrich, Christina Griessler, and Markus Rhomberg, 39–57. Zurich: Lit Verlag.

Guasti, Petra. 2013. "A Panacea for democratic legitimation? Assessing the engagement of civil society with EU Treaty reform politics." In *Democratising the EU from Below? Citizenship, Civil Society and the Public Sphere*, edited by Ulrike Liebert, Alexander Gattig, and Tatjana Evas, 135–163. Farnham: Ashgate.

Guibernau, Montserrat. 2009. "Towards a European Identity?" In *European Union and World Politics: Consensus and Division*, edited by Andrew Gamble and David Lane, 274–290. Basingstoke: Palgrave Macmillan.

Habermas, Jürgen. 2006. *The Divided West*. Cambridge: Polity Press.

Habermas, Jürgen. 2009. *Europe: The Faltering Project*. Cambridge: Polity Press.

Habermas, Jürgen. 2012. *The Crisis of the European Union: A Response*. Cambridge: Polity Press.

Haller, Max. 2008. *European Integration as an Elite Process: The Failure of a Dream?* Oxon: Routledge.

Havlík, Vratislav, and Ondřej Mocek. 2018. "Václav Klaus as a driver of Czech Euroskepticism." In *Reviewing European Union Accession: Unexpected Results, Spillover Effects, and Externalities*, edited by Tom Hashimoto and Michael Rhimes, 96–112. Leiden: Brill.

Hobolt, Sara B. 2016. "The Brexit vote: A divided nation, a divided continent." *Journal of European Public Policy* 23(9): 1259–1277.

Holmes, Douglas R. 2009. "Experimental identities (after Maastricht)." In *European Identity*, edited by Jeffrey T. Checkel and Peter J. Katzenstein, 52–80. Cambridge: Cambridge University Press.

Hughes, Edel. 2011. *Turkey's Accession to the European Union: The Politics of Exclusion?* London: Routledge.

Jansen, Thomas. 1998. *The European People's Party: Origins and Development.* Basingstoke: MacMillans.

Jonasson, Ann-Kristin. 2013. *The EU's Democracy Promotion and the Mediterranean Neighbours.* Oxon: Routledge.

Joppke, Christian. 2009. *Veil: Mirror of Identity.* Cambridge: Polity Press.

Kaina, Viktoria, Ireneusz Pawel Karolewski, and Sebastian Kuhn, eds. 2017. *European Identity Revisited: New Approaches and Recent Empirical Evidence.* Abingdon: Routledge.

Kauppi, Niilo. 2018. *Toward a Reflexive Political Sociology of the European Union: Fields, Intellectuals and Politicians.* Cham: Palgrave Macmillan.

Kennedy, Paul. 1987. *The Rise and Fall of the Great Powers: Economic Change and Military Conflict from 1500 to 2000.* New York: Random House.

Kupchan, Charles A. 2003. *The End of the American Era: US Foreign Policy and the Geopolitics of the Twentieth-First Century.* New York: Vintage.

Kupchan, Charles A. 2010. "The Potential Twilight of the European Union." Council on Foreign Relations, http://www.cfr.org/world/potential-twilight-european-union/p22934.

Lacroix, Justine, and Kalypso Nicolaïdis, eds. 2010. *European Stories: Intellectual Debates on Europe in National Contexts.* Oxford: Oxford University Press.

Lane, David. 2007. "Post-communist states and the European Union." *Journal of Communist Studies and Transition Politics* 23(4): 461–477.

Larivé, Maxime H.A. 2014. *Debating European Defense and Security Policy: Understanding the Complexity.* Farnham: Ashgate.

Laursen, Finn, ed. 2008. *The Rise and Fall of the EU's Constitutional Treaty.* Leiden: Martinus Nijhoff Publishers.

Lees, Charles. 2020. "Brexit, the failure of the British political class, and the case for greater diversity in UK political recruitment." *British Politics*, https://link.springer.com/article/10.1057/s41293-020-00136-6.

Magdaleno, Cristina. 2020. "Chomsky on Covid-19: The latest massive failure of neoliberalism." *Euractiv*, 25 April, https://www.euractiv.com/section/economy-jobs/interview/chomsky-on-covid-19-the-latest-massive-failure-of-neoliberalism/.

Mainwaring, Cetta. 2019. *At Europe's Edge: Migration and Crisis in the Mediterranean.* Oxford: Oxford University Press.

Marsh, Steve, and Wyn Rees. 2012. *The European Union in the Security of Europe: From Cold War to Terror War.* Oxon: Routledge.

Martill, Benjamin, and Uta Staiger. 2018. *Brexit and Beyond: Rethinking the Futures of Europe.* London: UCL Press.

Mayhew, Alan. 1998. "The European Union's policy toward Eastern Europe: Design or drift." In *The European Union in the World Community*, edited by Carolyn Rhodes, 105–126. Boulder, CO: Lynne Rienner Publishers.

McAllister, Richard. 1997. *From EC to EU: An Historical and Political Survey.* London: Routledge.

Mckenzie, Lisa. 2017a. "'It's not ideal:' Reconsidering 'anger' and 'apathy' in the Brexit vote among an invisible working class." *Competition & Change* 21(3): 199–210.

Mckenzie, Lisa. 2017b. "The class politics of prejudice: Brexit and the land of no-hope and glory." *The British Journal of Sociology* 68(S1): 265–280.

Mearsheimer, John. 1990. "Back to the future: Instability in Europe after the Cold War." *International Security* 15(1): 1–56.

Meier, Viktor. 1999. *Yugoslavia: A History of its Demise.* London and New York: Routledge.

Middlemas, Keith. 1995. *Orchestrating Europe: The Informal Politics of the European Union, 1973–1995*. London: Fontana Press.

Moravcsik, Andrew. 2010. "Europe, the second superpower." *Current History* 100(725): 91–98.

Morley, John, and Charlotte Taylor. 2012. "Us and them: How immigrants are constructed in British and Italian newspapers." In *European Identity: What the Media Say*, edited by Paul Bayley and Geoffrey Williams, 190–223. Oxford: Oxford University Press.

Oliver, Tim. 2018. *Europe's Brexit: EU Perspectives on Britain's Vote to Leave*. Newcastle upon Tyne: Agenda Publishing.

Parekh, Bhikhu. 2005. "Does Islam threaten democracy?" In *The Spiritual and Cultural Dimension of Europe*, edited by European Commission, 35–37. Brussels: European Commission.

Radeljić, Branislav. 2012. *Europe and the Collapse of Yugoslavia: The Role of Non-State Actors and European Diplomacy*. London: I.B. Tauris.

Radeljić, Branislav. 2014. "On European Identity." In *Debating European Identity: Bright Ideas, Dim Prospects*, edited by Branislav Radeljic, 1–20. Oxford: Peter Lang.

Radeljić, Branislav. 2019. "Tolerating semi-authoritarianism? Contextualizing the EU's relationship with Serbia and Kosovo." In *The Europeanisation of the Western Balkans: A Failure of EU Conditionality?* edited by Jelena Džankić, Soeren Keil, and Marko Kmezić, 157–180. Cham: Palgrave Macmillan.

Ridge-Newman, Anthony, Fernando León-Solís, and Hugh O'Donnell 2018. *Reporting the Road to Brexit: International Media and the EU Referendum 2016*. Cham: Palgrave Macmillan.

Riemer, Nick. 2015. "How to justify a crisis." *Jacobin*, 10 May, https://www.jacobinmag.com/2015/10/refugee-crisis-europe-zizek-habermas-singer-greece-syria-academia/.

Rios, Beatriz. 2020. "Commission chief, MEPs slam lack of EU solidarity in COVID19 crisis." *Euractiv*, 26 March, https://www.euractiv.com/section/coronavirus/news/commission-chief-meps-slam-lack-of-eu-solidarity-in-covid19-crisis/.

Rose, Richard. 2013. *Representing Europeans: A Pragmatic Approach*. Oxford: Oxford University Press.

Russack, Sophia. 2018. "Pathways for citizens to engage in EU policymaking." *CEPS Policy Insights* 14, https://www.ceps.eu/wp-content/uploads/2018/11/PI2018_14_SR_2CU%20chapter%20on%20Pathways%20for%20Citizens%20to%20Engage%20in%20EU%20Policymaking.pdf.

Said, Edward W. 1994. *Representations of the Intellectual: The 1993 Reith Lectures*. New York: Pantheon Books.

Salter, Brian. 2018. "When intellectuals fail? Brexit and hegemonic challenge." *Competition & Change* 22(5): 467–487.

Sanders, David, Paolo Bellucci, Gábor Tóka, and Mariano Torcal. 2012. "Conceptualizing and measuring European citizenship and engagement." In *The Europeanization of National Polities? Citizenship and Support in a Post-Enlargement Union*, edited by David Sanders, Paolo Bellucci, Gábor Tóka, and Mariano Torcal, 17–38. Oxford: Oxford University Press.

Sarotte, Mary Elise. 2014. *1989: The Struggle to Create post-Cold War Europe*. Princeton, NJ: Princeton University Press.

Shipman, Tim. 2017. *All Out War: The Full Story of How Brexit Sank Britain's Political Class*. Glasgow: HarperCollins.

Silvestri, Sara. 2012. "Comparing burqa debates in Europe: Sartorial styles, religious prescriptions, and political ideologies." In *Religion in Public Spaces: A European Perspective*, edited by Silvio Ferrari and Sabrina Pastorelli, 275–292. Farnham: Ashgate.

Smith, Anthony D. 1992. "National identity and the idea of European unity." *International Affairs* 68 (1): 55–76.

Spence, David. 1992. "The European Community and German unification." *German Politics* 1(3): 136–163.

Spoerri, Marlene. 2015. *Engineering Revolution: The Paradox of Democracy Promotion in Serbia*. Philadelphia, PA: University of Pennsylvania Press.

Stefanova, Boyka. 2018. "(Dis)trusting the European Union? On the evolving variety of Euroskepticism in Central and Eastern Europe." In *Reviewing European Union Accession: Unexpected Results, Spillover Effects, and Externalities*, edited by Tom Hashimoto and Michael Rhimes, 77–95. Leiden: Brill.

Stevis-Gridneff, Matina. 2020. "As Europe confronts the coronavirus, what shape will solidarity take?" *The New York Times*, 8 April, https://www.nytimes.com/2020/04/08/world/europe/eu-coronavirus-aid.html.

Surovell, Jeffrey. 1995. "Western Europe and the Western Alliance: Soviet and post-Soviet perspectives." *Journal of Communist Studies and Transition Politics* 11(2): 155–197.

Taylor, Paul. 1993. *International Organization in the Modern World: The Regional and the Global Process*. London and New York: Pinter.

Terzi, Özlem. 2010. *The Influence of the European Union on Turkish Foreign Policy*. Farnham: Ashgate.

Thatcher, Margaret. 1988. "The Bruges Speech." https://www.margaretthatcher.org/document/107332.

Tocci, Nathalie. 2011. *Turkey's European Future: Behind the Scenes of America's Influence on EU-Turkey Relations*. New York: New York University Press.

Torcal, Mariano, Eduard Bonet, and Marina Costa Lobo. 2012. "Institutional trust and responsiveness in the EU." In *The Europeanization of National Polities? Citizenship and Support in a Post-Enlargement Union*, edited by David Sanders, Paolo Bellucci, Gábor Tóka, and Mariano Torcal, 91–111. Oxford: Oxford University Press.

Trimikliniotis, Nicos. 2019. *Migration and the Refugee Dissensus in Europe: Borders, Security and Austerity*. Oxon: Routledge.

Valmorbida, Antonella, ed. 2014. *Citizens' Participation at the Local Level in Europe and Neighbouring Countries*. Brussels: Peter Lang.

Villaroman, Noel G. 2012. "The right to establish and maintain places of worship: The developments of its normative content under international human rights law." In *Religion in Public Spaces: A European Perspective*, edited by Silvio Ferrari and Sabrina Pastorelli, 295–322. Farnham: Ashgate.

Wall, Stephen. 2019. *The Official History of Britain and the European Community: The Tiger Unleashed, 1975–1985*. Oxon: Routledge.

Wallach Scott, Joan. 2007. *The Politics of the Veil*. Princeton, NJ: Princeton University Press.

Winlow, Simon, Steve Hall, and James Treadwell. 2017. *The Rise of the Right: English Nationalism and the Transformation of Working-Class Politics*. Bristol: Policy Press.

Zimmermann, Warren. 1996. *Origins of a Catastrophe: Yugoslavia and Its Destroyers – America's Last Ambassador Tells What Happened and Why*. New York: Times Books.

Žižek, Slavoj. 2020. "Barbarism with a human face." *Welt*, 19 March, https://www.welt.de/kultur/literarischewelt/article206829259/Slavoj-Zizek-on-Corona-Barbarism-with-a-Human-Face.html.

Between Past and Present

Jan Květina

2 The Polish Early Modern Republic as the Other Europe: The *Sarmatian* Moment of Jean-Jacques Rousseau in the Polish Political Discourse

The Western European perspective of the Polish society and statehood has often been laden with stereotypes and prejudices stemming from the need to highlight fundamental Polish contrasts in comparison with another, apparently better, system of values. For example, the depiction of Poland as a European troublemaker within the current European Union context, can also be interpreted as part of a more general treatment of Eastern Europe – an undesirable space, hell-bent on non-liberal democracy (Karolewski and Benedikter 2017; Zielonka 2018). However, this is not a recent trend; during the interwar period, the popular image of Poland was one of a land of dangerous chauvinists and extremists of all kinds, under the auspices of marshal Józef Piłsudski (Davies 1972, 553–561; Davies 2003, 173–174). Even more so, the stereotypes of Poland as the other Europe were also found among West European observers already in the early modern period (Bodin 1606; Connor 1698).

A crucial dimension of Polish historical otherness lies in the state's political constitution, with bizarre contours frequently highlighted by foreign intellectuals, as well as by the local noblemen. At home, the Polish otherness was often exploited for political aims, either as a symptom of backwardness and impuissance, or as an evidence of pure traditions of noble ancestors. Although it is plausible to identify the internal Polish debate about one's own distinctiveness as early as the birth of the so-called noble republican myth in the sixteenth century (Grześkowiak-Krwawicz 2012, 3–24), the main dispute over preservation or modification of the traditional constitution broke out no sooner than in the mid-eighteenth century, when the adherents to the European Enlightenment clashed with supporters of old-fashioned way of noble life, who were pejoratively called *Sarmats* (Faber 2018; Walicki 1989, 10). Furthermore, this was the time when foreign and domestic perspectives of Polish otherness started to shape one another, as important commentators – especially from France, with Jean-Jacques Rousseau at the forefront – stepped into the Polish political discourse.

In this regard, it should be mentioned that although Rousseau's 1772 *Considerations on the Government of Poland* may be considered his last political piece and thus some sort of testament, it is regularly omitted from his political theory and eclipsed by much more renowned writings such as the *Social Contract* and the series of *Discourses*. This lack of interest can be explained by the uncertainty of Rousseau's motivation to be intrigued in the Polish matters, when the contemporary Polish constitution stood

https://doi.org/10.1515/9783110684216-002

dominantly for a deterrent example of dysfunctional and arbitrary anarchy (Pyrrhys de Varille 1771, 21–23, 116–117, 121). Nonetheless, the main controversy of *Considerations* is due to the surprising message of Rousseau's words that seemingly do not correspond with the general corpus of his well-known political theory. Rousseau's surprising conclusions, when he urges Poles not to change their traditional constitution as it is precisely its essence that has enabled the Polish nation to become what it is (Rousseau 2005, 170), might provide us with the impression that he had transformed into a conservative defender of hierarchical status quo. So the crucial question is: How and why did Rousseau take part in the Polish political discourse, and, even more so, why would he have supported the Polish society based on "aristocratic arrogance" and serfdom, if today Rousseau is hailed dominantly as an adherent to principles of equality, general will, and popular sovereignty?

It is precisely the alleged contradiction between the reality of Polish politics and Rousseau's political theory which causes disputes concerning the right interpretation of his motives, but also his intentional message: is it possible to find anything remarkable about human society in general in *Considerations*? And if it so, then why did Rousseau choose the exotic conditions of the Polish-Lithuanian Commonwealth to prove universal remarks about politics as such? The question of coherence between the *Considerations* and the *Social Contract* resembles similar quandaries characterizing other authors' contradicting writings; for example, the ideological gap between *The Prince* and the *Discourses* by Niccolò Machiavelli is one of the most notorious instances of such a dilemma. Their discrepancy is permanently analyzed by political thinkers who strain to find a sustainable explanation of the author's intentions and to decide whether Machiavelli changed his political mind or used different genres for different purposes or, quite the contrary, defended the same principles – which are to be identified – all the time. Nevertheless, in order to frame the message of Rousseau's *Considerations* in a reasonable context, it is necessary to focus not only on the historical details of Rousseau's involvement, but also on the then Polish political culture and the image of Poland in Western European collective consciousness of that time. Only on this condition it would be possible to demonstrate that the then Polish features, including backwardness and feudal hierarchy, did not represent negation, but continuation of Rousseau's former political principles and his skepticism about the modern development of European civilization.

Hence, when trying to analyze the peculiarities of the Polish political context (that is the specific character of the so-called noble republic in crisis), it is necessary to reject all perennialist approaches that assume it is possible to identify a common philosophical heritage of different thinkers across various historical and cultural eras. On the contrary, if we accept the methods of the *Cambridge School* and its contextual approach (Pocock 2009; Skinner 1969), it is desirable to admit that Rousseau stepped into the broader and already existing debate that was led within the Polish Enlightenment discourse, which reflected the question of ancient republican traditions. On the basis of this approach, I will seek to address three main questions that are significantly inter-linked: Under which historical conditions did Rousseau write his Polish *Considerations* and how did his interpretation of Polish identity fit into the broader Western perception of East European space? Which were the principles representing the Polish republican tradition that Rousseau could have considered as an ideal structure for the realization of his social contract concept? Finally, how did the attitudes of Rousseau reflect the contemporary republican discourse of the Polish nobility with its inherent dilemma as to whether European patterns should be adopted or rejected?

Having Rousseau's involvement in the Polish affairs in mind, it is important to note that the general interest in East European borderland was not so sporadic; in 1770, Jean-Paul Marat wrote *Aventures du jeune comte Potowski*, and in 1774, Giacomo Casanova's *Istoria delle turbolenze della Polonia* appeared. Admittedly, this part of the continent served as a semi-mythical landscape whose depiction was used either for a diatribe against one's own society or as a proof that the Western concept of evolution was the right one. Needless to say, in the first case, Eastern Europe was identified with the idea of incorrupt space of chastity and virtue, whereas in the second case it was depicted mainly as a wild and dangerous area of barbarians that stood in strong opposition to the modern principles of progress and civilization. The same dichotomy is found in the dominant interpretation of Rousseau's *Considerations*, which is supposed to be compared to another French analysis of Poland – *Du gouvernement et des lois de la Pologne* by Gabriel Bonnot de Mably (1781), also commissioned by the representative of the revolting Polish government.

Although it will be possible to notice that the strict reading of Rousseau and de Mably as two antagonistic options is not as clear-cut as it might seem, the classical approach assesses de Mably as a harsh critic of the Polish statehood and a stan-dard-bearer of that concept which identified Polishness with obscure foolishness and a threat for the whole European continent. Thus, the only way to save Polish society from decay was through the acceptance of Western civilization, meaning that de Mably did nothing more but to expand on the formerly defended arguments, as in Charles Louis Montesquieu's 1777 *Spirit of Laws* and, somewhat more implicitly, in Voltaire's 1731 *History of Charles II*. If Voltaire – under the strong influence of his bonds with the court of Catherine the Great – presents Polish society as a seedbed of zealotry and religious bigotry, which corresponded with the Polish domestic Enlightenment discourse standing against the so-called *sarmatism*, Rousseau actu-ally offers an entirely different interpretation. Accordingly, the "Polish statements" of Rousseau are sharply anti-Voltairean, which means that his *Considerations* are not only benevolent regarding Polish oddities, but also strongly against the idea of Russian empire following Rousseau's older anti-Russian tones expressed in the *Social Contract*. Whereas in the *Considerations*, Rousseau labels Russia as "a cunning ag-gressor who, pretending to present you with the bonds of friendship, burdened you with the irons of servitude" (Rousseau 2005, 170), in *Social Contract*, he criticizes

Peter the Great who "wished to produce at once Germans or Englishmen, when he should have begun by making Russians" and warns that "[t]he Russian Empire will desire to subjugate Europe, and will itself be subjugated. The Tartars, its subjects or neighbors, will become its masters and ours" (Rousseau 2002, 184–185).

However, as suggested above, this kind of pro-Eastern Europe approach was not so unique among the milieu of the French philosophers. Anti-Russian attitudes of Rousseau, admiring the exotic conditions of Polish society, must be therefore linked to the older European tendencies of which Rousseau himself was aware. In 1761, the famous book *The History of the Polish King John Sobieski* was published and almost immediately banned as its author Gabriel-François Coyer used his admiration for Polish republicanism with the sovereignty of the noble estate and limited power of the king for a covert and subversive rejection of the domestic absolutism in France (Lukowski 2012, 122). In a very similar way, one can read the unfinished work *The History of Polish Anarchy* by Claude-Carloman de Rulhière, clearly showing that the image of Poland, as a land of hope instead of decay, had existed in the West before Rousseau's *Considerations*. What is more, Rulhière's reflections were based on his own personal experience from his visit to Poland in 1776, meaning that when he interpreted the Polish political manners as a possible way to revive the ancient values of the Roman republic (Lukowski 2012, 123; Wolff 1994, 272–278), he had been influenced by the Polish domestic narrative of the noble republicanism and *sarmatism*, which was also Rousseau's case later on.

Still, in terms of involvement, in contrast to his predecessors, Rousseau was asked for an advice on the Polish question by the delegation of Polish provisional government, whose members believed in Rousseau's intellectual capacity, thanks to the Polish nobleman Michał Wielhorski of the insurgent milieu Confederation of Bar, who had travelled to Paris to arrange for further political agreements with the French government. Although the original plans had failed, Wielhorski still succeeded in a quite different initiative – to secure input from the experienced French intellectuals in relation to the planned reform of the constitution that would strengthen the Polish capacities to maintain state sovereignty. His efforts led to the birth of two foreign analyses of aristocratic Poland: a critical essay by de Mably and a laudatory writing by Rousseau, who accepted Wielhorski's call while highlighting his allegedly non-professional approach and the lack of local knowledge: "A good institution for Poland can only be the work of the Poles or of someone who has studied well the Polish nation . . . A foreigner can hardly give anything but general views . . . Perhaps all this is only a heap of chimeras, but they are my ideas; it is not my fault if they resemble those of other men so little . . ." (Rousseau 2005, 169, 240).

Apart from the fact that both French philosophers were provided with several detailed papers concerning the Polish political matter (Michalski 2015, 19–38; Rousseau 2005, 169; Stasiak 2010, 721–722), Rousseau also possessed an earlier experience with Polish politics. Although he never travelled to Poland and even declined a personal invitation made by the Count Grigory Orlov (Richardson 1784,

400–7), once he had finished the *Discourses,* he was confronted by the nominal Polish king Stanisław Leszczyński who rejected almost all of his philosophical views about human nature and the progress of civilization (Leszczyński and Menoux 1751). Even though the debate between Leszczyński and Rousseau – who also seized the opportunity to react to the Polish king's objections (Rousseau 1823, 63–95) – revolved around the conclusions regarding the *Discourses on the Arts and Science,* and was thus not directly related to the Polish context, the fact that Rousseau had to communicate with the court of the Polish king equipped him with knowledge he later used in his *Social Contract.* There he quotes a work called *Głos wolny wolność ubezpieczający* (Leszczyński 1858) that, in Rousseau's era, was believed to be written by Leszczyński himself and whose main question treated the reform of the Polish constitution – so, precisely the same task that Rousseau handled several years later on, on his own. With all this in mind, Rousseau's engagement in Polish politics was not a purely accidental adventure and that is why the *Considerations* cannot be read as a purpose-built list of counsels, designated for Polish society in particular and Rousseau's striving for the admiration from local aristocracy.

The Myth of the Aristocratic Republic as a Symptom of the Polish Distinctiveness

For a sustainable interpretation of Rousseau's *Considerations* it is not decisive to consider modern historiographic debates – whether the Polish constitution was in accordance with oligarchy of magnates, democracy of nobles or dysfunctional anarchy (Butterwick 2001a) – but to get to the core of the then discourse and to understand how the Polish nobility perceived and described their own state. In this respect, one is supposed to take into account that from the mid-sixteenth century onwards, a very influential republican myth was enforced, whose essence depicted the Polish-Lithuanian Commonwealth as an heir of glorious and virtuous ancient republics (Czubek 1918a, 407), when the members of the noble estate identified themselves with modern Platos, Aristotles, and Ciceros (Grześkowiak-Krwawicz 2011, 59; Opaliński 2002, 147–166).

For the Polish nobility, their own estate was an aristocratic community and the only true modern republic, which could be compared to the vanished Rome or contemporary Venetian constitution, chosen by God to preserve the original virtues of a natural man and thus to save a fading European civilization. But how did this republican obsession of the Polish noble estate come into being? Why were they so fascinated with their own constitution so they themselves referred to their own state as *Rzeczpospolita,* which is the Polish version of the traditional Latin collocation *res publica,* or common matter? Of course, if we applied the modern meaning of the word republic, it would be highly absurd to equate early modern Poland with republicanism, because the Polish-Lithuanian Commonwealth was a monarchy for the whole time, with a king as the official representative of the government. But it is exactly the presence of a king that was so important for the humanist concept of republicanism and *monarchia mixta* (Frycz Modrzewski 1551; Orzechowski 1566; Przyłuski 1553), which tried to revive the Aristotelian-Ciceronian ancient tradition, as also stressed by Rousseau. From a nobleman's perspective, the triangle of a king, Senate and chamber of deputies (*izba poselska*) represented an arrangement, in which the first institution stood for the majesty of monarchy, elected and established by the act of citizen consent, the second pillar was regarded as an aristocratic principle of older and more experienced mediators between the sovereign and the people, and the last institution was supposed to defend democratic interests of all the noble "nation." Accordingly, the Polish mixed constitution, with its popular motto *inter maiestatem ac libertatem* struggling to avert any threat of *absolutum dominium* (Wolan 2010, 143), emphasized the republican character of the state by the clear delimitation of sovereignty as a basic principle of all the political power. In contrast to the centralization and absolutism in other European states of that time – even though these phenomena can be defined in a very broad way (Henshall 1992; Miller 1990) – it was the community of nobles in the Polish-Lithuanian Commonwealth that claimed the right not only to perform as the main spokesmen of the common good, but also to consider themselves as the *raison d'être* of the Commonwealth, whose existence was meaningful only on the condition that the state power was able to protect the liberties of the noble-citizen estate as well as of its individuals.

The obsession of the noble estate with its own freedom manifested itself on the institutional level, which should have ensured protection from the royal *potestas*, as well as on the individual level, where a symbolical myth of the so-called golden liberties had occurred, guaranteeing the noble title holders to be unlimited sovereigns at their domains. Concerning the sphere of political decision-making, liberty of a noble estate was expressed by the byword "lex regnat, non rex" (Radziwiłł cited in Przyboś and Żelewski 1974, 238–239), which highlighted a dominancy of legal authority that was supposed to rule over all subjects of the republic, including the king. Sovereignty of law and its limitation of royal power were put into practice by a complicated net of traditional agreements and acts, such as the *Heinrician Articles* and *Pacta Conventa* (Volumina legum 1860, 133–134, 150–153), which enabled nobility to maintain the principle of the elective monarchy. It was exactly this principle that strengthened the idea of a civic republic and promoted the essence of noble identity, although the fact the king kept being elected made the effectiveness of the executive power impossible and jeopardized the stability of the Polish state in the long run. In this regard, especially during the *interregnum*, the act of the elections was always threatened by the corruption and speculations from foreign powers. However, apart from the right to choose their own ruler, Polish nobility was allowed to control decision-making processes with its supremacy in legislature, which, in reality, protected their own private sphere (Lewicki 1891, 190; Volumina legum 1859, 137).[1] The interconnection between the public dimension of Polish noble liberty as political participation and its private sphere as freedom from any non-legal interferences into the individual interests of particular noblemen is, in fact, a key argument, explaining a strong republican tradition within the Polish political culture, with golden liberties fitting into the conceptual framework of liberty as non-domination (Pettit 2002). When flicking through the files of the *Sejm* sessions or political essays of that time, it is apparent that republican perception of liberty strengthened the exclusivist idea of Polish nobility as the chosen nation; the Polish community, therefore, assessed itself as the freest nation in the world (Kołudzki 1727, 285) and adopted the phrase that without liberty, a Polish nobleman was like a fish without water (Czubek 1918b, 94).

Another peculiarity of the Polish system, which supported domestic conviction of one's own uniqueness and was also highlighted by Rousseau, lay in the absence of formal stratification of the noble estate, consequently supporting the argument of equality of all citizens. In this regard, a very popular and in Polish also onomato-poetic phrase "szlachcic na zagrodzie równen jest wojewodzie [a petty nobleman on his own manor is equal to a palatine]" (Jablonowski 1730, 15) referred to the fact that unlike the other European noble communities, where diverse levels of noble descent on the basis of property differences existed, in Poland every man who was able to give evidence of his virtuous origin was accepted as an equal member of nobility irrespective of his possessions. Although this kind of total equality was valid only formally and behind its façade huge differences between great magnates and their poor noble clients could be found, a noble identity remained to be based on political and not on ethnic or religious attributes (Friedrich and Pendzich 2009, 1–16). A civic essence of identity enabled the concept of a unified republic based on a very colorful mosaic of different languages and confessions, protected by the un-precedented scale of religious tolerance as guaranteed by the enactment of the 1572 Warsaw confederation (Tazbir 1983, 56; Wyczański 1991, 147). All this made the Polish-Lithuanian Commonwealth look like a state without stakes – an oasis of religious freedom and peace, where the republican common good was supposed to frame all the cleavages and conflicts concerning identity; as a famous politician Jan Tarnowski uttered, "[t]he point of the republic did not lie in piousness, but in liberty" (cited in Sucheni-Grabowska 2009, 27).

Nevertheless, even the advocates of Polish republicanism admitted lots of pitfalls in an inherent character of the Polish constitution. The mechanism of *liberum veto*, the

---

1 For the Polish nobility, the following principles were crucial: the 1505 act of Nihil novi, which prevented the king from adopting any new constitution without a consent of the noble community, and the 1430 principle of Neminem captivabimus, which protected the members of a noble estate from arbitrary limitation of their liberty (for example, imprisonment on the king's decision).

right of every noble envoy to block the whole parliamentary procedure just by disapproving of particular agenda was probably considered as the most questionable principle. This institution was formed to maintain the most valuable republican attributes – civic liberty and equality, but it gradually declined into the dangerous means misused by foreign agents as well as domestic magnates to make parliamentary procedure ineffective (Lukowski 1991, 91–92; Wagner 1997, 58–63). The question of removing *liberum veto* from the system thus belonged to the most insistent requests of the eighteenth century reformers, even though a number of them, including Rousseau, were rightly concerned as to whether this would be a good move since they were able to recognize some of its qualities in the framework of the distinct Polish republicanism. However, the complex political environment, the geopolitical position of the Polish republic, and the mentality of the noble civic community had started to change and called for reconsideration of the then organization, which explains the reasons behind the Polish nobility's interest in Rousseau's opinions about the future of Poland. More precisely, since the mid-seventeenth century, Poland failed to withstand raids of foreign powers and their anti-Catholic behavior (Frost 2003, 2, 8–9), which has resulted in an increase of religious intolerance and the process of ethnicization of the Polish noble identity. Given the fact that a permanent Swedish threat was linked to the infiltration of Lutheranism, and ambitions of the Russian tsardom strengthened the influence of the Orthodox community, it was obvious that Poland would not remain an oasis of religious tolerance; in fact, as witnessed during Rousseau's era, numerous confessional groups started to be considered as dangerous "fifth columns" of the republic (Frost 2007, 274–275; Lukowski 1999, 19–24). Together with the erosion of social and religious stability, necessity of a political reform was becoming more urgent; accordingly, the crucial dilemma occurred: "Was the Polish republic supposed to get rid of its bizarre political constitution and follow the European way of modernism or was it a better idea to stay loyal to its own traditions of noble parliamentarism?"

The Dilemma of Europeanization in the Eighteenth Century Polish Political Debates

When Rousseau stepped into the then *milieu*, he became involved in a collision of two main ideological camps, although the contemporary reality was even more complicated, since the orientation of particular political groups as well as individuals kept changing all the time. On one side, there was a clique of the Enlightened reformists who wanted to transform the Polish republic into a modern and centralized state, by adopting time-proven patterns from Western Europe. At the forefront of this movement in the 1760s stood the *Familia*, a powerful faction associated with noble families of *Czartoryski* and *Poniatowski* which sought to build harmonious relationship with Russia – a support required for the realization of their own political visions

(Zielińska 1983). On the other side, there was a very diverse mixture of political attitudes, frequently labelled as part of the so-called *sarmatism*, that is the belief of those nobles who tried to preserve the traditional Polish constitution with all the accompanying characteristics (including the way of dressing). Nonetheless, one should mention it is quite difficult to identify *sarmatist* ideas more specifically as the term itself was created by its adversaries (the adherents to the Enlightened reforms) who depicted their opponents as foolish reactionaries naively believing that the Polish nobility came from the ancient tribe of *Sarmats* (Walicki 1997, 155–159; Michalski 1972, 284).

Furthermore, the internal dynamics of both camps was complicated so none of the agents was able to control the power and, what was even more challenging, all parties had to reflect not only the quandary of reformism against traditionalism, but also the desirable foreign policy and related agenda of religious minorities (Lukowski 1985, 559–564). This dilemma was typical of the *Familia*; while defending modernist and liberal attitudes of Western European Enlightenment, such as pluralism and individual freedom, it was simultaneously forced to sacrifice some of these principles, because they could not be applied in the Polish context without serious political repercussions. This was exactly the case of religious minorities that, from the liberal perspective of the European Enlightenment, were supposed to enjoy the same political status as the rest of citizens. But if many of non-Catholic noblemen had been tied with Polish mortal enemies such as Russia, their total emancipation would have fully wrecked the sovereignty of Poland. Therefore, parties such as the *Familia* had to balance between the loyalty to Russians, which often smelled of betrayal, and hard resistance against any foreign influence, which posed a risk of foreign invasion.

In 1764, the *Familia*, supported by the Russian diplomacy, enforced several important reformist acts at the so-called *Convocation sejm* (Kisielewski 1880), the proceedings of which resembled coup d'état as the Russian army was present and prevented the opposition from applying *liberum veto* (Stanek 1996, 136–136). Moreover, the Polish government was forced to accept the results of the Polish-Russian *Eternal Peace* from 1686 and thus to recognize Russia's supremacy over large Ukrainian territories (Staszewski 1998, 100). Nonetheless, a pragmatic and purpose-built alliance between tsarina Catherine the Great and the *Familia* was fragile, because the Russian diplomacy superficially supported the reformists' efforts; the Russians only did it for the sake of preserving their own dominant influence in Polish matters and desire to prevent other great powers from interference. In addition, Russia had to ensure that none of the modern reforms would be put into practice, because a consolidated Polish state would surely endanger the Russian position as it had already been the case at the beginning of the seventeenth century (Dunning 2001). As it happened, two years after the *Convocation sejm*, the Russian diplomacy changed tactics and it decided to fight for the rights and interests of dissidents (members of religious minorities), as announced at the *Sejm of Czaplica*, named after its Marshal (Speaker) Celestyn

Czaplic (Konopczyński 1918, 413). So, in contrast to their earlier strategy, when the Russians promoted the idea of modernization, their envoy Count Nikolai Vasilyeich Repnin now stubbornly defended the Polish traditional constitution and its golden liberties, which also included the civil rights for non-Catholics (Kraushar 1898, 215–222).

The clash between the *Familia* and Russia, largely supported by the Polish orthodox nobility, helped the formation of a political alternative, known later as the Bar Confederation, which would then get in touch with Rousseau. While the *Familia* supported the modern reforms, but for tactical reasons could not accept the rights of dissidents, and the Russian side blocked the reforms by insisting on religious rights, a strong conservative opposition emerged under the auspices of Adam Stanisław Krasiński, the initiator of the later Bar Confederation. It rejected both of the existing approaches and thus required not only that the influence of religious minorities be limited, but also the elimination of then reforms and disposition of the king. However, the political situation came to a deadlock, since the conservative Bar Confederation, similarly to the *Familia*, looked down on minorities, but then, thanks to the Russian support, it blocked the *Familia's* reformist approach.

In the then setting, one of the key figures was the nobleman Michał Wielhorski, who had previously used the 1766 *Sejm of Czaplica* to introduce himself as one of the most ardent defenders of the traditional constitution with *liberum veto* at the forefront. This might sound confusing, given that in the early seventies, the same politician served as an official exponent of pro-French policy against the influence of Russia; he even wrote about the desirable Polish reform (Wielhorski 1775) and shifted his views about *liberum veto*, and, therefore, his former advocacy of old and backward principles seemed to have made him fulfil the role of a *Sarmatian* fool and Russian useful idiot. In any case, the complicated circumstances of Polish political reality required the ability to enforce the same interests and ideas with radically different tactics – hence, if Wielhorski initially defended the noble sovereignty of Poland against the *Familia* with the support of Russia, he did not hesitate to promote the same approach a few years later, when it was deemed more beneficial to push Moscow back and rely on Paris.

Under the above circumstances, with the *Familia* having failed to complete its reforms, but cooperated with the conservative opposition to block the Russians instead, the Russian diplomacy initiated the support of confederations[2] in Słuck and Toruń by assembling the revolting Protestant and Orthodox noblemen. The prime example of Russian interference was the establishment of the Radom Confederation in June 1767,

---

2 Polish confederations were specific institutions, formed when sections of the nobility revolted against their own king. As part of the traditional constitution, *confederacies* had the legal right to declare that the then government was inimical to the common good of the republic. In that case, political power was held by the association of confederates and decisions were taken by a majority rule without the option of *liberum veto*.

which covered the whole territory of the Polish-Lithuanian Commonwealth and included not just confessional minorities, but also Catholics; by doing this, it merged the opposing standpoints against the Polish government in the name of the preservation of golden liberties. Accordingly, a solid number of noblemen, who favored a traditional republic with religious tolerance, but were willing to accept the temporary supremacy of Russia in order to gain capacity for renewal of the complete sovereignty, supported the Russian initiative. This became clear when the Russian envoy Repnin wrote a letter to be used by the official delegation of Polish noblemen to request Catherine the Great to take control over the unstable Polish government and to ensure the old constitution be revived (Konopczyński 1918, 415).

On the basis of the Russian involvement, the so-called *Sejm of Repnin* gathered in Warsaw in late 1767. From the beginning, its decision-making process was abused both by the presence of the tsarist army and manipulations of the local *sejmiks* by pro-Russian collaborators (Iłowajski 1871, 88), including the arrest of four opposition leaders, all former members of the Radom Confederation (Lukowski 1985, 568–570; Scott 2001, 182). In support of limited sovereignty, a set of the cardinal laws was passed, which represented irrevocable principles whose preservation was guaranteed by the tsarina herself. Needless to say, this package of laws included principles such as elective monarchy, conservation of *liberum veto* and the right to revolt against the government (Lukowski 1977, 224–227; Volumina legum 1860, 250–256). The *Sejm of Repnin* thus terminated not only the provisional reform victory launched by the 1764 *Convocation sejm*, but also a purpose-built alliance between the *Familia* and Russian diplomacy, although the Polish king Poniatowski still held his position and kept cooperating with the Russians (Butterwick 2001b, 201–202). It is, therefore, fully understandable that under these conditions the older forces of conservative opposition accepted the challenge and, instead of a peaceful parliamentary fight that was conducted at the *Czaplica sejm*, decided to instigate their own coup d'état.

In this regard, similarly to the procedure that was followed in the former case of the Radom Confederation, the insurgents formed their own Bar Confederation, in 1768. The members of this political-military union, whose legitimate establishment corresponded with the constitutional tradition, represented a very colorful spectrum of attitudes. The confederation gathered *Sarmatian* advocates of the myth of golden liberties, as well as moderate Enlightened reformers or even self-seeking magnates who considered the revolt as an optimal way of terminating the influence of the rival *Familia* and replacing the noble Czartoryskis in the government (Maciejewski 1977, 22). This means that it is quite untenable to draw a line between the adherents to the Bar Confederation and its opponents as if it were a matter of one social and political cleavage. Much more than just traditional reactionaries, the Bar confederates represented a very specific and an *ad hoc* coalition of contemporary political tempers altogether denying the results of the *Sejm of Repnin* and defending the vague ideals of Polish republicanism.

Nonetheless, in case of a problem with a definite political program, the leaders of the confederation were still able to agree that the successful resistance against the Russian menace depended on foreign aid. On the basis of older bonds and contemporary international circumstances, the main hope of Bar diplomacy lay in French foreign policy under the leadership of Étienne-François de Choiseul, who considered Russia to be the biggest threat to French interests in Eastern Europe. As a pivotal move of the Bar Confederation concerning French-Polish relations, was the October 1770 decision of its executive organ (*Generalność*) to dispatch an official emissary to Paris to negotiate with French officials an additional governmental support and an appropriate candidate for the Polish throne (Wolff 1994, 237). Michał Wielhorski was appointed to this position, having switched from being one of the most ardent advocates of *liberum veto* at the 1766 *Sejm of Czaplica* and part in the pro-Russia Radom Confederation, to defend anti-Russian interests of French policy with a belief that *liberum veto* had to be abolished. However, his diplomatic mission was a political fiasco; during his stay in Paris, the Duke of Choiseul – the main exponent of the pro-Polish foreign policy at the French court – was removed from the office (Black 1999, 116) and the then French-Bar alliance was fatally damaged. Still, Wielhorski's then failure in terms of political matters did not imply problems with his informal contacts; it was precisely at this point when he joined the *milieu* of the French Enlightenment and got in touch with Gabriel Bonnot de Mably and soon afterwards with Jean-Jacques Rousseau.

Rousseau and de Mably: The Dispute over the Right Course

In the circle of Paris intellectuals, Wielhorski sought to promote the Bar Confederation not as a political patchwork of Polish noble families competing for power, but as a virtuous revolt of heroic patriots fighting for their liberty (Michalski 1985, 199–214). He managed to convince both Rousseau and de Mably of his ideas, which was obvious from their consequent writings clearly showing appreciation for the myth of Polish republic, rather than the political reality. In any case, de Mably managed to hand in his manuscript *Observations sur la réforme des loix en Pologne* already in August 1770, which was tactically geared toward the needs of the Bar confederates, with its official version, *Du Gouvernement et des lois de Pologne*, published in 1781, in London. Rousseau, who was slightly slower, submitted his considerations to Wielhorski during the spring 1771, at which point the urgent request for help had already ended, as the Bar Confederation was nearly defeated by the Russians, leaving the Polish sovereignty at stake. As in the previous case, Rousseau's thoughts were intended as nearly private matters for the Polish clients, although their unpublished copies circulated even before they were finally published as *Considérations sur le gouvernement de Pologne* in 1782, in Geneva.

While the recommendations of Rousseau and de Mably came in late and did not serve their original purpose, this does not mean absence of a Polish episode of the French Enlightenment. Although the contemporary Western European political philosophy had been partially reflected in the Polish culture already before, when particularly Stanisław Konarski applied the modern trends to the older classical canon of noble republican discourse (Konarski 1762; Michalski 1973, 137–138; Symmons-Symonolewicz 1983, 36), perspectives of Rousseau and de Mably were the first cases when the Polish domestic tradition of political ideas was put into more abstract framework of European Enlightenment. Rousseau's *Considerations* were translated into Polish only in 1789 (Rousseau 1789), but still served as one of the influential sources for the reform of the Polish state. In this regard, it was especially Rousseau who was able to assess the local political model in a more general understanding of human evolution and use a symbolic depiction of the European civilization for the defense of his political and philosophical standpoints (Lukowski 2012, 130). Between 1788 and 1792, and in parallel with the French revolution, the so-called *Great sejm* was convened in Warsaw with the ambition to renew the Polish sovereignty and modernize political procedures. Its main achievement was the adoption of a completely new constitution, ratified in early May 1791 (being the first codified constitution in Europe). Here, it should be stressed that both parliamentary debates and the language of the constitution reflected not only a rich canon of Polish domestic adherents to the Enlightenment (Hoensch 1997, 423–451), but also principles formulated by foreign observers, such as Rousseau's concept of general will (Butterwick-Pawlikowski 2016, 36–37; Lukowski 1994, 65–87; Tarnowska 2018, 124–131). Furthermore, it should be stated that Rousseau's ideas left a significant trail not only in the Polish political thought (Leśnodorski 1967, 39; Lis 2017; Szyjkowski 1913, 122–156), but also in the Polish educational reform, when the "first ministry of education in Europe" was established in Warsaw (Kamińska and Szybiak 2012, 273–280).

In contrast to Rousseau, the impact of de Mably's thought on the Polish political discourse was less significant, possibly because of the fact that his word was not available in Polish. Both, however, adhered to the belief, which was far from self-evident at that time, that the salvation of the Polish society and political sovereignty was not only possible, but also desirable – a possibility conditioned by a set of external and unlikely circumstances, such as the victory of the Ottoman Empire against the Russians, which would consequently weaken the Russian diplomacy and its influence in the Polish-Lithuanian Commonwealth (de Mably 1794–1795, 89–90; Rousseau 2005, 237). The agreement concerning such an important aspect is a clear confirmation that the philosophers' ideological grounds were not so antagonistic, as it is commonly suggested. Contrary to the widespread interpretation, depicting Rousseau as a conservative advocating the status quo of the Polish question and de Mably as his genuine counterpart, it is fair to stress that their recommendations as to how to reform the Polish state stemmed from a shared standpoint, according to which, without some proper changes Poland would not be able to survive. But even in the case of state failure, the unique Polish society would still be there, with all the valuable features of a national community; as warned by Rousseau, "[y]ou might not be able to keep them [the Russians] from swallowing you; at least make it so they cannot digest you" (Rousseau 2005, 174).

Thinking about features that were supposed to be either preserved or eliminated, both Rousseau and de Mably were critical of the Polish community's harsh serfdom, in comparison with the contemporary Western Europe. As rightly observed by Rousseau (2005, 184), the Polish nation was composed of "the nobles, who are everything, the bourgeoisie, who are nothing, and the peasants, who are less than nothing." Since this state of affairs also irritated de Mably, both philosophers called for a more egalitarian constitution in relation to the determination of citizen rights, which would also boost military capacities of the endangered state (Lukowski 2012, 135). However, it was the problem of social injustice that actually exposed an important difference between the two, namely as to whether Poland should have completely subscribed to the western European civilization or preserved its dominant peculiarities to assist the layout of future European order. With regard to the abolition of serfdom, Rousseau was more sensitive than de Mably toward Polish traditions and available options; instead of the implementation of egalitarian Enlightenment with its animosity against noble titles, he recommended a process of gradual ennoblement of various Polish groups and individuals for patriotic merits (Rousseau 2005, 228–229). Moreover, he suggested a transformation of the former aristocracy of nobles by origin into the genuine aristocracy of the spirit: "Polish Nobles, be more, be men. Then alone will you be happy and free, but never flatter yourself for being so, as long as you hold your brothers in chains" (Rousseau 2005, 185). Rousseau was thus fighting for not only preservation, but fundamental extension of the original concept of the Polish nobility, when all the classes of Polish society accepted the values of civic loyalty to the republic. It is worth noting that Rousseau presented similar views also in his other writings, where he admitted that a good republic needs social stratification stemming from different merits, talents, and contributions of citizens (Rousseau 2002, 169).

Another similarity between Rousseau and de Mably is found in the thesis maintaining that the Polish constitution was weakened due to the fatal paralysis of legislation, which was not followed by consolidation of the executive power. Contrary to Western Europe, where the decline of then form of political assembly was caused mainly by the rise of absolutist and centralized governments, Poland lost its parliamentary efficiency by becoming a dysfunctional anarchy (Lukowski 2012, 130). Here, while Rousseau agreed with de Mably about the essence of the problem, they differed about the optimal solution; in fact, this is the point of proper clash between them, with de Mably favoring Europeanization and Rousseau promoting Polonization. While de Mably viewed the fragile political power as an inherent symptom of the old and obsolete Polish constitution, which, therefore, had to be replaced with time-proven examples from the Western world, Rousseau wanted to rescue Poland through the respect of the traditional patterns, such as the mythical republicanism of the ancient world. When de Mably proposed to establish a Polish hereditary monarchy in order to end the corrupted chaos of *interregna*, Rousseau defended the ancestral concept of sweet liberty: "They would like to combine the peace of despotism with the sweetness of freedom. I am afraid that they might want contradictory things. Repose and freedom appear incompatible to me; it is necessary to choose" (Rousseau 2005, 170).[3]

According to Rousseau, free elections represented a condition necessary to prevent the Poles from embarking on a journey of general European slavery. Moreover, another traditional tool he believed should be preserved was the institution of *confederacies*, capable of legitimizing potential fights against an oppressive government. Rousseau considered *confederacies* as emergency brakes that could protect republican liberty from foreign invasion, as well as from domestic despotism: "[I]f the Confederations saved the fatherland, it is the Dietines that have preserved it, and it is there that the true Palladium of freedom is" (Rousseau 2005, 190). As in other cases, Rousseau found inspiration in the ancient world; *confederacies* were compared to the institution of Roman dictatorships that were also supposed to protect civic constitution from being corrupted. His sympathy for *confederacies* is linked to his own attitude toward *liberum veto*; unlike de Mably who wanted to get rid of it, Rousseau recommended to keep it for constitutional questions only: "In itself the liberum veto is not a vicious right, but as soon as it passes its bounds it becomes the most dangerous of abuses . . . The liberum veto would be less unreasonable if it fell uniquely on the fundamental points of the constitution" (Rousseau 2005, 202–203). Rousseau used his social contract principles, which required unanimous concordance when establishing a political community, but not for everyday decision-making. In terms of the optimal reform of the Polish constitution, *liberum veto* was supposed to be abolished as an obstructive technique of individual envoys but preserved for the collective protest of the whole delegation of regional *sejmiks*. In the case that the electorate of a particular *sejmik* – in charge of the appointment of envoys – subsequently concluded that the application of *veto* was legitimate, Rousseau proposed that the envoys be honored for the rest of their life, but otherwise (if their *veto* turned out illegitimate) they were to be sentenced to death (Rousseau 2005, 205). With regard to honors, both Rousseau and de Mably showed animosity toward material rewards and gave priority to the ancient tradition of symbolic prizes instead (de Mably 1952, 177; Stasiak 2014, 63).

---

3 Aversion of Rousseau to the principle of hereditary power is also found in his *Discourses*: "[I]t is thus that chiefs, become hereditary, contracted the habit of considering their offices as a family estate, and themselves as proprietors of those communities, of which at first they were but mere officers; of calling their fellow-citizens their slaves; of numbering them, like cattle, among their belongings; and of calling themselves the peers of gods, and kings of kings" (Rousseau 2002, 132–133).

Finally, given his belief that the main problem of Poland was its paralyzed legislation and weak executive power, Rousseau viewed the federalization of the state as a solution. In fact, he was fascinated with the large extent and unified structure of the Polish-Lithuanian Commonwealth since, according to the then widely accepted classical theory, virtuous republics could flourish only within a context of strictly bordered city-states (Bellah 2002, 280). Still, while Rousseau defended the idea that popular sovereignty should be decisive even for large communities (Rousseau 2002, 219), he was very well aware of the fact that huge Polish territories were out of reach of the central government control. For this reason, he depicted a future Polish republic as an association of many sovereign states representing specific administrative units, *voivodeships*.[4] Accordingly, it was their delegations, rather than individual members, who would be allowed to exercise *liberum veto*. They would, therefore, be responsible for ensuring protection of the republic against centralized despotism and bringing about the realization of Polish general will, already achieved at the level of *voivodeships*. In compliance with the interests of the Bar Confederation and its chief ideologist Wielhorski, Rousseau was thus opposed to the reforms of the *Familia* from the 1764 *sejm*, when obligatory instructions of regional *sejmiks* were abolished (Volumina legum 1860, 18). Needless to say, when Rousseau called for the renewal of these instructions and the birth of a direct republican democracy in a Polish style, he was again in stark contrast with de Mably who saw the rescue of Poland in hard centralization and strengthening of a state-wide parliament at the expense of regional *voivodeships*.

Rousseau and Wielhorski: Who is to be Saved, Poles or Europeans?

Rousseau's adherence to traditional institutions such as *confederations, liberum veto*, and sovereignty of *voivodeships* was not an end in itself, but part of a specific agenda of the Polish society. In contrast to de Mably who was not convinced of the Polish society's competencies and thus insisted on the involvement of foreign experts (Lukowski 2012, 126), Rousseau kept warning the Poles against strange novelties and went on to encourage an even greater use of Polish language and expression of traditional manners. In his view, education was crucial not only because of its potential to produce a new generation of Polish patriots to serve the interests of their own community, but even more significantly, to serve the whole of Europe. By maintaining their education and public activities purely Polish, the Poles would

---

4 Rousseau told the Poles: "The first reform you need is that of your extent. Your vast provinces will never allow the severe administration of small Republics. Begin by compressing your boundaries if you want to reform your government. Perhaps your neighbors are considering doing this service for you . . . I would like, if it were possible, for you to have as many of them as of Palatinates" (Rousseau 2005, 183).

become the main standard-bearers and saviors of the ancient civilization and aristo-cratic citizenship within the spoiled and commercialized European society. In addi-tion, the Poles were urged to keep their outlandish costumes, ride horses as knights, and not allow any perverted and effeminate acting existing in Western Europe to be performed in their theatres (Rousseau 2005, 175–177). Still, his fascina-tion with East European principles was not intended to promote the Polish society as such; it served as a comparative tool to disparage Western Europeans. Therefore, Rousseau's acceptance of Polish discourse of *sarmatism* and aristocratic republican-ism, which was partially defended by Wielhorski as well, provided him with a solid example to support his general animosity toward modernity and his favor for a just social contract.

When encouraging the Poles to live according to the Ciceronian motto *ubi patria, ibi bene* and not to worry about the loss of their sovereignty as they were anyway capable of building a true republic in their hearts, Rousseau suggests that a genuine value of Polishness does not reside in an ethnic identity. Rather it exists in a civic tradition contrasting with the despicable Western European lifestyle (Rousseau 2005, 174–177). Indeed, Wielhorski's depiction of his motherland as a community where no-blemen were subjected to the republic, strongly resembles Rousseau's *Social Contract* and his striving for an association where people are united and free at the same time (Rousseau 2002, 163–167). But why was Rousseau so keen on preserving the original spirit of the Polish society despite the likely fall of its statehood? Such a need was due to his disdain for an archetype of the commercial man who was supposed to be replaced by a right citizen of older times. When Rousseau wrote that there were no French, English, Germans or Spaniards anymore, because all of them had the same goal – to chase gold and money, and to seduce women (Rousseau 2005, 175) – it was exactly this belief that he used to deny a modern man who had come to terms with the loss of his own liberty (Michalski 2015, 82–83). Conclusively, Rousseau expected to see the Polish society sacrifice profit for the republic and common good; otherwise, fighting for Poland would not have made sense.

Still, in order to gain a full picture of Rousseau's impact on the question of Poland, it is necessary to pay more attention to Wielhorski, since it was him who stood behind Rousseau's engagement. Several years after Rousseau's work, Wielhorski published *O przywroceniu dawnego rządu* in 1775, where he outlined his own vision of a desirable Polish reform, previously discussed with his fellow-patriots (Stasiak 2010, 721–722). It is believed that Wielhorski must have conveyed some of his beliefs to Rousseau back in 1770,[5] although Wielhorski completed his own work later. The dilemma as to whether his remarks were influenced by the French Enlightenment or whether

---

5 As Rousseau repeatedly highlighted, he read several manuscripts which Wielhorski had given him, and, from Rousseau's words, it was obvious that at least some of them were written by Wielhorski himself: "I must limit myself to giving him [Wielhorski] an account of the impressions made on me by the reading of his work and the reflections it suggested to me . . . The succinct

Rousseau worked under the impact of the Polish discourse is thus a false one: Rousseau was aware of the Polish noble republican myth and Wielhorski obviously adjusted this myth following his French experience.

Wielhorski's contact with the broader European perspective is immediately spotted in his *opus magnum*; he presented traditional arguments in a new fashion of modern European thought and moreover, he repeatedly referred to both French philosophers that he knew (Wielhorski 1775, 284–303). In this regard, it is intriguing that although Wielhorski had a closer relationship with de Mably,[6] his use and interpretation of the noble republican myth reflected Rousseau's points of view more. Even though one can find a very positive evaluation of a Polish nobleman in his writing, the point of his book lay in the central thesis about the golden times of the old republic and its ancestors, whose values should have been restored. A resolution to the crisis was, therefore, not in the adoption of foreign patterns – as de Mably suggested – but in the rediscovery of the Polish old and lost heritage, as also recommended by Rousseau. Similarly, Wielhorski called for the preservation of elective monarchy, while defending the federalization of a republic on the basis of traditional *voivodeships* (Wielhorski 1775, 271–284). From Rousseau, Wielhorski also adopted a positive attitude toward the legal revolts (*confederacies*), as well as the concept of noble citizens as loyal state servants who should be elected to their offices by the public assembly and then assessed according to their effectiveness (Wielhorski 1775, 320–321). When Rousseau, for example, suggested honoring Polish officials with the title *spes patriae* (Rousseau 2005, 223), Wielhorski offered his own, similar version, known as *emeritus civis* (Wielhorski 1775, 141).

Nonetheless, it is not possible to conclude that Wielhorski simply copied Rousseau's worldview and that his understanding of the Polish question was nearly the same. While Rousseau used his admiration toward the Polish traditional society to criticize the European society of his time, Wielhorski shared the appreciation for the Polish older period, but at the same time, was convinced that the salvation of noble manners from the past required the acceptance of modern social trends coming from Western Europe. This is the reason why Wielhorski occasionally ignored the Rousseauist way and prioritized the rhetoric of European utilitarianism. In the case of *liberum veto*, admittedly the most controversial part of the Polish constitution, Wielhorski appreciated it as a valuable tool of the past, but, unlike Rousseau, perceived it as a dangerous institution. He proposed

---

exposition of the morals of the Poles that M. de Wielhorski kindly passed on to me is not sufficient to make me well acquainted with their civil and domestic practices . . . Count Wielhorski proposes raising one Regiment per Palatinate" (Rousseau 2005, 169, 176, 218).

6 In 1777, de Mably visited Poland at Wielhorski's invitation, but it must be said that he was mostly confused by that experience as he found out that the myth of Polish virtuous aristocracy was a false illusion. After his arrival to France he promoted even more skeptical attitudes toward Poland than before, which one can identify in his letters to Rulhière (Lukowski 2012, 137; Wolff 1994, 275–276).

its abolition, even though he himself advocated its preservation several years earlier when it was useful to block the *Familia* (Wielhorski 1775, 80, 251). Moreover, in the case of *liberum veto* and Polish social structure, Wielhorski did not rely on Rousseau, but on "the famous Locke" and his concept of social contract (Wielhorski 1775, 85–88). For that reason, when expressing respect for the Polish ancient times, Wielhorski referred to the image of the Polish republic as a merit-based community of emancipated individuals, and not the depiction of Poland as a resurrection of the ancient *polis*. Concerning his approach, the citizens of the Polish republic were supposed to respect its laws not because of the vague concept of common good, but in order to protect their own life, liberties, and possessions (Stasiak 2010, 724). This argument abandoned the collectivist interpretation of Rousseau and gave priority to the older discourse and guidance of the Polish early modern republicans, including Stanisław Orzechowski (1563) and Andrzej Frycz Modrzewski (1551).

Conclusion

Rousseau's *Considerations* perhaps represent the attitudes of "the most foreign *Sarmat* of all the time" (Walicki 2000, 31), who – shortly before the final collapse of the Polish-Lithuanian Commonwealth in 1795 – believed that the salvation of the Polish society lay in the ideals of ancient republics, the restoration of which could have saved the European society as a whole. The dilemma of whether to change Poles into Europeans or Europeans into Poles was not a simple one, since Poland and Western Europe were communicating vessels for Rousseau and Wielhorski. However, it is possible to conclude that the philosophical dispute over desirable Europeanness was strongly linked to political questions about the Polish republic, with the participants in that debate being expected to reflect on its future heading. Today, almost 250 years later, the essential tension between Rousseau and de Mably's points of view is still traceable in the Polish discourse, with the question of heading at the very forefront. As the Polish conservative thinker Andrzej Nowak puts it, there is still some kind of "eternal imprisonment" of Poland, moving between the Polish self-perception of an ordinary European nation catching up with the West and the romantic image of Poland as a standard-bearer of unique civilization (Nowak 2004, 391).

After the failure of the Soviet bloc and subsequent decline of both overly optimistic or extremely pessimistic predictions (Fukuyama 1992; Huntington 1997), when it became clear that national questions would also go into the twenty-first century, the urgency for a new interpretation of the Polish history and the state's national interest increased dramatically. During the nineties, when the idealist vision of homecoming to Europe prevailed in East-Central European region – with its countries competing for the best Europeanness candidate status – a new wave of the so-called Enlightened discourse occurred in Poland. Its main advocates claimed it was necessary to get rid of the Eastern manners and to abandon the old dreams about the Polish mission and sovereign empire; in their view, there were more important tasks, such as to find the easiest and fastest way to the Western Europe, which was deemed the only true Europe (Tunander 1997, 17–45). In the words of Aleksey Miller, "instead of a river with two banks, Russia and the West, that would enable Eastern European ships to choose where to anchor . . . there is only one river of time carrying all the Eastern Europe together with Russia in one direction – toward the West" (Miller 2002, 81). Nevertheless, the pro-Occidentalist optimism was quickly confronted with questions concerning the nature of the Western European Enlightened development (Michalski 1996), as well as the Polish resignation in front of the moral dimension of its own identity and its historical heritage including the early modern patterns of republicanism (Gawin 2006), appreciated by Rousseau at the end of the eighteenth century. It is even intriguing that the reactions, with the conservative right as the lead, relied on the theoretical framework of postcolonial studies (Grzechnik 2014; Mayblin, Piekut, and Valentine 2016; Zarycki 2011, 2014). While known as a method of the European left, in the Polish case it has assisted the supporters of older traditions with their intention to deconstruct the dominant Western patterns of self-identification (Bill 2014, 107–127).

As during the Rousseau's moment, the contemporary discussions over genuine Polishness and its optimal relation toward Western Europe are full of mutual prejudices and stereotypes. In 2017, when one of the co-workers of Hillary Clinton, the former United States presidential candidate, posted a tweet about Polish citizens celebrating the Day of Independence – "60,000 Nazis marching today through Warsaw" (Lehrich 2017), he reflected ignorance and impetuous judgements characterizing many Western European intellectuals of the eighteenth century, who had never travelled to Poland, but used it for symbolic purposes and expression of their moral superiority. From the opposite side, one can find ideological assessments and purpose-built simplifications about the Western European society in the discourse of the ruling Polish elites, identifying themselves with the position resembling the *sarmatian* ideal of the Polish nation as a defender of pure morality. When one flicks through the controversial statements made by the leader of the Polish ruling party, Jarosław Kaczyński, about "a great offensive of evil" (Osiecki 2019) or "social diseases" (Sobczak and Florkiewicz 2018), it is not difficult to identify which threats he has referred to. Even more so, in one of his speeches preceding the 2019 election, he argued that for Poland to catchup with the most developed countries, it did not require to "copy those in the West . . . We do not have to stand under the rainbow flag, but under Poland's red and white banner" (cited in Cienski 2019).

The rhetoric depicting the EU as a dangerous hydra, which supports postmodern relativism, dangerous multiculturalism, and political correctness, stems from the similar patterns of the ancient *sarmatism*, according to which, the Polish Easterness represented moral and spiritual purity that had to be protected from the

Western decadence. Hence, the Polish appeal to preservation of national pride and otherness together with defiance against transnational capital cannot be read just as a protest of those who have been left behind the globalization process, but as a more general revolt against the Western Enlightenment with its all universalist tendencies. When one listens to the Polish far-right's position warning the Poles that if they do not return to their roots, they "will die as the nations of western Europe are dying" (Koper and Pempel 2019), they can identify a strong similarity with the calling for golden ancient *sarmatian* times and Rousseau's warnings about the decay of European civilization (Rousseau 2005, 175). Here, of course, we should be careful in order to avoid deducing false allegories or wrong conclusions about the heritage of the Polish Enlightened and *sarmatian* discourses that belonged to an entirely different context.

When we consider the contemporary debates about the Polish society's optimal heading, we should not neglect the fact that this kind of enquiry has strong historical roots. Therefore, it is false to imagine Poland as an isolated island of chastity in the dangerous European waters, and it is misleading to present the Polish society as a seedbed of fanaticism, irrationalism, and intolerance, in the need of uprooting by the right values of the civilized West. The Polish contemporary challenge is about finding a way to democracy and national identity that would not blindly embrace foreign patterns without respect for the Polish traumatic past, but also about finding a way to avoid war against European liberal heritage. After all, Rousseau wrote his apologia of the Polish *Rzeczpospolita* not as an adoration of status quo, but as a sum of recommendations to be pursued in order to restore ancient virtues not only for the future generations of Poles, but for the European society as a whole.

References

Bellah, Robert. 2002. "Rousseau on society and the individual." In *The Social Contract and The First and Second Discourses: Jean-Jacques Rousseau*, edited by Susan Dunn, 266–287. New Haven, CT: Yale University Press.

Bill, Stanley. 2014. "W poszukiwaniu autentyczności: Kultura polska i natura teorii postkolonialnej." *Praktyka teoretyczna* 11: 107–127.

Black, Jeremy. 1999. *From Louis XIV to Napoleon: The Fate of a Great Power*. London: Routledge.

Bodin, Jean. 1606. *The Six Books of a Commonweale*, edited by Richard Knolles. London: Adam Islip impensis G. Bishop.

Butterwick, Richard. 2001a. "Introduction." In *The Polish-Lithuanian Monarchy in European Context, c. 1500–1795*, edited by Richard Butterwick, 1–23. New York: Palgrave Macmillan.

Butterwick, Richard. 2001b. "The Enlightened Monarchy of Stanisław August Poniatowski (1764–1795)." In *The Polish-Lithuanian Monarchy in European Context, c. 1500–1795*, edited by Richard Butterwick, 193–218. New York: Palgrave Macmillan.

Butterwick-Pawlikowski, Richard. 2016. "Challenges for the Commonwealth: The Counsel of Jean-Jacques Rousseau." *XVIII amžiaus studijos* 3: 3–42.

Casanova, Giacomo. 1774. *Istoria delle turbolenze della Polonia*. Gorizia: Per Valerio de'Valerj.

Cienski, Jan. 2019. "Kaczyński's last hurrah: The PiS leader is preparing to step aside, but his party might not survive the ensuing power struggle." *Politico*, 10 April, https://www.politico.eu/arti cle/jaroslaw-kaczynski-last-hurrah-poland-election-pis/.

Connor, Bernard. 1698. *The History of Poland in Several Letters to Persons of Quality: Giving an Account of the Antient and Present State of that Kingdom, Historical, Geographical, Physical, Political, and Ecclesiastical*. London: Dan Brown.

Coyer, Gabriel Franciszek. 1761. *Histoire De Jean Sobieski, Roi De Pologne*. Varsovie and Paris: Chez Duchesne.

Czubek, Jan, ed. 1918a. *Pisma polityczne z czasów rokoszu Zebrzydowskiego 1606–1608, Vol. II*. Kraków: nakł. Akademji Umiejętności.

Czubek, Jan, ed. 1918b. *Pisma polityczne z czasów rokoszu Zebrzydowskiego 1606–1608, Vol. III*. Kraków: nakł. Akademji Umiejętności.

Davies, Norman. 1972. "Sir Maurice Hankey and the Inter-Allied Mission to Poland, July-August 1920." *The Historical Journal* 15(5): 553–561.

Davies, Norman. 2003. *White Eagle. Red Star, The Polish-Soviet War 1919–1920 and the Miracle on the Vistula*. London: Pimlico.

de Mably, Gabriel Bonnot. 1781. *Du gouvernement et des lois de la Pologne*. London: [s.n.]

de Mably, Gabriel Bonnot. 1791–95. "Du gouvernement et des lois de la Pologne." In *Collection complete des œuvres de l'abbé de Mably, Vol. VIII*, 1–336. Paris: Ch. Desbrière.

de Mably, Gabriel Bonnot. 1952. *Zasady praw, Vol. I*. Warszawa: PIW.

Dunning, Chester. 2001. *A Short History of Russia's First Civil War: The Time of Troubles and the Founding of the Romanov Dynasty*. University Park, PA: Penn State University Press.

Faber, Martin. 2018. *Sarmatismus. Die politische Ideologie des polnischen Adels im 16. und 17. Jahrhundert*. Wiesbaden: Harrasowitz Verlag.

Friedrich, Karin, and Barbara Pendzich. 2009. *Citizenship and Identity in a Multinational Commonwealth Poland–Lithuania in Context, 1550–1772*. Leiden: Brill.

Frost, Robert. 2003. *After the Deluge: Poland – Lithuania and the Second Northern War, 1655–1660*. Cambridge: Cambridge University Press.

Frost Robert. 2007. "The nobility of Poland-Lithuania, 1569–1795." In *The European Nobilities in the Seventeenth and Eighteenth Centuries, Vol. II: Northern, Central and Eastern Europe*, edited by Hamish M. Scott, 183–222. New York: Palgrave Macmillan.

Frycz Modrzewski, Andrzej. 1551 (1857). *O poprawie Rzeczypospolitej*. Przemyśl: Nakł. Michała Dzikowskiego.

Fukuyama, Francis. 1992. *The End of History and the Last Man*. New York: Free Press.

Gawin, Dariusz. 2006. *Blask i gorycz wolności*. Kraków: OMP.

Grzechnik, Marta. 2014. "The missing second world: On Poland and postcolonial studies." *Interventions* 21(7): 998–1014.

Grześkowiak-Krwawicz, Anna. 2011. "Noble republicanism in the Polish-Lithuanian commonwealth." *Acta Poloniae historica* 103: 31–65.

Grześkowiak-Krwawicz, Anna. 2012. *Queen Liberty. The Concept of Freedom in the Polish-Lithuanian Commonwealth*. Leiden: Brill.

Henshall, Nicholas. 1992. *The Myth of Absolutism: Change and Continuity in Early Modern European Monarchy*. London: Longman.

Hoensch, Jörg. 1997. "Citizen, nation, constitution: The realization and failure of the constitution of 3 May 1791 in light of mutual Polish-French influence." In *Constitution and Reform in Eighteenth-century Poland. The Constitution of 3 May 1791*, edited by Samuel Fiszman, 423–451. Bloomington: Indiana University Press.

Huntington, Samuel. 1997. *The Clash of Civilizations and the Remaking of World Order*. New York: Touchstone.

Iłowajski, Dmitrij. 1871. *Sejm Grodzieński roku 1793. Ostatni sejm Rzeczypospolitej Polskiej.* Warszawa: Żupański.

Jabłonowski, Jan Stanisław. 1730. *Skrupuł bez skrupułu w Polszcze albo Oświecenie grzechów narodowi naszemu polskiemu zwyczaynieyszych a za grzechy nie mianych.* [s.l.] [s.n.]

Kamińska, Janina, and Irena Szybiak. 2012. "Idee wychowawcze Jeana-Jacques'a Rousseau w przepisach dla szkół Komisji Edukacji Narodowej." *Przegląd Filozoficzny – Nowa seria* 84(4): 273–280.

Karolewski, Ireneusz P., and Roland Benedikter. 2017. "Europe's new rogue states, Poland and Hungary: A narrative and its perspectives." *Chinese Political Science Review* 2(2): 179–200.

Kisielewski, Władysław Tadeusz. 1880. *Reforma książąt Czartoryskich na sejmie konwokacyjnym roku 1764.* Sambor: [s.n.]

Kołudzki, Augustyn. 1727. *Thron Oyczysty albo Pałac Wieczności, w krotkim zebrániu monarchow, xiążąt y krolow polskich.* Poznań: Jan Tobiasz Keller.

Konarski, Stanisław. 1762. *O skutecznym rad sposobie albo o utrzymywaniu ordynaryinych seymow.* Warszawa: w Drukarni J.K. Mci i Rzeczypospolitey u XX. Scholarum Piarum.

Konopczyński, Władysław. 1918. *Liberum veto. Studyum Porównaczo-Historyczne.* Kraków: S. A. Krzyżanowski.

Koper, Anna, and Kacper Pempel. 2019. "Polish far-right groups march on independence anniversary." *Reuters*, 11 November, https://www.reuters.com/article/us-poland-independence-march/polish-far-right-groups-march-on-independence-anniversary-idUSKBN 1XL22R.

Kraushar, Aleksander. 1898. *Książę Repnin i Polska w pierwszem czteroleciu panowania Stanisława Augusta (1764–1768),* Vol. I. Kraków: G. Gebethner.

Lehrich, Jesse. 2017. "60,000 Nazis marched on Warsaw today." *Twitter*, 11 November, https://twit ter.com/jesselehrich/status/929451829657853952.

Leśnodorski, Bogusław. 1967. "Idee polityczne Jana Jakuba Rousseau w Polsce." In: *Wiek XIX; prace, ofiarowane Stefanowi Kieniewiczowi w 60 rocznicę urodzin,* edited by Stefan Kieniewicz – Barbara Grochulska – Bogusław Leśnodorski – Andrzej Zahorski, 29–48. Warszawa: Państwowe Wydawnictwo Naukowe.

Leszczyński, Stanisław, and Joseph Menoux. 1751. *Réponse au discours de Mr Rousseau, qui a remporté le prix de Académie de Dijon, sur cette question: si le rétablissement des sciences et des arts a contribué f épurer les moeurs.* [s.l.] [s.n.]

Leszczyński, Stanisław. 1858 (1743). *Głos wolny wolność ubezpieczający.* Kraków: Wydawnictwo Biblioteki Polskiej.

Lewicki, Anatol, ed. 1891. "Przywilej Brzeski przez Władysława Jagiełłę za przyrzeczenie uznania królem jego syna Władysława nadany." In *Codex epistolaris saeculi decimi quinti,* Vol. II: *1382–1445,* 187–192. Kraków: Nakładem Akademii Umiejętności Krakowskiej.

Lis, Rafał. 2017. "Polish republicanism of the Four Year Seym at a doctrinal crossroads." *History of European Ideas* 43(7): 762–775.

Lukowski, Jerzy. 1977. *The Szlachta and the Confederacy of Radom, 1764–1767/68. A Study of the Polish Nobility.* Rome: Institutum Historicum Polonicum Romae.

Lukowski, Jerzy. 1985. "Towards partition: Polish magnates and Russian intervention in Poland during the early reign of Stanisław August Poniatowski." *The Historical Journal* 28(3): 557–574.

Lukowski, Jerzy. 1991. *Liberty's Folly: The Polish-Lithuanian Commonwealth in the Eighteenth Century, 1697–1795.* London: Routledge.

Lukowski Jerzy. 1994. "Recasting utopia: Montesquieu, Rousseau and the Polish constitution of 3 May 1791." *Historical Journal* 37(1): 65–87.

Lukowski, Jerzy. 1999. *The Partitions of Poland, 1772, 1793, 1795.* London: Longman.

Lukowski, Jerzy. 2012. *Disorderly Liberty. The Political Culture of the Polish-Lithuanian Commonwealth in the Eighteenth Century*. London: Continuum.

Maciejewski, Janusz. 1977. "Pojęcie narodu w myśli republikantów lat 1767–1775." In *Idee i koncepce narodu w polskiej myśli politycznej czasów porozbiorowych*, edited by Janusz Goćkowski and Andrzej Walicki, 21–41. Warszawa: Państwowe Wydawnictwo Naukowe.

Marat, Jean-Paul. 1770 (1847). *Les Aventures du jeune comte Potowski*. Paris: Le Siècle.

Mayblin, Lucy, Aneta Piekut, and Gill Valentine. 2016. "'Other' posts in 'other' places: Poland through a postcolonial lens?" *Sociology* 50(1): 60–76.

Michalski, Cezary. 1996. *Powrót człowieka bez właściwości*. Warszawa: Casablanca Studio.

Michalski, Jerzy. 1972. "Stanisław Konarski wobec sarmatyzmu i problem europeizacji Polski." In *Polska w świecie: szkice z dziejów kultury polskiej*, edited by Jerzy Dowiat et al., 277–284. Warszawa: Państwowe Wydawnictwo Naukowe.

Michalski, Jerzy. 1973. "Sarmatyzm a europeizacja Polski w XVIII wieku." In *Swojskość i cudzoziemszczyna w dziejach kultury polskiej*, edited by Zofia Stefanowska, 113–168. Warszawa: Instytut Badan Literackich PAN.

Michalski, Jerzy. 1985. "Idee reformatorskie sekretarza konfederacji barskiej. Dyskusja Ignacego Bohusza z Gabrielem Mablym." *Miscellanea Historico-Archivistica* 1: 199–214.

Michalski, Jerzy. 2015. *Rousseau and Polish Republicanism*. Warsaw: Instytut Historii PAN.

Miller, Aleksey. 2002. "Europa Wschodnia – potrzeba nowej wizji." *Arcana: kultura, historia, polityka* 44(2): 76–82.

Miller, John, ed. 1990. *Absolutism in Seventeenth Century Europe*. New York: Palgrave Macmillan.

Montesquieu, Charles Louis. 1777. *The Complete Works of M. de Montesquieu*. London: T. Evans.

Nowak, Andrzej. 2004. "From empire builder to empire breaker, or there and back again: History and memory of Poland's role in Eastern European politics." In *Od imperium do imperium: Spojrzenie na historię Europy Wschodniej*, edited by Andrzej Nowak, 356–393. Kraków–Warszawa: Arcana–Instytut Historii PAN.

Opaliński, Edward. 2002. "Civic humanism and republican citizenship in the Polish renaissance." In *Republicanism: A Shared European Heritage, Vol. I: Republicanism and Constitutionalism in Early Modern Europe*, edited by Martin van Gelderen – Quentin Skinner, 147–166. Cambridge: Cambridge University Press.

Orzechowski, Stanisław. 1859 (1566). *Policyja Królestwa Polskiego na kształt Arystotelesowych Polityk wypisana*. Poznań: Merzbach.

Orzechowski, Stanisław. 1919 (1563). *Rozmowa albo Dyjalog około egzekucyjej Polskiej Korony*. Kraków: Akademia Umiejętności.

Osiecki, Grzegorz. 2019. "Walka z 'wielką ofensywą zła' i obrona 'polskiej rodziny'. Ale co z pieniędzmi?" *Dziennik*, 8 July, https://wiadomosci.dziennik.pl/polityka/artykuly/602021,kaczynski-konwencja-pis-program-pieniadze-lgbt.html.

Pettit, Philip. 2002. *Republicanism: A Theory of Freedom and Government*. Oxford: Clarendon Press.

Pocock, John. 2009. *Political Thought and History: Essays on Theory and Method*. Cambridge: Cambridge University Press.

Przyboś, Adam, and Roman Żelewski, eds. 1974. *Albrycht Stanisław Radziwiłł: Memoriale rerum gestarum in Polonia 1632–1656, Vol. IV: 1648–1656*. Wrocław: Zakład Narodowy im. Ossolińskich.

Przyłuski, Jakub, 1553. *Leges seu statuta ac privilegia Regni Poloniae omnia*. Kraków: [s.n.]

Pyrrhys de Varille, César Félicité. 1771. *Lettres sur la Constitution actuelle de la Pologne et la tenure de ses diétes*. Paris: Chez Delalain.

Richardson, William. 1784. *Anecdotes of the Russian Empire in a Series of Letters*. London: W. Strahan and T. Cadell.

Rousseau, Jean-Jacques. 1782. "Les Considérations sur le gouvernement de Pologne et sur sa réformation projeté." In *Collection complète des œuvres de J.J. Rousseau*, 255–442. Genève: Paul Moultou and du Peyron.

Rousseau, Jean-Jacques. 1789. *Uwagi o rządzie polskim oraz nad Odmianą, czyli Reformą onego projektowaną* (translated by Franciszek Karp). Warszawa: Nakładem i Drukiem Michała Grölla.

Rousseau, Jean-Jacques. 1823. "Réponse de Jean-Jacques Rousseau au roi de Pologne, duc de Lorraine, Sur la Réfutation faite par ce prince de son Discours." In *Oeuvres de J.J. Rousseau, Vol. IV*, edited by Victor-Donatien Musset-Pathay, 63–95. Paris: Chez P. Dupont.

Rousseau, Jean-Jacques. 2002. *The Social Contract and the First and Second Discourses*. New Haven, CT: Yale University Press.

Rousseau, Jean-Jacques. 2005. *The Plan for Perpetual Peace, on the Government of Poland, and Other Writings on History and Politics*. Hanover and London: The University Press of New England.

Rulhière, Claude-Carloman. 1807. *Histoire de l'anarchie de Pologne*. Paris: Desenne.

Scott, Hamish. 2001. *The Emergence of the Eastern Powers, 1756–1775*. Cambridge: Cambridge University Press.

Skinner, Quentin. 1969. "Meaning and understanding in the history of ideas." *History and Theory* 8(1): 3–53.

Sobczak, Paweł, and Paweł Florkiewicz. 2018. "Defiant Kaczynski says Poland must avoid EU's 'social diseases'." *Reuters*, 2 September, https://www.reuters.com/article/us-poland-politics /defiant-kaczynski-says-poland-must-avoid-eus-social-diseases-idUSKCN1LI0J2.

Stanek, Wojciech. 1996. "Konfederacja a ewolucja mechanizmów walki politycznej w Rzeczypospolitej XVIII wieku." In *Między barokiem i oświeceniem. Nowe spojrzenie na czasy saskie*, edited by Krystyna Stasiewicz and Stanisław Achremczyk, 133–139. Olsztyn: Ośrodek Badań Nauk. im. W. Kętrzyńskiego.

Stasiak, Arkadiusz Michał. 2010. "Republican and monarchical patriotism in Polish political thought during the Enlightenment." In *Whose Love of Which Country? Composite States, National Histories and Patriotic Discourses in Early Modern East Central Europe*, edited by Balász Trencsényi and Marton Zászkaliczky, 711–733. Leiden: Brill.

Stasiak, Arkadiusz Michał. 2014. "Czy Polski radykalny republikanizm przełomu lat 60 i 70 XVIII wieku miał charakter rewolucyjny?" *Teka Komisji Historycznej* XI: 56–68.

Staszewski, Jacek. 1998. *August II Mocny*. Wrocław: Zakład Narodowy im. Ossolińskich.

Sucheni-Grabowski, Anna. 2009. *Wolność i prawo w staropolskiej koncepcji państwa*. Warszawa: Muzeum Historii Polski.

Symmons-Symonolewicz, Konstantin. 1983. *National Consciousness in Poland: Origin and Evolution*, Meadville: Maplewood Press.

Szyjkowski, Maryan. 1913. *Myśl Jana Jakóba Rousseau w Polsce XVIII wieku*. Kraków: Akademia Umiejętności.

Tarnowska, Anna. 2018. "To which constitution the further laws of the present Sejm have to adhere to in all . . . Constitutional precedence of the 3 May system." In *Reconsidering Constitutional Formation II Decisive Constitutional Normativity: From Old Liberties to New Precedence. Studies in the History of Law and Justice, Vol. XII*, edited by Müßig Ulrike, 113–172. Heidelberg: Springer.

Tazbir, Janusz. 1983. *Kultura szlachecka w Polsce: rozkwit, upadek, relikty*. Warszawa: Wiedza Powszechna.

Tunander, Ola. 1997. "Post-Cold War Europe: A synthesis of a bipolar friend-foe structure and a hierarchic cosmos-chaos structure?" In *Geopolitics in Post-Wall Europe: Security, Territory and*

Identity, edited by Ola Tunander, Pavel K. Baev, and Victoria Ingrid Einagel, 17–44. London: Sage.

Voltaire. 1731 (1908). *History of Charles II*. London: J. M. Dent & Sons.

Volumina legum. 1859. *Prawa, konstytucye y przywileie Królestwa Polskiego, Wielkiego Xięstwa Litewskiego y wszystkich prowincyi należących na walnych seymiech koronnych od Seymu Wiślickiego roku pańskiego 1347 aż do ostatniego Seymu uchwalone, Vol. I*. Petersburg: Nakładem i drukiem Jozafata Ohryzki.

Volumina legum. 1860. *Prawa, konstytucye y przywileie Królestwa Polskiego, Wielkiego Xięstwa Litewskiego y wszystkich prowincyi należących na walnych seymiech koronnych od Seymu Wiślickiego roku pańskiego 1347 aż do ostatniego Seymu uchwalone, Vol. VII*. Petersburg: Nakładem i drukiem Jozafata Ohryzki.

Wagner, Wenceslas J. 1997. "Some comments on old 'privileges' and the 'liberum veto'." In *Constitution and Reform in Eighteenth-Century Poland. The Constitution of 3 May 1791*, edited by Samuel Fiszman, 51–65. Bloomington: Indiana University Press.

Walicki, Andrzej. 1989. *The Enlightenment and the Birth of Modern Nationhood: Polish Political Thought from Noble Republicanism to Tadeusz Kościuszko*. Notre Dame, IN: University of Notre Dame Press.

Walicki, Andrzej. 1997. "The idea of nation in the main currents of political thought of the Polish Enlightenment." In *Constitution and Reform in Eighteenth-Century Poland. The Constitution of 3 May 1791*, edited by Samuel Fiszman, 155–174. Bloomington, IN: Indiana University Press.

Walicki, Andrzej. 2000. *Idea narodu w polskiej myśli oświeceniowej*. Warszawa: Polska Akademia Nauk Instytut Filozofii i Socjologii.

Wielhorski, Michał. 1775. *O przywroceniu dawneho rzadu według pierwiastkowych Rzeczypospolitej ustaw*. [s.l.] [s.n.]

Wolan, Andrzej. 2010. *De libertate politica sive civili. O wolności Rzeczypospolitej albo szlacheckiej*, edited by Maciej Eder and Roman Mazurkiewicz, Warszawa: Neriton.

Wolff, Larry. 1994. *Inventing Eastern Europe*. Stanford, CA: Stanford University Press.

Wyczański, Andrzej. 1991. *Polską Rzeczą Pospolitą Szlachecką*. Warszawa: PWN.

Zarycki, Tomasz. 2011. "Orientalism and images of Eastern Poland." In *Europe: Discourses from the Frontier*, edited by Anna Gąsior-Niemiec, 162–184. Warsaw: Oficyna Naukowa.

Zarycki, Tomasz. 2014. *Ideologies of Eastness in Central and Eastern Europe*. New York: Routledge.

Zielińska, Zofia. 1983. *Walka 'Familii' o reformę Rzeczypospolitej 1743–1752*. Warszawa: Państwowe Wydawnictwo Naukowe.

Zielonka, Jan. 2018. *Counter-Revolution: Liberal Europe in Retreat*. Oxford: Oxford University Press.

Marius-Mircea Mitrache

3 The Pursuit of France's Milieu Goals (1871–1925): The French Mental Mapping of East-Central Europe

In his 1983 article "Un Occident kidnappé ou la Tragédie de l'Europe Centrale," published in the French intellectual periodical *Le Débat*, the Paris-exiled Milan Kundera contemplated about the difficulties in geographically locating the region of Central Europe and concluded that "[i]t would be senseless to try to draw its borders exactly. Central Europe is not a state, it is a culture or a fate. Its borders are imaginary and must be drawn and redrawn with each new historical situation" (Kundera 1983, 8–9). Thus, he explained that Central Europe is not so much a state in itself, but rather a state of mind whose existence is consubstantial to a certain culture, imagination, and memory, or, in the words of French scholar Jacques Le Rider, "a mental map" (Le Rider 2008, 156). Kundera's essay retains all its intellectual vigor and value, becoming a useful Rosetta Stone in its endeavor of deciphering the Central European cultural Geist and its geopolitical stakes. For instance, only by mentioning the term Central Europe in an age when the Cold War divided the continent between Eastern Europe and Western Europe, Kundera already captured the concept's subversive nature and its anti-imperial implications. To speak of Central Europe in 1984 instead of Eastern Europe was an act of defying an arbitrary geopolitical order that would not go unnoticed; it actually accentuated the conflict between Eastern Europe as a reality of the Yalta order and Central Europe as an idea.

When dealing with Central Europe, scholars tend to either highlight its imperial legacy or outrightly consider it a substitute for the defunct Austro-Hungarian Monarchy. Few, however, explore the fact that the genesis of the concept and the birth of the states composing this region have deep-seeded anti-imperial roots. Initially the historiography dealing with the intellectual history of the region focused either on the Habsburg Monarchy's civilizational heritage, as in William Johnston's *The Austrian Mind* and Claudio Magris's *Danube*, or on the cultural crisis, known as the Vienna Secession, as in Carl Schorske's *Vienna fin-de-siècle: Politics and Culture* and Jacques Le Rider's *La modernité viennoise et crises de l'identité*. However, the fall of the Iron Curtain brought a fresh interest in the newly communist-free countries of Central Europe; once again, the region became a mental map, both intellectually and (geo)politically, as it had already been the case during the interwar period as well as the period preceding the Great War, when French geographers and policymakers invented the term 'Central Europe' and used it for

---

Note: Dedicated to my grandmother, Lenca.

https://doi.org/10.1515/9783110684216-003

an anti-imperial purpose. As rightly observed by Antoine Marès, one of France's leading historians on the region, the way France imagined Central Europe says more about the French than the other way around (Davion 2013, 22).

Because it is a concept situated at the crossroads of political history and the history of ideas, there are many ways to deal with Central Europe, either historically or culturally. During the early decades of the Cold War, French historiography favored a historical approach to the region, using the more ideologically neutral term 'Danubian Europe' to designate it, like in the case of Victor-Lucien Tapié's *Monarchie et Peuples du Danube* and Jean Bérenger's *L'Europe danubienne de 1848 à nos jours*. Still, the politically charged term 'Central Europe' never really vanished, as illustrated by Jacques Droz's *L'Europe Centrale: L'évolution historique de l'idée de Mitteleuropa*, whose sympathetic accounts of federalist attempts of region might be perceived in hindsight as a rebuttal of the Iron Curtain's status quo. Moreover, during the 1980s, the world's interest and enthusiasm for the events of Poland, with the emergence of the movement *Solidarność*, brought further attention to the region. In addition to Kundera's article, other works popular among the French *intellighentsia* included Vaclav Havel's 1984 speech, prepared for the University of Toulouse-Le Mirail where he was awarded the title of *doctor honoris causa*, and Danilo Kiš's 1987 essay "Variations sur le thème de l'Europe Centrale."

With the fall of the Berlin Wall, French researchers' interest in Central Europe shifted toward the region's cultural dimension. Among the noticeable scholarly works on the subject we find Gerard Beauprêtre's collection *L'Europe Centrale: Réalité, mythe, enjeu, XVIIIe-XXe siècles*, Bernard Michel's *Nations et nationalismes en Europe Centrale XIXe-XXe siècles*, Chantal Delsol and Michel Masłowski's *Histoire des idées politiques de l'Europe Centrale*, and Catherine Horel's *Nations, cultures et sociétés d'Europe Centrale aux XIXe et XXe siècles*. Furthermore, the cultural synergies and the mirrored relationship between France and the nations in the region were explored in Horel's *Cette Europe qu'on dit centrale: Des Habsbourg à l'intégration européenne, 1815–2004*, Olivier Chaline, Jarosław Dumanowski and Michel Figeac's edited volume *Le Rayonemment français en Europe Centrale du XVIIe siècle à nos jours*, and, most recently, Antoine Marès's *La France et l'Europe Centrale: Médiateurs et médiations*. With regard to the very process of mental mapping, the overall discursive mechanisms in charting a cognitive geography are eloquently explained in Larry Wolff's *Invention of Eastern Europe: The Map of Civilization on the Mind of the Enlightenment*, and Maria Todorova's *Imagining the Balkans*.

A Mental Map in Search of a Name

One of the early definitions of a cognitive map states that "a cognitive map is a mental construct that we use to understand and know an environment . . . Cognitive maps, however, are not just a set of spatial mental structures indicating relative position; they contain values of attributes and meanings" (Kitchin 1994, 2). Moreover, it can be argued that "a cognitive map refers to a specific set of beliefs, and their interconnectedness, as they exist in the mind of the decision maker concerning some aspects of the environment" (Rosati 1995, 56–57). In turn, this set of beliefs concerning the environment is being gradually formed as a result of a process called cognitive mapping or cognitive cartography. According to one of the most encompassing definitions, "the individual receives information from a complex, uncertain, changing and unpredictable source *via* a series of imperfect sensory modalities, operating over varying time spans and intervals between time spans. From such diversity the individual must aggregate information to form a comprehensive representation of the environment. We view cognitive mapping as a basic component in human adaptation, and the cognitive map as a requisite both for human survival and for everyday environmental behavior" (Downs and Stea 2011, 313).

There are similarities between the terms cognitive map and mental map; however, one of the main differences is that a mental map is a representation that the political wishes to apprehend, being easily reduced to the following formula: mental map = perception + imagination. As the term mental map came into use in foreign policy analysis and the field of international relations, in his 1980 article "The Geographical 'Mental Maps' of American Foreign Policy Makers," Alan Henrikson defined the mental map as "an ordered but continually adapting structure of the mind – alternatively conceived as a process – by reference to which a person acquires, codes, stores, recalls, reorganizes, and applies, in thought and in action, information about his or her large-scale geographical environment, in part or in its entirety . . . They may be thought of as 'triggered' when a person makes a spatial decision . . . They give some guidance in situations, if comparable, that are new. They are not merely recordings of experience; they are anticipation of it" (Henrikson 1980, 498). In his view, a mental map has a trigger and offers anticipation of the future from past experience, such being the case when French intellectuals, and afterwards politicians, diplomats, and generals began their process of mental mapping of East-Central Europe as a result of their own historical trigger – the defeat of Sedan in 1870 during the Franco-Prussian war, and France's later rivalry with the newly established German Empire.

When dealing with this subject one must ask if the term 'Central Europe' is synonymous with that of *Mitteleuropa*? More precisely, what is the difference between *Mitteleuropa* and *Zentraleuropa* and when should we use the term Eastern Europe? We can agree that this region, a zone of friction of empires, does not belong to a well-defined geographical reality. Popularized with Friedrich Naumann's 1915 book with the same name, the term *Mitteleuropa* is rather a definition for the diffusion of Germanophone culture at eastern borders of the Holy Roman Empire. Later, this term came to embody the German expansionist tendencies or pan-Germanism (in the broad sense of the term), first economically and then territorially, with *Mitteleuropa* having become a geopolitical concept, explained as part of German foreign policy before 1945. Understandably, German historians and politicians are now rather reluctant to use it and prefer the terms of *Zentraleuropa* or *Ostmitteleuropa* instead, since they are free from the negative connotations of the past and also closer to the English term of East-Central Europe. Similarly, in France, Marès proposed the use of the more neutral *Europe médiane* instead of the politically charged *Europe Centrale* (Davion 2013, 24), despite the public's preference for *Europe Centrale-Orientale*, which is a translation of the Anglo-Saxon form, East-Central Europe.

As Polish historian Krzysztof Pomian has sought to clarify it, "[t]he term *Mitteleuropa* has unpleasant connotations for a center-European ear, because it associates itself very strongly with the idea of a German Central Europe; German, if not in ethnic-cultural terms – although there was this view of central and eastern Europe, linked to German colonization – at least in economic terms. In this perspective, *Mitteleuropa* plays the role of hinterland necessary for the German economy. So, the term is not particularly nice for anyone with a historical memory. I would not really like to introduce Naumann as an inspiration for Governor General Frank's policy, but it must be said that his ideas were implemented by the Nazis in the way we know" (Pomian 1994, 15). Still, if *Mitteleuropa* or *Zentraleuropa* designates the existence of a German-Austrian sphere of influence, there is nonetheless another definition of East-Central Europe designating an identity, this time conceived precisely against this German-Austrian influence. In 1915, almost at the same time when Naumann published his book, at the height of the First World War, in London, Tomáš Masaryk, leader of the Czechoslovak independence movement, wrote an article "Independent Bohemia" in which he denounced the expansionist drifts of what at the time was called the *Drang nach Osten* of the Germans. Masaryk later became a professor at King's College London thanks to his friend and expert on Central Europe, Richard Seaton-Watson (Peter 2004, 655–679), and used his inaugural lecture to talk about "The Problem of Smaller Nations in the European Crisis," during which he deplored the fact that among the four great multinational empires, in this eternal zone of friction, there are nationalities striving for their independence (Hayashi 2008, 11).

If the concept of *Mitteleuropa* has German connotations and East-Central Europe has rather Anglo-Saxon ones, that of Eastern Europe is rather close to Russia's vision of the region, especially before of the Iron Curtain's fall. Even so, it seems that the term Eastern Europe was used by the French observers as early as in the mid-eighteenth century, namely by the philosophers of the Enlightenment. As explained by the historian Larry Wolff, "it was the intellectual work of the Enlightenment to bring about the modern reorientation of the continent which produced Western Europe and Eastern Europe. Poland and Russia would be mentally detached from Sweden and Denmark, and associated instead with Hungary and Bohemia, the Balkan lands of Ottoman Empire, and even with Crimea on the Black Sea" (Wolff 1994, 5). Just as Western philosophers declared Western Europe to be the epicenter of civilization, they invented Eastern Europe as a backward counterpart, both politically and culturally in complete reversal with the Roman antiquity when since Tacitus, Europe was divided between North and South, between the Roman civilization and that of the non-Roman barbarians. In doing so, the age of Enlightenment placed a new line of demarcation between the West and the East through philosophical geography, with the new reconstructed world containing a paradox of both exclusion and inclusion that has continued until today (Wolff 1994, 7–12). Although for the philosophers of the Enlightenment the vast region of East-Central Europe did not belong to the space of Western civilization and, therefore, needed to be civilized, a synergy of both attraction and rejection took place between France and this new Europe that strived to forge its own identity through both opposition and mimetism of Western Europe. It is not by chance that Kiš, the Yugoslav exiled writer, later said that in Paris "[he] spiritually moved to Central Europe" (cited in Cornis-Pope and Neubauer 2004, 5).

French Intellectuals and the Mental Mapping of East-Central Europe

In order to understand the dynamics of the relations between France and East-Central Europe from the second half of the nineteenth century to the First World War, we must make clear distinctions between the notion, the idea, and the concept of East-Central Europe, and the meanings each of these came to embody through various mediators in specific historical contexts.

To begin with, the notion of Central Europe appeared for the first time in 1876 as a mere geographical expression used by Auguste Himly. Thinking about the region, he remarked that "except the vague term of Central Europe, there was no word to define it, interposing itself physically and politically between the neighboring groups of East and West, of North and South, more as the product of a successive elimination rather than of a strongly defined individuality . . . It was a region intermediary in every way . . . where all converges, equalizes and compensates;" according to him, it regrouped Austria, Prussia, Switzerland, the Netherlands and Belgium (cited in Marès 1991, 3). Another geographer, Elisée Reclus, adopted the term of Central Europe in his 1878 *Nouvelle géographie universelle* saying that "it consists of Switzerland, Austria-Hungary, and Germany," while stressing the importance of the Danube in the formation of Austria-Hungary. Furthermore, the term appeared in *La Grande Encyclopédie* of 1887, together with Eastern Europe (*Europe orientale*), roughly corresponding to Russia, whereas Central Europe was a region between the Rhine and the Dniester rivers (quoted in Marès 1991, 3). However, to fully grasp the relevance of the idea of East-Central Europe for the French historiography we must resort to the diachronic and synchronic analyses of the

Begriffgeschichte methodology and apply both Fernand Braudel's paradigm of *la longue durée* and Pierre Renouvin's les *forces profondes* to explore the historical events and the geopolitical context which fueled French intellectuals' interest in East-Central Europe and gave birth to the idea that this region, previously a geographical notion, might have been of great interest to the French.

Initially, it was the Austrian Empire (and since 1867 the Austro-Hungarian Empire) which shaped the understanding of Central Europe in French official circles and among public intellectuals, since when they looked at the map of the region, they saw the Danubian Monarchy. From a geostrategic point of view, Paris's vision toward it was rather favorable, the empire being seen as a balancing factor, against the Russian Empire's expansionist tendencies, but also against the increasing hegemony of Prussia. An important landmark was the 1866 battle of Sadowa, when the Prussian troops won a decisive victory over the Austrian ones, marking the beginning of Prussian leadership among the German states and the shift of the Austrian Monarchy to a second place. Normally, this moment would have offered the opportunity of a Franco-Austrian alliance against Berlin, but this opportunity was missed; a meeting between Napoleon III and Franz-Joseph, which eventually took place in Salzburg, did not lead to any *rapprochement* between Paris and Vienna. Later, the French defeat of Sedan in 1871 and the collapse of the Second Empire would be perceived as the logical outcome of Sadowa (Deschênes 2006, 96). It was precisely at this point, also marked by the proclamation of the German Empire in Versailles, when everything changed. This was the beginning of a great geopolitical change of vision whose consequences would last throughout the twentieth century. As cleverly observed elsewhere, if France had previously known the Germany of Ideas, now she was about to encounter the Germany of Force (Marès 1991, 3).

Given the circumstances, France's impression was that only Russia could be a reliable partner in the face of the German danger; the preference for pan-Slavism over pan-Germanism was sealed with the 1892 Franco-Russian alliance. Nevertheless, from a political point of view, the involvement of the French governmental circles in East-Central Europe diminished, mainly because of the diplomatic isolation imposed by Otto von Bismarck, but also because of the political establishment's ambition to pursue a colonial expansion. On the other hand, in the context of accentuated Slavophilia, the interest of scholars started to increase and, in contrast to the period before 1871, when they interpreted the map in relation to a particular empire and dynasty (i.e. the Habsburgs), from now onwards, they invested effort in researching nationalities of the region and their political claims. The main reason for this sudden Slavophilia, as poignantly confessed by one of the leading Slavists in France, Ernest Denis (cited in Kecskés 2005, 21), was the following: "[After 1871] we were in full distress, very afflicted by our ignorance; we wanted to find support in Europe, and to whom could we turn if not toward the Slavs?" The role of scholars and scientists would prove essential in crystallizing the French perception of the complexities shaping East-Central Europe – a crystallization achieved through the vector of Slavophilia, seen as necessary to counter the dangers of pan-Germanism.

As to the question of how France should deal with Austria-Hungary, the French public intellectuals were divided into two main schools of thought. One school, with Adrien Leroy-Beaulieu and the Viscount of Vogüé as the most active members, promoted a policy of accommodation and friendship with respect to the Dual Monarchy, thus much in line with the official government policy. The other school, which attracted Slavists such as Louis Léger, Ernest Denis, and Louis Eisenmann, believed that France should put pressure on the Dual Monarchy by championing the cause of nationalities within the empire, especially the cause of the Slavs (Marès 1991, 6). Indeed, their approach contributed considerably to the formation of the French public opinion about the nationalities of East-Central Europe, since they were the first ones to scientifically and systematically develop the argument that the milieu goals of France's foreign and security policy go through East-Central Europe. More specifically, they vigorously promoted the idea of an East-Central Europe whose destiny is inextricably linked to France's fate, being pioneers of a cognitive cartography that will last until the First World War, at the end of which this region will become a mental map for French foreign policy.

For example, Louis Léger, the initiator of the study of Slavic languages and civilizations in France, admitted that "[his] ambition would be to naturalize definitively the Slavic studies in our country" (cited in Marès 1991, 4). In contrast to people who feared pan-Slavism, Léger, on the other hand, saw in the flourishing of the Slav nationalities of Austria-Hungary a real opportunity for France to find partners in East-Central Europe against the German danger. Léger became interested in the Slavs after the Polish revolutions of 1863, when he established contacts with many Slavs exiled from Russia and the Habsburg Empire. In his first book (co-written with the Czech Josef Vaclav in 1867), *La Bohême historique, pittoresque et littéraire*, he attacked the Austrian Empire, in which he saw an outpost of German-Prussian expansionism (Droz 1986, 39). At the Sorbonne, Léger taught Russian grammar and the literary history of the Czechs, Poles and Serbs, followed by appointments at the School of Oriental Languages and the Collège de France. After the defeat of Sedan, he began to write for *Correspondance Slave*, a newspaper articulating the aspirations of the Czechs for greater *rapprochement* with the French culture in order to diminish German influence. Indeed, Léger believed in the existence of a united Danubian Europe, but not necessarily under the Habsburgs. In his book, *L'Histoire d'Autriche-Hongrie*, he took a very critical position toward it: "[A]s long as it has not found the secret of granting to all its peoples the fair use of the same freedoms and grouping them in a harmonious balance, Austria-Hungary will remain a provisional state and play a rather negative than a positive role in European politics" (cited in Deschênes 2006, 100).

Ernest Denis was another Slavist who used his position of the chair of modern history at the Sorbonne to advocate for closer relations between the Slavs of Central

Europe and the French. His friend Louis Eisenmann said that it was "a natural sympathy which had attracted Denis to the Slavs, dictated by the clear awareness of the solidarity of interest that unites them to France in the defensive struggle against the ambitions and aggressions of Prussian-Germanism. He never varied in this sympathy, nor in the conviction of serving France well, endeavoring to make it known to the Slavs, and to make them known to it" (cited in Deschênes 2006, 100). For Denis, the Danubian basin should have been organized only according to the criterion of self-determination of nationalities, and while rejecting the experience of 1848 and the Austro-Hungarian compromise of 1867 (the *Ausgleich*) as durable solutions, he rather encouraged a form of Austro-Slavism by progressive recognition of the rights of the Slavs within the empire. In fact, Eisenmann who, unlike Léger and Denis, began his academic career by studying the Hungarians and the impact of the defeat of Sadowa and the consequent 1867 compromise on the dual empire's future, perceived the then dualism as the cause weakening the Danubian Monarchy, foretelling its possible disappearance, and therefore causing a disruption in the European balance of power. Some of the solutions he proposed, such as having national autonomies within a unitary framework, were assessed favorably even by the Social-Democrats of Austria-Hungary. For him, the ultimate goal would have been the creation of a democratic federation, a sort of the United States of Austria, replacing the influence of Berlin with that of Paris (Deschênes 2006, 103).

Here, it must be said that until the First World War, none of these Slavists thought about the total destruction of the Dual Monarchy; on the contrary, they tried and reasoned in finding a solution between the aspirations of the Slavs and the constraint of keeping the multinational empire alive, despite their often critical attitude. Among all its nationalities, they considered that the interests of France were better represented by the Slavs, a priori considered Germanophobes, rather than by the Hungarians who were judged too close to Berlin, not to mention the Austrians, on whom the French did not harbor any illusion. They simply wanted a federation including East-Central Europe where the Francophile Slavs could play an important and effective role in blocking German influence. However, with the progression of the First World War, Léger, Denis, and Eisenmann reevaluated their positions and commenced campaigning for the dissolution of the Dual Monarchy. Léger and Denis supported the claims of Czech leaders, Tomáš Masaryk and Edvard Beneš. In his *La liquidation d'Autriche-Hongrie*, Léger argued that by its vassalage toward the German Empire, and by its weakness in front of Berlin's militarism, the Danubian Monarchy failed its mission and, therefore, had to be replaced with new states, in accordance with the right to self-determination (Deschênes 2006, 106).

For his part, Denis used his standing to popularize the claims of Masaryk and Beneš, and in 1915, published two books *La Guerre: Causes immédiates et lointaines, l'intoxication d'un peuple, le traité* and *La Grande Serbie*, expressing his support for the principle of self-determination, which he also considered in favor of France's interests (Ferencuhova 1993, 32). In addition, thinking of the post-war arrangements, he maintained that "Austria must be divided into independent states: the Serbo-Croat-Slovene kingdom on the one hand, extending as far as the Danube between Vienna and Raab, and the Czechoslovak state on the other, extending from the Danube to Poland and Russia. These little states are too weak to run adventures, [they] threaten no one, but will watch over Germany. They will be able to spare the sensibilities of other ethnic groups because of their own experience. The Czechs and Slovaks will live in intelligence because they are brothers" (cited in Deschênes 2006, 107). Finally, with regard to Eisenmann's position, at the beginning of hostilities, he hoped that France would replace the German hegemony in the Danubian basin because "the French cultural influence represents a national strength and wealth, the French weapon can be the most precious in the competition of nations . . . It is in this moral and intellectual order, by affirming and extending our traditional mission of protectors and arousers of young, weak and oppressed nationalities, that we will find, with our original role, the most reliable guarantee of our influence, of our authority in Europe and in the world" (Marès 1996, 231–232). Obviously, as in the decades preceding the Great War, for France, East-Central Europe remained a region whose stability directly concerned its own security. But by this time, Vienna was being replaced by Prague; the post-war East-Central Europe order necessitated a Paris-Prague axis, with the new Czechoslovak state being the keystone of the East-Central Europe and French security systems. As a matter of fact, the tireless efforts deployed by scholars such as Léger, Denis, and Eisenmann, who had dedicated entire decades to the cause of the Slavs, weighed considerably to crystallize the French attitude concerning the reorganization of this region after the dissolution of the Dual Monarchy.

East-Central Europe and the Postwar Peace Planning

As far as the actual positions of the French political elites about the post-war reorganization of East-Central Europe are concerned, things were more nuanced, with the period 1917–1918 as decisive. At the beginning of the war, French leaders did not consider supporting the nationalities of East-Central Europe for two reasons: first, they did not seek the disappearance of Austria-Hungary, but hoped for the federalization and democratization of the Dual Monarchy and its use as a counterweight to Germany, and second, the bringing up of the question of nationalities, especially the Polish one, would have caused difficulties to its precious ally in the East, the Russian Empire (Soutou 1993, 702–703). Nevertheless, the situation changed radically following the February 1917 liberal revolution in Saint Petersburg, when the Russian Provisional Government issued a declaration in late March with regard to the Polish independence, as part of a Russian-Polish alliance. The taboo being lifted, France decided to instrumentalize the Polish question, but without harming its relations with Russia; it did so by setting up a Polish army on French soil, authorized by

French President Raymond Poincaré, and by recognizing a Polish virtual state, with the Polish National Committee as its representative. Still, the event that mattered the most was the Bolshevik revolution that brought Vladimir Lenin to power, whose demand for a separate peace with the Central Empires meant the collapse of the Eastern Front. Suddenly, France lost its *alliance de revers* with Russia, with the Central Empires concentrating their offensive toward the Western Front (Deschênes 1999, 521–522). During this period, Pierre de Margerie, the political director at the French Ministry of Foreign Affairs, drew up a memorandum in which he sketched the contours of a future East-Central Europe designed to encircle Germany and to block the expansion of Russian anarchy. According to him, "Poland reconstituted by the action of the Allies must form in Eastern Europe the best bulwark against Germanism with the help of enlarged Romania, against the attempts of German and Austro-Hungarian expansion toward the East. Even if one envisages the maintenance of the Russian alliance during and after the war, Poland with access to the [Baltic] sea will constitute the best barrier between an organized and organizing Germany and a weakened, defective, perhaps even fragmented Russia. A center of Western culture, Poland will be the wedge between Germanic culture and Slavic culture, able to quickly develop . . . From politico-military point of view and in an immediate order of ideas, the constitution of Poland . . . would be of considerable significance for the Slavic countries of Austria-Hungary that aspire to independence. Bohemia, Slovakia and North Moravia would be encouraged by demands that the Allies could also support, making it possible to envisage the constitution of new states, likely to complete the eastside of the bulwark against the Germanic expansion" (cited in Castelbajac 1995, 87).

Following the separate peace of Brest-Litovsk and with Russia being increasingly seen as an enemy, another memorandum produced at the French Ministry of Foreign Affairs reiterated the need to create a Czechoslovak state and an independent Poland, considering that "one of the essential elements of the future European balance is that the restored Poland, touching in the south to Romania . . . [with] the Czech people also granted their independence, will constitute the indispensable barrier between Germanism, on the one hand, and the Balkan countries and Eastern countries, on the other" (cited in Castelbajac 1995, 92–93). The two memoranda set forth the future goals of the French foreign policy, largely implying a security architecture in which Germany would be surrounded by states faithful to France. Thus, deprived of the *alliance de revers* with the Czarist Empire and disappointed with its hopes of seeing the Dual Monarchy transformed into a democratic federation – additionally eroded after the Spa conference when Austria-Hungary fully tied its fate to Germany's through a treaty of close economic cooperation – France began thinking of the region's future in the context of the principle of self-determination of nationalities since the creation of new states seemed a good post-war strategy to control the defeated, but still threatening, Germany (Kecskés 2005, 24). Moreover, the disappearance of the Czarist Empire permitted the Allies to move fast with the Polish question; in fact, in June 1918, the constitution of a Polish state was declared a condition *sine qua non* for a just and lasting peace, with an independent Poland being recognized as an allied belligerent power during the transfer of the command of the Polish army from the French government to the Polish National Committee. As far as the Czechs and the Slovaks of the Dual Monarchy were concerned, also in June, the Georges Clemenceau government recognized the Czechoslovak Council as a de facto government and then later in October, went on to recognize the newly formed Provisional Government of Czechoslovakia (Kecskés 2005, 25). This political and diplomatic turning point benefited from the strong support of the public opinion and the academic community, especially from the lobby advocating the cause of nationalities, with scholars like Léger, Denis, and Eisenmann being prominent figures in the process.

The Paris Peace Conference provided for a solid connection between scholars and policymakers. Through the works of the so-called *Comité d'Etudes*, scholars were able to participate as experts and had the opportunity to deploy activities in favor of the causes they felt strongly about. Proposed by President Poincaré, the *Comité d'Etudes* was a semi-official study group attached to the prime-minister's office, whose task was to conduct research and produce studies on key issues with respect to France's interests in the post-war order. Poincaré initially asked the center-right and conservative deputy Charles Benoist to handle its creation, but back in 1915 Benoist declined the offer since he deemed it too early to plan ahead. However, some scholars, including Denis and the geographer Emmanuel de Martonne, had already begun meeting in 1916 within the *Société de géographie* to discuss post-war borders, either between France and Germany or in terms of future states in East-Central Europe. Asked again in 1917, Benoist agreed to assemble a group of scholars, scientists, and academics, with the great historian Ernest Lavisse as the chairman, the geographer Paul Vidal de la Blache in the role of vice-president, de Martonne as the secretary, Slavists like Denis and Emile Haumant among members. Their mission was to produce dossiers or mémoires founded upon scientific information about Europe and the Middle East, and especially, while bearing in mind the war goals pursued by the French leadership, to help guide the French position in times of peace planning after the defeat of the Central Powers (Jackson 2013, 124–125). The presence of Lavisse and Vidal de la Blache, as well as the composition of the study-group clearly suggested that France's post-war claims were based on history and geography, thus on an impartial scientific background provided by professional and truly objective historians and geographers, whom the French politician André Tardieu referred to as "the pride of French science" (Tardieu 1921, 95), albeit nearly all of the *Comité d'Etudes* members were actively engaged in wartime propaganda (Prott 2016, 29–30).

Once the *Comité d'Etudes* had gathered the data, it transmitted them to the reviewing commissions and assisted the relevant ministries in drawing the final conclusions. At the Paris Peace Conference, the high-ranking official Jules Laroche oversaw the so-called European ethnographic issues and represented France in the

Committee on Political Clauses. The Chairman of the Polish and Czechoslovak Affairs Committee was Jules Cambon (the former French ambassador to Berlin), especially instructed to monitor French interests concerning the two future states, while in a similar manner, the aforementioned Tardieu served as the Chairman of the Committee on Romanian and Yugoslav Affairs (Davion 2009, 38–39). As in the case of the Poles and the Czechoslovaks, the Romanians also found a strong lobby to support their position; one of the most active and constant advocates of their cause was de Martonne, the son-in-law of Vidal de la Blache. At the beginning of the conference, he had just returned from the United States where he exchanged ideas with influential American officials and geographers, which subsequently explained the concord of Franco-American standpoints on the issue of borders in the Balkans and Eastern Europe. In fact, during his visit, de Martonne realized that the American experts had already considered the principle of self-determination and he went on to advocate for the dissolution of the Austro-Hungarian Empire (Prott 2016, 45–47). De Martonne himself had the opportunity to provide data and expertise to specialized commissions and subcommittees, and to participate in their sessions, notably those dedicated to Romanian and Yugoslav affairs (Bowd 2011, 114). His analysis and arguments were rooted in Vidalian geography (named after his father-in-law, Vidal de la Blache), favoring the poor and rural areas with a predominant Romanian presence (Boulineau 2001, 363).

Ultimately, the influence of the *Comité d'Etudes* on policymaking was somewhat limited, with the academics being unable to condense their vast research into practical summaries for diplomats and civil servants, so they could effectively use them during the 1919 conference (Prott 2016, 32). However, its importance lies in the fact that its members greatly contributed to the process of mental mapping of East-Central Europe, crystallizing it as a concept and its relevance in French foreign policy in a new post-war European order. Indeed, as rightly concluded elsewhere, their epistemic selectivity exemplified "how the use of science and expert knowledge [to] underpin strategic action leads to hegemonic patterns in the way in which (scientific) expert knowledge is related to particular claims of policies and facts" (Vadrot 2017, 61).

From the Intellectual to the Military and Diplomatic Mental Mapping

In reality, what genuinely mattered was France's goal to consolidate its foreign policy in East-Central Europe. After Poland and Czechoslovakia, Paris was counting on an enlarged Romania and a new kingdom of the South Slavs (the future Yugoslavia) to strengthen its security apparatus against both Germany and Russia, hoping to create the so-called *cordon sanitaire*, which was imagined to stretch from the Baltic

Sea to the Adriatic Sea and the Black Sea. At this point, the French Army's influence was decisive in giving new attributes and values to the concept of East-Central Europe, as we can gradually observe a transition from an intellectual mental mapping to a military and diplomatic mental mapping of the region (Jackson 2013, 367–368).

After the Great War, in the early 1920s and well until the 1925 Treaty of Locarno, the French Army was divided between two powerful informal pressure groups, the House of Pétain and the House of Foch. The former was organized around Marshal Philippe Pétain and favored a concentration of forces and resources on the defense of the Rhine, and, in accordance with its understandings, promoted a strictly defensive military policy toward Germany, which was shortly after embodied by the notorious and ultimately useless Maginot Line. The second group, formed under the supervision of Marshal Foch, actively lobbied for the establishment of a *cordon sanitaire* against Bolshevism and an alliance against Germany with the new states of East-Central Europe (Davion 2007, 23). More precisely, the junction between the hawkish diplomats of the time (such as Philippe Berthelot, secretary-general and *éminence grise* of the French Ministry of Foreign Affairs) and the military lobby of the House of Foch set up a security system in the new East-Central Europe through a horizontal implementation of bilateral treaties with Poland in 1921, with Czechoslovakia in 1924, with Romania in 1926, and with the Kingdom of the Serbs, Croats and Slovenes in 1927, and through a vertical implementation of the *cordon sanitaire* strategy by guaranteeing the Little Entente of 1921 and the Polish-Romanian alliance of 1921. The politico-diplomatic efforts were followed by a policy of economic penetration, an attempt to make French capital compete with German or British capital. The results achieved in this domain were mixed; in his study, Georges-Henri Soutou describes the whole initiative as "the imperialism of the poor," because of the French side's weaknesses in front of the German economic presence in the region (Soutou 1976, 219–220).

In his 1962 analysis of a country's foreign policy, Arnold Wolfers drew a distinction between "possession goals" and "milieu goals," and while the former are related to territorial gains and self-regarding, the latter refer to "other-regarding," in that "nations pursuing them are not to defend or increase possessions they hold to the exclusion of others, but aim instead at shaping conditions beyond their national boundaries" (Wolfers 1962, 73). Following this classification, one can conclude that East-Central Europe represented the cornerstone of France's milieu goals-oriented foreign policy, which unofficially started with the Slavists' inauguration of mental mapping, and then progressed to become part of the official approach, with the elaborate plans of French diplomats and army generals, all for the purpose of shaping the European order and containing the German threat. However, looking back, by the early 1920s, the *air du temps* had been changing, with and a paradigm shift impacting on the traumatized and exhausted French psyche. As it would be proved, consequences of the profound socio-cultural changes were felt throughout the interwar decades. For example, the rise of pacifism among European and French public opinion, especially in the context of the hostility in relation to the brief occupation of the Ruhr by French troops (1923), showed that Europe was not ready to risk a new war because of the Franco-German rivalry. In fact, in the period 1921–1923, a new generation of diplomats was admitted to the French Ministry of Foreign Affairs, many of whom came from the elite *École National Supérieure* and were influenced by the pacifist ideas of the philosopher Alain (his real name being Émile Chartier), a professor and a *maître à penser* for an entire generation (Sirinelli 1988, 273–274). Having witnessed the horrors of war first-hand, the new intake of civil servants favored a pacifist approach to international relations by actively promoting the doctrine of "juridical internationalism" and the principles of collective security, therefore relying more on the mechanisms of the League of Nations for solving potential crises (Jackson 2013, 428–430). In other words, France's milieu goals stopped passing through the mental map of East-Central Europe.

In May 1924, the victory of the left-wing *Cartel des Gauches*, led by Édourd Herriot, introduced important changes in France's policies, one of them being the official recognition of the Soviet Union in October, which ended its status of a pariah on the international stage. Still, the real turning point came with the 1925 Treaty of Locarno, a culmination of Aristide Briand and Gustav Stresemann's efforts directed toward a Franco-German *rapprochement.* The treaty stipulated that while Germany recognized and guaranteed its Western borders, when it came to the ones in the East, namely with Poland and Czechoslovakia, they were open to territorial revision. Understandably, East-Central European capitals were outraged by what they perceived, a betrayal from the British and the French, who had been regarded not only as their allies, but also their protectors (Wandycz 1962, 364–366). As it happened, in less than two years, the two main reasons for France's diplomatic involvement in East-Central Europe – the German menace and the Bolshevik threat – were gone. Moreover, what once was considered the Holy Grail of the post-war order – epitomized by the new arrangements and security alliances with East-Central European states – now became a burden, hindering Paris's new diplomatic initiatives (Jordan 2002, 48). This was the beginning of French disengagement from East-Central Europe and the intricate network of alliances it helped establish; in Soutou's words, the new preoccupation of the French leadership was actually "*comment s'en débarasser* [how to get rid of them]" (Soutou 1981, 295–296).

In spite of the previous standpoint, in 1933, when the Nazis came to power and the German menace surfaced, East-Central Europe once again became a mental map for French diplomacy. Louis Barthou, Minister of Foreign Affairs, attempted a revival of the *alliances de revers*, with Germany and the Soviet Union included, seeking to reach a "Locarno of the East" to guarantee the eastern borders of Europe (Duroselle 1962, 533–534). After his assassination in Marseille in 1934, the ties between French diplomacy and East-Central Europe were quickly loosened. Pacifism paved the way to appeasement toward Berlin, both in Paris and London, and the

French Army's defensive policies eventually prevailed. <IBM12>However, the watershed moment of France's failure to protect East-Central European states occurred during the 1938 Munich Agreement, when it sided with Berlin, London, and Rome, in forcing Czechoslovakia to give its Sudetenland to Nazi Germany – a move defended as imperative for preserving the peace in Europe. In many respects, from the French point of view, Czechoslovakia's fate was sealed months earlier when the Permanent Committee of National Defense concluded in one of its reports that it would be impossible to come to Prague's rescue in case of an armed conflict with Germany (Adamthwaite 1979, 59).

At the time, the Munich Agreement was perceived rather favorably, both by the public and the political spectrum from left to right. The days when Slavists, such as Louis Léger and Ernest Denis, and diplomats, such as Philippe Berthelot, arduously defend the pro-Czech cause were over. Quite the opposite, there was a prevailing feeling of hostility toward the states of East-Central Europe (and Czechoslovakia in particular), because of their potential of bringing France in an unwanted conflict with Nazi Germany. Revealing in this respect are press articles whose authors rhetorically questioned as to why should France "fight for a pot-pourri of elements and most diverse races that will never succeed in melting and unifying" (*Le Matin*), or "be in favor of something similar to the Republic of San Marino, isolated in the middle of powerful enemies" (*Le Petit Provençal*), with some going as far as to write that "all the Czechs are not worth the bones of a single French soldier" (*Éclaireur de Nice*), and generally argue that Czechoslovakia was an artificial and unviable state from the start, while ironically forgetting France's own contribution in its creation (all cited in Marès 1979, 113). Anatole de Monzie, a center-right politician and vehemently anti-Czech, captured the prevailing feeling when exclaiming (cited in Dessberg 2013, 192): "To die for Jan Huss? No!" Strangely enough, the same expression was used in May 1939, when Poland became the target of Nazi's ultimatum concerning the city of Gdańsk and the left-wing pacifist politician (turned appeaser and then Nazi collaborator) Marcel Déat wrote an article entitled "Why Die for Danzig?" (Hucker 2016, 161), in which he promoted French non-involvement in East-Central European conflicts.

East-Central Europe and the French School of Possibilism

If there was one area in which France kept weighing its prospects during the Paris Peace Conference, that was the one concerning the borders of East-Central Europe. Here, a certain geographical spirit (the Vidalian geography) prevailed – known as "possibilism" from 1922 onwards. Besides its diplomatic and military influence, France also manifested an epistemic influence, since the post-war Europe, including the newly created states, was, to a certain extent, a product of the French school of political geography, and a nexus of geographers, diplomats, and generals, altogether contributing to the reification of East-Central Europe. Although the French school of political geography did not experience the fame assigned to the British and German schools, the influence of the founder of modern geography in France, Paul Vidal de la Blache, was considerable. Lucien Febvre used the term "possibilism" to argue that "each human community lives in symbiosis with its space and in relations which are so intimate; yet, even in similar natural conditions, each environment can change and become distinct, as it is based on different exploitation choices and values" (cited in Holt-Jensen 2009, 66), with the fundamental postulate being the following: "Whatever touches the individual is contingent" (cited in Courville 1995, 14).

In order to understand possibilism we must define what it tries to refute, that is to say, the Ratzelian determinism, as advocated by Friedrich Ratzel, the founder of the German school of human geography, according to whom the physical environment is the one that determines, directly or indirectly, the individual's behavior, their actions, their habitat, and their lifestyles. For the followers of determinism, the environment is superior to the individual, who is merely an actor whose decisions are subjected to the external factors of the environment. For determinists, history, culture, lifestyles, as well as the stages of social group development are considerably regulated by the environment, reflecting a stimulus-response relationship. Student of the philosopher, biologist and naturalist Ernest Haeckel, Ratzel was a zoologist by training and consequently much influenced by Darwinist and Malthusian ideas, which he used in his enterprise to complete a biogeography that placed the notion of "vital space" at the very core (Hussy 1993, 437), although he gradually abandoned Darwin's theories of natural selection and became more convinced by the idea of spatial evolution (Sanguin 1990, 585). It is from his training that Ratzel embraced the term living space, *Lebensraum*, which is "a geographical area required to support a living species in the normality of its demographic size and its mode of existence" (cited in Sanguin 1990, 589). These ideas were later recovered and, to some extent, distorted, by the Weimar Republic, to justify its policy of revising borders, and by the Nazi regime, which added a strong racial connotation.

In contrast to the German naturalistic thought impregnated by the Ratzelian determinism, Vidal de la Blache affirmed that the individual can control the physical environment thanks to his culture and technology, and can escape any predestination, regardless of whether such a move is conditioned by the physical environment or not (Ribeiro 1968, 661). Departing from the analysis of the individual-environment relationship, he borrowed Ratzel's binary opposition, but then placed the individual's adaptation to their environment at the center of his research, emphasizing the symbiosis of the individual with his space, and not the domination of the latter over the former. Three great dimensions constitute the Vidalian geography or possibilism: the environment, for which the individual is simultaneously a master and an associate, thus not a mere submitter, the concept of the way of life, concerned with how people live in terms of habits and practices and how they use resources of their community for their needs, and, finally, the ongoing circulation, as a consequence of contacts and exchanges between different environments (Courville 1995, 15–16). In sum, in the view of possibilism, nature does not impose a certain path that the individual is supposed to follow, but it provides opportunities (different paths) to choose from. For its supporters, the state organization is not the exclusive realization of the physical environment's external action, but it is created as a result of the choices and the physical and intellectual efforts of a society, composed by individuals as either masters or choosers (Rana 2008, 387).

The Vidalian geography emphasized the possibility for the individual to shape their destiny independently from the irrevocable conditionality of the environment, thus trying to reduce the scope of the Ratzelian thought's deterministic postulates (Ribeiro 1968, 651). This principle found its complementarity with the principle of self-determination of nationalities and the capacity to govern without the need of a tutelage from a ruling power (Parker 2000, 959). This very much explains the epistemic link between the beliefs of French geographers present at the Paris Peace Conference and the political aspirations of the nationalities from the disintegrating empires who were trying to gain independence through the right of self-determination. There is a symbiotic relationship between the scientific vision of the Vidalian geographers and other scholars (such as the Slavists), altogether playing a lead role in the birth of new East-Central Europe, perceived as the realization of possibilism, bringing the Vidalian ideas into the plane of immanence. Indeed, in accordance with the Vidalian view of political geography, "in the French thought which inclines to neo-Kantianism, the state is conceived less as the expression of an integrative power than as the result of hereditary habits of collective life, of common work, of the need for protection" (Muet 1998, 58). It is precisely in the new East-Central Europe where the French school of political geography found the object of its study and research, as well as the validation of its theories and a new paradigm anchored in the right of self-determination of nationalities, since "these national aspirations were not only legitimate, but also in congruence with the new course of history" (Muet 1998, 60).

Conclusion

From Auguste Himly's early mention of Central Europe in 1876 to Emmanuel de Martonne's 1930 *L'Europe Centrale*, the term evolved from a geographical notion to a geopolitical concept. Even before the Great War, although not fully conceptualized, this region served as a mental map for those intellectuals that entertained the idea that it was here where France could find future allies in its rivalry with the German Empire, perceived as an existential threat. Alongside Henrikson's understanding, any mental map needs a trigger, and for the intellectuals of the French Third Republic it was the defeat of Sedan and the annexation of Alsace-Lorraine.

At first, they believed that the Habsburg Monarchy, could serve as an ally. However, such a view slowly dissipated in favor of the idea that the nationalities of the multinational empire, especially the Slavs, could act as allies in the future, with Slavists such as Louis Léger, Ernest Denis, and Louis Eisenmann, acting as chief advocates of the idea and thus a democratized Habsburg Monarchy. The First World War made it clear that the only way to win the conflict was the dissolution of the empire and formation of independent states based on their self-determination rights. It was throughout this period that the region of East-Central Europe established the reputation of a geopolitical concept, and part of France's post-war security plans and pursuit of its milieu goals, as defined by Arnold Wolfers. Moreover, it is worth stressing that during this cognitive process – the construction of otherness – the discourse was never about dominance or superiority; on the contrary, the Slavs were presented as depositaries of France's hopes to neutralize the ever-haunting German threat. Therefore, the otherness of East-Central Europe was not born out of a binary opposition, but out of a triangulation, forcing the French to look for a friendly other to counterweight the menacing other. In many ways, something similar happened in the 1980s, when the Soviet Union represented the menacing other whereas the region of Central Europe, trapped behind the Iron Curtain, was the friendly other. Back then too, the West welcomed the Polish and Czechoslovak struggle for freedom, showing enthusiasm about the rejuvenation of this part of Europe, just like a century ago, the then French Slavists were amazed by the vitality of the same Slavs.

As it was pointed out, a mental map has values and attributes, and East-Central Europe's were primarily anti-imperial, either against the German Empire or the Soviet Union. Even in the aftermath of the Great War, the words used by the French establishment to describe the region – a bulwark (against German influence) or a *cordon sanitaire* (against the Bolshevik virus) – indicated its double function. In pursuing its milieu goals and trying to keep the new states out of Germany's sphere of influence, France spared no means, in the form of cultural influence, military presence, economic penetration, as well as an entire network of treaties for setting a security system to prevent the new post-war states from sliding toward Berlin. As Luis da Vinha has put it, "[d]ecision makers' mental maps are never static. Policymakers are constantly re-charting policy issues, constructing and reconstructing different places and spaces" (da Vinha 2017, 69). This was the case after the 1925 Treaty of Locarno, when the existential threat of the menacing other (Germany) was replaced with a narrative of cooperation and friendship; in many ways, this point marked the birth of the idea that only a historical reconciliation between the concerned feuding nations could bring a lasting peace in Europe. In the aftermath of this paradigm shift, the region transformed itself into a mental map with negative connotations, a burden that France needed to unload. Thus, East-Central Europe became an almost unwanted other Europe, and in the geopolitical game of the Great Powers, the countries in the region turned into a bargaining chip – a constant leitmotiv throughout their history.

Ironically, with many nationalities having achieved statehood after the First World War, the concept of East-Central Europe came to occupy a specific place in the mental mapping of French politicians, diplomats, and generals, while simultaneously remaining abstract and constrained vis-à-vis the rigors of *Realpolitik* thinking or *raison d'État* policy making. As history showed, the latter did not feel the same attachment as the former, which was largely due to a different cause and perception of the region in terms of the national interest. According to the mental mapping by triangulation, for Western democracies, the people of East-Central Europe, projected as the friendly other, were always part of the West in sharing its ideals and aspirations, but had the misfortune to fall under the captivity, often literally, of the menacing other and thus, in Milan Kundera's terms, appear as "kidnapped." Following this discursive narrative, it was the moral obligation of the West, that incidentally also veiled geopolitical interests, to enable them to fulfill their potential, either through the 1919-promoted right to self-determination or by supporting their efforts to tear down the Iron Curtain in 1989. Eventually, with their accession to NATO and the European Union, it seemed that nations of East-Central Europe rejoined the Western family of values and principles from which they were separated since 1945.

However, with history making its comeback, East-Central Europe has witnessed a new narrative develop since the 2010s, one of illiberal democracy. Promoted by the populist national-conservative governments of the so-called Visegrád Group (Czechia, Hungary, Poland, and Slovakia), the tenets of illiberal democracy espouse a political and cultural narrative in surprising collusion with the milieu goals of authoritarian regimes with few regards for the rule of law. In a remarkable reversal of values, in 2020, for the rightwing national-conservative governments in Budapest or Warsaw, the menacing other has become either the European Union as a whole, with its alleged interference in their internal affairs, or any other state or non-state actor, including non-governmental organizations, who are in favor of the West. The revival of East-Central Europe demonstrates that regardless of its place in the mental mapping of Western diplomats, the region has, since the First World War, presented itself as a geopolitical gambit on the international relations stage; as Halford Mackinder famously observed in his 1919 *Democratic Ideals and Reality*, "[w]ho rules East Europe commands the Heartland; who rules the Heartland commands the World-Island; who rules the World-Island commands the world" (Mackinder 1919, 113). Interwar French geopoliticians were not far behind these assumptions, tying France's fate and Europe's peace to that of East-Central Europe, launched at the Paris Peace Conference as a combination of the balance of power and the right to self-determination rights. As de Martonne prophesied, "[o]ne wonders if the world peace will not depend on what will happen in a few decades from now in Central Europe" (de Martonne 1931, 3). It transpired he was right, as the collapse of the Versailles-orchestrated European order set the stage for the beginning of the Second World War, ultimately confirming that in the never-ending game of shifting alliances and changing geopolitical orders, East-Central Europe will always be a coveted prize.

References

Adamthwaite, A. P. 1979. "Le facteur militaire dans la décision franco-britannique avant Munich." *Revue des études slaves* 52(1–2): 59–66.

Allain, Jean-Claude. 2005. "L'affirmation internationale à l'épreuve des crises (1898–1914)." In *Histoire de la diplomatie française, tome II: De 1815 à nos jours*, edited by Jean-Claude Allain, Pierre Guillen, and Georges-Henri Soutou, 214–279. Paris: Perrin.

Beauprêtre, Gerard, ed. 1991. *L'Europe Centrale: Réalité, mythe, enjeu, XVIIIe-XXe siècles*. Warsaw: Editions de l'Université de Varsovie.

Bérenger, Jean. 1976. *L'Europe danubienne de 1848 à nos jours*. Paris: PUF.

Boulineau, Emmanuelle. 2001. "Un géographe traceur de frontières: Emmanuel de Martonne et la Roumanie." *L'Espace géographique* 30(4): 358–360.

Bowd, Gavin. 2011. "Emmanuel de Martonne et la naissance de la Grande Roumanie." *Revue Roumaine de Géographie* 55(2): 103–120.

Chaline, Olivier, Jarosław Dumanowski, and Michel Figeac, eds. 2009. *Le Rayonemment français en Europe Centrale du XVIIe siècle à nos jours*. Pessac: Maison des sciences de l'homme d'Aquitaine.

Cornis-Pope, Marcel, and John Neubauer. 2004. "General introduction." In *History of the Literary Cultures of East-Central Europe: Junctures and disjunctures in the 19th and 20th centuries. Volume IV: Types and Stereotypes*, edited by Marcel Cornis-Pope and John Neubauer, 1–9. Amsterdam: John Benjamins Publishing Company.

Courville, Serge. 1995. *Introduction à la géographie historique. Géographie historique*. Québec: Presses Université Laval.

da Vinha, Luis. 2017. *Geographic Mental Maps and Foreign Policy Change: Re-Mapping the Carter Doctrine*. Oldenbourg: De Gruyter.

Davion, Isabelle. 2007. "Les projets de Foch à l'est de l'Europe." *Cahiers du CESAT* 8: 23–29.

Davion, Isabelle. 2009. Mon voisin, cet ennemi: La politique française face aux relations polono-tchécoslovaques entre 1919–1939. Bruxelles: Peter Lang.

Davion, Isabelle. 2013. "The concept of Central Europe in French historiography in the 20th century." *Historyka: Studia Metodologiczne* XLIII: 21–33.

de Castelbajac, Ghislain. 1995. "La France et la question polonaise (1914–1918)." In *Recherche sur la France et le problème des Nationalités pendant la Première Guerre Mondiale*, edited by Ghislain de Castelbajac, 41–108. Paris: Presses de l'Université de Paris-Sorbonne.

de Martonne, Emmanuel. 1931. *Europe Centrale – Généralités – Allemagne: Géographie Universelle, Volume IV, Part One*. Paris: Armand Colin.

Delsol, Chantal, and Michel Masłowski. 1995. *Histoire des idées politiques de l'Europe Centrale*. Paris: PUF.

Denis, Ernest. 1915. *La Grande Serbie*. Paris: Librairie Delagrave.

Denis, Ernest. 1915. *La Guerre: Causes immédiates et lointaines, l'intoxication d'un peuple, le traité*. Paris: Librairie Delagrave.

Deschênes, Dany. 1999. "Rupture et équilibre: Les options de la Realpolitik française face à l'Autriche-Hongrie lors de la Première Guerre Mondiale." *Études internationales* 30(3): 521–545.

Deschênes, Dany. 2006. "French intellectuals and the image of Austria -Hungary." *Hungarian Studies Review* 33(1–2): 93–120.

Dessberg, Frédéric. 2013. "Les motivations politiques d'un ministre 'munichois:' Anatole de Monzie." In *Expériences de la guerre, pratiques de la paix: Hommages à Jean-Pierre Bois*, edited by Guy Saupin and Eric Schnakenbourg, 181–194. Rennes: Presses Universitaires de Rennes.

Downs, Roger M., and David Stea. 2011. "Cognitive maps and spatial behavior: Process and products." In *The Map Reader: Theories of Mapping Practice and Cartographic Representation*, edited by Martin Dodge, Rob Kitchin, and Chris Perkins, 312–317. New York: John Wiley and Sons.

Droz, Jacques. 1960. *L'Europe Centrale: L'évolution historique de l'idée de Mitteleuropa*. Paris: Payot.

Droz, Jacques. 1986. "Les historiens français face à la Double Monarchie." In *Relations franco-autrichiennes: 1890–1970*, edited by Félix Kreissler, 63–70. Rouen: Presses Universitaires de Rouen et du Havre.

Duroselle, Jean-Baptiste. 1962. "Louis Barthou et le rapprochement franco-soviétique en 1934." *Cahiers du monde russe et soviétique* 3(3–4): 525–545.

Ferencuhova, Bohumila. 1993. "Les slavisants français et le mouvement tchécoslovaque à l'étranger au cours de la Première Guerre Mondiale." *Guerres mondiales et conflits contemporains* 169: 27–36.

Havel, Václav. 1984. "Politika a svědomí." Děkovný projev k udělení čestného doktorátu Univerzity Toulouse-Le Mirail (14 March).

Hayashi, Tadayuki. 2008. "Masaryk's 'Zone of small nations' in his discourse during World War I." *Acta Slavica Iaponica* 15: 3–20.

Henrikson, Alan K. 1980. "The geographical 'mental maps' of American foreign policy makers." *International Political Science Association* 1(4): 495–530.

Holt-Jensen, Arild. 2009. *Geography: History and Concepts*. London: Sage.

Horel, Catherine. 2006. *Nations, cultures et sociétés d'Europe Centrale aux XIXe et XXe siècles*. Paris: Editions de la Sorbonne.

Horel, Catherine. 2009. *Cette Europe qu'on dit centrale: Des Habsbourg à l'intégration européenne, 1815–2004*. Paris: Beauchesnes.

Hucker, Daniel. 2016. *Public Opinion and the End of Appeasement in Britain and France*. London: Routledge.

Hussy, Charles. 1993. "Y aurait-il deux Friedrich Ratzel." *Cahiers de géographie du Québec* 37(101): 435–440.

Jackson, Peter. 2013. *Beyond the Balance of Power: France and the Politics of National Security in the Era of the First World War*. Cambridge: Cambridge University Press.

Johnston, William. 1983. *The Austrian Mind*. Berkeley, CA: University of California Press.

Jordan, Nicole. 2002. *The Popular Front and Central Europe: The Dilemmas of French Impotence 1918–1940*. Cambridge: Cambridge University Press.

Kecskés, Gusztáv. 2005. "Le grand tournant de la politique française envers l'Europe centrale et orientale au cours de la Première Guerre Mondiale." *Öt Kontinens* 1: 21–26.

Kiš, Danilo. 1987. "Variations sur le thème de l'Europe Centrale." In *Homo Poeticus: Essays and Interviews*, edited by Susan Sontag, 95–114. New York: Farrar Straus & Giroux.

Kitchin, Robert M. 1994. "Cognitive maps: What are they and why study them?" *Journal of Environmental Psychology* 14(1): 1–19.

Kundera, Milan. 1983. "Un Occident kidnappé ou la tragédie l'Europe centrale." *Le Débat* 5 (27): 3–23.

Le Rider, Jacques. 1990. *La modernité viennoise et crises de l'identité*. Paris: PUF.

Le Rider, Jacques. 2008. "Mitteleuropa, Zentraleuropa, Mittelosteuropa: A mental map of Central Europe." *European Journal of Social Theory* 11(2): 155–169.

Léger, Louis. 1879. *Histoire de l'Autriche-Hongrie*. Paris: Hachette.

Léger, Louis. 1915. *La liquidation d'Autriche-Hongrie*. Paris: Librairie Félix Alcan.

Léger, Louis, and Josef Vaclav. 1867. *La Bohême historique, pittoresque & littéraire*. Paris: Librairie Internationale.

Mackinder, Halford J. 1919. *Democratic Ideals and Reality: A Study in the Politics of Reconstruction*. London: Constable and Co.

Magris, Claudio. 1986. *Danube*. Milan: Garzanti.

Marès, Antoine. 1979. "La question tchécoslovaque devant l'opinion française en 1938." *Revue des études slaves* 52(1–2): 109–122.

Marès, Antoine. 1991. "La vision française de l'Europe Centrale du XIXe au XXe siècle." *Les Cahiers du Centre de Recherches Historiques* 7: 1–12.

Marès, Antoine. 1996. "Louis Eisenmann et l'Europe centrale (1897–1937)." In *Regards sur l'indomptable Europe du Centre-Est du XVIIème siècle à nos jours*, edited by Jerzy Kloczowski, Daniel Beauvois, and Yves-Marie Hilaire, 223–242. Lille: Editions Revue du Nord.

Marès, Antoine. 2015. *La France et l'Europe Centrale: Médiateurs et médiations*. Paris: Institut d'Etudes Slaves.

Masaryk, Tomáš G. 1915 (1943). "Independent Bohemia." In *Masaryk in England*, edited by R. W. Seton-Watson, 116–134. Cambridge: Cambridge University Press.

Michel, Bernard. 1995. *Nations et nationalismes en Europe Centrale XIXe-XXe siècles*. Paris: Aubier.

Muet, Yannick. 1998. *Les géographes et l'Europe. L'idée européenne dans la pensée géopolitique française de 1919 à 1939*. Genève: Editions de l'Institut européen de l'Université de Genève.

Naumann, Friedrich. 1915. *Mitteleuropa*. Berlin: Georg Reimer.

Parker, Geoffrey. 2000. "Ratzel, the French School and the birth of alternative geopolitics." *Political Geography* 19(8): 957–969.

Peter, László. 2004. "R. W. Seton-Watson's changing views on the national question of the Habsburg Monarchy and the European balance of power." *Slavonic and East European Review* 82(3): 655–679.

Pomian, Krzysztof. 1994. "L'Europe Centrale: Essais de définitions." *Revue germanique internationale* 1: 11–23.

Prott, Volker. 2016. *The Politics of Self-Determination: Remaking Territories and National Identities in Europe, 1917–1923*. Oxford: Oxford University Press.

Rana, Lalita. 2008. *Geographical Thought: A Systematic Record of Evolution*. New Delhi: Concept Publishing Company.

Ribeiro, Orlando. 1968. "En relisant Vidal de la Blache." *Annales de Géographie* 77(424): 641–662.

Rosati, Jerel A. 1995. "A cognitive approach to the study of foreign policy." In *Foreign Policy Analysis: Continuity and Change in the Second Generation*, edited by Laura Neack, Patrick J. Haney, and Jeanne A. K. Key, 49–70. Englewood Cliffs, NJ: Prentice Hall.

Sanguin, André-Louis. 1990. "En relisant Ratzel." *Annales de Géographie* 99(555): 579–594.

Schorske, Carl. 1979. *Vienna fin-de-siècle: Politics and Culture*. New York: Alfred A. Knopf.

Sirinelli, Jean-François. 1988. "Alain et les siens: Sociabilité du milieu intellectuel et responsabilité du clerc." *Revue française de science politique* 38(2): 272–283.

Soutou, Georges-Henri. 1981. "L'alliance franco-polonaise (1925–1933) ou comment s'en débarrasser?" *Revue d'Histoire Diplomatique* 2(3–4): 295–348.

Soutou, Georges-Henri. 1976. "L'impérialisme du pauvre: La politique économique du gouvernement français en Europe Centrale et Orientale de 1918 à 1929. Essai d'interprétation." *Relations internationales* 7: 219–239.

Soutou, Georges-Henri. 1993. "Les grandes puissances et la question des nationalités en Europe Centrale et orientale pendant et après la Première Guerre Mondiale: Actualité du passé?" *Politique Étrangère* 3: 697–711.

Tapié, Victor-Lucien. 1969. *Monarchie et Peuples du Danube*. Paris: Fayard.

Tardieu, André. 1921. *La Paix*. Paris: Payot.

Todorova, Maria. 1997. *Imagining the Balkans*. Oxford: Oxford University Press.

Vadrot, Alice B. M. 2017. "Knowledge, international relations and the structure agency debate: Towards the concept of 'epistemic selectivities.'" *Innovation: The European Journal of Social Sciences Research* 30(1): 61–72.

Wandycz, Piotr Stefan. 1962. *France and Her Eastern Allies, 1919–1925: France-Czechoslovak-Polish Relations from the Paris Peace Conference to Locarno*. Minneapolis, MN: University of Minnesota Press.

Wolfers, Arnold. 1962. *Discord and Collaboration: Essays on International Politics*. Baltimore, MD: The Johns Hopkins Press.

Wolff, Larry. 1994. *Inventing Eastern Europe: The Map of Civilization on the Mind of the Enlightenment*. Stanford, CA: Stanford University Press.

Jasmin Hasanović

4 Mirroring Europeanization: Balkanization and Auto-Colonial Narrative in Bosnia and Herzegovina

The shadow of old Europe has entered the spirit of the new Balkans. Initially used as a denominator of a mountain chain also known by its antique name of Haemus and later expanded to cover the entire peninsula, the term 'Balkans' has transformed from a geographical category into a derogatory metaphor standing for hatred, instability, and savagery. Maria Todorova notices how the new name of an old mountain and a part of Southeastern Europe – Balkan(s) – stands for Eastern legacy, as well as how the Ottoman elements mostly invoked the current stereotypes about the Balkans as an abstract symbol of violence (Todorova 2009, 12). However, the Balkan region does not just separate but it also stands for a bridge between the East and the West, as perhaps most symbolically illustrated in Ivo Andrić's *The Bridge on the Drina*, for which he won the Nobel Prize in 1961. Whether a border or a bridge, the region appears as the Other that in order to include, has to also imply exclusion. Understanding Europe as the cape of Asia, and the Balkans as the cape of Europe, Katarina Luketić believes that "the Balkans are a double margin, the edge of an edge. However, it does not share in the European pattern, it does not move away from the margin, from the remote cape into a cultural or social center. Its symbolic geography and spatial potency are completely different from those of Europe" (Luketić 2013, 14). In this manner, the idea of otherness has additionally inspired the archaic and stereotypical notions, which are exceedingly beyond the rational, becoming so metaphysical that they are no longer attempted to be explained.

In the dawn of the unfortunate events of the 1990s, the portrayal of the region as backward, stuck in ancient hatreds, and dominated by violence and deep divisions, began to increasingly color the academic discourse. The enjoyment in "the subsequent reverse and retroactive ascription of the ideologically loaded designation to the region, particularly after 1989" (Todorova 2009, 7) was obvious.[1] Not only does the Balkans shift outside the historical time, which leaves them outside of the civilized world, but they are now being understood outside the political

---

[1] This is how, for example, the fateful predestination of the Balkans as the source of instability is attempted to be explained in the spirit of Samuel Huntington's 1993 study "The Clash of Civilizations," presenting the Balkans as a space, or in other words, as the interspace of the lines of civilizational divide. The nature of such divisions, according to Huntington, is rooted in the very identity of the people, whose conflicts are, due to fundamental identity questions, at stake, long-lasting, ferocious and bloody, and therefore, impossible to be resolved by means of negotiations or compromise.

https://doi.org/10.1515/9783110684216-004

realm, as well – doomed to an eternal reproduction of hate. Alongside this view, a number of authors have offered constructions, according to which, the people of the Balkans are at each other's throats just like cats and dogs (Durham 1905), they have nothing in common (Fields 1999), their cruelty is so primitive that it is compared to the Amazon Janamo tribe (Nicholson 1994), and the savage mystery of this unfortunate peninsula has turned it into a restless corner of the world as an example of animosity and hate (Winchester 1999). Such exotic notions of the animosities of the Balkans were noticed by Richard Holbrooke in his memoirs, where he defines them as one of the factors that helped misinterpret the Yugoslav crisis. Their political power was especially noticeable in the book *Balkan Ghosts* written by an American author and journalist Robert Kaplan that had a profound impact on the Clinton administration (Holbrooke 1999, 22). In this way, the Balkans came to represent an identity and a pejorative geopolitical object defined by the simplified commentaries of the West leaving the impression that war was inevitable. Ultimately, the geographical determinant of the Balkans was demonized as a barrel of gunpowder, as something not belonging to the West, or in other words, as something Eastern.

The Balkan region has been blurred by its negative imagination, with its imaginary projections being the dominant image within which it is interpreted. In a time when borders have become newly important, its boundary position and the question of identity of the Balkans are increasingly expressed in the context of the ever intensifying global multipolarity. In this manner the region is pervaded through new geopolitical narratives, imaginations, and discourses. At the same time, the negative symbolism of the Balkans is intended to be overcome, but by doing so, it is actually being acknowledged and confirmed. The construction of the Western Balkans as a new geo-identity is an example of such an attempt, a dialectic equal to that by which the negative image of the new Balkans had been created. However, the position of the Western Balkans, its name and geopolitical positioning, has very little to do with the Balkans as such. In its background lies a discourse of power refracted through the objectivization of the Balkans, where the mapping of space also follows the imposed identity constructions. Accordingly, the term 'Western Balkans' will be problematized in the context of space and identity, as well as power and geopolitics.

The Western Balkans between Space and Identity

The meaning of the Balkans as a geographical region is lost. Undoubtedly dominant are its metaphorical images constructed from the outside, such as the Western Balkans itself. On the other hand, it is to be asked whether these external and fictional imaginations of the Balkans, some in closer and some in further episodes of our history, were really imaginary and fictional. Were they constructed based on false and imaginary perceptions of the passive beholders of the Balkans, or were they a true depiction of the immanent reality of this region? After all, gaining their lives in retrograde nationalistic politics in the Balkans, can such imaginations still be perceived only as imaginations? The understanding of the geopolitical position of the Balkans is, therefore, inseparable from the attempt to define it within identity, as well as metaphorical determinants comprehended with the new notion of the new Balkans – the Western Balkans. It could be said that the Western Balkans, as a geopolitical phenomenon, is geopolitical due to the constructions it draws from its otherness, the new Balkans as an abstract symbol of violence.

I will seek to explain the understanding of the Western Balkans by defining it from two perspectives – spatial and identity – where the spatial follows the identity as much as the identity spatial. In general, the space of the Balkans and its identity pervade each other. Not only did its space influence its identity, but its identity as such determined the spatial meaning of the Western Balkans as a geopolitical determinant as well. Geography itself, according to Gearóid Ó Tuathail, is a form of writing the Earth inseparable from culture, discourse, and power (knowledge): "All geography is cultural geography and all geopolitics a cultural geopolitics" (Tuathail 2005, 65). In this manner, the identity belonging of the Western Balkan's non-belonging seems like a mirror image of the geopolitical aspirations of both new and old global actors which determine its curse on the windwards of identity wanderings and to them, related geopolitical pretensions. I shall join those authors who do not perceive space as a given reality, but rather as a constructed social product, thus defining it in the context of its colonization by social activity (Colás and Pozo 2011; Hubbard 2005; Parker 2008). Although they may act as synonyms, it is different from place, which is understood through the prism of the existence of an emotional relationship with a certain space – place is the space where we live, a location defined by the lived experiences – a sort of "fields of care," as accentuated by the Chinese-American geographer Yi-Fu Tuan, in his work *Space and Place*. As such, space necessarily produces various fragmentations within itself, depending on the relation between social, political and economic power. Phil Hubbard, while relying on the work of Henri Lefebvre, speaks of the impossibility of the existence of an absolute space, due do the fact that every single way of production produces its own space, where he "distinguishes between the abstract spaces of capitalism, the 'sacred' spaces of the religious societies that preceded it and the 'differentia' spaces yet to come" (Hubbard 2005, 42).

Noel Parker, however, sees that as a kind of geometry of centers and margins in which "space and the entities 'in' it can be conceived as 'arrangements of objects or parts.' Furthermore, unless there is perfect equality between entities, some of the positions in the geometry in and around them . . . will be central, a some marginal" (Parker 2008, 4). Although the relation between the center and the periphery is present even outside the geographical categories amidst globalization flows, nonetheless, its territorial dimension is still dominant. The experience of power that determinates the central position is obvious on two levels, geographical and economical. These two levels are mutually dependent, as well as historically intertwined. The double marginality of the Balkans, as spotted by Luketić, is not solely geographical – its marginality is determined by the political and economic discourse of power. Historically and geographically, the territory of the Balkans has been (and still is) the edge of Europe; it divided and connected, but simultaneously, it had been dominated by external and alien hegemon in whose narratives its image had been constructed as an image of otherness. Therefore, the Balkans could not be realized as an independent (geo)political subject, the Balkans, as well as their marginality, is a direct product of the historical and geographical position being reproduced continually by Eurocentric fetishisms constructing it and them as a geo-political object(s) – as otherness in relation to their own dominant position. The Balkans is neither Western, nor Eastern enough (Said 1978).

However, isn't the common denominator of various pejorative categories about the Balkans and their people their continual objectivization by the dominant geopolitical centers, rather than exotic pugnacity and conflict? Such views had created an external identity of imagination, transforming the Balkans from space into a negative place. It is a perverted image of regional identity as something which is being created in connection with specific places, both territorial and social, where the importance of territorial location and history are obvious to its molding (Keith and Pile 1993). The construction of the subject's identity is, therefore, perceived "not as marking out some inherent or essential features (e.g. reason, racial characteristics, class position, etc.) but as a fractured, overlapping, sometimes unstable condensation of various social influences" (Martin 2005, 99). One should not fall into a trap here. It is impossible to generalize identity as the feeling of belonging. It is both a plural and a fluid category, where an individual can simultaneously have multiple identities. Respecting this perspective, this chapter is focusing on a single, particular identity, just one of its episodes expressed in the feeling of belonging to the Balkans as a geographical category, the Balkans as a region, space, or place.

The Balkans is rarely mentioned separately from negative stereotypes – its dynamic existence in the public discourse is present in Balkanization, Balkanism or the Balkanic. Such projections are not surprising considering that the dominant Eurocentric discourse, which created the narrative of the new Balkans, is neglecting the centuries of isolation and submission of the Balkans, equally to the East, as to the West. Over time, the historical border between the Habsburg and Ottoman Empire, stretching through the region, shaped their identities under the direct influence of its external presence and factors, differentiating them according to certain categories.[2] Taking care not to fall into historical, anthropological or social problematization, the identities, as such, obtained their specific

---

2 History has shown that the animosity in the Balkans was produced each time the colonizer favored and privileged one cultural, religious or ethnic group over others. Such favoritism created

valorization and affirmation later, by the establishment of national states. Therefore, they are not inherently as the Westerncentric understanding of the Balkans would have depicted them, binding a particular place with metaphysics; it is rather that their mutual antagonisms should be looked for in the external, colonial marking of space and their population. Precisely because of this, the Balkans cannot be reduced solely to balkanism as the dominant strategy of Western thought of its Eastern-European peripheral space, nor can it be generally explained by the Western categorical apparatus. This is not due to its alleged anachronism, timelessness or dissymmetry, but because the identity of the Balkans had been constructed and interpreted as a geopolitical object through the narrative of a geopolitical subject. The Western, Eurocentric discourse of the Balkans is the discourse of the core; the discourse of the center which cannot observe the Balkans as its edge differently than through the imperial imagination, within which it is reproduced as inferior, alien and other. The problematization of the Balkans has always, and wrongly so, dealt with the consequences, rather than the causes. It is here that Todorova identifies their spatial interposition, the in-betweenness as their transitionary character which could have "made them simply an incomplete other; instead they are constructed not as other but as incomplete self" (Todorova 2009, 18). In this manner, the Balkans have been prevented from their own imagining of the future.

Finally, based on the ideas developed by John Agnew and Stuart Corbridge (1995), according to which the geopolitical order is a political economy of spatial practice – that is, a hierarchical organization of space and the geopolitical discourse the geopolitical idea of that hierarchical organization of space, which has the interpretation of that space in its center – then, undoubtedly, the Balkans is a geopolitical category, a geo-identity that had been transformed from its original, neutral geographical determinant to a significant identity and metaphorical meaning (Ćurak 2016, 40). In its spatialization, the Balkans is being set up as the object of the economy of spatial practice of global powers that hierarchically shape and create space as an idea of their own imagination. Therefore, the geo-identity of the Balkans is a new objectivization of space, and according to that relation, the Balkans is been interpreted.

---

virtual antagonisms, artificial and imaginary differences being later used and materialized by national projects and politics verifying their alleged individuality. Aleksandar Kjosev sees the sources of antagonisms among the peoples of the Balkans, despite a large number of heterogenous similarities, in the strong religious identity during the Ottoman reign: "The strength and the rigidity of these identities can be illustrated with the fact that in the medieval Ottoman towns ethnic groups and religious communities lived in close proximity for centuries, neither mixing nor merging their identities. They lived in different neighborhoods, celebrated different holidays, observed mutual rites, wore different clothes, and were often – despite everyday communication, labeled pejoratively, and even, hated one another" (Kjosev 2003, 208).

Spatializing Identity: The Western Balkans as the Europe's Repressed

The dilemma is whether the Balkans can ever be free from the Balkans within. Its imagination now becomes the alibi for its new objectivization, for the overcoming of the existing and the construction of a new identity of the Balkans as a positive place. The idea is in nearing the Balkans to the West – in the nomenclature of the Western Balkan region which draws its determination as a response to the negative place. Having in mind Nietzsche's allegory of Overman (Übermensch), the Western Balkans (man) is a rope stretched from the primordial, Eastern, primitive and the archaic Balkans (animal) to the civilized Europe as the non-Balkans (superman). The Balkans is to be humanized, civilized and tamed, which is only possible if it becomes Westernized. Therefore, the Western Balkans is, essentially, not a new category – it bases and relates its determination to the simplified interpretations of the Balkans and materialized antagonisms from the previous war, so it can be understood only through their reproduction. As noticed by the linguist Ljiljana Šarić, it wants to be construed as a new geopolitical identity: "The war has become proof and it had confirmed the fact that the idea of the Balkans is fundamentally different from that of Western Europe. Discussing the barbarity of the Balkans and the need for intervention, the European Union had created a feeling of joint identity and purpose based on a preconceived notion of a civilized Europe and the wild Balkans" (Šarić 2004, 391).

Accordingly, the Western Balkan region is neither other nor its own – it is somewhere in-between, meaning that it does not belong to the East, nor the West; rather, it represents the residue of the East and the surplus of the West. It does not represent a coherent geographical entity or a geographical category as such, thus appearing as a geopolitical fault line (Mankoff 2017) or a common denominator for a group of post-communist countries in Southeast Europe (Albania, Bosnia and Herzegovina, Kosovo, Macedonia, Montenegro, and Serbia), coalesced with the spirit of the predefined new Balkans. The understanding of the Balkans is reduced by this insight as it becomes geographically bordered and value specified. The Western Balkans is not imaginary but is construed by the imaginary Balkans. This shows a new discourse of power, a new Westerncentric objectivization and interpretation of space: "With the term Western Balkans, one is left under the impression that a third imaginary position between Europe and the Balkans had been created, under the assumption that the Balkans and Europe are two imaginary areas between which we must choose. Not quite Western and incompletely Eastern space – 'no man's land.' Still, this also leaves the possibility of understanding it as belonging both to the Balkans and to Europe simultaneously" (Beširević 2013, 103–104). Moreover, the Western Balkans appears as a geopolitical category functioning as a spatial geographic metaphor. As noticed by Andjelko Milardović it is "a social construct because this toponym is not found on the official map of the world or the globe itself. As a construct, it had been derived from Western political ideology, power, and the violent reconstruction of identity" (2009, 9). In other words, the Western Balkans is a geopolitical pun of the West in terms of a post-Cold-War strategy of approaching the countries of the former Yugoslavia, and vice versa. However, the matter of identity of the Western Balkans as a term and their countries had not been resolved by this. Construed as a new paradigm of geopolitical discourse toward the Balkans, the Western Balkans became the subject of another external objectivization. Its non-belonging and the inability of imaging its ownness are now used in the raging era of multipolarity to legitimize new future throws toward the Balkans that it had not been able to construct by its own.

Samuel Huntington (1993) defined the West as one of the seven or eight identified civilizations. To him, it is a cultural entity which he understands on the basis of their mutual divisions based on history, language, culture, tradition, and religion. Consequently, he perceives the domination of the West by accentuating its fundamental ideas such as "individualism, liberalism, constitutionalism, human rights, equality, the rule of law, democracy, free markets, the separation of church and state" (Huntington 1993, 40). The essence of the Western civilization is further elaborated in Huntington's article "The West Unique, Not Universal," where he identifies the key points that make the West what it is: the Classical legacy, Western Christianity, European languages, separation of spiritual and temporal authority, rule of law, social pluralism and civil society, representative bodies, and individualism (Huntington 1996, 30–33). The concept of Western auto-reflection is best seen among Huntington's attitudes – the West constructs itself immanently in relation to the Other by which it assumes a dominant position in this comparison. It could be said that every Other makes the West – West (a formulation which Huntington names as West vs. Rest). Although an elusive term (Koker 2006, 21), the contemporary geopolitical interpretation of the West had mostly been shaped by the latest outcomes in which the West is a political, economic, civilizational and cultural community of all those countries that share certain ideological foundations such as liberal democracy, free market, the rule of law and human rights. It could also be claimed that the contemporary West is speaking in the voice of NATO – NATO shaped the Western world during the Cold War, and it is still, except for certain immediate deviations such as those based on Turkey's example, politically, ideologically and militarily keeping it together. Geopolitically, the West can't even be thought of outside NATO as the unifying factor of Western values and interests, and as the primary framework of its defense (Sloan 2016).

If digging deeper, one would notice that fear is the founding stone of the West.[3] It is not a symbolic or an abstract fear, but rather, the memories of past, lived

---

3 Defining the West as a political identity shortly after the Cold War is presented in Owen Harries's text "The Collapse of the West," also published in 1993. Here, the author presupposes the West as a

European experiences. As the cradle of the West, Europe is a bloody continent – written with the pen of war, blood, and violence, it cultivated fear, both from the inside toward European countries, as well as externally, outside toward the other. The old Europe seeks to end its latest episodes of internal fear with the Second World War, turning itself into a continent of peace and possibilities by erasing its own negative memories, as well as by suppressing the fear toward its borders. Such experiences transformed the old Europe, under the significant domination of the United States, into the West: "They [desperation and fear] have been the forces that have driven Europeans to unite among themselves and to associate with the United States under the banner of 'the West' . . . For, once in being, 'the West' has always and necessarily been dominated by the United States, a country long viewed by many Europeans as unsophisticated in international affairs" (Harries 1993, 47). The symbolism of Europe as a bloody continent is overcome and the old Europe wants to be suppressed. Fear and danger moved beyond the West, toward the geopolitical Other which, in order to define it positively, has to be outside the West.[4] This is notable in the following claim about the Balkans: "Usually, the perception of the Balkans, as well as the term 'Balkanization' are related to that what Europe claims to have already overcome or mastered (this is why both of these terms contain the idea of humiliation and degradation): war (especially between neighboring countries), traditional hostility between nations and countries in the same region, brutality and bloodshed . . . the Balkans is the Europe's repressed, the phantasmal constructed as Europe's past" (Kolozova 2003, 297).

---

political and military entity. However, according to him, "political 'West' is not a natural construct but a highly artificial one. It took the presence of a life-threatening, overtly hostile 'East' to bring it into existence and to maintain its unity" (Harries 1993, 42). The division between East and West experienced its most dominant forms in three historical episodes – the first being the division of the Roman Empire into the Eastern and the Western Roman Empire; the second being the division between the Ottoman Empire and Christian Europe; and the third being the construction of a bipolar world architecture after the Second World war. As written by Norman Davies: "There is the line of the Roman limes, dividing Europe into one area with a Roman past and another area without it. There is the line between the western Roman Empire and the eastern Roman Empire. In more modern times there is the Ottoman line, which marked off the Balkan lands which lived for centuries under Muslim rule. Most recently, until 1989, there was the Iron Curtain. There is the line of the Roman limes, dividing Europe into one area with a Roman past and another area without it. There is the line between the western Roman Empire and the eastern Roman Empire. In more modern times there is the Ottoman line, which marked off the Balkan lands which lived for centuries under Muslim rule. Most recently, until 1989, there was the Iron Curtain" (Davies 1996, 27).

4 Such cases can also be found in other peripheral regions of the world, ranging from Africa, across the Middle East and all the way up to the Near Neighborhood; all of these regions having in common the fact that they had been construed as geo-political objects, being dominated by others, which is something that had almost been neglected and ignored in the understanding of conflicts and violence within them. Such attributions, due to the creation of their own identities had also expanded on other Others, which were not necessarily historically objectivized.

Through the Western Balkans neologism, the Balkans want to be the future of Europe, therefore, the Western Balkans is perceived as a concept, as the debalkanization of the Balkans, that is, as its Europeanization. But then, how are we to explain the fact that the first step of such a Europeanization; the escape from the dark Balkans into the bright civilizational circle of Europe and the West, led to that what has been understood as Balkanization? Here, I aim to question this contradictory and seemingly paradoxical, complex relationship between Europeanization on the one hand, and Balkanization on the other. Were not the historical experiences of a conflicted, divided and disharmonized Europe a "Balkanism" as such, long before the term was forged to describe our own experiences? The Balkans is, thus, with the creation of new national states on the basis of war, violence, ethnic cleansing, religious wars and genocide, truly Europeanized in the original, repressed sense. The political order created after the breakup of Yugoslavia represents a strategy of reconstructing the post-Yugoslav space, which is thought of from the outside, it is being objectified all over again through its naming and defining throughout the Western Balkans. The Balkans still remain outside of history, it does not exist in the present, but it is determined by the past and the legacy of the wars. As Todorova explains, "the non-westerner is always living in another time, even when he is our contemporary" (Todorova 2005, 155). To thus constructed Balkans, it is possible to imagine a predestined future; by which dialectics it will become Western, overcoming the categories of ancient hate, deep division, and conflict.[5] Being present it its absence, Europe is present only in the future of the Western Balkans. Thus, Europe is becoming more fashionable than the anachronic construction of the Balkans. It functions as its ontological negation, a positive and progressive otherness confronting oldness and regression symbolically summarized in the notion of the Balkans.

In his book *Eurosis: A Critique of the New Eurocentrism*, the Slovenian cultural scientist Mitja Velikonja notices how those infinitely reproduced mantras function as a "new Eurocentric meta discourse," catching up and becoming uncritically normalized as a moral concept "within all spheres of social life: in politics, in the media, in mass culture, in advertising, in everyday conversations. Prattle about the Europeanism of just about everything – politics, behavior, product quality, creativity, knowledge and so on – has permeated every pore of public discourse" (Velikonja 2005, 8). The entire Western orgies over the nomos of the Balkans cannot be understood as neutral, but

---

5 This attempt, as observed by Kolozova, is the birth of a new name, the Southeastern Europe: "In a single given moment, with a surgical procedure, the term 'Balkans' had been removed, and 'Southeastern Europe' had been abruptly imposed substituting it with the promise of reconstruction and stabilization of the region together with the announcement of the Stability Pact. The name Southeastern Europe prevailed (on the name scene) as the denominator of a brighter future of the region, in terms of its 'Europeanization'. The term 'Balkans' (at least in the official and legitimate talks in the international scene) is now practically dead" (Kolozova 2003, 299). The new identity of Southeastern Europe imposed itself as politically correct.

rather, as ideologically burdened. The Western Balkans, having been associated to wars, is not an affirmative category; its determinant is positioned as an answer to a reversed question – what it is not. Undoubtedly, the answers are the European Union and NATO. Doesn't this case then, simultaneously, also define another important question – what Europe wants not to be? In order for the new Europe to break free from its centuries-long heritage of conflicts, wars and colonialism, its identity had to be repressed by the creation of an abstract symbol of violence as an object of the re-pressed self in which it is to deposit all of its darkness. Hence, the Balkans needs to be Europeanized, as the East had already been Orientalized, thereby, in both cases, neglecting their already existing colonial objectivity, by which they are now being sub-jectivized – they are being affirmed as extremes through the symbolic border con-structed by the relations of power. The marking of the centennial of the end of the Great War in Sarajevo with the manifestation "Sarajevo, Heart of Europe" under the sponsorship of the European Union, best depicts the logos of such an objectivization by which colonialism is reproduced anew. Completely neglecting its historical heritage of century-long colonial objectivity along whose coordinates imperial borders had been rendered and oftentimes changed, Sarajevo is *put in the focus of fin de siècle*, as the place which began and concluded the twentieth century in war, and the place which has now been offered the idea of reconciliation of the Balkans by the European Union, within its framework. With the intention of normalizing those assumptions, the organizer, as well as the sponsor, consciously ignore the Yugoslav transnational and socialist concept(s) of togetherness that existed in the region for almost half a century. It seems that the Balkans has to die from the Balkans *so that Europe could be* born in it, which is exactly what happened in the 1990s: "Sarajevo is the place where a fatal shot drove Europe off its tracks and into the First World War, to end the era of great empires and establish the New World Order. Here European political history traumati-cally purged itself of its symptoms . . . So is because the truth of Europe is evil itself" (Laibach 1995).

Along this ironic time-space line, the present of the Balkans is Europe's re-pressed past. The Balkans, as an objectivized identity, can hardly be perceived just as the accidental and spontaneous avantgarde of Europe in its contemporary slip to-ward the regressiveness of ethnonationalism and racism, but rather, as in one Lacanian analysis, functions as Europe's unconscious: "The Balkans is structured like the unconscious of Europe, das Unbewusste Europas. Europe puts, projects all of its dirty secrets, obscenities and so on into the Balkans, which is why my formula for what is going on in [the Balkans] is not as people usually say, they are caught in their old dreams . . . No, I would say they are caught into dreams but not into their own dreams, into European dreams" (Žižek 2008). This way, it seems that the Balkans cannot die away from the Balkans; it must continue functioning as a deter-minant of the otherness of post-historic Europe which, by laying it aside, proclaimed history ended in the name of universal modernity, depended on reproducing the co-lonial discourse which is not only metaphorical, but also extremely materially founded: "In the aftermath of these conflicts, Western governments sought to encourage the region's states to ease their ethnic divisions through a program of economic and political reforms, pushing them forward by dangling the prospect of deeper integration into the Euro-Atlantic community" (Mankoff 2017). Therefore, it does not come as a surprise that this region is still being contemplated from a security aspect, as a post-conflict area.

Postcolonial Reading of Transition: Auto-colonial Reproduction of Victimhood in Bosnia and Herzegovina

As Tanja Petrović notices in the book *Yurope*, ignoring and distancing from Yugoslav heritage is part of a wider ideological plan of Europeanization itself. By associating the Western Balkans to the wars preceding the breakup of Yugoslavia and its leak into the mundane, everyday space of communication, it "functions as a sort of a euphemism for ex-Yugoslavia . . . where it is not recommended to mention the name Yugoslavia, because it could awaken the memory of the common past" (Petrović 2012, 112). When it is mentioned or referred to, its heritage is discredited and criminalized, be it ideologically – through the "spectre of communism," temporally and spatially – as an archaic and backward "externality," or both. Such use was, among others, depicted in 2015 by promoting the Reform Agenda for Bosnia and Herzegovina, backed by the EU and the International Monetary Fund, within which the amendments to Labor Law were of essential importance. In that context, the then Head of the EU delegation in Sarajevo, Lars-Gunnar Wigemark, claimed how "the currently existing system in Bosnia and Herzegovina is something left over from the time of Tito, and we must ask ourselves whether we wish to go back to the past, or whether we wish for something more modern" (cited in *Fokus* 2015).

With such an attitude that strives to civilize and rationalize them from the outside, post-Yugoslav states are believed to be incomplete; the eternal periphery incapable of any kind of self. A postcolonial frame of observation is, therefore, necessary for the paternalizing view of the Balkans in order to identify and demystify hierarchical power relations, but also, to enlighten the patterns by which they are sustained, legitimized and reproduced. The voldemortization of Yugoslavia creates collective cracks in memory, especially among younger generations, thus ensuring the lack of alternatives when it comes to Europeanization. If we understand it as a form of speech and a semiological system transforming and distorting reality and meaning into form – as Roland Barthes does – the colonial narrative of Europeanization operates like a myth, functioning as ideology of the bourgeois class with the purpose to transform reality into an image and history into nature, being a speech justified in excess (Barthes 1991, 140–141). Applied in this manner, Barthes's interpretation of myth unravels a complex relation between the colonizing Europeanization on one hand, and the Balkan ethnonationalism responsible for the breakup of Yugoslavia on the other. Since its failure most tragically overwhelmed the fate of Bosnia and Herzegovina – previously seen as "little Yugoslavia" or "Yugoslavia in miniature," it is most convenient to read this relation on the canvas of Bosnia and Herzegovina, now being perceived as a paradigmatic example of a divided society, a case study for eternal hatred and conflicts, as well as a scientific safari for post-conflict research, ethnical tensions, political, institutional or social transition and state building.

The dissolution of Yugoslavia was based on two fundamental principles. The first was the dismantling of antifascist heritage on which it was based, which was only possible by referring to its opposites and countervalues, primarily – to the collaborationist and pro-fascist movements of the Second World War whose elements have now become the building tissue of great-(mono)national state projects of the 1990s. Blending the yesterday's working class into an ethnonational mass gave ethnopolitical leaders legitimacy to begin the process of restoring the capitalist order. The process was based on disempowering the previous model of social ownership by nationalizing it; establishing thus a framework for latter, suspicious and corrupt privatization processes, further contributing to the accumulation of both political and economic power in the hands of warlords. Unquestionably, the second principle lay in the neo-liberal attitude toward self-managing socialism as a backward and unsuccessful authentic economic model of a failed regime becoming so crucial in the ethno-national idea of decomposing socialism and finally, establishing mono-national states from its ruins.

In other words, the economic transition toward the restoration of capitalism went hand-in-hand with war, so it is not surprising that its legacy is an indispensable legitimizing factor of the ethno-political establishment to preserve the conditions of the primitive accumulation of capital. It was especially notable in the context of Bosnia and Herzegovina, where the majority of Yugoslavia's heavy industry was located, together with the aggressive political divisions being constructed through ethnic or religious lines. That is why reproduction of the symbolic omnipresence of the previous war is an important part of the very legitimacy of the post-Yugoslav nationalisms, it is being affirmed as an aspiration for a lasting social and political standardization, as an axiological category that sucks in every liberty and non-predetermined expression.

While accused of being bribed to support the nationalist candidate Abdulah Skaka and the opposite candidate from the one his political party had agreed to back in the election for the Mayor of Sarajevo, Almedin Miladin, one of the City Councilors in the City Council of Sarajevo, and the then member of Social-Democrat Party (SDP), justified his political move by referring to (his participation in) the war: "I could not vote for someone who spent the war in Belgrade . . . Supporting someone who has spent all the time of the aggression in Belgrade, SDP has shown to me that we don't operate according to the same principles" (Almedin Miladin cited in *Klix* 2020). A similar approach had already existed one year earlier, when a moderate majority was established in the Kanton Sarajevo led by the liberal Prime Minister, Edin Forto from Our Party (Naša Stranka). Leaving the leading Bosniak political party out in opposition, their MP's in the Cantonal Assembly attempted to politically discredit Forto, setting the moral political principle within "the question of where he was during the aggression against Bosnia and Herzegovina," as well as by asking him "to read the names of the ministers in the [new] Cantonal Government, together with their ethnical background" (*Klix* 2018). The chief editor of the critical left-liberal portal *Prometej*, Franjo Šarčević, sees those disqualifications as an attempt of the ruling Bosniak leadership, not only to cover up its bad political moves and criminal background, but also to catch their political opponents in a dangerous game of self-justification by which they are just accepting the dirty rules of a dirty play, normalizing the image of predestined guiltiness of every Other (Serb, Croat, atheist, communist, liberal, etc.) until they prove otherwise. Šarčević describes this totalitarian attitude of blood and soil as "a self-humiliating cleansing ritual in which (s)he proves that (s)he loves this country, how Bosnia and Herzegovina is also his/hers homeland, how (s)he fought in the Army of Bosnia and Herzegovina or how – at the very least – (s)he worships Army of Bosnia and Herzegovina and its commander-in-chief" (Šarčević 2019). War, as the measure of all things, establishes itself as an important political qualification for Bosniaks, and by analogy, for Bosnia and Herzegovina as well, with which, unlike the other two constituent peoples, they identify most with justifying so their claims on it. It is the same political narrative that has been visible in Serbia or in Croatia for years, with the question of "Where were you in 1992?" as part of a broader, social and cultural, impact. In this way, space is being painted in the colors of colonial discourse by which Western authors attempted to explain the 1990s as a necessary consequence of ancient hate, where conflicts are, simply, inevitable.

The identification of (post)Yugoslav nationalism with the imaginary Balkans becomes obvious in that which Dodds (2007, 85) recognizes as the basic expression of the creation and consolidation of a unique national identity sentiment, which includes referencing geopolitical tradition, visual culture and national history. While the Balkans is "in Macedonian, Bosnian, Serbian, and Montenegrin media . . . oftentimes used for geographic self-positioning" (Beširević 2013, 103), the narratives about escaping from the Balkans (Močnik 2003; Čiorojanu 2003) and returning to Europe (Lindstrom 2008) are also frequent, especially in the post-Cold War context and the new global redesign in the 1990s. The escape from the Balkans is, therefore, only possible if the Balkans is previously understood outside of its geographical determinant, as a balkanism. Such practices were most apparent in the 1990s in the Croatian and Slovenian example when the escape from the Balkans was equal to returning to Europe.[6] The Balkans is thus perceived as a non-European identity determined by external notions. The constant moving of the Balkans is also noticeable in the construction of a passive escaping from the Balkans, it is continually moving away from its own national borders toward the neighboring ones: the Balkans is always in the neighborhood, never at home. As rightly observed elsewhere, "while, to the Slovenian media, the Balkans begins beyond the Slovenian border, i.e. in Croatia, to the Croatian media the Balkans is always somewhere else, outside of Croatia" (Beširević 2013, 103). With such a creation of uniqueness, the Balkans is affirmed as a melting pot of negative stereotypes – the Balkan use of external perceptions about the pejorativity of its own geo-identity points out how the objectivization, which in those utilizations began to appear real, was accepted, whether for getting away from its violence or affirming it through nationalism. Nicole Lindstrom argues that "the persistence of Balkanist discourse can also be attributed to Balkan elites actively reproducing these negative representations against their own neighbors to the south and east. Leading up to and following the dissolution of Yugoslavia, one can observe in the region an endless chain of internal differentiations, whereby national leaders construed their nation as more civilized (or European) in contrast to their more primitive (and less European) neighbors – what Bakić-Hayden . . . terms 'nesting orientalisms'" (Lindstrom 2008, 196).

The climax of Balkan stereotypes ends in genocide, and as a process, they reproduce Balkanization, fragmentation for the sake of creating new ethnonational states. Stipe Šuvar (2003) observes that, although the term Balkanization was initially used in a positive context in the era of Africa's decolonization during the 1960s, it had originated in the nineteenth century within a wider, so-called Eastern question framework in order to resolve the Balkan question. With the slogan "the Balkans to the Balkan people," Balkanism is a colonial pun of instrumentalizing the Balkans that was Balkanized "in the First and Second Balkan Wars of 1912 and 1913, when four Balkan states – Greece, Serbia, Bulgaria and Montenegro – brought Turkey to its knees and banished it from the Balkans" (Šuvar 2003). This is how Balkanization corresponded to the strategy of colonial power, primarily European; in order to get rid of the Ottoman Empire that had threatened their colonial interests in the Mediterranean and the Middle East for centuries, they contributed "to the emergence of small (national) countries by which the peninsula would be politically 'divided'

---

6 In the case of Croatia, its first president, Franjo Tudjman, insisted that "Croatia must fight a difficult diplomatic battle against those who (still) attempt to place it in the Balkans," as well as that "[the Croatian authorities] have received assurances of the unreserved support of the United states that Croatia belongs to Central Europe, not the Balkans" (cited in Močnik 2003, 113). In the case of Slovenia, it is worth mentioning the slogan "Evropa znaj!" (Europe know!) accompanied the first multiparty elections in 1990. Moreover, the then Prime Minister of Slovenia, Janez Drnovšek also stated for *Dnevnik*: "This is a choice between Europe and the Balkans" (cited in Močnik 2003, 114).

and 'crumbled' in order to resolve 'the Balkan question'" (Šuvar 2003). Not only is the term of Balkanization a *déjà vu* of colonialism, but it had also been influenced by its centuries-old subordination, the periphery is subjectivized as an object within the framework of capitalist modernity based on the principles of sovereignty and in the form of a national state. This is where one can notice how the processes of modernization and Europeanization on one hand, and ethnonationalism and Balkanism on the other, are not mutually exclusive or opposite. On the contrary, the colonial context is reproduced by ethnonationalism in a victimological narrative as a form of auto-colonialism – being the very narrative of the colonizer, it is its localized ideological normalization that legitimizes its objectivity in constructing its own subjectivity. Through auto-colonialism, colonial assumptions about the Balkans are being reproduced and sustained; they are becoming a part of its identity. Hence, ethnopolitical identities in the post-Yugoslav context are only possible by excluding the Other as their homogenizer. As written by Alfred Arteaga, auto-colonialism is the omnipresence of the colonizer in the heart of the colonized, a situation in which "the colonist never goes home, that is . . . internal colonialism" (Arteaga 1997, 76). The vectors of differentiation and distraction are instruments of recognition which construe an image of community, a new political body that has to exist in fear. Its subjectivity is based on the defense of the group; hence, every deviation is named by the Other as a pejorative denominator, it is the opposite and the threatening – cancerous to the healthy national tissue from which it must be removed and disposed of. Furthermore, in the victimological, the permanence of war is the contemporaneity of fear; man is deprived of his future, so he inevitably exists in the past as her imaginary retrostruction. Believing how we are constantly living in the future, because the past is yet to come, while the present is always illusive, the German Marxist theoretician and philosopher Ernst Bloch (1986) believes that the present is practically non-existent. As the future is not perceived as the temporal, but rather as an empty space that could be filled with either fear, or hope; fear is what is erasing the horizon of time, filling the outcome of the future and displacing it into the imaginary space of the present. The illusive present functions as both the past and the future, establishing itself as the meta-state of the eternal. Constructed in a such way, identity must exist in perpetual vulnerability, it needs a narrative of war by which the political production of a paternalizing ethos is demanded – war did not just happen, it is still smoldering and threatening, fear is lurking from the future.

Referring to one of the political crises in Bosnia and Herzegovina in 2017 (related to a possible secession referendum of the entity of Republic of Srpska), the Serbian ultra-right daily *Informer* (2017) accused the Bosniak political leader Bakir Izetbegović by writing "Bakir Would Slaughter Again." Threats are also being fabricated as the explanations for all current affairs through the prism of never-ending conflict among the peoples of the Balkans and, in particular, Bosnia and Herzegovina. Chief editor of the Bosniak nationalist and conservative weekly magazine *Stav*, writing under his pseudonym, jams into the same pot judiciary, the growing migrant crisis, post-election majorities and their ideological background as a scenario that "wants to fatally weaken, paralyze and neutralize Bosniaks as a relevant factor and political subject capable of action and reaction for some major event to happen in the future, such as a possible secession, or that Bosnia and Herzegovina, or rather the Bosniak majority populated areas, want to be modeled after some of the unlucky Muslim-majority states governed by the minority and the illegitimate 'enlightened and progressive' regimes being accepted as partners because they control the annoying 'Muslim majority'" (Drnišlić 2019). In this nationalistic perception, auto-colonial attitudes want to be perceived as anti-colonialism, a dangerous silhouette that easily starts to haunt beyond the political spectrum of the right. This is seen in the extreme rightist statements of SDP's 2018 election presidency candidate, Denis Bećirović, not only during the election campaign, but also before and afterwards. The sacralization of the state, as perceived by him, is always endangered, therefore, it is to be constantly alert in the peacetime war against Bosnia and Herzegovina: "We have to be awake and careful. We must never again allow the protagonist of big-state ideologies to surprise us, whether they act openly or whether they are camouflaged . . . As in the times of aggression against the state of Bosnia and Herzegovina, propagandists replace theses, twist the truth, fabricate unspoken sentences, market lies, label, cheat, denigrate, accuse" (cited in *Dnevni avaz* 2019). By confirming the dominance of colonial perceptions, auto-colonialism serves as an affirmative factor of power for those who are maintaining power by using such narrations.[7] This explains the paradoxical relation of ethnonational leaders toward Yugoslavia as a dungeon, while the process of Europeanization is, mostly, observed favorably, as an expression of freedom and liberation.

The most intense materialization of spatializing mono-national states, being their bloodiest projection, was experienced on the territory of Bosnia and Herzegovina. Ending the conflict, the 1995 Dayton Peace Agreement shaped the contemporary Bosnia and Herzegovina under international patronage, maintaining the architecture of war as the new reality of peace, verifying its wider legacies, together with the political, economic and social structure that it has established. Violence and horrific crimes, the discharging and homogenizing of territories by ethnic cleansing and genocide, had institutionalized the exclusion of ethno-territories through administrational and territorial (re)organization of the country, thus retaining war within the political

---

7 The parallels between the past and the future seeks to produce a mutual continuity between leaders and the people, between the living and the dead, mainly perceived as victims. In such an algorithm, auto-colonialism is doomed to conserve the status quo by the victimological narrative. Being the subject of political misuse, the ethno-territory is being marked by the victims, they are constantly (re)counted defining responsibility and distinguishing crime from the victim. Thus, ethnonational politics cannot recognize the difference between individuality and collectivity, so, it is insisted upon the collective guilt of the entire nation instead of its nationalist politics, creating a position that essentially discards and rejects the possibility of any compromise, admitting any guilt or ones dissociation of such politics, while the war continues to be projected into the future.

structure as an integral part of the existing reality. This is evident in the administrative and territorial organization and division of Bosnia and Herzegovina into entities (as well as Brčko District later on), which are reflecting, in a way, the territorial distribution of the conflicted, armed forces in the period of signing the peace agreement (ARBiH and HVO as Federation of Bosnia and Herzegovina, VRS as Republic of Srpska), and on the other hand, nearly ethnically homogeneous areas as their consequences.[8] Only being part of the peace agreement, although it promises basic principles of a democratic state such as the rule of law, free elections and the protection of human rights, opposed to the classical liberal-democratic tradition and political theory, the Constitution of Bosnia and Herzegovina does not define the (abstract) citizen as the holder of its sovereignty, nor institutions, but rather, it defines Bosniaks, Croats and Serbs as constituent peoples who establish the constitution, placing them in the Preamble not only above Others, but well above the category of "citizens of Bosnia and Herzegovina" as well. Functioning as a post-sovereign entity, the presence and mission of the so-called international community through the Dayton agreement manifest numerous colonial tendencies toward Bosnia and Herzegovina (Hasanović 2016).

With the external mission to democratize Bosnia and Herzegovina, it is approached as a sort of consensual ethnocracy which produced a fruitful political environment for the preservation of the same political actors and narratives from the 1990s in peacetime, socializing its society along the ideological apparatus of ethno-deterministic biopolitics in order to appear deeply, traditionally and ethnically divided. Reducing the political subjectivity from citizens to ethnicities tends to be compensated by their constituency within a new political order together with the clientelist mechanisms of ethnopolitical elites by using the public sector as a partocratic mechanism in securing loyalty while ensuring social peace and maintaining the status quo. On the other hand, biopolitical reproduction of post-Dayton reality is grounded by administering life along ethnopolitical lines, atomizing individuals through its institutional practices, normalizing and adapting the separateness of Bosnia-Herzegovina society, homogenizing them and defragmenting against others. Within such geometry, any questioning or critique of the dominant narratives is being discredited by accusations of betrayal, mostly national oriented, or relativization, serving as a moral cover for the

---

8 The Presidency of Bosnia and Herzegovina, as a collective body, consists of three members – one Bosniak and one Croat elected directly from the territory of Federation of Bosnia and Herzegovina, and one Serb being directly elected from the territory of Republic of Srpska. The ethno-determinate structure also defines the country's legislature, where the bicameral Parliamentary Assembly of Bosnia and Herzegovina consists of the House of Peoples of Bosnia and Herzegovina with 15 members being equally distributed among three ethnic groups, two thirds being from the Federation of Bosnia and Herzegovina (5 Bosniaks and 5 Croats) and one third, that is, 5 Serbs from Republic of Srpska, making sure that no law is passed unless all three peoples agree on it. Beside this, one must not forget the nature of the electoral law which, based on this matrix, reflects and shapes the political culture in Bosnia and Herzegovina – the dominance of ethnopolitical parties within a political system of low state power in favor of those on the entity level.

(re)production of the conditions necessary in maintaining the existing relations of power as well as the wealth accumulated in the hands of the ruling classes. Any deviating must be put back within the dominating framework of interpretation, into the ideological framework of political schizophrenia that constructs the reality of imaginary, creating thus a state of apathy and passivity, mental discouragement and demotivation of any type of progress beyond the existing.[9] Protests of disgruntled citizens in two cases of suspicious and unsolved murders, those of David Dragičević in Banja Luka and Dženan Memić in Sarajevo, unconsciously, planted a serious political germ of mistrust in the current system, questioning it for the first time beyond the entity divides for the very same reason – in accusing their political elites for protecting the criminals and derogating political institutions alienating them from the citizens (Hasanović 2020). This provided not only an insight into the same logic of preserving the political order, but also opened an empty space for sharing and producing the most basic and common visions of fundamental values like justice or equality from below, from the people, ignoring their ethnical or territorial lines, illuminating the opportunities in reaching social and political catharsis. From a symbolic point of view, such attempts of procreating transethnic solidarity that parodies the entity-based realm of Bosnia and Herzegovina, briefly merging its divided society, simultaneously being aware of all the limitations and inconsistencies within, is an unforgivable threat for the system itself, far greater than its actual political reach. Very soon, protesters on both sides were discredited and accused for anti-constitutional actions and coup, labeled as foreign mercenaries in the case of Republic of Srpska while in the Federation of Bosnia and Herzegovina, mostly among Bosniaks, the question of David's father, Davor and his war legacy soon arose, verbally attacking those who were in solidarity with the Dragičević family and Banja Luka as traitors, reminding them of their own victims and the suffering of Bosniak children during the war. In both cases, the discreditation and accusations defocused from the causes of despair and discontent, suffocating the breath of possible political and social catharsis.

The legacy of the 1990s has been embedded in the ideological framework of the Right. Rationalizing the political and economic validity of the breakup of the former state union, auto-colonial symptoms became epidemic by the awakening of the retrogarde and great-state projects out of the political abyss, the dark ghosts of Chetniks, Ustashas, and Handschars from the beginning of the last century. By establishing continuity among them, especially through the symbolics of victimhood and historical revisionism, further fosters the illusions of perpetual and eternal hostilities. It is no wonder why the retrograde political ideas in the context of post-Yugoslav transition encourage the conservation of the status quo, especially in Bosnia and Herzegovina

---

9 In this context, for insights into how ethnodeterminist currents influence cultural policies in Bosnia and Herzegovina may be significant, by shaping and using culture as its political weapon for socializing Bosnian and Herzegovinian society as a divided society (Bakić 2013).

whose Dayton ethno-entityization is purifying its socialist and anti-fascist hinterland. Subjectification of this kind is, undoubtedly, a "process of producing the so-called 'transitional' or 'peripheral' subjectivity . . . and colonial placement of (half)peripheral subjectivity into the global capitalist hierarchy of exploitation by which neoliberal narratives and practices . . . serve as supplement to the auto-colonial logic of subjectification" (Tatlić 2018, 42–46). Auto-colonialism is being preserved by the victimological narrative, and vice versa, which is best described within the political habitus of the contemporary, post-Dayton Bosnia and Herzegovina. Having failed to produce any affirmative value for over twenty years, the fetishistic lack of future is masked up by an excess of confirmation of its own status of victimhood and endangerment, so the only legitimizing potential of ethnopolitics is being drawn from the past.[10] Successfully implementing the process of collective lobotomization, as Hajrudin Hromadžić calls the process of erasing socialist heritage, and internalizing the peripheral perception of its own infirmity and irrelevance "it is significantly easier for the national comprador elites to implement the hegemony of consensual policies, as is, for example, the self-explanatory thesis of the 'necessity' for the 'margin' to obey the economic and political demands of the 'center', and to install neo-liberal agendas of privatization, legal deregulation, cuts in public expenditure, 'austerity measures', 'painful cuts', and 'tightening the belt'" (Hromadžić 2019).

The justification of Bosnia and Herzegovina's path in the Euro-Atlantic integrations is more often found in the legacies of war, aggression and genocide than in other, more recent arguments. Their significance is being perceived through the past, speaking in the name of the future, stemming from the experiences of the 1990s – which can be seen, for instance, from a statement from the Association of Generals of Bosnia and Herzegovina, affirming the whole process because of NATO's "stopping of anti-civilizational and criminal activities in the implementation of great-state projects and stopping of serious violations of international humanitarian and war law during the aggression against Bosnia and Herzegovina" (*Klix* 2019). Perceived as the only way through "civilizational and democratic values," Bosnia and Herzegovina is affirmed as being out-of-civilization, as a place without the ability to articulate its own significance. It is only through its modernization, thus through Europeanization and Euro-Atlantic integrations, that it receives its importance, its "voice in the process of jointly deciding on significant global issues" (Mašović 2019). Without it, Bosnia and Herzegovina is in danger of "becoming a failed state . . . on [the European] doorstep" (Falatar 2019). The localized use of the

---

10 For example, in his early 2018 appearance in the Croatian talk show "Nedjeljom u 2," when asked about the heated political situation in the country and potentially a new conflict or division of Bosnia and Herzegovina, Bakir Izetbegović, the former Bosniak member of the Presidency of Bosnia and Herzegovina, said that given the previous atrocities, such as those in Srebrenica and Tomašica when so many innocent civilians were murdered, it was very obvious "who is responsible for every single Balkan war [the Serbs]" (Izetbegović 2018).

very narrative of the EU, normalizes and enables the reproduction of the image it wants to construct: "The EU continues to underline that Bosnia and Herzegovina needs to see tangible economic reforms, making the BiH economy fit for Europe. We stand ready to support BiH authorities on all reforms they undertake to advance the country's modernization and its ability to take on the obligations of EU membership" (EU Delegation 2020). Here, however, one must be cautious given that the dominant and existing counter-narratives to Euro-Atlantic integration in the Balkans and Bosnia and Herzegovina are equally immersed in the victimological and nationalist claims. Representing auto-colonialism as anti-colonialism, such rhetoric is the prevailing political narrative that can be found within the, for example, Serbian political discourse, which, under the cloak of anti-imperialist argumentation, finds its allies in the far-right excluding and regressive nationalist policies. The reason for their anti-NATO sentiment lies mostly in the NATO bombing of Serbian positions and Serbia during the Slobodan Milošević regime, thus identifying it as the intervention and conspiracy against Serbia and the whole Serbian people and not because of the crimes that have been committed in their name during the 1990s.

Collective feelings and internal perceptions of infirmity, smallness, irrelevance and general powerlessness are charted as pre-determined social anomalies of the region by which, among others, phenomena such as corruption, nepotism, social and political devastation, inequality or poverty try to be explained, while ignoring their class background and structural conditionality. In the absence of political imagination, no authentic vision of sociability has been forged, so Euro-Atlantic integration became an external substitute for the ineffectiveness of ethnopolitical regimes. By agreeing to auto-colonial discourse, the state of inferiority manifests itself through all pores of social life. Such perceptions strengthened the referencing of the colonial matrix, contributing to the firming of distances between the European and the Balkan. The possibility that, for instance, the "European Union empowers anti-corruption in Bosnia and Herzegovina" has also been legitimized by the needs of the other side – it is not important only because "fighting corruption is a key issue for BiH's progress toward the EU" (Tiro 2020) but also so "that the citizens of BiH want and have the right to live in a healthy country with functioning, reliable and efficient public institutions" (EU Delegation 2019). Thus, achieving a healthy political society is being imposed as only possible by the process of Europeanization, as a process that is needed not only for fulfilling abstract political goals, but because of the very interest of the people who are not able to achieve it on their own. In order for the idea of progress to be located in Europe, its opposite must exist, the backwardness and anachronism of the displaced Other, shaped and legitimized by its objectifying performance. At the same time, progress is future-focused, which implies modernization without alternatives in the transition toward capitalist modernity. Hence, the Balkans must continue to be imagined beyond time, in the symbolism of its geography – held peripheral by the (auto-) colonial mystification of Europe's repressed place, as an abstract symbol of violence, incomplete and incapable of its own subjectivity.

Conclusion

After the war in Bosnia and Herzegovina, in an article written for the British *Guardian*, journalist Julian Borger underlined the Western, colonial perception toward Bosnia and Herzegovina, as well as the Balkans in general, implying that one of the reasons why the Balkan chaos emerged could be seen in the absence of any great powers to which the nations could appeal. In this manner, he states how a "'benign colonial regime' was necessary for democratic development in Bosnia" (cited in Petrovič 2011). Supervising, parenting, or in other words – governing the Balkans is related to its perception of immaturity and primitivity that has to be raised. Considered subordinated, spoken in political terms, it must be civilized, domesticated and brought back to the reins of world history. Thus, the tendency of promoting and imposing Europeanism as the only and universal, preferred concept of life presupposes the existence of an external object of change, immanently being its opposite, non-European subject. But, the process of becoming more European-like is not only a cultural phenomenon, as adopting European features in culture, life, education or thought, but it is also a political pattern of change, whose main protagonist today is the European Union. The Yugoslav writer Miroslav Krleža brilliantly exposes this attitude cynically in his 1935 novel *Europe Today*: "Standing to its knees in the blood of its own slaughterhouse, Europe is paying an extraordinary amount of attention to proper lacing of the collar, spreading of tablecloths, questions of napkins, oysters, fishes . . . Europe today, after all, still does not know whether it thinks with its own head or not, still prone to believe how its way of thinking is of a divine, supernatural origin."

As a negative place constructed due to its constant, centuries-long objectifications by external, colonial actors and the perception of their border area, the Balkans functioned as a spatial but also a temporal margin and periphery. In this manner the question of the existence of categories, such as eternal hatred, conflict and backwardness, being attributed to the Balkans are to be considered as the residue of a colonial attitude toward the subject of objectification. It is not hard to see the awakening of the Balkan spirits every time a global order bents over its fate – their first awakening was in the Great War as the cry of a dying era of colonization and Great Empires, the second awakening occurred through collaborationist regimes in the Second World War, and lately, the last awakening we witnessed after the tearing down of the Iron Curtain and the end of the Cold War. Nationalist policies in the Balkans, coming to power and politically benefiting from the collapse of communism, produce and use the very rhetoric of external perceptions toward themselves, in a form of auto-colonialism; the local appropriation of colonial imaginations toward themselves to legitimize their policies and the necessity for the disintegration of trans-ethnic Yugoslavia being an impossibility in favor of small mono-national states. The de-memorialization of Yugoslavia is being reproduced by a fetishistic, victimological stand of over-memorializing the legacy of the last war, reviving traumas and continuous threats lurking from the uncertain future. Memorializing conflict in everyday life, thus, cannot be overcome within the post-Yugoslav societies on their own, as conflict is in their immanence, so it can be only done externally. In the years following the collapse of communism, Europeanization became transition; the Western, capitalist triumph over the communist East, as an institutional, post-communist transformation of societies. This process is mutually dependent "influenced by the preferences of domestic actors that are involved in policy making. On the other, the emerging institutions are significantly affected by Europeanization forces which increase competition among different types of capitalist systems and the adaptation pressures on national varieties of capitalism as a result of globalization" (Cernat 2006: 3).

Still, new questions arise: Is the Balkan region disappearing from the Balkans as the process of Europeanization is being done? Can the process be ever done and will the Balkans, both as a region and as countries, still be objectivized within the European Union? Finally, it is up for questioning whether the European Union will continue to exist after Brexit and other turbulences, both local and global? For example, Croatia's accession to the European Union shows that it has, narratively and symbolically speaking, thrown itself out of the Balkans; but still, it reproduces the same narratives that fall into the category of Balkanization. In order to answer the above questions, we need to consider two aspects. Firstly, the current European Union is not what it was and pretended to be in the 1990s, nor is it what it presents itself as to the potential members and candidates in its ideological image, which was equally sharpened by their auto-colonial perceptions toward the European Union. While promoting human rights, tolerance, openness, freedom or democracy and asking the same from their potential members, at least for the sake of the idea of a common market, those values are being seriously threatened by extreme far-right populist policies and neo-fascist tendencies which are mushrooming within the European Union. Such discrepancies are best seen in the example of the border. The migrant crisis has shown to us that such tendencies are not only isolated islands of political outsiders, but that they are also being backed by European Union policies as well. Instead of the ideal of a smooth and homogeneous space, the liveliness of the border, best being materialized in the EU border agency Frontex, is fortificating the European Union. As noted by the Greek political theorist Stathis Kouvelakis, the free movement of people, which is an integral part of the very essence of the European integrationist project, even among EU nationals does not uniformly apply, producing an even more complex picture in the relation of the Schengen Area to EU territory, and both to the rest of Europe, especially to the European countries that are neither in the EU, nor in the Schengen area, such as the Balkan states and the western zones of the former Soviet Union, including Russia and Ukraine (Kouvelakis 2018, 8–9). As seen by Kouvelakis, the Schengen rules allow the temporary re-establishment of internal border controls by member states, visible in the controlling of migration, but also in the autonomous closure of the borders by national states in the outbreak of the COVID-19 pandemic, reviving authoritarian tendencies under the carpet of a global quarantine. What is important here is the reference on the border as seen by Balibar (2004, 101–115) as a historical institution and the need to transform them in a democratic manner. In the liberal democratic regimes of a post-historic world, equalized with capitalism, every crisis of capitalism has also become a crisis of democracy. Thus, European periphery (Offe 2015) such as Spain, Greece or Italy became an internal border of the European Union as laboratory for brutal austerity policies after the financial crisis in 2008, while the so-called Balkan route confirmed a spatial, and biological border between the European Union and the Balkans as its periphery, in both cases re-affirming their objectifications and borderline to the European core. The later additionally affirmed the auto-colonial tendencies on the Balkans by the antemurale Christianitatis discourse, in presenting themselves as a demarcation line, a bulwark constituting the border between civilization and wilderness in order to legitimize their place inside the European civilization. Tanja Petrović describes the antemurale Christianitatis as a tool the European periphery uses "to emphasize that they are European" which becomes "a means of producing the 'nesting orientalisms'" (Petrović 2015, 113).

Secondly, the previously asked questions enlighten the existence of a paradox mediation between Balkanism and Europeanization. Europeanization seeks Balkanism as its Otherness, while Balkanism is being reproduced within the post-Yugoslav ethno-national reality by accepting external attitudes in constituting itself as a subjectivity. Nationalist moments appropriate within themselves the colonial content of a state of emergency within which the Balkans is being situated, as a place of impossibility and conflict by which imaginary vectors of differentiation and distraction are being legitimized, making conflict inevitable, omnipresent and permanent, while the future becomes impossible without an external presence. Nesting colonial perceptions toward the Balkans, Europocentric in this context, aim to leave a void in the collective memory of the people and break the continuity with the opposite, positive values and discourses that were to be found under the idea and historical experience of socialist Yugoslavia. This short epoch when a sort of political entity, with all its flaws and inconsistencies, has been independently constructed – coinciding with a half-century of peace in the Balkans – deludes the negative prepositions on which the Balkans is being predominantly perceived today, showing its historical possibility beyond Balkanism. The question of the victimological as the founding element of community is found in the previous, socialist regime through the cult of heroism, the myth of the national liberation struggle, and socialist revolution. However, the difference is in the fact that the victim, as well as the society is retroactively heroized through the victim, and not self-victimized. The brotherhood and the unity of all peoples was what was demanded of it, community as the building block of a new socialist society, which was supposed to have been built and preserved for the sake of their glory.

In the 2003 German film *Good Bye Lenin!*, after the mother (a passionate supporter of East German regime) of the main protagonist, Alex Kerner, has a heart attack the night before the fall of the Berlin Wall and somehow unexpectedly survives, her family is advised that even the slightest excitement could prove itself fatal. This was a tragi-comic experience used to show that even though the rule of communism was over, it still continued to penetrate the reality. In this discrepancy between imagination and reality, as Alex ultimately admits at the end of the movie, the German Democratic Republic – one that had never existed before but had always been imagined by the people participating in the gameplay for his mother – was born. This is today the nostalgic potential of Yugoslavia – not the nostalgia due to what had happened, but rather a displaced nostalgia toward what could have happened in given circumstances. Yugoslavia shifted from the political to cultural field, affecting music, culture, interaction, and memories (Abazović and Velikonja 2014; Luthar and Pušnik 2010; Perica and Velikonja 2012; Velikonja 2008). Hence, the only way to grow up and overcome immaturity and primitivity behind is by surpassing the conditions we are in, by demystifying and resisting dominant relations of power, as well as by ruthless criticism and discouragement of those values on which the order is based and being maintained, simultaneously and heretically invoking and building new heterotopias within its liminality.

Our current powerlessness in producing new and sustainable political narratives and actions is certainly based on our loyalty and fidelity to the legacy of the 1990s, to the auto-colonial perceptions that, by passing over positive historical experiences of common past, produce historical revisionism as a de-memorializing process of reducing of any kind of imagining counter-hegemonic concepts, such as the anticipating possibilities beyond the status quo. Hence, the current problems we are witnessing, that in turn stem from ethno-nationalistic narratives, cannot be resolved within them. Deeply conditioned by the framework in which they occur, they seek and wish to hear the answers which solely continue to reproduce them, coincidingly, in this manner only deepening their own vitality, and, therefore, the logic of solving them is at a deadlock. As long as they exist, it is impossible to escape the predicament of this region. This is not a Eurosceptic emphasis, but a critique of the ethno-nationalist counterrevolutionary policies that reproduce colonialism, as well as of the colonial, triumphalist discourses of post-ideological capitalist (post)modernity, ignoring and keeping aside any form of plurality of alternate social or political experiences, as common socialist modernity is in this case.

References

Abazović, Dino, and Mitja Velikonja. 2014. *Post-Yugoslavia: New Cultural and Political Perspectives*. London: Palgrave Macmillan.

Agnew, John, and Stuart Corbridge. 1995. *Mastering Space: Hegemony, Territory, and International Political Economy*. London: Routledge.

Arteaga, Alfred. 1997. *Chicano Poetics: Heterotexts and Hybridities*. Cambridge: Cambridge University Press.

Bakić, Sarina. 2013. "Kulturna politika u Bosni i Hercegovini: Mjesto susreta države i kulture." *Sarajevski žurnal za društvena pitanja* 1(1): 113–128.

Balibar, Éthiene. 2004. *We, the People of Europe? Reflections on Transnational Citizenship*. Princeton, NJ: Princeton University Press.

Barthes, Roland. 1991. *Mythologies*. New York: The Noonday Press.

Beširević, Nataša. 2013. *Vanjska politika Europske unije i Zapadni Balkan*. Zagreb: Fakultet političkih znanosti Sveučilišta u Zagrebu.

Bloch, Ernst. 1986. *The Principle of Hope, Vol. I*. Cambridge, MA: MIT Press.

Cernat, Lucian. 2006. *Europeanization, Varieties of Capitalism, and Economic Performance in Central and Eastern Europe*. New York: Palgrave Macmillan.

Colás, Alejandro, and Gonzalo Pozo. 2011. "The value of territory: Towards a Marxist geopolitics." *Geopolitics* 16(1): 211–220.

Cvrtila, Vlatko. 2003. "Geopolitičko odredjenje jugoistočne Evrope." *Godišnjak Šipan* 1: 126–137.

Čiorojanu, Adrian. 2003. "Nemoguće bekstvo: Rumuni i Balkan." In *Balkan kao metafora: Izmedju globalizacije i fragmentacije*, edited by Dušan I. Bjelić and Obrad Savić, 244–269. Beograd: Beogradski krug.

Ćurak, Nerzuk. 2011. *Izvještaj iz periferne zemlje: Gramatika geopolitike*. Sarajevo: Fakultet političkih nauka.

Ćurak, Nerzuk. 2016. *Rasprava o miru i nasilju*. Sarajevo and Zagreb: Buybook.

Davies, Norman. 1996. *Europe: A History*. Oxford: Oxford University Press.

Dnevni avaz. 2019. "Bećirović se oglasio nakon optužbi Gradske organizacije SDP-a Banja Luka." 6 December, https://avaz.ba/vijesti/bih/533595/becirovic-se-oglasio-nakon-optuzbi-gradske-organizacije-sdp-a-banja-luka.

Dodds, Klaus. 2007. *Geopolitics: A Very Short Introduction*. New York: Oxford University Press.

Drnišlić, Mustafa. 2019. "Bošnjaci pod opsadom." *Stav*, 17 June, https://stav.ba/bosnjaci-pod-opsadom/.

Durham, Edith. 1905. *The Burden of the Balkans*. London: Thomas Nelson.

EU Delegation. 2019. "European Union empowers anti-corruption in Bosnia and Herzegovina." https://europa.ba/?p=64171.

EU Delegation. 2020. "Statement by the EU Delegation/EUSR in BiH following the meeting with the BiH Presidency." http://europa.ba/?p=67591.

Falatar, Boriša. 2019. "Bosnia is at risk of becoming a failed state: Does the EU want that on its doorstep?" *The Guardian*, 12 November, https://www.theguardian.com/commentisfree/2019/nov/12/bosnia-crisis-eu-europe.

Fields, Jason. 1999. "Historical perspective: Yugoslavia, a legacy of ethnic hatred." *Associated Press*, 19 Febraury, http://www.wire.ap.org/Apnews/center_package.html?Packageid=flashpointyugo.

Harries, Owen. 1993. "The collapse of 'the West'." *Foreign Affairs* 72(4): 41–53.

Hasanović, Jasmin. 2016. "Geopolitički kontekst postdejtonske igre suvereniteta: Izmedju suverene i postsuverene Bosne i Hercegovine." *Pregled* 57(1): 163–182.

Hasanović, Jasmin. 2020. "Dijalektika etnodeterminizma: Biopolitičko konstruiranje narativa otpora." *Politička misao* 57(1): 26–47.

Holbrooke, Richard. 1999. *To End a War*. New York: The Modern Library.

Horvat, Srećko, and Igor Štiks. 2015. *Welcome to the Desert of Post-Socialism: Radical Politics After Yugoslavia*. London: Verso.

Hromadžić, Hajrudin. 2019. "Leksikon tranzicije: Autokolonijalizam." *Novosti*, 2 May, https://www.portalnovosti.com/leksikon-tranzicije-autokolonijalizam.

Hubbard, Phil. 2005. "Space/Place." In *Cultural Geography: A Critical Dictionary of Key Concepts*, edited by David Atkinson, Peter Jackson, David Sibley, and Neil Washbourne, 41–49. New York: I. B. Tauris.

Hungtington, Samuel P. 1993. "The clash of civilizations?" *Foreign Affairs* 72(3): 22–49.

Hungtington, Samuel P. 1996. "The West: Unique, not universal." *Foreign Affairs* 75(6): 28–46.

Informer. 2017. "Strašna poruka lidera Bošnjaka: Bakir bi opet da kolje!" 14 November, http://informer.rs/vesti/srbija/357012/samo-informeru-strasna-poruka-lidera-bosnjaka-bakir-opet-kolje.

Izetbegović, Bakir. 2018. "Nedjeljom u 2." *YouTube*, February 2018, https://www.youtube.com/watch?v=fCbDeCoJvQs.

Keith, Michael, and Steve Pile, eds. 1993. *Place and the Politics of Identity*. London: Routledge.

Kjosev, Alexander. 2003. "Mračna intimnost: Mape, identiteti, činovi identifikacije." In *Balkan kao metafora: Izmedju globalizacije i fragmentacije*, edited by Dušan I. Bjelić and Obrad Savić, 200–227. Beograd: Beogradski krug.

Klix. 2018. "Zastupnici SDA 'rešetali' Fortu: Gdje ste bili za vrijeme agresije, da li ste pobjegli." 26 December, https://www.klix.ba/vijesti/bih/zastupnici-sda-resetali-fortu-gdje-ste-bili-za-vrijeme-agresije-da-li-ste-pobjegli/181226047.

Klix. 2019. "Oglasilo se Udruženje generala BiH: NATO je zaustavio nastavak agresije i genocida u BiH." 27 August, https://www.klix.ba/vijesti/bih/oglasilo-se-udruzenje-generala-bih-nato-je-zaustavio-nastavak-agresije-i-genocida-u-bih/190827141.

Klix. 2020. "Miladin o ulozi u aferi 'Asim:' Nisam glasao za Sabinu Ćudić jer je u ratu bila u Beogradu." 3 March, https://www.klix.ba/vijesti/bih/miladin-o-ulozi-u-aferi-asim-nisam-gla sao-za-sabinu-cudic-jer-je-u-ratu-bila-u-beogradu/200303057.

Koker, Kristofer. 2006. *Sumrak Zapada*. Beograd: Dosije.

Kolozova, Katerina. 2003. "Identitet /jedinstva/ u izgradnji: O smrti 'Balkana' i rodjenju 'Jugoistočne Evrope'." In *Balkan kao metafora: Izmedju globalizacije i fragmentacije*, edited by Dušan I. Bjelić and Obrad Savić, 295–307. Beograd: Beogradski krug.

Kouvelakis, Stathis. 2018. "Borderland: Greece and the EU's southern question." *New Left Review* 110: 5–33.

Laibach. 1995. "Speech in Sarajevo." *YouTube*, https://www.youtube.com/watch?v=EL8KcXQ4-wA.

Lindstrom, Nicole. 2008. "Boundary-making in Europe's southeastern margin: Balkan / Europe discourse in Croatia and Slovenia." In *The Geopolitics of Europe's Identity: Centers, Boundaries, and Margins*, edited by Noel Parker, 195–206. Basingstoke: Palgrave Macmillan.

Luketić, Katarina. 2013. *Balkan: Od geografije do fantazije*. Zagreb: Algoritam.

Luthar, Breda, and Maruša Pušnik, eds. 2010. *Remembering Utopia: The Culture of Everyday Life in Socialist Yugoslavia*. Washington, DC: New Academia Publishing.

Mankoff, Jeffrey. 2017. "How to fix the Western Balkans." *Foreign Affairs*, 7 July, https://www.foreignaffairs.com/articles/southeastern-europe/2017-07-07/how-fix-western-balkans.

Martin, James. 2005. "Identity." In *Cultural Geography: A Critical Dictionary of Key Concepts*, edited by David Atkinson, Peter Jackson, David Sibley, and Neil Washbourne, 97–103. New York: I. B. Tauris.

Mašović, Senad. 2019. "Ulaskom u NATO BiH bi dobila pravo glasa na globalnom nivou." *Dnevni avaz*, 30 November, https://avaz.ba/vijesti/bih/532126/ulaskom-u-nato-bih-bi-dobila-pravo-glasa-na-globalnom-nivou.

Milardović, Andjelko. 2009. *Zapadni balkon*. Zagreb: Pan liber.

Močnik, Rastko. 2003. "Balkan kao element u ideološkim mehanizmima." In *Balkan kao metafora: Izmedju globalizacije i fragmentacije*, edited by Dušan I. Bjelić and Obrad Savić, 98–138. Beograd: Beogradski krug.

Nicholson, Michael. 1994. *Natasha's Story*. London: Pan.

Offe, Claus. 2015. *Europe Entrapped*. Cambridge: Polity Press.

Parker, Noel. 2008. "A theoretical introduction: Spaces, centers, and margins." In *The Geopolitics of Europe's Identity: Centers, Boundaries, and Margins*, edited by Noel Parker, 3–23. Basingstoke: Palgrave Macmillan.

Perica, Vjekoslav, and Mitja Velikonja. 2012. *Nebeska Jugoslavija*. Beograd: Biblioteka XX vek.

Petrovič, Nikola. 2011. "Thinking Europe without thinking: Neo-colonial discourse on and in the Western Balkans." *Eurozine*, 22 September, https://www.eurozine.com/thinking-europe-with out-thinking/.

Petrović, Tanja. 2012. *Yuropa: Jugoslovensko nasledje i politike budućnosti u postjugoslovenskim društvima*. Beograd: Fabrika knjiga.

Petrović, Tanja. 2015. "On the way to Europe: EU metaphors and political imagination of the Western Balkans." In *Welcome to the Desert of Postsocialism: Radical Politics after Yugoslavia*, edited by Srećko Horvat and Igor Štiks, 103–123. London: Verso.

Prošić, Slobodan. 2016. *Kartografija nestajanja*. Novi Sad: Mediterran.

Said, Edward. 1978. *Orientalism*. New York: Vintage Books.

Sloan, Stanley R. 2016. *Defence the West: NATO, the European Union and the Transatlantic Bargain*. Manchester: Manchester University Press.

Šarčević, Franjo. 2019. "Dokle ćemo živjeti pod nasiljem i ucjenama onih koji su 'nosili puške'?" *Prometej*, 15 December, http://www.prometej.ba/clanak/osvrti/franjo-sarcevic/dokle-cemo-zivjeti-pod-nasiljem-i-ucjenama-onih-koji-su-nosili-puske-4198.

Šarić, Ljiljana. 2004. "Balkan identity: Changing self-images of the south Slavs." *Journal of Multilingual and Multicultural Development* 25(5-6): 389–407.

Šuvar, Stipe. 2003. "'Balkanizacija' kao instrument globalizacije." *Hrvatska ljevica*, March, https://web.archive.org/web/20071105160112/http://www.geocities.com/ljevica13/arh/br2.htm.

Tatlić, Šefik. 2018. "(De)historizacija u toku: Kapitalistička modernost, autokolonijalizam i ekses socrealizma u bivšoj Jugoslaviji." *Sindikalizacija* 1: 33–55.

Tiro, Bakir. 2020. "Turković: Borba protiv korupcije ključno pitanje za napredak BiH na putu ka EU." *Anadolu Agency*, 25 February, https://www.aa.com.tr/ba/politika/turkovi%C4%87-borba-protiv-korupcije-klju%C4%8Dno-pitanje-za-napredak-bih-na-putu-ka-eu-/1744755.

Todorova, Maria. 2005. "The trap of backwardness: Modernity, temporality, and the study of Eastern European nationalism." *Slavic Review* 64(1): 140–164.

Todorova, Maria. 2009. *Imagining the Balkans*. New York: Oxford University Press.

Tuan, Yi-Fu. 2001. *Space and Place: The Perspective of Experience*. Minneapolis, MN: University of Minnesota Press.

Tuathail, Gearóid Ó. 2005. "Geopolitics." In *Cultural Geography: A Critical Dictionary of Key Concepts*, edited by David Atkinson, Peter Jackson, David Sibley and Neil Washbourne, 65–72. New York: I. B. Tauris.

Velikonja, Mitja. 2005. *Eurosis: A Critique of the New Eurocentrism*. Ljubljana: Mirovni Inštitut.

Velikonja, Mitja. 2008. *Titostalgia: A Study of Nostalgia for Josip Broz*. Ljubljana: Mirovni Inštitut.

Fokus. 2015. "Wigemark: Novi Zakon o radu je bolji, stari je iz vremena Tita." 24 July, https://www.fokus.ba/vijesti/globus/eu-fokus/wigemark-novi-zakon-o-radu-je-bolji-stari-je-iz-vremena-tita/92572/.

Winchester, Simon. 1999. *The Fracture Zone: A Return to the Balkans*. London: Viking.

Žižek, Slavoj. 2008. "Euronews talks films and Balkans with Slavoj Žižek." *Euronews*, 12 September, https://www.euronews.com/2008/09/12/euronews-talks-films-and-balkans-with-slavoj-zizek.

Kürşad Ertuğrul

5 Turkey and Europe: The Eternal Suspense

Modern Europe, now widely represented in the form of the European Union, is a political and cultural construct, which has absorbed the geographical designation inherent
to the term. Admittedly, from the end of the Enlightenment onwards, the concept of
Europe has denoted Western Europe as the political, economic and cultural center of
the modern civilization, with spatial designation of other parts of Europe having implied geographical inclusion but also measured proximity to and distance from the
center. With this in mind, the "demi-Orientalized Eastern Europe" (Wolff 1994), the
Balkans as the "incomplete self" (Todorova 1997), and Turkey and Russia, both representing the antinomic others, are corollaries of the said construction in the dawn of
European modernity. They have haunted Europe, politically and culturally, since
then. The reinvigoration of these conceptions in the wake of EU enlargement and thus
membership applications of the former communist countries in Central and Eastern
Europe in the 1990s is striking. For example, in their voluminous work on Eastern
Europe, Robert Bideleux and Ian Jeffries, define the spatial designation of other
Europe as Central-Eastern Europe, Eastern Europe, and Southeastern Europe – a clar-
ification resulting from their criticism of the label Central Europe, which, as they have
claimed, implies "being at the heart of Europe." Moreover, as they continue to argue,
it "overlooks the major extent to which they have been part of European 'periphery' in
medieval times and again since the later seventeenth century" (Bideleux and Jeffries
1998, xi).

The major line of distinction between the West and the East in Europe concerns
the character of the nation-state and citizenship. In the former, civic, liberal, and inclusive understanding of the nation and citizenship coincides with a tolerant, pluralist,
and differentiated civil society, whereas in the latter, authoritarianism, illiberal behavior, ethnic-exclusive preference, organic understanding of the nation, and weak civil
society sector, are the dominant features (Bideleux and Jeffries 1998, 7, 13). The representation of Europe as such has implied a scale of development in which all the countries located in these designated spaces "were tied into the overarching structure of a
decrease in modernization the further east one went" (Offe 1996, 136). The development, late-development and non-development of capitalism could be invoked here as
a constituent dynamic of this structure. However, the problem with the above conceptions is not that they are totally, factually wrong, but that the presented distinctions
are neither as pure as assumed nor they are immutable. Moreover, the designated ge-
ographies of other Europe are not clearly distinguishable and self-contained neutral

https://doi.org/10.1515/9783110684216-005

entities. As Marie-Janine Calic points out, when considering the complex category of Southeastern Europe, "interactions, interrelationships, and experiences that transcend borders" indicate more "multifaceted" pictures than the stereotypical conceptions of "otherness" (Calic 2019, 3). Still, they are imaginary and conceptual parts of the very structure they purport to define – a structure which has affected the social, political, economic, and cultural history of other Europe to a significant degree in terms of relating to, reacting against, and negotiating the otherness. For instance, the Hungarian political scientist Attila Agh has insisted that the history of Central Europe is characterized by the contradictory phases between "the waves of Europeanization-Westernization" and "the periods of Easternization" since the sixteenth century (Agh 1998, 4, 33).

Turkey, while being in the furthest east of this structure, has represented the so-called incomplete other of the center. Modern Turkish history, which is generally assumed to have begun with the late Ottoman reformism, in the first half of the nineteenth century, is deeply shaped by the process of westernization and its consequences in respect of social, political, economic and cultural reactions and responses to it. The Turkish state and society have been involved in an ongoing process of negotiation of both their otherness in relation to Europe and Europe's otherness, a process which has been accompanied by questioning, constituting, and projecting of their identity. Therefore, modern Turkish politics represents an arena in which various possibilities and modalities of self and other relationship, with the West (and Europe), are in contestation. This political and cultural confrontation has largely defined the modern ideologies and policy positions in the Turkish political scene throughout. Accordingly, this paper discusses the case of Turkey in this extensive context arguing that Europe-Turkey relationship remains in an eternal suspense in which the otherness has been negotiated in various ways but still has not been overcome. By looking at the inner political dynamics of modern Turkey, it is maintained that the key reason as to why this limit still holds is that westernization has not been experienced in the form of a modern identity and existence through self-transformation of the social and political subjectivities in terms of their self-constitution. The experience of westernization has remained top-down or at the level of synthetic projection, and partial at best, and as such it is characterized by insecurity and ensuing skeptical distance. Interestingly, the recent experience of self-transformation from political Islam toward a Western type neoconservatism adopting liberal reformism, as in the case of the Justice and Development Party (AKP), has given a glimpse of going beyond this condition. This, nevertheless, proved to be abortive by the authoritarian turn of the party's leadership with the heavy baggage of reclaiming Ottoman imperial authority in domestic and foreign policy.

Tanzimat and the Early Republic: From the Western Civilization as the Other to the Common or Universal Civilization

The modern history of Turkish society and politics is shaped by the westernization project, with its origins dating back to the late-Ottoman reformism, aimed at strengthening of administration and military capability against the West. The reformist process – initiated and controlled by the members of the state establishment – was announced following the 1839 Edict of *Tanzimat* (reordering). The state edict declared that "the old disordered system had to be replaced by one based upon new laws" and that the new laws "would be based upon the inviolability of life, property, and honor as legal fundamentals" (Berkes 1964, 145). In his study, the renowned scholar of the late Ottoman era, Şükrü Hanioğlu, uses the word accession, which somewhat resonates with its contemporary connotation concerning membership in the EU, to emphasize how the edict was intended toward European ears. In fact, it was used for the sake of promoting accession of the Ottoman Empire to the Concert of Europe at the time (Hanioğlu 2004, 73). The edict expressed a vision of "an imperial administration based on universal laws" as "the first step toward the transformation of hitherto Muslim, Christian and Jewish subjects into Ottomans" (Hanioğlu 2004, 74).

Back then, the centralist structure of the French public administration was taken as the model for reforming the organs of central and local government. The offices such as notary, solicitorship, and attorneyship were established. In 1858, a penal code was introduced by adopting the French penal code of 1810. A land code (*Arazi Kanunnamesi*), which regulated property and inheritance, was promulgated containing "articles that would be deemed as secular" (Ortaylı 1983, 161–162). Moreover, the new Western type schools and institutions were founded, including *Mekteb-i Sultani* (Galatasaray Lyceum), *Mekteb-i Mülkiye* (School of Public Administration), *Tıbbiye* (School of Medicine) and, as part of the Ministry of Foreign Affairs, *Tercüme Odası* (Translation Room), altogether seeking to raise "an elite group of Ottoman intellectuals" (Ortaylı 1983, 215). The reforms in the field of education were directed toward centralization and standardization, and were partly inspired by the secular reform program in France, with a vision of "a new educational system featuring preparatory, middle and high schools, as well as colleges with modern curriculum, including European languages" (Hanioğlu 2004, 102). These reforms introduced the concepts of "teacher, school, desk, blackboard, chalk, etc.," either for the first time or made them prominent (Sakaoğlu 1989). The beginning of the *Tanzimat* era also coincided with the first free trade agreement that the Ottoman authorities signed with the then United Kingdom of Great Britain and Ireland, in 1838. It opened and exposed the Ottoman economic and social structure, which was predominantly pre-capitalist, to the free movement of the British capital. The emerging Kemalist-nationalist left labeled this era as *Tanzimat* Westernism, defining it as an imitative, superficial, and elitist process, turning the Ottoman Empire into a colony of the Western imperialism through an unprecedented liberal economic policy (Berkes 2005; Eroğul 2013). It is in the wake of the social and economic disintegration, brought about by the nineteenth century, that a certain kind of soul-searching among the Ottoman intellectuals started, with the question 'Who are we?' as the most preoccupying one (Berkes 2005, 46). This self-questioning in search of an identity was clearly experienced in response to the westernization process. The group Young Ottomans, led by Namık Kemal, sought to develop an Ottoman identity, which would combine the basic institutions of the Empire, (Sultanate and Sharia) with sections of Western liberalism (essentially, a constitution and a parliament); such an identity was also imagined as receptive to the science and technology of the West. The Young Ottomans' political project went on for two years only, before it was suppressed by the Sultan's conservative reaction, in 1878. Indeed, the subsequent period was named after the Sultan, known as the Hamidian reaction restoring the absolutist monarchy. While supportive of Western science and technological achievements, the Hamidian regime was not appreciative of political liberalism. More specifically, it aimed to resolve the identity issue through Islamism.

What characterized the so-called longest century of the Empire was the variety of attempts to configure and construct a social, political, and cultural identity in response to the rising hegemony of the Western civilization. It is this encounter with the other (the West) that led to the self-questioning and ensuing attempts to project a new identity (one could say modern, due to the explicit constructionist character of the process) primarily among the Ottoman elites. Though significant differences did exist, the administrative reformism and economic liberalism of the *Tanzimat* bureaucrats, limited political liberalism and Ottomanism of the Young Ottomans, and Islamism of Hamidian regime, altogether shared one vital assumption: the Western civilization was not only the other, but it was also like a toolbox from which one could borrow what they needed and wanted to catch up with (law and institutions, as well as industry, science, and technology). This way, the instrumental-strategic relationship with the other was not demanding a self-transformation (in social, cultural, political and economic spheres), but it was just a synthetic assemblage. Therefore, although the relationship with the Western civilization inspired attempts of construction of the self (a new one), it did not imply a self-making through self-transformation but a fantasized projection of an image – a combined, assembled self. With this in mind, we could actually question its modernity. As one eminent scholar of Turkish intellectual life has put it, this era was an age of "duality in thought and life" (Ülken 1998, 49), which suggests that the noted attempts could only reproduce the duality from which they had originally departed.

The republican project can be defined as the radical elimination of the duality between Eastern and Western ideas, institutions and even lifestyles of the Turkish state and society. The institutions, norms, and values constituting and regulating the structure of power and public sphere were adopted from the Western civilization, and social and cultural life were subject to an imposed westernization. Since the dominant discourse of the time was about modern civilization, the Western civilization was accepted as "the civilization of the century" and "the common civilization" (Tunaya 1996, 119). Mahmut Esat Bozkurt, a prominent member of the ruling elite of the Early Republic and the author of a series of twelve articles, commonly known as "The Principles of Turkish Revolution," remarked that the republic was determined to resolve "the problem of duality" and make "the new Turkey" a European state (Uyar 1993). The revolutionary dynamism of the early republicanism took place in an authoritarian political framework through the monopoly of the Republican People's Party (CHP).[1] A special 1925 law, *Takrir-i Sükun* (Law on the Maintenance of Order), provided the government with the authority to ban all organizations and publications which were deemed as destabilizing of the public order, for two years. The focus was on the pursuit of reforms and revolutions, including the closure of *tekke*s and *zaviye*s (the gathering places for the members of the Islamic sects), prohibition of the fez and its replacement with the hat, the adoption of the Swiss civil code and the European calendar, and so on. Mustafa Kemal Atatürk, whose name is synonymous with the foundation of the secular Turkish Republic, maintained that the authoritarian character of the regime in the Early Republic was just an instrument used "to lead Turkish nation to the status they deserve in the civilized world" (Atatürk 1982, 897). For instance, in Atatürk's view, the adoption of the hat was "necessary to show that the mentality of Turkish nation was not different from that of the civilized social life" (Atatürk 1982, 895). He consistently distinguished between the European powers against which the war of liberation had been fought and the idea of Europe as the locus of modernity. As documented, in his 1920 letter of protest sent to the representatives of the powers occupying Istanbul, apart from describing their behavior as going "against dignity and honor," Atatürk himself insisted on a clear distinction between "the official Europe and America," and "the Europe and America of science, culture, and civilization," from which they drew their own inspiration (Atatürk 1982, 417).

The republican project of westernization and modernization followed from the previous attempts and corresponding reflections and reconstructions of identity. Here, it should be stressed that the political elite of the Early Turkish Republic did not perceive the European civilization as the other; on the contrary, it was regarded as common or universal. Therefore, the foundation of the republic did not represent yet another attempt of combination or assemblage of different values and principles, but a project of total transformation and break with the past. In order to join and feel part of the overarching civilization, a new state and society (meaning a new identity constructed through the process of nation-building) were absolute

---

1 Following the foundation of the Turkish Republic, the former People's Party was renamed to the Republican People's Party, in November 1923. It favored "democracy, modernization, and the rule of law," and defined "the people" as a homogenous body, without class divisions and privileged groups (Tunçay 1992, 58).

prerequisites. So, if the dominant ideology of the early republican era is labelled as Kemalism, it should not be forgotten that "it was not only about nationalism, national liberation or independence, but also nation-building and struggle for recognition, both by the world and its own self" (Berkes 2005, 119). However, the early republican project remained top-down and authoritarian; in this sense, it was not a process of self-transformation and self-constitution but a proper imposition from above, resulting in a long-lasting skepticism and gap between the leadership and people. Still, several aspects of Western civilization formed an integral part of the new Turkish society; indeed, the goal of becoming part of the common or universal civilization has been a constant theme in Turkish politics and socio-cultural life since then.

The Center-Right and Economic Westernization

The single-party regime's geo-political decision to develop closer relations and integrate with the Western bloc in the aftermath of 1945 – an approach consistent with the overall westernization drive of the Early Republic – and the subsequent transition to the multi-party politics through a process of limited democratization was a turning point for the modern Turkish politics and ideological life. The foundation of the Democratic Party (DP) in 1946 and its rise to power in the 1950 election (with the 53.35 percent of the vote), largely thanks to a popular social and political mobilization, exposed the frailty of the republican project of building a secular, Western and modern nation. The DP founders had split with the CHP and, in terms of their program, they shared the geo-political choice and policy of repression of the left. Moreover, they were committed to the foundational principles of the republic. However, the DP's turn to the people to obtain their support initiated a popular mobilization against what CHP used to stand for (radical secularism, the bureaucratic elite's oppression of the people, and economic problems, including black market and scarcity during the war years) (Eroğul 2013, 133–134). The politics of the DP throughout the 1950s is the basis of the modern center-right in Turkey; its understanding of westernization is essentially linked to the economic aspects, with a particular emphasis on an opening toward foreign capital and financial aid, as well as a more solid economic integration with the West. On the other hand, there is a certain social and cultural conservatism which supports the visibility and promotion of religious values in the public sphere and life together with a critical distancing from the excessive secularism of the Early Republicand CHP. The DP approach represented a liberal-conservative antidote to the top-down transformative ambitions of the CHP. It was certainly non-revolutionary in its populist exaltation of the traditional and religious values of the people and its liberalism took the private property rights as the foundational principle of the economic activity. DP's understanding of the identity of Turkish nation, hence, differed from the early republican promise; it is viewed as a society which is predominantly pious and committed to the traditional values and life that should not be forced to change, and it is a society which is eager to participate in economic development and enjoy prosperity through free economic activity. It was with this economic-based westernization perspective that the DP applied for membership to the then European Economic Community (EEC) in 1959. Together with Greece, Turkey was one of the first countries to apply for a membership in the EEC, which back then only included the six founding members.

The 1960 military intervention ended the ten-year long DP rule. The chief of staff had sent a letter to the prime minister a month before the coup, in which he criticized the ruling party's authoritarian repression of the opposition, judiciary, media reporting, and the higher education sector, consequently requesting certain democratizing reforms (such as the abrogation of anti-democratic laws) and the release of the political prisoners (Eroğul 2013, 235). The military junta changed the constitution which, paradoxically, both reinforced the bureaucratic, judicial, and military oversight over the regime through "extensive checks and balances" by creating "a senate with power to delay execution of laws and a constitutional court with authority to invalidate laws, . . . and a National Security Council . . . to give the military a forum to share their views with civilian authorities" (Harris 2011), and provided an extended space for fundamental rights and freedoms and political participation through the proportional representation (Gözler 2000, 77–92). Following the 1961 election, CHP-led coalition governments were in charge until 1965, and it was during this period when the Ankara Association Agreement between Turkey and the EEC was signed (1963), marking the official beginning of the still ongoing accession process. While the DP's application for this agreement depended on an economic understanding of westernization, the CHP, though fulfilling what DP had already begun, emphasized the political significance of the agreement and thus invoked the post-Second World War geopolitical positioning of the republic toward the Western civilization. In his 1962 address to the parliament, Feridun Cemal Erkin, Minister of Foreign Affairs, clearly expressed such a perspective. He first pointed out that "the economic integration of the Western Europe" depended on "a deep political consideration" and as such it actually represented "the beginning of the political integration" (cited in Çayhan 1997, 38). Then, he went on to define the Western orientation of the country as a "national policy," which was shared by all the political parties since the foundation of the republic, and underline that Turkey joining to the European Common Market was just a step in the pro-Western direction: "As our country has oriented itself toward the Western civilization since the foundation of the republic . . . and it has supported the Western solidarity in the post-Second World War division of the world into two blocs, it is futile to talk more about this issue [the Association Agreement]" (cited in Çayhan 1997, 38). When the agreement was initialed, both the Dutch foreign minister Joseph Luns, representing the Council, and Walter Hallstein, the president of the European Commission, emphasized the background of the whole Turkey-EEC process in similar terms. Luns, in his remarks, praised the efforts of Turkey for joining to the Common Market as "a walk in Atatürk's way," , and Hallstein, in addition to stating that "Turkey is a part of Europe," observed that "there is an impact of the strong personality of Atatürk and his European reforms in every field on each progressive step in Turkey" (cited in *Milliyet* 1963).

Against the CHP-led coalition governments, the opposition Justice Party (AP) – founded in 1961 to revive the legacy of the DP – managed to come to power following the 1965 general election. Its popularity was beyond expectation (with 53 percent of the vote); apart from mobilizing the organizational network of the DP across the country, it had also become the center of the opposition, not only in relation to the military intervention but also to the republican project of creating a secular and Western-like nation-state (Demirel 2004, 28–30). As such there was Islamist and radical nationalist factions within the party, the split of which, by the end of the 1960s, would define the political spectrum of the modern Turkish politics since then. The main ideological line of the party was similar to the DP, including a combination of economic liberalism and sociocultural conservatism. Still, its economic liberalism was framed in order to fit in with the new constitutional order, which envisioned a planned economy to promote the development of a nascent industrial bourgeoisie through import substitution – an approach the DP had been against since its liberalism fostered the interests of the big landowners and commercial bourgeoisie, and disadvantaged the interests of the rest of the population.

The AP did not reject westernization but, in its view, the CHP's representatives were on the wrong side of it (Demirel 2004, 101). Similar to the DP's understanding, for the AP, westernization could not be taken and implemented as a forced change of the nation's lifestyle, which was shaped by the religious values, symbols, and rituals; accordingly, westernization implied a certain relationship with the Western civilization so that progress in the field of domestic economics and financial resources, as well as science, technology, and infrastructure would eventually take place. Süleyman Demirel, the leader of the party, was a self-made man, forward looking engineer, engaged in professional business in the United States, but still appreciative of his countryside origins including the traditional and religious values that characterized his upbringing. His response to the criticism of the representative of the Labor Party of Turkey (TİP) on the occasion of the 1965 parliamentary debate concerning the newly defined government's program is noteworthy. Confronted with the question about the Turkish dependency on the international capitalist relations and their institutions (EEC, General Agreement on Tariffs and Trade, International Monetary Fund, and Organization for Economic Cooperation and Development), he said: "We should do justice to these institutions; they are useful to the humanity and for Western civilization's appeal" (cited in Çayhan 1997, 55–56). As it has been broadly interpreted, it is the economic and financial incentives that formed the basis of Turkey's Western aspirations, according to the AP leadership.

The Turkish Left and Rethinking of Westernization

A significant feature of the post-military intervention was the emergence of the Turkish left, which tried to stir the republican project in the direction of (democratic) socialism, time and conditions permitting. The 1961 foundation of the Labor Party of Turkey – which caused political repositioning of the CHP as the left-of-center party in mid-decade – and some vivid activism of prominent intellectuals started to influence public debates despite the control of the political power by the AP. More precisely, the critique of the CHP's westernizing reforms in the Early Republic, the liberal economy-based westernization understanding of the DP-AP, and the beginning of the EEC accession negotiations became the main themes in the left-wing political and intellectual renaissance. The Labor Party of Turkey's opposition to the Ankara Association Agreement and the accompanying process, initially taking place outside the parliament and then inside, from 1965 onwards, expressed a rather critical assessment of the structural underdevelopment of the country and the corresponding class relations. The key point of their declaration against the 1963 agreement was that the inclusion of Turkey in the Common Market could only reinforce the socioeconomic structure with big landowners and commercial bourgeoisie in charge of foreign capital. Given that the purpose of the Customs Union was largely understood as the continuation of "colonialism with new means," in such a union, Turkey "would be faltering eternally like a semi-colony in capitalism" (Çayhan 1997, 49).

One of the leading intellectuals was Doğan Avcıoğlu; in his role of a journalist, he was the founder of the magazine *Yön [Direction]*, a significant intellectual and ideological platform of the Turkish left, and in his role of an intellectual, he was a member and representative of the CHP during the drafting of the new constitution in 1961. Avcıoğlu was critical of the revolutions of the republic, depicting them as "revolutions in the superstructure" on a socio-economic basis that was not transformed. This base was an underdeveloped structure dominated by the merchants and landowners whose actions epitomized the pre-capitalist order. In fact, the republican revolution did not challenge their power; on the contrary, it depended on them to institute the revolutions in the superstructure, meaning that the reform policies of the Early Republic were constrained. These classes (or their fractions) enjoyed and participated in the superstructural change, yet they simultaneously blocked its diffusion to the rest of people, even if the large section of the society were eventually westernized. After the Second World War, the class alliance among the big landowners, commercial bourgeoisie and foreign investments was both welcomed and promoted by the *Tanzimat* Westernist wing of the bureaucratic apparatus which exposed Turkey to the American influence (Avcıoğlu 1998 [1968], 545–546). In Avcıoğlu's view, the weak and dependent capitalist class believed that the EEC membership could bring about the industrial economic development of the country – a standpoint defended by the bureaucrats and politicians who had an understanding of *Tanzimat* type of Westernism – and therefore, the 1963 Ankara agreement was not substantially different from the 1838 free trade agreement, signed between the Ottoman Empire and the United Kingdom of Great Britain and Ireland, regulating international trade (Avcıoğlu 1998, 925).

Another leading left-wing intellectual and politician İsmail Cem introduced an overall critique of westernization covering *Tanzimat*, the Early Republic and the DP-AP line. As a journalist in the 1970s, he served as the general director of the Turkish Radio and Television during the CHP-led coalition government, then in the 1980s, he was a member of the parliament and, finally in the late 1990s, Minister of Foreign Affairs during the coalition governments led by the Democratic Left Party (DSP). In addition to the earlier points about Turkish underdevelopment and a particular socioeconomic framework, he also highlighted the social and cultural differences of the Turkish people. He traced the legacy of the Ottoman economic order in shaping the worldview of the people and cultivating a certain type of man. Accordingly, this order constrained individualism through communitarianism (Cem 1997, 77). Moreover, the characteristics of "the type of man" of this social and historical domain were "not to be greedy, to be mild and to comply with the interests of the community and the society," and in this sense, "he" is different from "the type of man of the Western civilization" (Cem 1997, 111–112). More precisely, "the type of man" of the latter is "a single, creative, dynamic individual of the Western civilization constituted by ancient Greece, Rome and Christianity" (Cem 1997, 118). The westernization launched by the *Tanzima Tanzimat t* dissolved the sociocultural basis of this order and abused it, while serving to the economic interests of the bureaucrats, merchants, and the influential members of the society, who collaborate with the Western economic powers. According to Cem, during the process of westernization, continuing through the single party rule and getting rooted among the people through the DP-AP's line of rule, it was assumed that the transfer of economic, political, and legal institutions of Europe would elevate Turkey to the welfare level of Europe. However, "since the circumstances were completely different," this process resulted in "groundless institutions, confused reactions, an abused culture and a society whose qualities are uncertain" (Cem 1997, 313).

The left-wing rethinking of westernization, including the early developments with regard to the European integration process, as well as the concerns of sustaining the planning-led import-substitution industrialization, contributed to the CHP's turn toward center-left concerning the Turkish accession to the EEC in the second half of the seventies. The CHP-led coalition government in 1978, under the leadership of Bülent Ecevit, promised to renegotiate the country's transition (required as part of the accession process), which had already commenced by the 1970s. As the then leadership used to put it, Turkey's relations with the EEC "make it difficult to follow a foreign trade policy compatible with the economic and political interests of Turkey against the developed countries;" this relationship, in the government's view, also hindered the development of Turkey "in the fields of agriculture and industry" (Çayhan 1997, 198). The goal, as the official standpoint went on to promote, should be an independent Turkey, which eventually resulted in the Ecevit administration's decision to freeze the obligations of Turkey in the framework of its transition for five years. Following the resignation of the government in 1979, due to the defeat in the by-elections, the newly-founded Justice Party and its Demirel-led right-wing coalition with the Islamist National Salvation Party (MSP) and ultra-nationalist Nationalist Action Party (MHP) lifted the freeze, but the resumed process was short-lived, as it was interrupted by the 1980 military intervention.

According to the center-right adherents, the relations with the Western civilization and, more specifically, the EEC were to be grounded in economic cooperation, whereas the social and cultural authenticity of the Turkish system and society were to be preserved. Such an approach had been adopted back in the 1950s and restated ever since. However, in terms of the Turkish left, the case was somewhat reversed, as the sixties and seventies were also a period of a strong presence of center-left orientation. For the left, the economic relations with the West, led by the rules of free market, could only lead to semi-colonization that would prevent any possibility for an autonomous industrial economic development. With this in mind, such a relationship could only sustain further the backward social and economic structure of Turkey. The West, and the EEC in particular, represented the economic other; yet, the Turkish left did not reject or oppose the westernization reforms or revolutions of the republic which were seen as superstructural. They were rather seen as incomplete without a transformation of the predominantly pre-capitalist landowners and comprador commercial bourgeoisie, altogether dominating the socioeconomic structure. In this sense, the Turkish left was modernist in its relation to the Turkish society in terms of aspiration to see total transformation of both the base and superstructure, but in order to remain an autonomous modern industrial society. However, this could have only implied a more radical revolution than what the authoritarian Early Republic pursued and achieved. The revolutionary imaginary of the left could only have delivered its promises to the extent that it could have initiated a self-transformation of the Turkish people if it had not repeated the bureaucratic elite vs. people fault line of the Early Republic and remained a limited top-down project. This possibility, however, was halted and turned to be an ever-fading utopia after the anti-left military coup in 1980.

The Anti-Western Islamist Opposition and Its Transformation

The ultra-nationalist radical right in Turkey, represented by the Republican Peasants National Party (CKMP) in the period between 1958 and 1969, and the Nationalist Action Party (MHP), since 1969, did not consistently object to the westernization project of the republic and Turkey's decision to pursue the European integrationist process. In fact, the CKMP supported the EEC membership application. Later, especially from the 1990s onwards, the MHP embraced a Eurosceptic stand against the EU, since the political accommodation with the so-called Copenhagen criteria asked for a revision of the party's stance in relation to minority rights (for example, the Kurdish issue, which the party's view represented as a real terror). Moreover, the EU's position on the Cyprus problem and well-known nationalist anxiety about national sovereignty and identity exacerbated the MHP's skeptical standpoint. However, once in coalition with the Democratic Left Party (DSP) and the Motherland Party (ANAP), between 1999 and 2002, MHP members neither blocked nor approved the passing of the first (three) harmonization packages prescribed by the Copenhagen political criteria; so, as some observers put it, they represented an "emotional opposition," but did not actually hinder the process of integration (Güneş-Ayata 2003, 211).

In Turkey, the radical right's opposition to westernization and the European integrationist project has been represented by the political Islam and facilitated by the establishment of an Islamist party after the split within the AP. An outright opposition to Turkey's involvement in the European economic integration stood at the core of its agenda. Necmettin Erbakan, the founder of this new political track, was in charge of the Union of Chambers and Commodity Exchanges of Turkey (TOBB), which is an umbrella public institution composed of the local-provincial chambers of business and trade. Back then, the TOBB was supportive of the AP's policy, but because of his views that the AP came to promote the interests of big financial and industrial business at the expense of the vast Anatolian small-to-medium entrepreneurs, Erbakan was forced to resign (Demirel 2004, 54–55). He was elected an independent deputy in the 1969 general election and then founded the National Order Party (MNP), the first of a series of parties representing the political Islam in Turkey known as the National Outlook Movement.[2] His 1970 parliamentary address concerning the Turkey-EEC relations, set the politico-ideological direction of the movement for the decades to come: "The social structure, worldview, historical course and consciousness of Turkey prevents its integration with the Westerns European countries in a political formation" (cited in Çayhan 1997, 70). Besides, he went on to argue, "there are huge differences in the levels of economic development between Turkey and Western countries, [and therefore] integration with the Common Market would make Turkey a colony and worker of the Western countries" (cited in Çayhan 1997, 70). What was needed, Erbakan concluded, was an alternative common market, one of "the Eastern countries with which Turkey is connected historically and culturally" (Çayhan 1997, 70). Later on, in one of his manuscripts, he claimed that the EU membership was "a Kemalist plot to convert Turkey to Western Civilization" that "would prevent the growing influence of political Islam" (cited in

---

2 The MNP was closed down in 1971 by the Constitutional Court. In its place, the National Salvation Party (MSP) was founded in 1972 but closed down in 1980 together with all other political parties, as the result of the military intervention. Subsequently, the Welfare Party (RP) was established in 1983 and closed down in 1998 by the Constitutional Court. The Virtue Party (FP) was formed in 1997 and closed down in 2001 by the Constitutional Court. The ruling Justice and Development Party (AKP) was founded through a split with the FP, before its closure.

Duran 2004, 127). Again, in the early 1990s, in a manifesto of the just order, which was the politico-ideological statement of the Welfare Party, Erbakan kept promising a form of a new order without unjust taxes and interest rates, and one with sound money with an abundance of credit for everyone "who can do useful business." The cornerstone of this order is a common market consisting of Muslim countries, with Turkey as an active participant and supplier of these countries' needs; on the basis of this new order, Turkey "will be one of the strongest countries of the world" (Erbakan 1996, 13–14). Accordingly, the National Outlook Movement was proposing a hegemonic role, as a mirror image of the new imperialism, in which Turkey, in contrast to being subjected to a membership process of the EEC, would play a key role in the Islamic world through an alternative common market.

The watershed event in the history of this movement has been their coming to power as the major partner in a coalition government with the center right True Path Party (DYP), in 1996. However, in a year, the mobilization of the secular establishment through the National Security Council and segments of civil society, trade unions, and business organizations against "the supposed Islamization" of Turkey brought about the collapse of the government (Cizre and Çınar 2003, 309). While expecting the closure of the RP by the Constitutional Court, the movement found yet another party, the Virtue Party (FP). The FP's political discourse reflected a significant turn in the history of the movement, favoring democracy, protection of human rights, and a pro-EU agenda for Turkey. Ruşen Çakır, a prominent journalist with an interest in the movement, referred to this turn as "the political Islam's westernization" that was "compulsory" for them to survive (Çakır 1999). In the wake of the closure of the FP in 2001, the movement split into two along the division between the reformers and traditionalists. The Justice and Development Party was founded by the reformers in August 2001 and, under the leadership of Recep Tayyip Erdoğan came to power during the following year's snap election amidst political fragmentation of the center left and right, as well as the economic crisis.

The AKP and European Integration: A Case of Unfulfilled Self-Transformation

The reformists of political Islam defined their ideology as conservative democracy while rejecting Islamism – one of the available interpretations of neoconservatism in the Turkish context. It was broadly an ideology combining social and cultural populism through the discourse of conserving and representing the religious values of the people and nation as the basis of the political authority in domestic and foreign politics with a neoliberal understanding of free market economy. The then ideologue of the AKP, Yalçın Akdoğan, took the American and German cases of neoconservatism as the model, replicating their basic concern which is dedicated to "restoring authority in social life while defending the free market and the expansion of the domain of freedom in economic relations" (Ertuğrul 2012, 163). This was an intrinsically authoritarian ideology. With an Islamist background and later concerns of survival, the AKP resorted to democratization reforms, closely related to the country's EU membership perspective, which in return provided a new space for the exercise of neoconservative vision in an attempt to reshape Turkey. Still, the AKP, while representing the other of the secular Western-oriented republican establishment, exhibited a strong case of self-transformation of the Islamist-conservative social and political dynamics of Turkey in terms of adoption of the EU's normative framework and revamping of their ideology by looking toward the West. In this sense, the AKP was westernizing politically and ideologically while affirming its representation of cultural and religious otherness.

During its first term, the AKP's political agenda was in close connection with the fulfilment of the Copenhagen political criteria, necessary in order to begin negotiations for EU accession. Here, we should stress the importance of a facilitating background for the AKP's reformist and democratizing political endeavor; Turkey, following the neoliberal transformation of its economic structure in the eighties and early nineties (Şenses 2016), was included in the Customs Union by 1996, through an agreement with the EU. This arrangement is mainly about changing the regulations and legislations which were in force in Turkey – about the economic rights (protection of the copyright, patent rights, brand names, etc.) of the trading and producing actors (either of material goods or goods of thought and conception), customs policies, technical standards, and regulation of competition – and their adaptation to the ones which were in force in the EU. The point of the agreement put in place was the creation of an extended area for free trade within the EU, the elimination of commercial public monopolies, and the opening up of the public procurement to the firms from the EU. In fact, in its substance, the agreement has been integrating Turkey into the single market. As Cem Duna, a Turkish representative during the negotiation process, has sought to underline its importance in the long-lasting westernization process: "[With this agreement] you are gaining the title of a European country. You are achieving an integration in practice. Once you do that, you have to prepare the political superstructure of it" (cited in *Milliyet* 1995).

The multi-party coalition government formed by the center-left Democratic Left Party, the center-right Motherland Party, and the ultra-nationalist Nationalist Action Party, also took significant steps toward the opening of EU negotiations during their rule (1999–2002). It was thanks to their efforts that Turkey was granted a candidate status of the membership process at the 1999 Helsinki Summit of the European Council and consequently adopted three harmonization packages with the perspective of meeting the Copenhagen political criteria. So, when the AKP came to power, the government pursued a vigorous policy of reforms, and in addition to the areas tackled through the previous harmonization packages, went on to address the question of freedom of expression and abolition of capital punishment without exception to civilian-military relations (Ertuğrul and Akçalı Yılmaz 2018). In response, upon the recommendations of the European Commission, the Brussels administration agreed to open up the negotiation process for EU membership. In parallel, the AKP authorities have also complied with the IMF standby agreement, which came into existence one year before their coming to power. The goal of this program was to integrate Turkey into the finance-led global capitalism by establishing autonomous regulatory agencies and imposing tight fiscal policies. With the AKP's commitment to a Western-oriented economic policy, it can be concluded that the government went beyond the center-right tradition of Turkey by promoting not only economic westernization but also adaptation to the European civic-normative order, and by recrafting its ideology by showing clear appreciation for Western neoconservatism. In retrospect, this may look highly controversial, if not even paradoxical, but the AKP was the most westernist and self-westernizing (hence self-transforming) political agent in the modern Turkish history.

However, from the AKP's second term onwards, there has been a progressive reversal, including the return to political Islam and the building of an authoritarian regime. This tendency has been accompanied by a civilizational discourse; the AKP started to reclaim the Ottoman-Islamic legacy and to use the former Ottoman territorial conquests as the basis of its global leadership ambitions. The AKP's affirmation of cultural and religious otherness and its use as the core element of political mobilization served as a response to the westernist-secular establishment, both in terms of the party's struggle for recognition by the then establishment and a confirmation of the status of otherness in front of the wider European context. Yet, the tendency to reclaim the Ottoman-Islamic legacy went beyond this early affirmation; it was indicative of the urge to be a new center of power. The highly pretentious, as well as ahistorical and quasi-imperial discourse has been aimed at restoring a lost pre-modern hegemony under the conditions of the early twenty-first century. It is competitive against the EU at times, but more importantly, it signals diversion from the EU's civic-normative order. Ahmet Davutoğlu, serving as the Minister of Foreign Affairs between 2009 and 2014, and the Prime Minister between 2014 and 2016, can be considered as the ideologue of this new foreign policy vision. In his book, published before he pursued a political career, there are clear reflections of this new ideological orientation of Turkish foreign policy. He maintains that Turkey cannot evade the cultural and civilizational identity, which has been constituted by the Ottoman legacy, in the international relations, especially in the post-Cold War era (Davutoğlu 2008, 17–23). Later, in a speech delivered on the occasion of a conference with Turkey's ambassadors in 2011, he restated this vision even more pointedly, with a proper reference to the Balkans and the Middle East. Davutoğlu first criticized the Orientalist (and European) perception of the two regions as the arenas of eternal bloody conflicts ("blood-thirsty nations") and then emphasized the often-ignored long period of peace which they had experienced under the Ottoman rule, until the end of the nineteenth century. Moreover, he claimed that a new, yet similar Pax Ottomana could be possible if the historical links and heritage were revived whether with the Balkans in the EU, by forming a new basin, or outside of it, given the economic crisis and uncertainty about the future of the EU itself (Davutoğlu 2011). Concerning the Turkish economic policy orientation, it also went through a certain diversion, if not a proper reversal. In fact, medium-sized Islamic or conservative enterprises constituted the socioeconomic backbone of the AKP from its beginning; they were supported through privatization programs, public and municipal tenders, and credit facilities within the limits of disciplinary and rule-bound neoliberalism in the first term of AKP in power. After the termination of the IMF standby agreement in 2008 under the conditions of the global economic crisis, the Turkish leadership turned toward explicit favoritism of new big businesses with political allegiance to the party and its leader. The new entrepreneurs were expected to use part of the financial resources, which were made available to them, in the media sector to support and promote the activities of the government (Buğra and Savaşkan 2012).

In the AKP's move toward authoritarianism the 2010 constitutional referendum was a turning point. Having survived the public prosecutor's case for closing down the party in the trial by the Constitutional Court in 2008, thanks to the EU-oriented political reformism and support of the Brussels administration, the AKP used the referendum to acquire authority to control appointments in the higher judiciary. With a strong popular support and enhanced authority over the state politics and institutions, the party sought to install a new political setting, which would result in an end of the long-standing parliamentary democracy model. The AKP submitted the first proposal for a new constitution to the Constitutional Committee of the Parliament in November 2012, which was rejected by the opposition parties. In 2017, another proposal for a similar constitutional change was approved in the parliament, with the support of the Nationalist Action Party, and then ratified by a controversial and disputed referendum in 2017 (with 51.4 percent of the vote). In the proposed system, the president is the locus of political power. In the view of the Venice Commission, the amendments "lead to an excessive concentration of executive power in the hands of the President and the weakening of parliamentary control of that power" (Venice Commission 2017, 12). According to the constitutional amendments, the president can rule by presidential decrees and holds the power to control higher judiciary and public bureaucracy through appointments. In addition to having the authority to annul the parliament and call for elections, the president can remain a member of the party which gives leverage to control the parliamentary group of the party. Therefore, the proposed model has been about the unification of power in the post of the president, spoiling the basic democratic principle of separation of powers.

The key event causing the fatal departure of the AKP government from the EU civic-normative order was the 2013 Gezi insurgency, which clearly exposed the existence of political and sociocultural divisions between an authoritarian government enjoying conservative popular support and all those groups and individuals experiencing oppression under the radicalizing neoconservatism of the AKP. Those protesting against the AKP and rejecting the type of order it aimed to establish were mostly un-organized, unaffiliated, and diverse in terms of socioeconomic background, gender, and age; in fact, the majority of them did not have any previous experience of activ-ism or politicization (Bilgiç and Kafkaslı 2013; KONDA 2013; Yörük and Yüksel 2014). The government's response was to increase the severity of authoritarianism through violent dispersion of the encampment in the occupied Gezi Park and forceful suppres-sion of the protests across the country, which resulted in the killing of several young participants – Ahmet Atakan, Mehmet Ayvalıtaş, Abdullah Cömert, Berkin Elvan, Ali İsmail Korkmaz, and Ethem Sarısülük – whose names consequently became the pan-theon of social and political resistance in Turkey. Suppression of plurality, media freedom, and freedom of expression and organization have become the new norm since then. Indeed, all these issues were identified by both the European Parliament and the EU's Progress Report, which expressed concerns over "an overall absence of dialogue" between the civil society and the administrative power (Ertuğrul and Akçalı-Yılmaz 2018, 63).

The then Primer Minister (and since August 2014, President) Erdoğan's threat of a counter-mobilization of his supporters in the early days of the Gezi insurgency, sig-naled that the problem was beyond "an absence of dialogue," as illustrated by a press conference during which he boldly stated that "we are hardly keeping at least the 50 percent of this country at their homes," suggesting that if they wanted to, they could let them go out and confront the protestors (*Hürriyet* 2013). He positioned him-self as the leader of at least the majority of the Turkish society, which was an imagi-nary homogeneous community of pious Muslims living in accordance with the traditional morality and respecting their leader. In fact, the authoritarian turn of the AKP strongly depended on Erdoğan's self-positioning, a move that came to represent the sole ground of the claimed need for a (pseudo-)presidential regime. Accordingly, his campaign in the first direct election of the head of state in 2014 (held within the limits of a still-present parliamentary regime) presented him through the slogan Man of the Nation and as somebody in search of a new Turkey. Erdoğan's explanation of the idea of a new Turkey did nothing more but to indicate the absorption of the AKP's ideological elements, in both domestic and foreign policy, with his role of the president as directly representing the values and morality of the nation and the pre-republican Ottoman and Islamic legacy, while seeking to eliminate the residues of the military and bureaucratic tutelage. In his speech on the occasion of the beginning of the new legislative year of the Turkish parliament in October 2014, after having won the first direct election of the head of state, Erdoğan's stated that the notion of a new Turkey implied "continuity in terms of reconciliation with our civilizational roots [Ottoman and Islamic] and historical geography [Pax Ottomana]" and "break with the understanding of politics and society" (Erdoğan's 2014). By the latter, he re-ferred to "the participation of the long-othered parts of this society [pious conserva-tives] in politics," and it is within the framework of "a new sociology" – positioned against "the tutelage spots [within the state] of old Turkey" – that he sought to shape his political direction and consolidate future power (Erdoğan 2014). The political and ideological repositioning of the AKP from a seemingly Western-like neoconservative party to a Turkish-type (or native, as in the jargon of AKP representatives) authoritarian and right-wing populist party, which is largely subsumed by the personality of Erdoğan himself, ended up with the constitution of the so-called native form of presidential regime in 2017.

The failed coup attempt of the Gülenist-led[3] putschists in 2016 deepened the already increasing authoritarianism. Throughout the course of the state of emergency more than 130,000 public employees were purged (*BBC* 2018). The government's purge campaign was extended from the Gülenists to the broader opposition, and especially to academics and intellectuals, with a few hundred academics – signatories of a petition condemning the government's security operations and human rights violations in Southeastern Turkey, and inviting the state authorities to seek solutions through dialogue and peaceful means – being purged by the government decrees. Their passports were confiscated, and they were banned for life from employment in public institutions (TİHV Akademi 2019). In fact, the 2018 EU's evaluation of Turkey underlined that the state had fallen back from compatibility with the Copenhagen political criteria. In its summary, the European Commission used the word 'backsliding' to describe the situation in the areas concerning freedom of expression, assembly, and association, as well as the rule of law and property rights (European Commission 2018). In the view of the Brussels administration, the suppression of civil society, the closure of rights-based organizations, the transfers of power to the presidency through emergency decrees, and the replacement of municipal executives and elected representatives aimed at the weakening of local democracy, were detrimental features of the Erdoğan regime, suggesting that "Turkey has been moving away from the EU" (European Commission 2018, 3). However, one aspect received positive comments; Turkey was praised for its performance in the area of migration and asylum policy and its commitment to the 2016 EU-Turkey Statement (European Council 2016) about the control of "the migratory flows along the Eastern Mediterranean" (European Commission 2018, 41). Here, the report and similar subsequent assessments have revealed some proper cynicism with regard to the character of the relationship between EU and Turkey, with the former evaluating the Ankara leadership not only in the context of civic-normative behavior but also its capacity to block refugees and migrants on their way to the EU. In such a strategically driven arrangement, Turkey has not only remained a distant and incomplete other, but has also moved further away.

---

3 A religious sect which is known for its dissimulating members (apparently modern, yet followers of the cause of a religious organization) with positions in public institutions, including the army. They were raised and promoted throughout decades to advance to be able to control the state apparatus.

Conclusion

Westernization and the process of European integration shaped the modern history of Turkey by creating, and in a sense constituting, the terrain of political and ideological contestation, with policy preferences broadly affecting the pathways of Turkish economic and sociocultural development. Alongside this understanding, three significant political and ideological trends can be identified. The first concerns the Turkish left including the CHP; while the CHP was the top-down transformative political agent of the westernization project of the Early Republic, from the mid-1960s onwards it transformed into a left-of-center party, with concerns about Turkey's autonomous development in light of its economic relationship with the West and the EEC. This CHP's turn can only be fully understood in the context of the left-wing political and intellectual renaissance of the 1960s during which the critique of the limited superstructural westernization policy of the Early Republic, the economic westernization of the center-right, and the beginning of the EEC membership process were of utmost relevance. The key point related to the structural underdevelopment of Turkey and the difficult way out of this condition within the then terms of westernization and relations with the West. The second trend concerns the center-right tradition in Turkey which has been represented by the DP-AP line between 1950 and 1980, which understood the economic integration with the West and the European Common Market as a necessity for Turkey's economic development. It also promoted a social and cultural conservatism against the CHP's excessive westernization, hence representing a long-lasting conservative populism. The third trend concerns political Islam, the historical course of which has been characterized by abrupt breaks and turns. It was represented by the political parties of the National Outlook Movement since 1969, gathered around an outright rejection of Turkey's westernization and involvement in the European integrationist project – a position which lasted until the end of the 1990s. However, their transformation toward a new political agency with an emphasis on EU-oriented democratization program was crucial for the opening of EU accession negotiations. This was achieved by the AKP, founded after a split with the National Outlook Movement, which has shaped the Turkish political scene since the early 2000s. Its post-2010 authoritarian turn toward the establishment of a pseudo-presidential regime has fully eroded its early achievements bringing about the beginning of Turkey's EU negotiation process.

With everything taken into consideration, the 'What's Next?' question is the most pressing one. The European Commission's assessments concerning the economic criteria have suggested a future which is possible regardless of the cumbersome political limits; as observed, "the Turkish economy is well advanced" and it has achieved "good level of preparation to cope with the competitive pressures of market forces within the EU ... in terms of both trade and investment" (European Commission 2018, 7, 58). During the March 2019 local election and the controversially repeated İstanbul metropolitan municipality election in June, the opposition – consisting of the center-left CHP, secular nationalists, Kurdish groups, and pious Muslims, altogether rejecting the authoritarianism of the AKP-MHP power vertical – won the public vote in some of the biggest cities in Turkey, all being centers of the Turkish economy (including İstanbul, Ankara, İzmir, Adana, and Antalya). The joint participation of an alliance of heterogeneous forces against the authoritarian regime in the local ballot, despite the repression and unequal political competition, can also be viewed as an aftereffect of the Gezi movement. There has been no successful political articulation and representation of the diverse demands, identities, and new subjectivities constituted and unleashed by the Gezi insurgency. Yet, the whirlpool of Gezi transformed the political and social landscape; it has now been apparent that there are diverse, vibrant, and reckless groups of opposition, altogether vocal about their demands despite all the control and interference engineered by the ruling elite. The attempt of the CHP, as the main opposition party, to create an anti-authoritarian platform of opposition without claiming to represent it ideologically, yet to provide logistical organization for promotion of local leaders with a catch-all capacity, has paid off in this new conjuncture.

The long, unfinished, and somewhat eternal relationship between Turkey and the European Union, in the face of its problems, has nevertheless contributed to the development of a burgeoning civil society at the back of an advancing economy, which is broadly integrated into the European single market. Leaving aside the lengthy and complex debates about westernization and the degree of economic integration, the Turkish society and politics have reached a new stage – one that is characterized by a resistant civil society with (self-) transformative capacities against an anachronistic authoritarian regime which has no ideals and values but is solely preoccupied with self-preservation. Overcoming this political condition is a significant step toward overcoming the incomplete otherness of Turkey in the European civic-normative order.

References

Agh, Attila. 1998. *The Politics of Central Europe*. London: SAGE.

Atatürk, Mustafa Kemal. 1982. *Nutuk*. İstanbul: Milli Eğitim Basımevi.

Avcıoğlu, Doğan. 1998. *Türkiye'nin Düzeni*. İstanbul: Tekin Yayınevi.

BBC. 2018. "OHAL sona erdi: İki yıllık sürecin bilançosu." 19 July, https://www.bbc.com/turkce/hab erler-turkiye-44799489.

Berkes, Niyazi. 1964. *The Development of Secularism in Turkey*. Montreal, QC: McGill University Press.

Berkes Niyazi. 2005. *Batıcılık, Ulusçuluk ve Toplumsal Devrimler*. İstanbul: Kaynak Yayınları.

Bideleux, Robert, and Ian Jeffires. 1998. *A History of Eastern Europe: Crisis and Change*. London: Routledge.

Bilgiç, Esra E., and Zehra Kafkaslı. 2013. *Gencim, Özgürlükçüyüm, Ne İstiyorum? #direngezi Anketi Sonuç Raporu*. İstanbul: İstanbul Bilgi Üniversitesi Yayınları.

Buğra, Ayşe, and Osman Savaşkan. 2012. "Politics and class: The Turkish business environment in the neoliberal age." *New Perspectives on Turkey* 46: 27–63.

Calic, Marie-Janine. 2019. *The Great Cauldron: A History of Southeastern Europe*. Cambridge, MA: Harvard University Press.

Çakır, Ruşen. 1999. "İslamcıların Batıcılaşma Süreci." *Birikim* 128: 50–51.

Çayhan, Esra. 1997. *Dünden Bugüne Türkiye-Avrupa Birliği İlişkileri ve Siyasal Partilerin Konuya Bakışı*. İstanbul: Boyut Yayıncılık.

Cem, İsmail. 1997. *Türkiye'de Geri Kalmışlığın Tarihi*. İstanbul: Can Yayınları.

Cizre, Ümit, and Menderes Çınar. 2003. "Turkey 2002: Kemalism, Islamism and politics in the light of February 28 process." *The South Atlantic Quarterly* 102(2–3): 309–332.

Davutoğlu, Ahmet. 2008. *Stratejik Derinlik*. İstanbul: Küre Yayınları.

Davutoğlu, Ahmet. 2011. "Dışişleri Bakanı Sayın Ahmet Davutoğlu'nun IV. Büyükelçiler. Konferansı vesilesiyle Trakya Üniversitesi Balkan Kongre Merkezi'nde Yaptığı Konuşma, 29 Aralık 2011, Edirne." Ministry of Foreign Affairs, http://www.mfa.gov.tr/disisleri-bakani-sayin-ahmet-davutoglu_nun-iv_-buyukelciler-konferansi-vesilesiyle-trakya-universitesi-balkan-kongre-merkezi_nde.tr.mfa.

Demirel, Tanel. 2004. *Adalet Partisi, İdeoloji ve Politika*. İstanbul: İletişim.

Duran, Burhanettin. 2004. "Islamist redefinition(s) of European and Islamic identities in Turkey." In *Turkey and European Integration*, edited by Mehmet Uğur and Nergis Canefe, 125–146. London: Routledge.

Erbakan, Necmettin. 1996. *Adil Ekonomik Düzen*. Ankara: Refah Partisi.

Erdoğan, Recep Tayyip, 2014. "Türkiye Büyük Millet Meclisi'nin 24'üncü Dönem 5'inci Yasama Yılı Açılışında Yaptıkları Konuşma." 1 October, https://www.tccb.gov.tr/konusmalar/353/2941/tur kiye-buyuk-millet-meclisinin-24uncu-donem-5inci-yasama-yili-acilisinda-yaptiklari-konusma.

Eroğul, Cem. 2013. *Demokrat Parti, Tarihi ve İdeolojisi*. İstanbul: Yordam.

Ertuğrul, Kürşad. 2012. "AKP's neoconservatism and politics of otherness in Europe-Turkey relations." *New Perspectives on Turkey* 46: 157–186.

Ertuğrul, Kürşad, and Öznur Akçalı Yılmaz. 2018. "The otherness of Turkey in European integration." *Turkish Studies* 19(1): 48–71.

European Commission. 2018. *Turkey 2018 Report*. 17 April, https://ec.europa.eu/neighbourhood-enlargement/sites/near/files/20180417-turkey-report.pdf.

European Council. 2016. "EU-Turkey statement." 18 March, https://www.consilium.europa.eu/en/press/press-releases/2016/03/18/eu-turkey-statement/.

Gözler, Kemal. 2000. *Türk Anayasa Hukuku*. Bursa: Ekin Kitabevi Yayınları.

Güneş-Ayata, Ayse. 2003. "From Euro-scepticism to Turkey-scepticism: Changing political attitudes on the European Union in Turkey." *Journal of Southern Europe and the Balkans* 5(2): 205–222.

Hanioğlu, Şükrü. 2004. *A Brief History of the Late Ottoman Empire*. Princeton, NJ: Princeton University Press.

Harris, George S. 2011. "Military coups and Turkish democracy, 1960–1980." *Turkish Studies* 12(2): 203–213.

Hürriyet. 2013. "Başbakan: Yüzde 50'yi evinde zor tutuyorum." 4 June, http://www.hurriyet.com.tr/basbakan-yuzde-50-yi-evinde-zor-tutuyorum-23429709.

KONDA. 2013. "Gezi Parkı Araştırması: Kimler, neden oradalar ve ne istiyorlar?" June, https://konda.com.tr/tr/rapor/gezi-parki-arastirmasi-kimler-neden-oradalar-ve-ne-istiyorlar/.

Milliyet. 1995. "Cem Duna interviewed by Nilgün Cerrahoğlu." 5 March, http://gazetearsivi.milliyet.com.tr/Arsiv/1995/03/05.

Milliyet. 1963. "Turkey-EEC relations." 13 September.

Offe, Claus. 1996. *Varieties of Transition: The East European and East German Experience*. Cambridge: Polity Press.

Ortaylı, İlber. 1983. *İmparatorluğun En Uzun Yüzyılı*. İstanbul: Hil.

Sakaoğlu, Necdet. 1989. "Tanzimat Okulları." *Tarih ve Toplum* 12(72): 346–350.

Şenses, Fikret. 2016. "Turkey's experience with neoliberal policies since 1980 in retrospect and prospect." In *The Making of Neoliberal Turkey*, edited by Cenk Ozbay, Maral Erol, Aysecan Terzioglu, and Z. Umut Turem, 15–32. Farnham: Ashgate.

TİHV Akademi. 2019. "Barış İçin Akademisyenler Vakasının Kısa Tarihi," 11 January, http://www.tih vakademi.org/wp-content/uploads/2019/03/Barisicinakademisyenlervakasi.pdf.

Todorova, Maria. 1997. *Imagining the Balkans*. Oxford: Oxford University Press.

Tunaya, Tarık Zafer. 1996. *Türkiye'nin Siyasi Hayatında Batılılaşma Hareketleri*. İstanbul: Arba.

Tunçay, Mete. 1992. *T.C.'nde Tek Parti Yönetimi'nin Kurulması (1923–1931)*. İstanbul: Cem Yayınevi.

Uyar, Hakkı. 1993. "Türk Devrimini Teorileştirme Çabaları: M. E. Bozkurt Örneği-II." *Tarih ve Toplum* 20(120): 329–336.

Ülken, Hilmi Ziya. 1998. *Türkiye'de Çağdaş Düşünce Tarihi*. İstanbul: Ülken Yayınları.

Venice Commission. 2017. *Opinion on the Amendments to the Constitution Adopted by the Grand National Assembly on 21 January 2017 and to be Submitted to a National Referendum on 16 April 2017.*

Wolff, Larry. 1994. *Inventing Eastern Europe*. Stanford, CA: Stanford University Press.

Yörük, Erdem, and Murat Yüksel. 2014. "Class and politics in Turkey's Gezi protests." *New Left Review* 89: 103–123.

William Jay Risch
6 Heart of Europe, Heart of Darkness: Ukraine's Euromaidan and Its Enemies

People of Maidan, you have a dream that unites you. Your dream is Europe. Not the Europe of accountants, but the Europe of values. Not the Europe of bureaucrats, but that of the spirit. Not the Europe that is tired of itself, that doubts its mission and its meaning, but an ardent, fervent, heroic Europe . . . You give to the word and to the idea of Europe a meaning that is not 'purer,' as a French poet said, but more precise and richer. And that is why I believe that the real Europe is here. That is why the real Europeans are those who have come together here in Maidan. That is why Ukraine is not a vassal of the Russian empire begging to be joined to Europe. It is, at least for the moment, the beating heart of the continent, and Kiev is that continent's capital.
French philosopher Bernard-Henri Lévy, speaking to the Kyiv Maidan, 9 February 2014
(Lévy 2014)

The Heart of Europe Beats in the East!
Far-right activists' banner, Kyiv, 2 July 2016 (Goble 2016)

Ukraine's Euromaidan Revolution, or the Revolution of Dignity (2013–2014), inspired all sorts of visions for not just this former Soviet republic, but for Europe as a whole. Like British playwright George Bernard Shaw touring the Soviet Union under Stalin in the 1930s, visitors to Independence Square (the Maidan) in Kyiv saw what they wanted to see. In the age of the Internet, smart phones, and the social network, there were many such admirers from even further distances, across the globe. At a time when confidence in European Union (EU) institutions was in decline in EU states, the anti-government protests in Ukraine, commonly called the Maidan, encouraged some EU citizens like the French philosopher Bernard-Henri Lévy to believe that Ukrainians could revitalize the mission of European unity. Lévy expressed these hopes when he spoke to crowds at the Kyiv Maidan, home to a protest camp that had stood for nearly three months, through what became a very cold winter. Maidan protesters stood not for economic interests, but for values that were European. Lévy's speech expressed naïve emotional responses to the Maidan, yet several books on Ukraine (Shore 2017; Snyder 2018; Wynnyckyj 2019), ignoring press materials in Russian and Ukrainian (which came out every day, if not every hour), yet claiming to deal closely with Maidan events, express similar myths. This chapter challenges these myths about Ukraine's Revolution of Dignity and its war with Russia, suggesting that the fight for European values was far from the liberal, multicultural utopia presented by its Western admirers. It relies on Ukrainian online press materials, social network postings, *YouTube* videos, recent scholarship in sociology (curiously ignored or dismissed by all three books mentioned above), as well as the author's own field observations and oral interviews with participants. While the Parisian philosopher Lévy lent intellectual cachet to Kyiv's protest camp, equating its struggles with a struggle for Europe, others who claimed to be the heirs

https://doi.org/10.1515/9783110684216-006

of the Kyiv Maidan viewed this struggle for Europe differently. Right-wing activists who organized a conference on a geopolitical alliance called Intermarium in July 2016 claimed, "[t]he heart of Europe beats in the East" not as how Lévy saw it – as a struggle for the rule of law, multiculturalism, and individual rights – but as a struggle for a "real" Europe that was free of the multiculturalism, liberalism, and "neo-Marxism" of the EU and the "neo-Bolshevism" of Vladimir Putin's Russia (Kott 2017).

Rather than being a monolithic entity centered on a Europe of "the spirit," the Euromaidan protests were a "floating signifier" (a term from Lévi-Strauss 1987) that meant different things to different people. Far-right nationalists there did not want integration with the EU as much as a national revolution for Ukrainians as an ethnically homogeneous nation. An escalating cycle of violence, perpetrated by the Yanukovych regime, yet sustained by unruly Maidan protesters, undermined civil protest. Efforts to contain the violence and return the Maidan to nonviolent protest failed by late February 2014; the Maidan protest camp had become too militant and uncompromising, while the Yanukovych regime only further escalated the violence by using hired thugs, riot police, and Berkut special forces to disrupt, if not crush, the protest camp. The lack of leadership and viable institutions limited the Maidan's vision and appeal and made it vulnerable to the far right. The violence that broke out in late February 2014 ultimately caused the Yanukovych regime to implode, yet it also shattered a state and gave free expression to far-right nationalist groups and their discourse. Real fears of right-wing extremists coming to their cities and towns fueled support for Antimaidan forces and then pro-Russian separatists, while local elites and Russians from across the border channeled these fears into unrest that eventually led to war in the Donbas region. By summer 2014, the Maidan had legitimated far right forces allegedly fighting for the freedom of not just Ukraine, but the whole continent. As far-right groups and their volunteer militias acted with impunity in Ukraine, drawing in fellow thinkers from abroad, Ukraine became a heart of darkness as well as the heart of a Europe Lévy and his fellow thinkers championed.

The Battle for Europe

This battle for Europe began with the Euromaidan, a protest movement that emerged spontaneously on 21 November 2013, when President Viktor Yanukovych suspended plans to sign an Association Agreement with the EU at its summit in Vilnius, Lithuania. While the Association Agreement was a mere trade agreement signed with many countries, it had acquired political significance in Ukraine, and for Russia, it had acquired geopolitical significance, threatening its sphere of influence (Gessen 2018). The Yanukovych administration, in power since 2010, had degenerated rapidly into a regime plagued with unprecedented corruption. It had overthrown the country's 2004 constitution and imprisoned a major political rival (former Prime Minister Yulia Tymoshenko). Theft, bribery, and expropriation had created a circle of overnight billionaires, known as the Family, around Yanukovych, while police, courts, tax inspectors, and auto inspectors abused their power and compelled exorbitant bribes from ordinary citizens. The Association Agreement offered Ukrainians a chance to escape this with Europe's help. While the country's political opposition was weak and divided, activists, journalists, and politicians who had been activists managed to organize the first protests.

The first protests were small, and the power of social networks to mobilize protesters was in fact limited (despite claims made in Shore 2017). It took student rallies in the western Ukrainian city of Lviv, followed by Kyiv, to provide much of the energy and the numbers for the protests (Junes 2016). More traditional networks, such as party organizations and civic movements, brought record crowds later (between 80,000 and 100,000 according to organizers) at a rally the opposition held in Kyiv on 24 November 2013 (Onuch and Sasse 2016). Despite European integration being the general theme of these protests, demonstrators participated out of various motives, and primarily they were socioeconomic ones (Junes 2016; Onuch and Sasse 2016), rather than the abstract European values heralded by early commentators (Kotsyuba 2013). After the Vilnius summit ended on 29 November, the protests in Kyiv appeared to be dying out, and then in the early hours of the following day, Berkut security forces stormed the Maidan and cleared it with brute force, mercilessly beating anyone who was on the square or nearby (Koshkina 2015, 59–84). Opposition leaders and activists organized a rally to retake the Maidan on 1 December 2013. While Mychailo Wynnyckyj refers to this event as the "March of millions" (even while admitting there were not even one million there), it was a watershed event in the Maidan protests (Wynnyckyj 2019, 72–73). For Marci Shore, "'Maidan' had become an impassioned protest against brutality, corruption, and rule by gangsters. It had become a revolt against *proizvol* – a Russian word combining arbitrariness and tyranny, the condition of being made an object of someone else's will" (Shore 2017, 40–41). The Maidan protest against police brutality and corruption reached metaphysical proportions because participants gave empirical content to the philosophical concept of Europe. Europe now had ideals philosopher Edmund Husserl yearned for in the 1930s as an antidote to the irrationality and barbarism he saw his native Germany and other parts of the continent descending into (Shore 2017, 156–157).

This metaphysical moment was dubious at best. As opposition leaders set up a National Resistance Headquarters and occupied the Trade Unions Building, radical nationalists, including football ultras, attacked the Presidential Administration building up the hill. Activists from the far right-wing party *Svoboda* (Freedom), led by journalist Tetiana Chornovol, attacked and occupied Kyiv City Hall on Khreshchatyk Street. The attack on the Presidential Administration building suggested a provocation, with videos showing radical protesters and police intermingling. A far-right provocateur with connections to Russia, Dmytro Korchynskyi, soon fled Ukraine after he had been spotted in the crowd (Koshkina 2015, 88–98; Wynnyckyj 2019, 75–77).

Such incidents may have been provocations to discredit the Euromaidan protests and link them to far-right violence. Yet this view deprives the participants of agency. Already tensions had been high after the 30 November Berkut crackdown. Crowds threatened to smash windows of a police bus and would have, had not one civic activist and a journalist intervened (Interview 2). People with far-right views and enraged protesters, not just provocateurs, contributed to the violence of the next day. Those attacking security forces in front of the Presidential Administration building included football ultras who soon joined far-right organizations on the Maidan. One of them recalled being caught up in the emotions of the crowd that day (Spirin and Konopkin 2019). Young men from the neo-Nazi organization, Patriot of Ukraine, were there wearing the yellow armbands that bore the neo-Nazi wolf's hook symbol in dark blue (Shekhovtsov 2014b).

Those *Svoboda* party activists who occupied Kyiv City Hall included members of the neo-Nazi organization C14. Led by Ievhen Karas, this group claimed their name was *Sich*, the name of the self-governing community of Ukrainian Cossacks important to Ukraine's national history, and that the number 14 referred to the founding of the Ukrainian Insurgent Army – an army that fought the Soviet Union and Nazi Germany for Ukraine's liberation, yet whose leaders collaborated with Third Reich leaders throughout the war – on 14 October 1942. In fact, the Cyrillic spelling for "*Sich*" is "C14," betraying its neo-Nazi affinities, as the "14" stands for the words of white supremacist David Lane: "We must secure the existence of our people and a future for white children" (*Bellingcat* 2019). C14 activists epitomized the merging of Ukraine's liberal and far-right protest forces over the years leading up to the Maidan. The *Svoboda* party had encouraged the development of youth groups like C14 to attract followers among young people in Kyiv (Gonta 2015). Right-wing political organizations like *Svoboda* were thus far better at developing grassroots organizations, while other political parties opposed to Yanukovych relied on paid party workers to mobilize voters. In the process, from 2010 on, *Svoboda* became a key ally of these other opposition parties as they organized resistance to the Yanukovych regime (Ishchenko 2016). In 2013, C14 activists joined a protest movement against illegal construction sites in Ukraine's capital, "Protect Old Kyiv," and by tearing down fences to illegal construction sites and clashing with police, they earned the admiration of Ukrainian journalists and civic activists, including liberals (Gonta 2015). C14 activists participated in rallies with football ultras, and *Svoboda* activists provided ultras with legal help; thus, ultras became friends and allies of C14, since they shared a common enemy, the police (Gonta 2015). Yet C14, as well as most football ultras, shared the ideological markers of the far right, including racism and xenophobia, and openly professed white supremacist ideals, for instance, holding a "Youth Football Cup" in 2011 that they said was for white children only (*Bellingcat* 2019; Gonta 2015). Just before the Euromaidan protests, C14 activists broke into Kyiv City Hall, allegedly to show city council members how easy it was for Kyiv citizens to enter their building and bring to justice council members involved in corrupt land deals. C14 activists thus led the fight against corruption and promised justice. Over the course of 2013, the Kyiv city government had lost legitimacy already, given that Yanukovych had appointed a state administrator instead of allowing mayoral elections, and the Kyiv City Council, too, failed to hold elections. Still, these visitors to City Hall proudly displayed their black flag with a white Celtic cross, a universal symbol of white supremacists (Gonta 2015).

When the Euromaidan began, activists from C14, *Svoboda*, and Right Sector (an umbrella organization uniting several small far-right groups, including Patriot of Ukraine) bullied and intimidated leftist opponents. Between 24 and 28 November 2013, there were at least four attacks on the left, two against Euromaidan activists rallying for women's rights and two against civic and trade union activists who made socioeconomic demands on the Maidan (Shekhovtsov 2014b; Shore 2017, 54–55). As reported by *Levyi Bereg*, another such attack on trade union activists happened on 4 December, and this time right-wing extremists did not act alone. One video shows Maidan organizers from the main stage urging men to get together and stop these "Communist" provocateurs, and up to 100 were part of the mob breaking up the trade union activists' information stand (Maidan online 2013). Far-right organizations such as *Svoboda*, Right Sector, and C14 were numerically few on the Maidan, yet far right activists, especially those affiliated with *Svoboda* and its youth organizations, and later Right Sector, were the most active in confrontational and violent protests and were also highly organized (Ishchenko 2016). The 4 December attack on trade union activists suggests early collusion between the far right and the Maidan's leadership. Rather than being dupes of the Kremlin or Yanukovych, far-right activists gained prominence as tensions escalated on the Maidan and as the Maidan became militarized.

Observers later claimed that the Maidan embodied new politics, emphasizing such values as civic engagement, personal responsibility, friendship, altruism, and organizing societies without hierarchy (Snyder 2018, 127–131; Wynnyckyj 2019, 307–338). Yet, by December 2013, the Maidan protest camp was part of a strategy to remove Yanukovych from power, not an alternative community with institutions to perpetuate its values. After the Berkut crackdown of 30 November, Maidan activists, politicians, and their financial supporters entered a "coalition of inconvenience" that produced greater cooperation in the end, yet failed to give the protest camp meaningful leadership (Onuch and Sasse 2016). Activists and politicians became adversaries as they offered competing plans to negotiate with the Yanukovych regime (Interview 1). When Maidan politicians and activists formed what became known as the All-Ukrainian Maidan People's Association, with a governing council (known colloquially as the Maidan Council) on 22 December 2013, they excluded and marginalized competing plans to form a grassroots organization independent of the politicians. One activist thus claimed that both the political opposition and Yanukovych were part of the same political class, not interested in civil society or the people (Sinchenko 2013). When Euromaidan activists from Ukraine's different regions held a forum in Kharkiv, in mid-

January 2014, to coordinate the activities of regional Euromaidans more effectively, opposition politicians claimed Yanukovych's Presidential Administration had sponsored it to divide the national resistance movement (Chistilin 2014; *Facenews* 2014). One civic activist complained that the Maidan Council failed to meet for important decisions, and that the National Resistance Headquarters mostly served opposition political parties' interests (V'iatrovych 2014).

As the Maidan protest camp developed, the Yanukovych regime mobilized opposition to it, called the Antimaidan. Some of its protesters were athletes, often trained in the martial arts, who were paid to provoke fights at opposition events. The most infamous of such paid protester-athletes was Vadym Titushko, and on 18 May 2013, he and some other athletes (ten in total), clashed with protesters and journalists at an opposition rally in Kyiv. The Ukrainian media came up with the term *titushka* (plural form: *titushky*) in Ukrainian for any hired thug paid to disrupt rallies and intimidate activists. The term soon also referred to anyone paid to attend a demonstration on behalf of the Yanukovych regime (Mazanik 2014). The Yanukovych regime made greater use of Antimaidan rallies, employing such *titushky*, from mid-December 2013 onward, first on European Square, then in Mariinskyi Park near Parliament. Participants were "mainly workers from industrial enterprises who had received paid 'vacations' to Kiev" (Kozachenko 2014). In any case, by mid-January 2014, the Maidan had failed to unite Ukraine against Yanukovych. Antimaidan rallies did not prove this, but polling data did; according to a Research & Branding Group poll, conducted in early December 2013, a total of 49 percent of respondents, when asked if they supported the Euromaidan, said yes, while 45 percent said no, and 6 percent said they could not give an answer (Research & Branding Group 2013a). Despite media reports about a night-time standoff between Maidan protesters and security forces (10–11 December), as well as stories about activists and journalists under attack, polling data indicated support for the Maidan had declined. In a Research & Branding Group poll conducted in late December, 45 percent said they did support the Euromaidan, while 50 percent said they did not, and 6 percent said they could not answer the question. When asked if the Euromaidan should disband or continue, 59 percent said it should disband, while only 41 percent said it should continue. In the meantime, a plurality of Ukrainians, but not a majority, viewed integration with the EU favorably. When asked what entity Ukraine should integrate with, 43 percent said the EU, while only 30 percent said the Eurasian Customs Union sponsored by Russia. An additional 20 percent said Ukraine should maintain its current status (not associated with either the Eurasian Customs Union or the EU), while 7 percent said they could not answer the question (Research & Branding Group 2013b). Thus, while considerable numbers of Ukrainians continued to support integration with the EU, most did not support the Maidan protest camp and preferred seeing it disband. Moreover, the Maidan was not winning over supporters in Ukraine's south and east, either; while in Ukraine's southern regions, 23 percent supported the Euromaidan (down from 4–9 December by 10 points), 73 percent did not, and 4 percent could not answer the question, in Ukraine's eastern regions, 17 percent supported the Euromaidan, 76 percent did not, and 7 percent could not answer the question (Research & Branding Group 2013b).

The Maidan at War

Clashes with security forces rescued the Maidan from historical oblivion. On 16 January 2014, hardliners from the Party of Regions and the Communist Party of Ukraine forced through the Supreme Rada a set of laws known as the Dictatorship Laws. Signed that very evening by Yanukovych, the laws made protesting illegal, and they even criminalized specific acts of protest practiced by the Maidan (Koshkina 2015, 162–169). Maidan participants had already shown a willingness to fight security forces. On the night of 10–11 January 2014, as they protested the sentencing of three members of the neo-Nazi organization Patriot of Ukraine for crimes they did not commit, Maidan Self-Defense activists, activists from Automaidan (a protest movement using vehicles to support the Maidan), and other Maidan supporters blocked police forces and made Berkut soldiers in one bus walk out and suffer humiliation. For the first time, demonstrators, without weapons, assaulted police, and the night's clashes gave confidence to protesters that they could fight the security forces and win (Wynnyckyj 2019, 101; Interview 11). A few days later, such crowds brought that fighting spirit to the Maidan itself. At this Maidan assembly, the audience booed political opposition speakers for refusing to assert leadership over the protest movement and respond decisively to the Dictatorship Laws. An Automaidan activist called on the Maidan to march on the Supreme Rada by way of European Square and Hrushevskyi Street and have the Supreme Rada rescind the Dictatorship Laws. Stopped by police barricades near the entrance to the Kyiv Dynamo football stadium, the protesters argued with riot police and started pushing back police buses blocking the street. Police fired teargas, stun grenades, and later rubber bullets. A line of young men (aged 17–20) with paramilitary dress, masks, and black-and-red armbands, later identified as Right Sector activists, arrived and threw pavement stones and Molotov cocktails at the riot police, and shortly after, set the buses on fire. It was not just Right Sector activists leading the fight against security organs; the crowd itself organized resistance, and Maidan Self-Defense forces, organized to protect the protest camp, joined them as well (Interviews 5, 8, and 11).

The battle for Hrushevskyi Street captured international headlines, as protesters not only lobbed Molotov cocktails, but fired off projectiles from a medieval-style catapult and even resorted to firing off arrows at police. Riot police responded by firing stun grenades and rubber bullets, intentionally wounding people, including medics helping the injured (Interview 10). The neighborhood of the Kyiv Dynamo stadium became blackened with smoke from piles of tires protesters lit to keep riot police from advancing. The night of 20–21 January 2014, Automaidan activists and Maidan protesters went after *titushky* who allegedly were about to attack the Maidan, in what *Ukrains'ka Pravda* called a "Titushko Safari." They hunted down these young men and brought them to the Trade Unions Building, where they filmed them and questioned them. The next day, they let them go, but they had to pass through the Maidan in a "march of shame." Live stream videos of this "safari" on Hromadske TV suggested that, far from engaging in European politeness, Automaidan activists taunted and swore at their prey, often in Russian. It was far from clear that any of the young men captured threatened the Maidan. However, the following day, the clashes on Hrushevskyi Street became lethal, with three protesters shot near the barricades, all eventually dead. All three shootings were suspicious; forensic evidence made public indicated that all three were shot at close range – between 3 and 4 meters away – on the protesters' side, when the riot police were at least 20–25 meters away. While Sonia Koshkina claimed this was a provocation by the Yanukovych regime, to stir up violent resistance and legitimate a forceful clearing of the Maidan, she offers no proof that any of the shooters came from the regime's side (Koshkina 2015, 178–192). Later video released demonstrated that burned out busses blocked one victim from the riot police side, making it impossible for them to have been the killers anyway. Hearsay evidence, but only hearsay evidence, suggests Right Sector groups shot and killed two of the protesters (Katchanovski 2020, 13).

Activists' lives were threatened far from the Maidan. Already dozens of activists had suffered from various forms of assault and intimidation, as noted by the leader of the *Svoboda* party for the Zhytomyr Region in early January 2014 (*Espreso TV* 2014). Such incidents led one Kyiv observer to speculate on whether the *titushky* were soon to become like the death squads of Latin America, terrorizing opponents of the Yanukovych regime (Hrabovs'kyi 2013). Then two Maidan activists were kidnapped in the early morning hours of 21 January, at a Kyiv hospital as one of them was undergoing treatment for wounds received in Hrushevskyi Street clashes. As *Ukrains'ka Pravda* noted, unknown men took them to a forest outside Kyiv, where they were beaten and interrogated and then left for dead. One of them, Kyiv activist Ihor Lutsenko, found help later that evening and survived, while the other, Lviv activist Iuriy Verbytskyi, was found dead the next day. By 23 January, Automaidan leader Dmytro Bulatov had gone missing, but surfaced a week later in a village outside Kyiv, badly beaten, with part of an ear cut off. As *Radio Free Europe/Radio Liberty* reported, Bulatov told reporters his captors had even tried to crucify him. Reports of kidnappings, torture, and killings of activists reached fantastic proportions by the last week of January 2014, while fake stories about morgues filled with dead bodies and rumors about body parts tied to railroad tracks (the victims run over by trains) appeared on the social networks. In the end, these stories about dozens or even more Maidan activists being kidnapped and killed turned out to be no more than wild rumors. Yet the medium became the message, and the message was powerful. The Maidan was under assault and death squads threatened conscious Ukrainians. Lutsenko claimed *titushky* beat up Verbytskyi more than him because Verbytskyi was from the western Ukrainian city of Lviv and thus a "Banderite" (referring to followers of Stepan Bandera, leader of the Organization of Ukrainian Nationalists, which cooperated with the Third Reich for much of the Second World War). Bulatov claimed that Russians speaking Russian accents from Russia – that is, foreign citizens from Russia – had kidnapped him, implying that the Kremlin was behind such atrocities (Stadnyi 2014).

This wave of shootings, kidnappings, assault, torture, and humiliation, as well as other forms of intimidation, such as setting activists' cars on fire (Wilson 2014, 75), radicalized and militarized the Maidan. They drove more liberal and moderate elements into the arms of the far right, not exactly the "Maidan friendship" Snyder probably had in mind as a new form of Ukrainian politics (Snyder 2018, 130). Both *Liga.net* and *Ukrains'ka Pravda* featured stories about protesters in western Ukrainian cities blocking riot police and Berkut forces in their bases on 20–21 January, to keep them from coming to Kyiv to crush the rebels on Hrushevskyi Street. After the first fatal Maidan shootings on 22 January, protesters in the capitals of ten regions of western and central Ukraine seized control of regional state administration buildings, demanding resignations of regional governors Yanukovych had appointed. As one opposition politician later noted, the National Resistance Headquarters had coordinated these uprisings as part of a "regional offensive," to sap the regime of security forces needed to crush the Maidan and keep Yanukovych from declaring a state of emergency (Koshkina 2015, 183). Within days, protesters seized control of Ukrainian House, a major conference center on European Square, forcing the riot police inside to leave (Koshkina 2015, 185–188). As Maidan protesters expanded the territory of the protest camp, activists from the far-right group, Common Cause *(Spil'na Sprava)*, according to *Ukrains'ka Pravda*, seized control of the Ministry of Agriculture building (24 January) and then the Ministry of Justice building (26 January), both which were near the Maidan. The Maidan's political leaders denounced these occupations as provocations. Common Cause left the Ministry of Justice building on 27 January, and then activists from *Svoboda* forced them out of the Ministry of Agriculture building. By the beginning of February, Oleksandr Danyliuk, the leader of Common Cause, had fled Ukraine.

The Maidan and the Far Right

As Maidan protesters felt encircled and hunted by security organs and *titushky,* the voices of the far right gained further appeal. As noted earlier, the neo-Nazi group C14 had already become allies of activists and politicians opposed to Yanukovych before the Euromaidan began. The symbols of Ukraine's radical right, as well as neo-Nazi movements, gained popularity in Maidan demonstrations, primarily through football ultras' participation (Interview 1). For instance, the chant, "Glory to Ukraine!" *(Slava Ukraini!)*, followed by "Glory to the Heroes!" *(Heroiam slava!)*, had its origins in Ukraine's national revolution of 1917–1920, but it became widespread as a slogan under the wing of the Organization of Ukrainian Nationalists (OUN) under the leadership of Stepan Bandera. By 1941, the Bandera wing of the OUN had embraced the ideals of fascism and Nazism, emphasizing militarism, one-party rule, and the cult of the leader. It had adopted as its party banner a red-and-black flag that embodied the fascist values of "blood and soil" *(Blut und Boden)*, and its leaders on the eve of the Second World War argued for removing Poles, Jews, and Russians from Ukraine. While the Nazis persecuted Bandera and other leaders for attempting to set up a satellite state in Lviv, both factions of the OUN (one under Bandera, the other under Andriy Melnyk) collaborated with Nazi Germany on and off until the war's end (Rossolinski-Liebe 2014). Some radicals chanted a slogan that was not from the OUN, but from neo-Nazi movements in independent Ukraine: "Ukraine above all!" *(Ukraina – ponad use!)*, a Ukrainian version of *"Deutschland über Alles!"* and "Glory to the nation! Death to the enemies!" *(Slava natsii! Smert' voroham!)* (Sharhovs'ka 2013).

The red-and-black flag, as well as the chant, "Glory to Ukraine! Glory to the Heroes!," and even the neo-Nazi slogan, "Ukraine above all!," became ubiquitous at Maidan demonstrations. For more liberal Maidan participants, these symbols took on new meaning as security forces and *titushky* attacked and killed protesters. Artist Olexa Mann, who took part in Maidan Self-Defense, posted his thoughts on this transformation of the symbol, "Glory to Ukraine!" on 26 January 2014, just after some of the most heated battles between protesters and security forces on Hrushevskyi Street; he wrote: "When you are surrounded by smoke from burning tires, and clouds of purple gas, through which you can't see a damn thing, hear the cry 'Glory to Ukraine' from an approaching group of fellow soldiers, and hear thousands of voices respond with 'Glory to the Heroes!,' it becomes clear that the paradigm of the cry has changed. You understand that the berserkers are charging to help you." "It is now a battle cry," Mann asserted. "A battle cry of an undefeated and organized people, which makes the pigs [i.e., the riot police and Berkut] shake in their boots." "Glory to Ukraine!" united people of all ethnic groups, all professions and levels of education, all political backgrounds, and even all sexual orientations, against one existential evil. Such symbols may have taken on new meaning for Mann, yet at the same time, far-right organizations who first spread these symbols now started making public claims that they spoke for the Maidan. Right Sector, an umbrella organization for several marginal far-right groups, gained widespread media attention after their young activists had taken part in the 19 January 2014 clashes with riot police on Hrushevskyi Street. Toward the end of the month, its leader Dmytro Iarosh, a veteran of far-right groups from the 1990s, gave a press conference, with two comrades present, in the Trade Unions Building, where Right Sector occupied the fifth floor, during which Iarosh called on all prisoners to be freed, a request repeated in a later interview with *Ukrains'ka Pravda*.

He said that Right Sector was going to compel both the political opposition and the Yanukovych regime to listen to the demands of the people of the Maidan. While he stressed that he was not a fascist or a racist, Iarosh cited Bandera's approach to dealing with Ukrainians' enemies, waging merciless war against them, as one of his principles (Bilozerska 2014; Naiem and Kovalenko 2014). He also omitted mention of any of his remarks made against other races, globalization, and liberal democracy in his collection of essays, *Nationalism and Revolution*, which he had published in 2012 (Iarosh 2012).

The rise of Right Sector as spokespersons for the radical Maidan made it competitors with *Svoboda* and C14, whose members also claimed to be defending the Maidan against its enemies, including the police and alleged death squads. Maidan activists recalled C14's interrogation room in the basement of Kyiv City Hall, a torture chamber where "Nazis" beat up and sprayed tear gas at *titushky* and policemen they captured (Shore 2017, 54). C14's leader, Ieven Karas, admitted in an interview to *Levyi Bereg* on 8 February 2014, that they roughed up and humiliated drug addicts, pedophiles, and thieves that posed a danger to the Maidan, including writing "THIEF" *(VOR)* and "DRUG ADDICT" *(NARKOMAN)* on their foreheads. On 25 January 2014, as reported by *Levyi Bereg*, C14 activists who were in Maidan Self-Defense forces assaulted and seized three policemen on the Maidan, taking them to their interrogation room and beating them up there. Ministry of the Interior sources indicated that one of the policemen had been stabbed and underwent hospitalization. Karas in his interview with *Levyi Bereg* claimed that these policemen seized had been members of a "death squad" organized by Ukraine's Ministry of the Interior and one state anti-terrorist unit that, as he put it, was grabbing Euromaidan activists, taking them out to nearby woods, and interrogating them (and, by implication, torturing them as well). He said that these same policemen had followed and persecuted activists the previous year, even attacking them during the spring of 2013. Interestingly enough, a *Livejournal* (2014a) blog for the user "v_n_zb," published on the same day of the assault on policemen has photos claiming to be those of a body tied up and left out in the snow to die, one of the victims of Minister of the Interior Vitaliy Zakharchenko's "death squad."

Groups like Right Sector and C14 made up only a marginal portion of those forces defending the Maidan by early February 2014. By late January 2014, Right Sector was just one of several Maidan Self-Defense hundreds *(sotni)* protecting the Maidan protest camp, but by the time of the clashes on Hrushevskyi Street, its members made greater publicity for themselves, aiming to become a major political force on the Maidan (Koshkina 2015, 174–175). C14 activists likewise just made up one Maidan Self-Defense hundred, known as the Sviatoslav the Brave Hundred of Maidan Self-Defense, affiliated with *Svoboda* (Gonta 2015; Movchan 2017). The namesake for this hundred, Sviatoslav the Brave, only further demonstrates the group's neo-Nazi affinities; Sviatoslav the Brave, Grand Prince of Kyivan Rus, defeated the Khazars, a Jewish people near the Black Sea, back in 965. Radical nationalists from Eastern Slavic nations like Ukraine thus called him a hero out of anti-Semitic motives. This C14 hundred did the dirty work for *Svoboda,* a key political force on the Maidan, kicking Common Cause activists out of the Ministry of Agriculture building they had occupied in late January, even firing non-lethal pistols at them (Gonta 2015). They intimidated leftists aspiring to take part in the Maidan's self-defense. On 9 February 2014, around 150 people connected with *Svoboda* Maidan Self-Defense organizations (including C14), armed with bats, wearing helmets, surrounded a group of anarchists, antifascists, and other young men who, assembled not far from Kyiv City Hall, were about to swear an oath to their new hundred, the Black Hundred *(Chernaia Sotnia)*, and have it registered with the Maidan Self-Defense leadership. Besides claiming that the Black Hundred's ideology was harmful to the Maidan, C14 and other *Svoboda* activists made a racial slur: they complained that the Black Hundred had people of Caucasian nationality (*"khachi"* in Russian) in its ranks. The Black Hundred activists left, realizing they were outnumbered, and the *Svoboda* crowd chanted anti-Communist slogans as they left (presumably such hostile ones as "Lynch the Commies!" (*Komuniaky na hiliaky!*)). While no violence erupted, and Black Hundred activists later returned to the Maidan that night peacefully, it was clear that the "Maidan friendship" between leftists and those on the far right, envisioned by Mann in his 26 January post, did not really exist (*Avtonomnoe deistvie* 2014).

C14 and Right Sector were just two of several Maidan Self-Defense hundreds on the Maidan by early February 2014. Yet allying with the far right had become a necessity by the end of January 2014. As one social movement organization activist at the Kyiv Maidan admitted, the fighting on Hrushevskyi Street had marginalized the non-violent protests their organization had supported since the Maidan's beginning (Interview 9). Civic activists speaking off the record to Onuch and Sasse's research team said that from January 2014 on, they felt a need to "compete and even collaborate with the extremist groups in the Maidan zone when vying for the attention of possible recruits" (Onuch and Sasse 2016, 573). By early February 2014, most residents of the Maidan protest camp had no loyalty to far-right groups or political parties. As one poll indicated, 69.9 percent of Maidan protesters said they belonged to no political organization (union), while just 7.7 percent said they belonged to a political party, 8.4 percent said they were members of a public organization, and 14.2 percent said they belonged to a public movement (DIF and KIIS 2014). Most likely, these more moderate and liberal activists surveyed by Onuch and Sasse (2016) needed the support of far-right groups for coordination and leadership of the protests (whose role in this has been stressed by Ishchenko 2016).

A Militarized Maidan

Indeed, the confrontational tactics of far-right organizations like Right Sector and C14 exemplified the Maidan's growing militarization after clashes on Hrushevskyi

Street, and thus the need to include them in coordinating protests and maintaining order. As seen with Mann's post, what united protesters of all backgrounds was their war with the police, which involved injuring and maiming people, if not killing them. By early February 2014, Maidan Self-Defense was nothing like what I had seen on the Maidan in late December or early January. Video from 6 February 2014, released by *Radio Svoboda*, showed Maidan Self-Defense forces marching on the Maidan and along the government offices district (guarded by Berkut and riot police) with metal shields and a variety of helmets, sticks, and bats. The Maidan Self-Defense men from the 14th Self-Defense Hundred, "Free People" *(Vil'ni Liudy),* lined up in front of the Maidan stage with their steel shields gleaming in the afternoon sun, in photos posted on 8 February, by Euromaidan Press on *Facebook* (2014), were not the self-defense forces I had seen some three weeks earlier (where people at most wore helmets for protection). As already reported by *Radio Svoboda,* Maidan Self-Defense Council leaders had announced the expansion of their organization (which by then had as many as 12,000 volunteers) to all regions of Ukraine, as part of plans to form what they claimed would be an "active revolutionary army" of as many as 30,000–40,000 people. They were moving beyond the barricades to include all of Ukraine, and their self-defense hundreds were to engage in nonviolent resistance, defending local Euromaidan activists and exposing acts of corruption, as well as demand the removal of abusive officials from power and wage an information war (presumably against Russia and Antimaidan forces). If needed, they would come to Kyiv to oppose the regime. Maidan Self-Defense leaders admitted that turning to violence could cause a civil war that Russia would exploit through an invasion. Thus, these self-defense forces would be under a disciplined chain of command, with their leadership cooperating with the National Resistance Headquarters. Yet such rhetoric as "active revolutionary army" and referring to the model self-defense volunteer as "not just a guard, but also a revolutionary political soldier" *(ne lyshe okhoronets', a i revoliutsiynyi politychnyi soldat),* suggested the Maidan's further militarization.

While the Maidan Self-Defense forces exercised restraint by early February, restless elements among them had the potential to act on their own and attack opponents. Thus C14's Sviatoslav the Brave Hundred operated its own interrogation room and tortured people. Right Sector maintained an explosives laboratory on the fifth floor of the Trade Unions Building, as seen in Security Services of Ukraine (SBU) surveillance video presented by one controversial blogger (Sharii 2019) and as admitted to me (speaking off the record) by a political analyst with ties to security organs in Kyiv in late September 2014. The surveillance video suggests young activists were making more than just Molotov cocktails, but actual bombs for use against security forces. Provocations by questionable groups opposed to the Maidan either tested the Maidan Self-Defense ranks' patience or trained them for defense, or both, on a regular basis. The southern barricade on Khreshchatyk Street, near the Central Shopping Center (or *TsUM* in Russian), became a regular site for provocations, from the very same people, from December 2013 onward. A group called "For a Clean Kyiv," led by one Ivan

Protsenko, with possible connections to Viktor Medvedchuk's Ukrainian Choice organization (a civic organization opposed to the Maidan, which advocated close ties with Russia), claimed that they were gathering volunteers to take down those barricades. As reported by *Ukrains'ka Pravda* on 21 December, Protsenko had asked for permission from Kyiv City Hall to allow volunteers to conduct a Saturday clean-up *(subbotnik)* that day in the center of Kyiv, tearing down and removing Maidan barricades. According to *Ukrains'ka Pravda*, opposition politicians the day before had warned people that the Yanukovych regime was sending hundreds of *titushky* to try and storm Kyiv City Hall and provoke fights with Maidan participants. At the urging of a friend, who said *titushky* were coming to attack the Maidan, I went to the area near the southern barricades, only to hear it was a false alarm. Still, an early version of Maidan Self-Defense forces (wearing hardhats, but without any weapons) showed up to defend the barricades against *titushky*. Protsenko tried to take down the southern barricades again on Saturday, 18 January 2014. I happened to be there with a friend. Maidan Self-Defense forces now had actual formations with banners, and they paraded around the area near the barricades. Afghan War veterans were also out to guard the barricades. A few activists from Protsenko's side quarrelled with Maidan supporters in front of a flock of reporters, and while someone egged a middle-aged man from Protsenko's side, nothing else happened.

By February, these tests of will on Khreshchatyk Street had changed. Protsenko's group showed up on two successive Saturdays, 8 and 15 February. On the first occasion, *Ukrains'ka Pravda* passed along alarmist reports by opposition politicians that some 500 people, *titushky*, had gathered at Lev Tolstoy Square and were headed toward Khreshchatyk Street, yet the crowd that showed up at the barricades was 100 or less, judging by video from blogger Sergei Rulev (2014a). His video displayed hundreds of Maidan Self-Defense forces armed with bats, sticks, and pipes, as well as shields, bulletproof vests, and a variety of helmets. One Maidan politician was on a megaphone urging Maidan supporters not to give in to this provocation organized by the regime. Except for some shouting, pushing, and shoving, the incident ended peacefully. The Saturday of 15 February did not end so peacefully. A *Livejournal* (2014b) blog published that same day by flackelf, who took part in the march, reported Maidan Self-Defense forces, led by Ieven Karas and other types from C14, attacked and beat them, some of the victims lying on the pavement as they flailed them with sticks, bats, and maybe even pipes. One Kyiv office worker who either saw the march live or online said it was "really stupid," given that the protesters carried portraits of Stalin (Interview 13). Indeed, photos in flackelf's *Livejournal* blog indicate marchers brought posters that were inflammatory and highly insulting toward Maidan supporters, equating them with cockroaches, violent extremists, dupes of Washington and the EU, Nazis, and sheep, despite claims made by the march leaders (on video provided by flackelf) that they were there to engage in peaceful dialogue.

Still, the Maidan side responded with impunity. Just before attacking the demonstrators, Karas smiled and laughed at flackelf and reminded him that they knew where he lived in Kyiv. There were no police around to protect the demonstrators, though Sergei Rulev, also there to film events, reminded two men standing to the side that they were plainclothes policemen (Rulev 2014c). Perhaps most disturbing was that while friends on *Facebook*, most of them living abroad, condemned this attack on peaceful demonstrators, one Maidan supporter from Ukraine who apparently took part in Maidan protests saw this attack as justified: "You know what I felt when I observed the video, when people in camouflage with sticks beat up demonstrators lying on the ground? *Schadenfreude (Zlovtikhu)*. What a ruined guy *(Otakyi zipsovanyi)*. I personally have wound up more than once in a similar situation only the attackers were official state organs of repression or people who are now acceptable to call '*titushky*.' Yes, during a conflict, perspectives on the world are divided into 'ours' and 'theirs,' any psychologist will tell you this. And using violence becomes almost automatic, I won't say that is good, but it's natural. Look at the Maidan right now, it's practically become a besieged fortress with the psychology that comes with it. People there think they are in a war, however outside analysts look at it. They in fact are combatants. And here we come to the moral question of if there are wars and participants in them that are pure from an ethical point of view? In my opinion, any war is a complete crime. And then everyone should decide for themselves whether to be pacifists at whatever the cost and moralizing sissies *(moralizatory-chystopliui)*, or be a part of the conflict." This comment to a friend's post on *Facebook* conveyed the sense of desperation that supporters of the Maidan had reached by mid-February 2014. Though presumably convinced that history was on their side, they perceived that they were surrounded by government forces or their hired thugs, and that anyone taking part in defending it was endangered. Violence was justified, as this was a time of war. It was not a time for the "European values" of the early Maidan.

The man's comment conveyed the general mood at the Maidan by this point in time. According to a set of polls studying the attitudes of Maidan protest camp inhabitants in early February 2014, as many as 50.4 percent said they were willing to take part in setting up "armed units independent of authorities." The number supporting such an activity had more than doubled over the course of a month (21.3 percent on 20 December) and more than tripled since early December 2013 (15 percent on 7–8 December). The number of protesters from Kyiv had decreased to 12.4 percent (down from nearly 49.8 percent on 7–8 December). The protest camp now consisted primarily of outsiders, who were overwhelmingly from provincial towns and villages: 42.4 percent were from small towns (small towns being less than 100,000 residents), and 20.3 percent were from villages. By early February, 54.8 percent of camp residents were from western Ukraine, while 23 percent were from central Ukraine, and 21 percent were from eastern and southern Ukraine. This was a Maidan that had the potential to become an armed camp willing to fight the Yanukovych regime; it was no longer willing to compromise with that regime. When asked the question "Do you agree with the proposition to conduct the negotiations round table with participation of the authorities, the opposition and public leaders with the mediation of the international organizations?" 63.1 percent answered: "There is no need to conduct any negotiations with the authorities." Only 27.4 percent answered that such negotiations were necessary, and just 9.6 percent said they could not answer the question. When asked what demands they supported, by far the most popular answer (more than one response was possible) was the resignation of President Yanukovych and conducting snap presidential elections (85.2 percent). When asked how long they intended to stay at the Maidan, an overwhelming majority said: "For as long as it would be needed" (86 percent) (DIF and KIIS 2014).

While some scholars equate the Maidan with Ukraine throughout the protest period (especially Shore 2017, Snyder 2018, and Wynnyckyj 2019), nationwide polling figures from the time suggest that by early February 2014, the cognitive dissonance between Maidan rhetoric and ordinary people's lives could not have been greater. Protesters' seizure of administration buildings in the provinces produced a backlash, not just by governors and Party of Regions politicians in southern and eastern Ukraine, and not just among Crimea's leaders, who openly discussed leaving Ukraine (all of which *Liga.net* reported extensively for late January and early February 2014), but among ordinary citizens. A Research & Branding Group poll conducted among residents of Ukraine's regional capitals *(oblastnye tsentry)*, including for Crimea and Sevastopol, in late January 2014, revealed that as many as 60 percent said they viewed negatively protesters' seizures of regional state administration buildings or attempts to do so. Most of those polled expressed some degree of certainty that a civil war would happen or could happen; a total of 8 percent said civil war "definitely will happen," 32 percent agreed that "a real danger exists," and 31 percent said that "the likelihood exists." Only 20 percent agreed with the statement "absolutely does not threaten," and 9 percent could not answer the question. Support for the Euromaidan remained as low as it had been before the protests had become violent. When asked if they supported the Euromaidan in Kyiv, a total of 51 percent said no, 44 percent said yes, and 5 percent were unable to answer the question. In the regional capitals of Ukraine's east, overwhelming majorities continued to state that they did not support the Euromaidan (81 percent).

While an overwhelming majority of Maidan protest camp inhabitants expressed no desire to compromise with the Yanukovych regime, ordinary Ukrainian citizens said otherwise. In a late January 2014 poll, conducted by Kyiv International Institute of Sociology (KIIS) and SOCIS (Center of Social and Marketing Research) in all parts of Ukraine, a vast majority (63.3 percent) said negotiations had to take place if the Euromaidan protests were to accomplish positive results, and only 11.1 percent said that the protesters needed to use force to achieve this goal (KIIS and SOCIS 2014). In other words, the spirit of compromise remained strong for most Ukrainians. Besides that, support for the Maidan protests remained sharply divided; while a total of 47 percent of those polled supported them (26.8 percent completely, while 20.9 percent most likely did), as many as 46 percent said they did not support them (of these, 31.3 percent did not support them at all, while 14.8 percent said they most likely did not support them) (KIIS and SOCIS 2014). In addition, it did not look like Yanukovych's base of electoral support had eroded at all by early February 2014, despite the wave of violence committed against activists, despite the so-called Dictatorship Laws. During the third week of January, when likely voters were asked whom they would vote for as president, a total of 28.9 percent said they would vote for Viktor Yanukovych in a hypothetical first round of elections (SOCIS 2014) – a figure which did not change at all from the previous poll, taken in late December 2013 (28.9 percent) (SOCIS 2013).

By mid-February 2014, the Maidan's political leaders reached a compromise with the regime, and their protesters and activists reluctantly went along with them. Already by the end of January, Yanukovych and the Supreme Rada agreed to repeal the Dictatorship Laws, remove Mykola Azarov as Prime Minister, pass an Amnesty Law for Maidan participants (which foresaw the release of Maidan prisoners), and begin negotiations for constitutional reform. In return, the Maidan's leaders had to leave all state administration buildings and open at least Hrushevskyi Street in Kyiv to traffic. By 16 February, Maidan protesters in Kyiv and in the provinces had complied with this; it looked as if some Maidan activists had decided it was time to return to nonviolent resistance and use it more effectively. A member of Civic Sector Euromaidan and a historian, Volodymyr Viatrovych, observed that the Maidan camp had become militarized and distanced from ordinary people, as the latter preferred not to risk their lives in the lethal battles taking place there. The compromise reached with Yanukovych through seizing administration buildings in late January did not achieve much of a compromise at all (V'iatrovych 2014). Viatrovych also noted that, as a result of the Maidan's violent attacks on the police, the police, rather than joining with the people, had become battle hardened and calloused toward protesters (V'iatrovych 2014). One blogger's 10 February video of Berkut and riot police forces on the other side of the Hrushevskyi Street barricades suggested ways in which they had dehumanized the protesters gathered on the other side. Among a collection of pieces of wood riot police had made into signs decorating one side of Hrushevskyi Street, one sign, pointing in the direction of the protesters, read in Russian, "APES 50 M[ETERS]" *(ABEZIANY 25 M)*, and another sign, pointing to the direction of the protesters, suggested they were born with defects, with the phrase, "Born in pain" *(Rozhdeny v mukakh)* on it. While the protesters' side included the red-and-black flag of the OUN, Soviet symbols stood out among the police handmade signs. One such sign, featuring an automatic rifle, had a slogan from the Soviet victory in the Second World War on it in Russian: "THANKS GRANDPA FOR THE VICTORY!" *(SPASIBO DEDU ZA POBEDU!)* (Rulev 2014b).

The police forces expressed determination to defend their own ranks, at whatever the cost (Shchotkina 2014). Once two worlds had collided on Hrushevskyi Street, it looked like neither had any chance to reconcile their differences soon, let alone form an alliance against the regime. Viatrovych faulted political opposition leaders for failing to coordinate protests more effectively. As noted above, the National Resistance Headquarters and the Maidan Council had failed to represent protesters. As for the People's Council *(Narodna Rada)*, which opposition leaders on 22 January 2014 declared would replace the Supreme Rada as the country's legislative branch, it only existed on paper. Politicians, reluctant to set it up in the first place, had abandoned it, preferring to work with colleagues in the Supreme Rada instead; this body was supposed to coordinate People's Councils that were to form in all of Ukraine's regions, but these bodies emerged haphazardly and failed to assert much leadership at all. Viatrovych urged Maidan supporters to focus on such efforts as boycotts, peaceful expansion of protest space throughout Ukraine, and a long-term nonviolent struggle for freedom (V'iatrovych 2014). So, despite Lévy's praise for a vibrant civil society that had sustained the protests for almost an entire winter, the Maidan by mid-February 2014 seemed isolated, restless, and angry, though determined to win. One Kyiv office worker recalled the 16 February Maidan assembly when opposition leaders explained their compromise with Yanukovych and announced plans for a march on the Supreme Rada, called the "Peaceful Offensive" *(Mirnyi nastup)*. Activists grumbled, making references to the political opposition committing "treason." At Kyiv City Hall, youths from a far-right group called "Warriors of Narnia" *(Voiny Narni)* (taken from C. S. Lewis's *The Chronicles of Narnia* series) stormed the building after Maidan protesters had left it, ransacking offices. Members claimed to be neither under Right Sector nor *Svoboda*; they wore paramilitary outfits, bulletproof vests, balaclavas, and face masks, and they wielded sticks and clubs, and when posing for journalists' cameras, they gave the *"Sieg, Heil!"* salute. The Warriors of Narnia also beat up policemen waiting outside the building, without facing any punishment. For this Kyiv office worker watching these events, which were reported by *Ukrains'ka Pravda* and *Vesti.ua* that same day, it seemed worse developments were coming. These warriors from "Narnia" were part of a whole army of young people who had been on the Maidan for months, whom the police were too afraid to arrest, and who saw no other way out than overthrowing Yanukovych. Otherwise, they were going to prison. More violent clashes were in the offing (Interview 13).

On the morning of 18 February, Maidan activists and self-defense forces began their Peaceful Offensive on the Supreme Rada. Demonstrators were to rally in Mariinskyi Park, near Parliament, to put pressure on it to return Ukraine to the Constitution of 2004, which reduced the President's powers considerably (thus spelling the beginning of the end for the Yanukovych regime). Maidan politicians and civic activists said the Maidan Council decided to organize this rally, because the Maidan was dying out, and it looked like government forces were gathering enough strength to clear the Maidan with force if needed (Koshkina 2015, 222–223). According to interviews with eyewitnesses and press accounts from *Liga.net* and *Ukrains'ka Pravda*, the march started out peacefully, with many pensioners in the procession (given that it was on a working day) (Interviews 3, 4, 6, 8, and 11; see also Koshkina 2015, 226–242). Yet violence soon flared up, with protesters picking fights with riot police along the route, which went along Instytutskyi Street, part of the perimeter of the fortified government offices district. Pitched battles broke out and protesters lobbed Molotov cocktails and pavement stones at riot police and burned vehicles that had blocked more direct access to Parliament, while riot police fired off stun grenades and bullets (rubber bullets, but also live ammunition). In Mariinskyi Park, what started as peaceful arguments between demonstrators and riot police turned violent as radical young protesters attacked police and began tearing down a metal fence between protesters and government forces (OrangeDoc 2014). *Titushky* from the Antimaidan camp nearby threw Molotov cocktails and fired live ammunition at the protesters, after which Berkut forces rushed in, bludgeoning anyone who crossed their path. *Titushky* followed in their wake, finishing off anyone left lying in the park. Not far from Parliament and Mariinskyi Park, a crowd egged on by investigative journalist Tetiana Chornovol (Derzhavne Biuro Rozsliduvan' 2020) set fire to the headquarters of the Party of Regions building (lobbing Molotov cocktails at its windows). Before security forces and *titushky* forced them out, an employee inside suffocated from the blaze and died. By evening, Berkut and riot police had closed in on the Maidan itself, with government officials warning protesters to disperse. Protesters set their protest city on fire to block security forces from entering the Maidan.

Despite all their discipline and bravery, Maidan Self-Defense failed to prevent its more radical members from going overboard and picking fights with the police. One of those men who set the Party of Regions building on fire allegedly told his ex-wife (one of my friends) that he felt they were "finally doing something." Yet provocateurs from within may have been stirring up some of the violence. Despite all their claims to be defending the Maidan against *titushky* and "death squads," members of C14 fled to the Canadian Embassy later that day and stayed there for the duration of the uprising. As reported by *Strana.ua* on 2 November 2017, a former C14 member, Dmytro Riznychenko, on *Facebook* claimed their leader, Ievhen Karas, had received a tip-off of plans to clear the Maidan from the SBU, with whom Karas had collaborated. Despite their absence, C14 activists online kept agitating people to fight the regime that night (Gonta 2015). One Maidan Self-Defense volunteer recalled that when the mayhem broke out in Mariinskyi Park, people near him were attacked from behind, suggesting there were provocateurs among the demonstrators that afternoon (Interview 6). As for Right Sector, its leader, Dmytro Iarosh, was nowhere to be seen. One participant in the battles along the government offices district recalled feeling as if no one was there to defend them. The Afghan War veterans had claimed they could send 1,500 volunteers to defend the Maidan in an hour and as many as 11,000 in a day, but no such numbers showed up to fight on Instytutskyi Street that afternoon or later that evening (Interview 4). Ordinary Kyiv residents chose to avoid the Maidan rather than help defend it that night. One eyewitness saw crowds of office workers walking away from the Maidan area that evening, preferring to make the journey home on foot for as long as three hours (due to the city metro closing and a complete traffic jam) rather than go to the nearby Maidan and support it (Interview 13). As for the "revolutionary army," Maidan Self-Defense, security forces and *titushky* had smashed it in Mariinskyi Park; only some of its hundreds, and some of its leaders, made it back to the Maidan that night to defend it (Interview 6). On the night of 18–19 February, the Maidan's defense depended on an unorganized group of politicians, activists, and ordinary protesters – a group willing to go to the end and use weapons. For one civic activist, that evening was the first time he saw people on the Maidan carrying rifles (Interview 7). Maidan politicians admitted that the day's events had compelled many to take up arms and that the country was moving closer to civil war (Koshkina 2015, 234). Even ordinary Kyivans with no combat experience had started considering more radical measures to defend the Maidan. One Kyiv businessman recalled that the following day, he and friends from a number of Maidan Self-Defense hundreds decided to make fertilizer bombs and test out their explosives in a university laboratory. The Yanukovych regime fell before they had a chance to use them (Interview 11).

The February uprising brought about the implosion of the Yanukovych regime and buried what had remained of nonviolent resistance on the Maidan. Over the night of 18–19 February, the Maidan lit up with fireworks, bonfires, and the flashes of stun grenades and Molotov cocktails. Protesters set ablaze an armored personnel carrier trying to force its way down Khreshchatyk Street, and the Trade Unions Building, home to the National Resistance Headquarters, caught fire, the blaze either set by the SBU's Alfa forces or Right Sector activists. Leaked documents from the Ministry of Justice suggest that radical activists had set the fire in several places inside, using materials from the explosives laboratory Right Sector ran, as Alfa forces reached the building (Sharii 2019). While opposition leaders and Yanukovych reached a truce on 19 February, the truce was short lived, since on the following morning, armed men with hunting rifles gathered near the Conservatory building on the Maidan and started firing on riot police from the Conservatory balcony, killing several. They started a firefight that caused security forces to retreat. As protesters advanced past the Maidan and up a street that went in the direction of the Hotel *Ukraina*, they came under fire from snipers. Nearly 50 people were shot and killed that day, before riot police and Berkut forces retreated (Wynnyckyj 2019, 122–125; Interview 6). They left the government offices district on 21 February, after the Supreme Rada met and ended all security operations, and after Yanukovych and the political opposition reached a settlement brokered by diplomats from Russia, France, Germany, and Poland. The political settlement included a return to the Constitution of 2004 and presidential elections at the end of 2014, as well as the formation of a new coalition government of national unity. While the settlement provoked heated arguments in the Maidan Council, and while protesters assembled on the Maidan denounced it and called for Yanukovych to resign the next morning, the regime was no more. Security forces, abandoning Yanukovych, pulled out of Kyiv (Higgins and Kramer 2015). Yanukovych fled Kyiv and soon Ukraine; on 22 February, the Supreme Rada removed him from power, appointed Oleksandr Turchynov as interim president, set up a new government, and scheduled presidential elections for 25 May. It also freed Yulia Tymoshenko from jail, and she spoke to the Maidan later that evening.

The February uprising caused a meltdown of the state that gave people free license to engage in violence and get even with their enemies. As the Maidan in Kyiv burned on the evening of 18 February, residents of the western city of Lviv, who watched the fires in Kyiv online, rose up against the state. In what local media called the "Night of Rage," crowds ransacked the regional headquarters of the Ministry of the Interior, the regional office of the Prosecutor General of Ukraine, and several district police stations. In another part of the city, they converged on a riot police base and set a soldiers' dormitory on fire (Holovko 2014). As they wrecked police stations, protesters took guns. The danger of armed protesters from Lviv coming to help the Maidan in Kyiv may have served as an additional justification for security forces to open fire on demonstrators on 20 February. Opposition politicians, while denying that arms were arriving from Lviv, used the occasion to warn that further violence would ensue if foreign diplomats did not stop Yanukovych from using more force on the Maidan (Higgins and Kramer 2015). The police disappeared from Lviv's streets, and citizens formed self-defense patrols to maintain law and order. Some of these patrols used the power vacuum to commit crime, hiding their identities with balaclavas and face masks, as one local journalist admitted (Interview 12). In central Ukraine, Maidan supporters in towns and villages assaulted their perceived enemies when trying to stop security forces and suspected *titushky* from reaching Kyiv by bus. In the Cherkasy Region, a number of incidents took place where crowds manning highway checkpoints attacked buses that were coming from or going to Kyiv. On the evening of 20 February, after the worst mass shootings in recent Ukrainian history had taken place in Kyiv, a crowd at a checkpoint near the entrance to the town of Korsun – Shevchenkivskyi stopped buses of Antimaidan participants returning to Crimea from Kyiv. A fight broke out; bus passengers threw stun grenades at residents and residents broke bus windows and destroyed their wheels and tires. They made bus passengers squat and march along piles of glass shards left on the road. They forced them to lie in a ditch as self-defense men screamed and cursed at them. One of them filmed a bus passenger making a promise never to show up in Kyiv again. These Antimaidan demonstrators may have provoked the incident, since they had attacked an earlier checkpoint. Still, amateur videos of the incident (circulated widely on the *Vkontakte* (2014) page for Typovyi Korsun' – Shevchenkivs'kyi), as well as eyewitness testimony, became material for a Russian documentary film justifying Russia's annexation of Crimea. Russia needed to return Crimea to its fold to save its people from such bestial "Banderite" crowds (Buniakina 2015, Information Group 2014). Scenes of Maidan supporters attacking, humiliating, and threatening their enemies (driven by the horror of the mass shootings on the Maidan) were hardly those befitting people who supposedly were bringing about new "European" values in Ukraine.

Descent into Darkness

While this chapter concerns the Euromaidan and opponents rather than the war that broke out between Ukraine and Russia, that conflict reified what the Kyiv Maidan allegedly stood for. In a series of protests aided by Russians from across the border, in what they called "Russian Spring," the violence unleashed at the Kyiv Maidan terrified and mobilized considerable numbers of people to protest the new government in Kyiv. These demonstrators demanded greater rights for their regions (in some more radical cases, independence from Ukraine and unity with Russia). The Maidan contributed greatly to such trends. Already, state authority had broken down in western and central Ukraine. Maidan activists and politicians had raised the specter of civil war as the fighting grew worse in Kyiv. On the eve of the February uprising, Maidan Self-Defense was already expressing aspirations to become a "revolutionary army," minus the weapons; thus, they had become a potential military institution challenging Kyiv's authority. Russian forces intervened in and engineered the annexation of Crimea in a matter of days after the Yanukovych regime had fallen (23 February – 18 March). Yet grassroots forces in Crimea, reacting to this power vacuum in Kyiv, supported by local pro-Russian movements and institutions, greatly facilitated this operation (Zeveleva 2019). The Crimea crisis highlighted the weakness of the Ukrainian state and suggested the new regime lacked legitimacy. In a leaked transcript of a 28 February meeting of the National Security and Defense Council, Kyiv's new leaders admitted that they had to rebuild not just the Ukrainian military, but also the Ukrainian state, because it had collapsed. Maidan protesters' seizures of administration buildings had given legitimacy to separatists' actions in Crimea. Extremists like Right Sector's leaders, who sported guns in public in defiance of the state, only weakened the government's authority further ("Polnaia stenogramma" 2016).

Spontaneous reactions against the Maidan and the violence and chaos it generated emerged in the Donbas region. In Donetsk, on 23 February, just a day after the Yanukovych regime fell, a demonstration erupted across from a Euromaidan gathering at a square down the road from the regional state administration building. Donetsk residents, wearing St. George ribbons, guarded their regional state administration building from what they said were radical nationalists allegedly from outside town. A *Radio Svoboda* video featured a man who said that they were standing in front of that building to prevent what had happened in Kyiv from happening there, in their city. This gathering, as one local journalist later noted, included people who angrily swore at local officials, Yanukovych, and members of the Party of Regions, and who failed to heed any leaders, breaking through a police barrier to try and attack the nearby Euromaidan rally (*Radio Svoboda* 2014a; Sizov 2014). In Kharkiv, residents expressed similar fears of Maidan activists threatening to plunge their city and region into bloodshed and chaos as they spoke to an assembly of Antimaidan supporters of Mayor Hennadiy Kernes and former Governor Mykhailo Dobkin on 1 March. That rally – comprised of locals and also guests from Russia – ended with an enraged mob storming the regional state administration building behind them, beating up Maidan activists who had occupied the building's first floor. They forced their Maidan captives to go through a "corridor of shame" and then endure humiliation and intimidation on their rally's stage (*Bloggeroks* 2014; *Radio Svoboda* 2014b; Zubr Belovezhskii 2014). The so-called Russian Spring turned into a series of clashes between local protesters and pro-Russian activists, aided by local elites, on one side and the Kyiv government on the other. While Russian influence in these disturbances cannot be denied, these conflicts, at least in their early form, expressed genuine grievances locals had with the new government, grievances that were inarticulate; they involved locals who lacked leaders who could represent them (Koshkina 2015, 385–386; Wojnowski 2014; Wojnowski 2017, 3–4). Russian military formations and Russian leaders played a crucial role in turning these conflicts between center and periphery into separatist movements that seized power in Luhansk and Donetskand started a war with Ukraine that continues to this day (Matveeva 2018, 39–188).

By mid-May 2014, the Maidan had defeated Yanukovych and the war in Donbas had just started. An international conference held then in Kyiv, "Ukraine – Thinking Together," brought academics, journalists, and policy analysts from around the world to Ukraine's capital. This conference, organized by historian Timothy Snyder of Yale University, highlighted what Ukraine's recent revolution signified to the rest of the world. Among guests speaking was Leon Wieseltier, former literary editor of *The New Republic*, who had published several works on Jewish themes. Reflecting on the dangers Russia posed to Ukraine at that point in time, Wieseltier suggested that the Maidan symbolized a wider struggle between the West and Russia that the West needed to support. Ukraine embodied the ideals of modern liberalism, civic nationalism, and multiculturalism, the polar opposite of Putin's Russia, the aggressor state, which valued nations as tribal entities centered on homogeneity and purity, where intolerance and conflict were signs of a nation's cultural wellbeing (Wieseltier 2014). Wieseltier's speech in Kyiv cast the emerging war in Ukraine as a battle for the heart and soul of Western civilization and its values. It resembled a similar appeal made by Czech writer Milan Kundera in 1984 on behalf of Central Europe, a diverse region that had contributed much to Western culture and civilization, yet during the Cold War had been subjected to the homogenizing and oppressive Soviet Union and had been abandoned by the West (Kundera 1984). Some Maidan advocates went further. Armed separatists who seized power in Crimea and the Donbas represented more than just Putin's Russia; they were terrorists who wished to snuff out civilization itself. Reflecting on Wieseltier's Kyiv speech, Mychailo Wynnyckyj wrote, "Ukraine matters because it represents a battleground between two civilizational paradigms – no less significant than the ongoing paradigmatic battle between ISIS and Al Quaeda on the one hand, and western civilization on the other" (Wynnyckyj 2019, 348).

Other, much darker, forces also saw Ukraine's Maidan and war with Russia inherently tied to the fate of European civilization. Already in early February 2014, Fredrik Hagberg, a member of the Swedish neo-Nazi organization Nordic Youth, spoke to protesters in Kyiv City Hall. Lamenting Europe's abandonment of traditional gender roles, traditional sexual orientations, and the white race, he urged Ukrainians waging revolution to choose their own path independent of the West and Russia (Moinyhan 2014). By 2016, Ukraine's war with Russia had attracted far-right activists supporting the geopolitical project of Intermarium, an alliance of Eastern European states between the Baltic and the Black Seas. Originally conceived by Polish leader Jozef Piłsudski between the world wars, Intermarium was a conservative nationalist alliance to counter the forces of Soviet Russia and Germany. Made up of lands formerly controlled by the Polish-Lithuanian Commonwealth, Poland was to play a leading role in it. Decades later, far-right groups in Ukraine, right-wing nationalist groups from other Eastern European countries, and more liberal politicians and academics revived this project as a defensive alliance against Putin's expansionist Russia. Yet this new far-right view of Intermarium was also aimed against the EU, its bureaucracy centered in Brussels, and the multicultural, neoliberal, secular, and feminist ideals the EU stood for (Kott 2017). In early July 2016, Andriy Biletsky, leader of the Azov Battalion that fought against Russian forces in the Donbas and former leader of the neo-Nazi Patriot of Ukraine, organized a conference in Kyiv on the prospects of forming an Intermarium alliance. The participants, who came from not just Ukraine, but the Baltic states, Belarus, Poland, and Central and South-Eastern Europe, included members of far right and fascist groups from the region. The conference included others not affiliated with such groups, making it seem more innocuous to mainstream audiences. Among the guests were employees of foreign embassies, academics, someone close to Lithuanian media, and even someone connected with a nonpartisan German academic institution, the Konrad Adenauer Foundation, an institution noted for its promotion of the liberal values of the EU. The banner for the conference, in Ukrainian and English, betrayed its organizers' affinities with a Europe that was racially pure, culturally conservative, and thoroughly anti-liberal: "Intermarium – The Heart of Europe Beats in the East" (Goble 2016; Kott 2017).

Despite the flights of fancy defenders of Ukraine resorted to after the Maidan's alleged triumph, this chapter has suggested that the Maidan hardly reflected their fantasies. As the Maidan drew in a variety of people whom activists and politicians failed to lead, it gave possibilities not just to those dreaming of Ukraine becoming part of the Europe of politeness, rule of law, civility, and multiculturalism. It gave license to more sinister voices that saw Europe as a white Christian civilization endangered by not just Russia, but by forces within the EU itself. Those forces included people of different races, genders, and sexual orientations. Biletskyi and his Patriot of Ukraine organization, whose members fought Yanukovych, then formed Azov Battalion to fight Russia, were just a few such examples. Iarosh of Right Sector and the activists from C14 were also in these ranks. To be sure, there were many other people on the Kyiv Maidan who shared none of these values. Yet as the Maidan became more and more a besieged fortress, facing a choice between overthrowing Yanukovych or winding up in prison, the far right became a crucial ally. The far right had fought with police before the Maidan, and they would fight them during it and even after. As war with Russia broke out, young men from the far right signed up for military service or formed their own volunteer battalions. Thus, forces on the radical right, such as C14, Right Sector, and what became known as Azov Battalion, who already claimed to be heirs of the Maidan legacy of violent resistance to Yanukovych, now became the sons and daughters of Ukraine determined to fight the Russian enemy. They also fought the alleged internal enemy in Ukraine. For C14, these "separatists" were anyone with views to the left of them, or even rival forces on the right who threatened their authority (Kondratova 2017; Movchan 2017). This made possible all sorts of alliances with far-right forces in Europe and elsewhere (Miller 2018). While the Maidan and its defense of European values brought out the most noble expressions of resistance to the Yanukovych regime, its descent into violence transformed it into one of twenty-first century Europe's darkest places.

References

Avtonomnoe deistvie. 2014. "Maidan: 'Shturm' komendatury ukrainskogo doma, narodnoe 'veche' i 'chernaia sotnia.'" 10 February, https://avtonom.org/news/maydan-shturm-komendatury-ukrainskogo-doma-narodnoe-veche-i-chernaya-sotnya.

Bellingcat. 2019. "Yes, it's (still) OK to call Ukraine's C14 'neo-Nazi.'" 9 August, https://www.bellingcat.com/news/uk-and-europe/2019/08/09/yes-its-still-ok-to-call-ukraines-c14-neo-nazi/.

Bilozerska, Olena. 2014. "Pravyi Sektor vysunuv vlasni vymohy do vlady." *YouTube*, 27 January, https://www.youtube.com/watch?v=isqPpJMKYY4.

Bloggeroks. 2014. "1 marta 2014 goda izvinenie boitsov 'Pravogo sektora' (banderovtsev) pered khar'kovchanami." 1 March, https://www.youtube.com/watch?v=aa63IjsaWIk#t=380.

Buniakina, Dar'ia. 2015. "Cherkashchany: Korsuns'kyi pohrom – vyhadka rosiys'kykh propahandystiv." *Radio Svoboda*, 16 March, http://www.radiosvoboda.org/content/article/26904323.html.

Chistilin, Vladimir. 2014. "Shto reshil forum Evromaidanov." *Glavnoe*, 13 January, https://glavnoe.ua/articles/a8693?fbclid=IwAR2ciu1c9aEu8hXmKgJhCAo8vCARMTh6jLXXkKeIh5o_5qZekEAjV8Tn8pk.

Derzhavne Biuro Rozsliduvan'. 2020. "Pidpal partiynoho ofisu u tsentri Kyieva ta smert' liudyny – DBR povidomylo pro pidozru v umysnomu vbyvstvi hromadiantsi (VIDEO)." 10 April, https://dbr.gov.ua/news/pidpal-partiynogo-ofisu-u-centri-kieva-ta-smert-lyudini-dbr-povidomilo-pro-pidozru-v-umisnomu-vbivstvi-gromadyanci-video.

DIF and KIIS. 2014. "Maidan-December and Maidan-February: What has changed?" Ilko Kucheriv Democratic Initiatives Foundation, 6 February, https://dif.org.ua/en/article/maidan-december-and-maidan-february-what-has-changed.

Espreso TV. 2014. "V militsii nemaie zhodnoi informatsii pro te, khto pobyv nardepa Illienka ta ioho advokata." 8 January, https://www.youtube.com/watch?time_continue=1&v=tVPVgDv-Ul0&feature=emb_title.

Facebook. 2014. "Euromaidan Press." https://www.facebook.com/euromaidanpress.en/.

Facenews. 2014. "Zachem 'Bat'kivshchyna' trollit Grazhdanskii sovet Maidana?" 13 January, https://www.facenews.ua/articles/2014/185455/.

Gessen, Keith. 2018. "The quiet Americans behind the US-Russia imbroglio." *The New York Times Magazine*, 8 May, https://www.nytimes.com/2018/05/08/magazine/the-quiet-americans-behind-the-us-russia-imbroglio.html.

Goble, Paul. 2016. "Intermarium: An idea whose time is coming again." *Euromaidan Press*, 5 July, http://euromaidanpress.com/2016/07/05/intermarium-an-idea-whose-time-is-coming-again/?fbclid=IwAR2Y0Bs2zfoMojUJ8BCU0QiVqeqbiUQzkMHvaCsqCTn-NqbNSAxAdD0czaw.

Gonta, Boris. 2015. "Medved'ko i C14: Ot bor'by s zastroikami k ubiistvu Buziny." *Bukvu*, 18 June, https://bykvu.com/ru/mysli/3197-medvedko-i-s14-ot-borby-s-zastrojkami-k-ubijstvu-buziny/.

Higgins, Andrew, and Andrew E. Kramer. 2015. "Ukraine leader was defeated even before he was ousted." *The New York Times*, 3 January, http://www.nytimes.com/2015/01/04/world/europe/ukraine-leader-was-defeated-even-before-he-was-ousted.html?_r=1.

Holovko, Bohdan. 2014. "Nich Hnivu. Shcho stalosia u L'vovi v nich na 19 liutoho?" *Zakhid.net*, 19 February, http://zaxid.net/news/showNews.do?nich_gnivu_shho_stalosya_u_lvovi_v_nich_na_19_lyutogo&objectId=1302802.

Hrabovs'kyi, Serhiy. 2013. "Chy peretvoriat'sia zahony 'titushkiv' na 'eskadrony smerti'?" *Tyzhden. ua*, 26 December, https://m.tyzhden.ua/column/97749.

Iarosh, Dmytro. 2012. *Natsiia i revoliutsiia*. Lviv: n.p.

Information Group. 2014. "The pogrom of Korsun." *YouTube*, 2 July, https://www.youtube.com/watch?v=0WzNZymJe84.

Ishchenko, Volodymyr. 2016. "Far right participation in the Ukrainian Maidan protests: An attempt of systematic estimation." *European Politics and Society* 17(4): 453–472.

Junes, Tom. 2016. "Euromaidan and the Revolution of Dignity: A case study of student protest as a catalyst for political upheaval." *Critique & Humanism* 46(2): 69–92.

Katchanovski, Ivan. 2020. "The far right, the Euromaidan, and the Maidan massacre in Ukraine." *Journal of Labor and Society* 23(1): 5–29.

KIIS and SOCIS. 2014. "'Nastroi Ukrainy' – rezul'taty spil'noho doslidzhennia KMIS ta SOTsIS." *Kyivs'kyi Mizhnarodnyi Instytut Sotsiolohii*, 7 February, https://www.kiis.com.ua/?lang=ukr&cat=reports&id=227&page=1&y=2014&m=2.

Kondratova, Valeriia. 2017. "C14: Kto oni i pochemu im pozvoleno bit' liudei." *Liga.net*, 15 November, https://news.liga.net/politics/interview/s14_kto_oni_i_pochemu_im_pozvoleno_bit_lyudey.

Koshkina, Sonia [Ksenia Vasylenko]. 2015. *Maidan: Nerozkazana istoriia*. Kyiv: Brait Star Pablishing.

Kott, Matthew. 2017. "A far right highjack of Intermarium." *New Eastern Europe*, 26 May, https://neweasterneurope.eu/2017/05/26/a-far-right-hijack-of-intermarium/.

Kotsyuba, Oleh. 2013. "Ukraine's battle for Europe." *The New York Times*, 29 November, https://www.nytimes.com/2013/11/30/opinion/ukraines-battle-for-europe.html.

Kozachenko, Ivan. 2014. "How social media transformed pro-Russian nostalgia into violence in Ukraine." *The Conversation*, 16 October, https://theconversation.com/how-social-media-transformed-pro-russian-nostalgia-into-violence-in-ukraine-33046.

Kundera, Milan. 1984. "The tragedy of Central Europe." *New York Review of Books*, 26 April, 33–38.

Lévi-Strauss, Claude. 1987. *Introduction to the Work of Marcel Mauss*. London: Routledge & Kegan Paul.

Lévy, Bernard-Henri. 2014. "Kiev's Independence Square: Where Europe hangs in the balance." *Huffpost*, 18 February, https://www.huffpost.com/entry/kievs-independence-square_b_4808629.

Livejournal. 2014a. v_n_zb, https://v-n-zb.livejournal.com/.

Livejournal. 2014b. flackelf, https://flackelf.livejournal.com/.

Maidan online. 2013. "Aktyvisty Maidanu zavadyly provokatoram-komunistam." 4 December, https://www.youtube.com/watch?v=j26OjtzZJl4&feature=emb_title.

Mann, Olexa. 2014. "Facebook Profile." https://www.facebook.com/olexa.mann?__tn__=%2Cd*F* F-R&eid=ARBYieZxPHwBpZ2Ni5KfeB3FQinRwM9p-dbGZVQQnq6e_2njjhEdd4QUE-dt _uNzcSr4yg7CYe9I4vUH&tn-str=*F.

Matveeva, Anna. 2018. *Through Times of Trouble: Conflict in Southeastern Ukraine Explained from Within*. Lanham, MD: Lexington Books.

Mazanik, Lesia. 2014. "Pokolenie titushek." *Gordon*, 1 February, https://gordonua.com/specpro jects/titushki.html.

Miller, Christopher. 2018. "Azov, Ukraine's most prominent ultranationalist group, sets its sights on US, Europe." *Radio Free Europe/Radio Liberty*, 14 November, https://www.rferl. org/a/azov-ukraine-s-most-prominent-ultranationalist-group-sets-its-sights-on-u-s-europe /29600564.html?fbclid=IwAR1g-Kg.

Moinyhan, Michael. 2014. "The Swedish neo-Nazis 'volunteers' of Kiev." *Daily Beast*, 28 February, https://www.thedailybeast.com/the-swedish-neo-nazis-volunteers-of-kiev.

Movchan, Sergei. 2017. "Nestandart BBC, abo sorom'iazlyvi terorysty." *Politychna krytyka*, 19 July, https://politkrytyka.org/2017/07/19/nestandart-bbc-abo-sorom-yazlivi-teroristi/.

Naiem, Mustafa, and Oksana Kovalenko. 2014. "Lider Pravoho sektoru Dmytro Iarosh: Koly 80% krainy ne pidtrymuie vladu, hromadians'koi viyny buty ne mozhe." *Ukrains'ka Pravda*, 4 February, http://www.pravda.com.ua/articles/2014/02/4/7012683/.

Onuch, Olga, and Gwendolyn Sasse. 2016. "The Maidan in movement: Diversity and the cycles of protest." *Europe-Asia Studies* 68(4): 556–587.

OrangeDoc. 2014. "George Sajewych interview in Kyiv, 20 March 2014." *YouTube*, 21 March, https://www.youtube.com/watch?v=J13CsoehWkM.

"Polnaia Stenogramma." 2016. "Polnaia stenogramma chrezvychainogo zasedaniia SNBU po Krymu (dokumenty)." *Ukrains'ki novyny*, 22 February, http://ukranews.com/news/411852-polnaya-stenogramma-chrezvychaynogo-zasedanyya-snbo-po-krymu.

Pyrih, Volodymyr. 2015. "V spravi pro vykradennia Bulatova nema ni svidkiv, ni pidozriuvanykh – MVS." *Zakhid.net*, 18 November, https://zaxid.net/v_spravi_pro_vikradennya_bulatova_ nema_ni_svidkiv_ni_pidozryuvanih__mvs_n1373390.

Radio Svoboda. 2014a. "Donets'kyi Ievromaidan vshanuvav pam'iat' zahyblykh . . ." 23 February, https://www.youtube.com/watch?v=bOFLlUGchRM.

Radio Svoboda. 2014b. "Kharkiv / 01.03.2014 / Priama transliatsiia." 1 March, https://www.you tube.com/watch?v=yJ210LicNgw.

Research & Branding Group. 2013a. "Ievromaidan – 2013." 10 December, http://rb.com.ua/rus/ projects/omnibus/8836/. (The page no longer exists as of 7 May 2020.)

Research & Branding Group. 2013b. "Prezentatsiia rezul'tatov vseukrainskogo issledovaniia 'Otsenka sotsial'no-politicheskoi situatsii v Ukraine.'" 30 December. (The original presentation, quoted by *Korrespondent.net*, is no longer available online as of 7 May 2020.)

Research & Branding Group. 2014. "Krizis v Ukraine: Mnenie zhitelei oblastnykh tsentrov." 3 February. (This press release is no longer available at the organization's website, www.rb. com.ua.)

Rossolinski-Liebe, Grzegorz. 2014. *Stepan Bandera: The Life and Afterlife of a Ukrainian Nationalist – Fascism, Genocide, and Cult*. Düsseldorf: Ibidem Press.

Rulev, Sergei. 2014a. "Banderovtsy napali na kievlianina, demonstratsiia sily, pesni UPA." 8 February, https://www.youtube.com/watch?v=2zEdC3tWwwc.

Rulev, Sergei. 2014b. "Na fronte zatish'e pered burei." 10 February, https://www.youtube.com/ watch?v=9qXzDXgW9kA.

Rulev, Sergei. 2014c. "Mirnaia aktsiia Ivana Protsenko podavliaetsia boevikami maidana."
    15 February, https://www.youtube.com/watch?v=adbV25ZBEP4.
Sharhovs'ka, Ol'ha. 2013. "'U UPA suchasni povstantsi maly b povchytysia zavziattia' – istoryk."
    Gazeta.ua, 6 December, https://gazeta.ua/articles/history/_u-upa-suchasni-povstanci-mali
    -b-povchitisya-zavzyattya-istorik/530240.
Sharii, Anatolii. 2019. "Laboratoriia mirnogo Maidana." 13 December, https://www.youtube.com/
    watch?v=thf43N6Z-mM.
Shchotkina, Kateryna. "Chuzhyi, shche chuzhishyi." *ZN,UA*, 7 February, https://dt.ua/internal/
    chuzhiy-sche-chuzhishiy-_.html.
Shekhovtsov, Anton. 2014a. "Ukrains'ki krain'opravi i Ievromaidan." *Ji*, 3 January,
    http://www.ji-magazine.lviv.ua/dyskusija/2014/Shehovcov_Ukr_krajn-pravi_i-
    Euromajdan.htm.
Shekhovtsov, Anton. 2014b. "A comment on the involvement of the Patriot of Ukraine in the
    Ukrainian revolution." *Anton Shekhovtsov's blog*, 31 December, at http://anton-shekhovtsov.
    blogspot.com/2014/12/a-comment-on-involvement-of-patriot-of.html.
Shore, Marci. 2017. *The Ukrainian Night: An Intimate History of Revolution*. New Haven, CT: Yale
    University Press.
Sinchenko, Dmytro. 2013. "Vorohy narodu Mezhyhir'ia." *Ukrains'ka Pravda*, 26 December,
    http://www.pravda.com.ua/columns/2013/12/26/7008573/.
Sizov, Vitalii. 2014. "Srabotaet li russkaia idea separatizma v ukrainskom Donbasse?" *Novosti
    Donbassa*, 1 March, http://novosti.dn.ua/article/4794-srabotaet-ly-russkaya-ydeya-
    separatyzma-v-ukraynskom-donbasse.
Snyder, Timothy. 2018. *The Road to Unfreedom: Russia, Europe, America*. New York: Tim Duggan
    Books.
SOCIS. 2013. "Suspil'no-politychna sytuatsiia v Ukraini hruden' 2013." 26 December, http://old.
    socis.kiev.ua/ua/press/suspilno-politychna-sytuatsija-v-ukrajini-hruden-2013.html.
SOCIS. 2014. "Dani zahal'noukrains'koho sotsiolohichnoho doslidzhennia monitorynhu 'Ukraina i
    ukraintsi.'" 31 January, http://old.socis.kiev.ua/ua/press/dani-zahalnoukrajinskoho-
    sotsiolohichnoho-doslidzhennja-monitorynhu-ukrajina-i-ukrajintsi.html.
Spirin, Ievhen, and Artem Konopkin. 2019. "'Koly liudy khodyly do universytetiv, my rubalysia z
    musoramy na barykadakh.' Dvoie ul'tras rozpovidaiut', iak bylysia na Bankoviy, valyly Lenina,
    voiuvaly ta izdyly v Honkong – velyke interv'iu." *Babel'*, 19 December, https://thebabel.com.
    ua/texts/39816-koli-lyudi-hodili-do-universitetiv-mi-rubalisya-z-musorami-na-barikadah-dvoe
    -ultras-rozpovidayut-yak-bilisya-na-bankoviy-valili-lenina-voyuvali-ta-jizdili-v-gonkong-velike-
    interv-yu?fbclid=IwAR1iNK_ITghfcsbQcsPEmbhAe3wFh_c_RZLuIuT3LqejLhqABD7LDX5bM8Y.
Stadnyi, Iehor. 2014. "Rosiys'kyi aktsent – zbroia proty Maidanu." *Lb.ua*, 31 January, https://lb.ua/
    blog/jegor_stadny/253913_rosiyskiy_aktsent-zbroya_proti.html.
V'iatrovych, Volodymyr. 2014. "Dovha doroha do voli." *ZN,UA*, 14 February, https://dt.ua/internal/
    dovga-doroga-do-voli-_.html.
Vkontakte. 2014. "Typovyi Korsun' – Shevchenkivs'kyi." https://m.vk.com/typical_korsun.shev
    chenkovsky?from=post.
Wieseltier, Leon. 2014. "'The Russian war on Ukraine is one of the proving grounds of principle in
    our time:' Remarks from Kiev." *The New Republic*, 19 May, https://newrepublic.com/article/
    117817/leon-wieseltier-remarks-ukraine-thinking-together-conference.
Wilson, Andrew. 2014. *Ukraine Crisis: What It Means for the West*. New Haven, CT: Yale University
    Press.
Wojnowski, Zbigniew. 2014. "Russian propaganda is fueling separatist sentiments in Donbass."
    Aljazeera America, 25 March, http://america.aljazeera.com/opinions/2014/3/protest-grows-
    indonbaseasternukrainenearrussia.html.

Wojnowski, Zbigniew. 2017. *The Near Abroad: Socialist Eastern Europe and Soviet Patriotism in Ukraine, 1965–1985*. Toronto, ON: University of Toronto Press.

Wynnyckyj, Mychailo. 2019. *Ukraine's Maidan, Russia's War: A Chronicle and Analysis of the Revolution of Dignity*. Stuttgart: Ibidem Verlag.

Zeveleva, Olga. 2019. "How ordinary Crimeans helped Russia annex their home." *Open Democracy Russia*, 14 March, https://www.opendemocracy.net/en/odr/how-ordinary-crimeas-helped-russia-annex-their-home/.

Zubr Belovezhskii. 2014. "Miting v g. Khar'kove 1. 03.2014 pereros v osvobozhdenie obl. administratsii." *YouTube*, 1 March, https://www.youtube.com/watch?v=RMt2U7qp8pI.

A Note on Interviews

Due to the politically sensitive nature of the Maidan protests even six years after their passing, all interviews are given here as anonymous. Interviews were conducted by the author, except for interviews archived at the Ukrainian Institute of National Memory in Kyiv. The author thanks the institute for these materials.

Interview 1: Two employees of a non-governmental organization, Kyiv, 21 December 2013.

Interview 2: A social movement organization activist, Kyiv, 22 December 2013.

Interview 3: A social movement organization activist, Kyiv, 17 March 2014.

Interview 4: A Maidan participant and former student, Kyiv, 18 March 2014.

Interview 5: A Kyiv university student and Maidan participant, Kyiv, 20 May 2014.

Interview 6: A Kyiv Maidan Self-Defense volunteer, Ukrainian Institute of National Memory, Kyiv, 23 July 2014.

Interview 7: A Kyiv civic activist, Kyiv, Ukrainian Institute of National Memory, 14 August 2014.

Interview 8: A Kyiv journalist, Kyiv, 10 November 2014.

Interview 9: A social movement organization activist, Kyiv, 11 November 2014.

Interview 10: A Maidan doctor, Kyiv, 28 November 2014.

Interview 11: A Kyiv Maidan participant and friend of Maidan Self-Defense forces, Kyiv, 15 December 2014.

Interview 12: A Lviv journalist, Lviv, 16 December 2014.

Interview 13: A Kyiv office worker, by Skype, 24 January 2016.

Between Present and Future

Lia Tsuladze

7 Managing Ambivalence: An Interplay Between the Wanted and Unwanted Aspects of European Integration in Georgia

This study deals with the perception of Europe and European integration as viewed by a small, in-between country with a rather vague position on the territorial and imaginary maps of Europe. It starts from the premise that Europe is a discursive construct that is constantly reinvented and negotiated from both inside (by the EU member states themselves) and outside (by the countries not belonging to the EU). Furthermore, the idea of Europe is "constructed with strategic goals in mind and the 'reality' that it designates is also used strategically" (Delanty 1995, 3). The strategic use of Europe reflects a tension between its diverse visions (della Porta and Caiani 2009, 24) as Europe "means different things to different people in different contexts" (Delanty 1995, 3), and hence "is fraught with ambiguity" (Nanz 2000, 282). This ambiguity is reflected in both different nations' discourses about Europe and the EU, and how different groups within society talk about the EU and European identity. It is these talks that disclose their narrators' "status insecurity" (Webber 2007, 5) or "positional insecurity" (Melegh et al. 2019) vis-à-vis the EU, as it is argued that "[t]o talk about 'Europe' is to enter a field of discursive struggle involving power relations typical of situations of social bargaining" (Nanz 2000, 289). Such power relations become increasingly notable in relation to the current shift from "permissive consensus" to "constraining dissensus" (Hooghe and Marks 2008) in public and even political support to European integration. Framing the above mentioned in the context of Georgian society, it is crucial to find out what discourses (political and popular) Georgians present about the EU and European integration, what they consider desirable and undesirable outcomes of Georgia's Europeanization, how they perceive their position and respective bargaining power in the hierarchical system of Europe, as well as how they negotiate their status vis-à-vis the EU and what strategies they use to represent their country as European in the context of current Europeanization. In this process, how do they reinvent Europe and their own Europeanness?

Acknowledgements: I would like to thank Professor Attila Melegh for his feedback and useful comments on this paper.

https://doi.org/10.1515/9783110684216-007

Georgia's European Integration in the Framework of Developmental Idealism

In his book *Inventing Europe: Idea, Identity, Reality*, Gerard Delanty argues that "every age reinvented the idea of Europe in the mirror of its own identity," and hence Europe "is an idea as much as a reality" (1995, 1; see also Larry Wolff's 1994 *Inventing Eastern Europe*). In the same vain, we can argue that every nation reinvents "the idea of Europe in the mirror of its own identity." Viewed through the lenses of historically inherited and shaped identity constructions of various elite and non-elite groups, the reinvented Europe is attributed those identity traits considered essential by a particular nation. These essential traits are primarily related to cultural norms and values; however, economic (such as free markets) and political (such as democratic institutions) features are equally crucial, as they make inseparable part of a country's profile, and hence its identity. Aspiring for European integration, a country attempts to resemble the cultural, economic and political features associated with Europe, thus creating a model for one's own development. This model constructed in the framework of teleological and hierarchical modernization is not a mere invention but is based on the vision and practices of the international community, mainly, the Western developed countries, regarding "the appropriate goals of development and the ends for achieving these goals" (Thornton, Dorius, and Swindle 2015, 277). This is how Developmental Idealism (DI) enters the realm of European integration generating certain motivations and respective action plans for the aspirant countries such as Georgia.

Indeed, the DI model defines Georgians' vision of European integration by viewing Europeanization, as their forerunner Central and Easter European countries did, as a break with the Socialist/Soviet past (Brusis 2001) and as a modernizing force (Kuus 2007; Melegh 2006), which is vividly demonstrated by the Caucasus Research Resource Centers' (CRRC) Georgia surveys on Knowledge of and Attitudes toward the EU in Georgia, in the period between 2009 and 2017. Georgians do perceive their European path as a precondition for the development of society in terms of democratization (especially with a focus on the protection of human rights), economic advancement, better functioning of political institutions, as well as improvement of various freedoms (Tsuladze et al. 2016). One more factor that Georgians consider a crucial outcome of the country's European integration is the defense of its security. Despite the fact that the EU is not a military union, it is perceived as Georgia's safeguard against Russian threats (Tsuladze et al. 2016, 183). In this sense, security as value (Dimitrova 2015) becomes an inseparable part of Georgians' DI model. The abovementioned aspects are in compliance with the general perception of the EU and Europeanization usually "seen as a product of culture," and "closely linked to the pursuit of economic interests . . . [and] also connected with militarism in the sense of Europe as a security agenda" (Delanty 1995, 9). Furthermore, it is widely acknowledged that "[t]he image of Europe becomes intertwined with the concept of democracy and citizens' rights" (della Porta and Caiani 2009, 23).

Social researchers argue that "DI provides guidance, sometimes in the form of prescriptions, regarding how to achieve the good life" (Thornton et al. 2015, 279). No doubt, Georgia's European aspirations presuppose the pursuit of a standard for modernity linked to "Europe" (Chakrabarty 2000), which is spread through three main mechanisms as listed by Thornton and his colleagues, namely, transnational actors; programs and institutions; and transnational interactions (Thornton et al. 2015, 290). In the case of Georgia's European integration, the first mechanism can be represented by the EU itself, the second one by an association agreement that provides the basic guiding principles for the associated countries, and the third one by the Eastern Partnership (EaP) that represents the framework of interactions for the EU and its neighborhood countries. The developmental model promoted by the EU in the form of association agreement among Georgia and other EaP countries gains legitimacy among the locals because of the normative power (Manners 2002) its disseminator possesses and because of the aspirant countries' asymmetrical dependence on the latter (Zhelyazkova et al. 2015, 20). Thus, the EU's strong bargaining position makes its developmental model appealing to those who aspire to join that "universally valid community" symbolized by the EU and "social and value patterns it represents" (Melegh 2006, 30). Therefore, its "DI beliefs are often taken for granted as unquestioned 'truths' or commonsense understandings about the world" by both local elites and population (Thornton et al. 2015, 279). These taken-for-granted truths, however, might still be resisted by the same local actors (whether governmental or not), who might act as critics in the process of implementing these standards (say, political parties with anti-EU sentiments or far-right nationalistic groups) or might try to adapt them to the local cultural practices (for instance, based on our research, the current and former government officials in Georgia advocate for the selective incorporation of EU standards and even criticize local NGOs for their uncritical attitudes toward adopting these standards). As a result, we encounter rather ambivalent views on the abovementioned norms and standards among politicians and population, in particular, both wanting and resisting them.

Thus, even in the case of country's strong European aspirations and attempts to follow EU standards, the latter might not be implemented with much eagerness or based on the desire to take after those countries considered more developed and democratic. That is, the reforms might not be driven by the mechanism of socialization but rather by the EU conditionality (Sedelmeier 2011; Schimmelfennig 2012) or even self-conditionality, which means that a country tries to take more responsibility than implied by EU regulations as a means to "seek legitimacy within the international community" (Thornton et al. 2015, 294). So, quite often, we can encounter a performative use of the DI model for positioning oneself as more progressive and oriented toward modernizing one's own society. On a declarative level, therefore, local political actors might express their readiness to be taught by the EU; while "in many cases policies [might be] endorsed without any intention for implementation"

(Thornton et al. 2015, 294). Thus, despite the declared ambition to modernize one's own society, the DI model might merely stay on paper.

In this context we should introduce the major frameworks for explaining attitudes toward the EU – the rational utilitarian and the identity and value-based ones (Toshkov et al. 2014, 20), which are closely intertwined with each other. Therefore, certain utilitarian or pragmatic (as will be termed in the rest of the paper) factors help better understand identity considerations and vice versa. The utilitarian/pragmatic framework relates to collective and individual benefits associated with the EU in terms of economic development, education and proper functioning of political institutions; in many cases, a security agenda becomes an important element of this list. The identity and value-based framework relates to the perceived cultural threats and respective identity concerns stemming from a country's European integration, as the latter obviously contributes to the redefinition of national identity. What does the existing body of research reveal about the perception of pragmatic and identity factors in the EU's new member states and aspirant countries such as Georgia? It reveals that the citizens of new member states do not expect immediate economic gains from European integration but rather certain benefits in terms of new opportunities and better functioning of democratic institutions (Doyle and Fidrmuc 2006, 541). Thus, evidence shows that the long-term democratic gains associated with European integration prevail over the short-term economic ones in the Eastern enlargement and aspirant countries, pointing to the prevalence of DI again. It also shows that elites and population expect different advantages and disadvantages associated with European integration. The key difference between the positions of elites and population is "the empowerment or loss of control that collective actors attribute to a transfer of national responsibilities and authority to the European level" (Best 2012b, 240), and hence the perceived threats related to national sovereignty, as well as the power asymmetry resulting from these changes. Concerning the identity and value-based considerations related to European integration, studies reveal that those exhibiting high national pride (Carey 2002) and intolerance to distinct religious and ethnic groups (especially migrants), as well as fearing the loss of national identity, express rather negative attitudes toward the EU and EU enlargement (Toshkov et al. 2014, 22). Thus, it is reasonably expected that the pragmatic factors be viewed predominantly in a positive light, while the ones related to identity concerns cause citizens' discontent with European integration. However, in contrast to such expectations our research shows that both identity and pragmatic considerations related to the country's European integration invoke rather ambivalent views among population and elites in Georgia, and this ambivalence is clearly reflected in their reinvented version of Europe and their own Europeanness.

The current research is based on a mixed-method approach integrating both qualitative and quantitative components. The target group consists of, on the one hand, politicians (the parliamentary majority and minority) and representatives of governmental and non-governmental sectors, that is, political and intellectual elites (31 respondents), who were probed based on in-depth interviews, and on the other hand, population residing in the capital and main cities of Eastern and Western Georgia (6 cities in total, 137 respondents), who participated in focus group discussions. Because the representative surveys by CRRC Georgia (2009–2017) show that younger age and higher education positively correlate with pro-European attitudes, our target population was divided into three age categories matching with their exposure to socialization in the Soviet and post-Soviet times: those aged 18–25, born and educated in the post-Soviet era, those aged 26–40, educated partly in the Soviet and partly in the post-Soviet times, and those aged 41–65, born and educated in the Soviet era (based on the abovementioned age categories, three focus groups were held in each target city, which makes 18 focus groups in total). We have incorporated Q methodology in both in-depth interviews with political and intellectual elites and focus group discussions with population. At the initial stage, the dominant political and popular discourses on Georgia's European integration were selected from the former research project with the same focus implemented in the period between 2014 and 2016. Furthermore, the most widespread discourses were transformed in 30 statements and given to the same target groups (political and intellectual elites and population), who were asked to assess these discourses/statements based on the provided Q grids. The target group representatives rated the statements on a 7-point scale (from – 3 to +3) based on their agreement/disagreement with the statements alongside rating their importance (–3 containing the most important statements the respondents disagreed to and +3 containing the most important statements the respondents agreed to). As a result, correlation and factor analyses were performed using the Ken-Q-Analysis software. Furthermore, the participants reflected on the most important statements/discourses they agreed/disagreed with and provided their views on key issues in the process of Georgia's European integration, which were subject to content and discourse analyses.

Pragmatic Considerations: Protection of Human Rights and Security Issues

As Georgians view European integration in the light of DI, it is important to find out what transformations the Georgian DI model envisages that are endorsed by political and intellectual elites and likewise supported by population. First of all, these transformations are seen in relation to the country's democratic performance, especially in terms of human rights' protection. As Q analysis reveals, the statement that Georgia's European integration will result in the better protection of human rights has the highest positive correlation among the interviewed MPs and representatives of governmental and non-governmental sectors, as well as population. Another statement with the highest positive value is the one on the EU seen as Georgia's safeguard against Russian threats. Based on Z-Score variance that measures the consensus-dissensus among various factors, the abovementioned two factors are closely correlated, which indicates that the democracy and security issues are perceived as interconnected. As Q analysis shows, in this respect, there is a high resonance between the political and intellectual elites' views and those of population under 40, especially young people aged 18–25. That the democracy and security matters are considered intertwined is confirmed by the interview data too. According to our respondents, improving the country's democratic performance is also a means of countering the Russian domination and especially its soft power. It is believed that the Russian propaganda targeting the "rotten West" (particularly demonizing homosexual relations and homosexuals whose rights are protected in the Western countries) will not bear any danger to Georgia if its democratic institutions are strong enough and human rights are protected not just on paper but in practice. As one of the MPs from the parliamentary majority notes, "getting closer to the European Family means that we have an ambition to reach a different level and be a country distinct from Russia in terms of its level of democracy, mentality, etc. That is why we need to be closer to the European Family, and Europe should also recognize this."

This rather concise quote provides quite interesting information on Georgians' perception of European integration: It is obvious that they consider their European aspirations as a means of societal modernization relative to the perceived Russian levels. This ambition is believed to take Georgians to a different level of development, including their "mental modernization" (The term coined by the research participants). The respondent stresses that "our society lacks the awareness that the EU has" and hence the latter should help Georgia develop it. Such a mental modernization is considered a necessary precondition for distancing oneself from Russia, which is evidently perceived as Europe's Other (Neumann 1998) and a semi-civilized force. Thus, the development of democratic institutions and its accompanying mental modernization are believed to be the strategies for both avoiding the Russian domination and getting recognition from Europe, which implicitly assumes that in the hierarchical system of power relations Georgia improves its position vis-à-vis both Russia and the EU.

The focus on democratic and mental developments does reveal the prevalence of DI model in the discourses of Georgia's Europeanization, as democratic institutions, protection of human rights, and educated citizenry are consisting parts of DI (Thornton et al. 2015, 282). Education as an instrument of mental modernization is considered vital for translating EU norms and standards from paper to practice. Indeed, the research participants, especially the population from different regions of Georgia, believe that the European integration process will be followed by the Georgian population's enhanced education and broadened worldview resulting in a greater acceptance of alternative positions, and hence increased tolerance. Such a perception is well evidenced by the following statement: "If Georgia integrates with the EU and becomes its member, human rights will be better protected as the level of education will increase" (Male, 18–25, Tbilisi). Thus, a linear connection is seen between the level of education and the improvement of human rights' protection (and hence the reinforcement of democracy). Although the above quote stresses the current lack of both education and awareness about human rights, it is also proudly announced that "humanist and democratic values were the guiding principles for Georgians back in 1918, when the first republic was founded" (Male, 26–40, Gori). However, it is believed that later these values were overshadowed by the socioeconomic hardships resulting from the Soviet rule. As this participant sadly notes, "we used to have tolerance but have somehow forgotten it because of economic problems . . . A lot is to be done though nothing is impossible." So, it seems the state of democracy would substantially improve as soon as Georgians assisted by the EU recalled their forgotten tolerance.

Despite the fact that there is a common agreement among political and intellectual elites and population that the EU raises Georgians' awareness about human rights and tolerance, concurrently one can see certain resistance to this idea among the same target groups. On the one hand, representatives of political elite would argue that it is extremely important to adopt EU regulations on human rights, as "the legislation will provide the framework for us to gradually learn how to respect others" (MP, parliamentary majority). Another politician provides a similar argument claiming that "those who cannot learn tolerance themselves, will be taught it by force" (government official). Thus, EU regulations are perceived as a necessary framework to teach Georgians how to respect human rights. Moreover, it is argued that some Georgians even need to be taught tolerance by force. On the other hand, the same respondents would argue that Georgians are historically tolerant, and hence the respect for human rights is their inborn feature (MP, parliamentary majority). Therefore, they do not need to be taught it by the EU. According to one of the government officials, "the focus on human rights is not imposed by the EU but is embedded in the Georgian identity, in particular, national traditions and Christianity." Thus, based on this quote, Georgians had known how to respect human rights long before they decided to integrate with the EU.

The same ambivalence to the EU's role in disseminating tolerance and respect to human rights is expressed in the population's discourses. On the one hand, the EU is called "a front-runner in defending human rights" (Male, 18–25, Batumi) and it is stressed that as a result of European integration, "we will have a better control on the protection of human rights, which we lack now" (Male, 26–40, Gori). It is hard to find a focus group participant of any age and any region who disagrees with this idea. However, simultaneously, there is a widespread argument that human rights have been historically respected in Georgia, which is especially characteristic to the participants of the older generation: "Human rights have always been protected in Georgia, at least to some extent, so it was absolutely unacceptable to adopt the anti-discrimination law in such a haste" (Male, 41–65, Kutaisi). Despite a confident beginning that "human rights have always been protected in Georgia," it seems the respondent is not quite sure himself, which is revealed by the use of the phrase "at least to some extent." It is worth noting that the participant tries to adjust his discourse to a socially desirable view, as he does not call "absolutely unacceptable" the anti-discrimination legislation itself but only the fact of adopting it "in such a haste."

Finally, one might question why it is absolutely unacceptable to adopt the anti-discrimination legislation even in a haste, if the protection of human rights has never been an issue in Georgia. Another participant against anti-discrimination legislation though, because of social desirability again, not daring to openly admit it, argues that Georgians "are fast in learning harmful things, while homosexuals appear so often even on the TV that some young people might try to take after them, just for the sake of popularity" (Female, 26–40, Kutaisi). This and other passages reveal that anti-discrimination legislation is primarily associated with the protection of homosexuals' rights, while Georgians' characteristic feature of easily acquiring undesirable things, as well as the motivation to protect younger generation from it, is used as an excuse for opposing the anti-discrimination law. In fact, the youngest participants (18–25) themselves believe that Georgians are in need of anti-discrimination legislation as they do lack tolerance toward various minorities, including the sexual ones. Moreover, they argue that the adoption of this legislation does not point to the fact that Georgian politicians and policymakers acknowledge its necessity but only shows that "in order to become a EU member, our legislation should be harmonized with theirs, and if not this motivation, Georgian politicians would have never thought of implementing lots of reforms, especially adopting the anti-discrimination law (Male, 18–25, Tbilisi).

According to this passage, the main motivation for adopting the anti-discrimination legislation is not the Georgian politicians' awareness of the need for a more tolerant society or their attempt to ensure equal rights for everyone but their pragmatic approach to earn a golden carrot, that is, EU membership. Despite the fact that young respondents from different regions often voice this idea, the older participants and also political elites share the view that Georgians used to have a European mindset long before they decided to integrate with the EU but, as noted above, it was oppressed when Russia occupied the country in the nineteenth century and forcefully imposed its own lifestyle on Georgians. However, it is believed that even the Russian influence could not deprive Georgians of their European mentality: "Despite the fact that Georgia was occupied by Russia and belonged to the Soviet Union, our historical heritage is European, our mentality is European" (MP, parliamentary majority). It is argued, therefore, that Georgians need to reactivate this mentality and the EU should help them to do so through the abovementioned process of mental modernization. Accordingly, mental modernization seems to be Georgia's civilizational choice as the country faces two alternatives: a positive pole is represented by Europe with its normative power and democratic performance, while a negative one by Russia as Europe's Other with its military power and undemocratic performance. Such a vision is well evidenced by one of the MP's words from the parliamentary majority stating that "Russia comes with force and destruction, while Europe comes with suggestions and it is up to you to accept or reject them. Besides, if we compare what happens in Russia and how it treats its citizens to how Europe treats its citizens, it is easy to make a decision, which one we would like to resemble." This quote illustrates that Georgia's European choice is considered indisputable, as there is a confidence about who "we would like to resemble." In this context, European democracy is usually juxtaposed with the Russian authoritarian regime, the European educational system with the Russian one whose quality is questionable, while the European constructive power with the Russian destructive one. The abovementioned quote also confirms the introductory statement that Georgia's European integration is predominantly viewed in the light of human rights' protection and defense against Russian threats, primarily via strengthening its democratic capacity.

We might naturally assume that because Georgia attempts to resemble Europe and such an attempt represents its civilizational choice, the main strategy for achieving this goal is socialization, which implies that the local actors see the advantages of European standards and do their best to embrace them in order to introduce desirable changes (Sedelmeier 2011, 15; Schimmelfennig 2012, 8). Surprisingly, it does not seem the case, as Z-Score variance shows that not only the population and NGO representatives but also the MPs and government officials doubt that Georgia would implement the present reforms without the EU's demands. Although the interviewed MPs and government officials try to offer socially desirable discourses declaring that EU standards are implemented because they are vital for the country's progress, the Q analysis reveals that they still acknowledge that EU demands represent the main driver for implementing them. This tendency is even more visible in the interview conversations, which sound rather ambiguous: On the one hand, the parliamentary majority and government representatives underline that "if not the EU, we could have recognized the need for these reforms and implemented them ourselves;" while on the other hand, they note that "EU demands accelerate certain things, . . . without them we might not have dared to risk, while the EU pushes us to do so" (MP, parliamentary majority). The passage sounds as if personal initiative and external demands harmoniously coexisted. The use of the word risk in relation to reforms is also noteworthy. We can infer that the ongoing reforms are perceived as somewhat risky and if not the push by the EU, the country might have not dared to implement them.

That Georgian politicians consider the abovementioned risk harmful to their political career is represented by an attempt to blame unpopular reforms upon the EU. According to one of the MPs, approximation with the EU implies the introduction of new regulations in all the spheres followed by new obligations, "which cannot be pleasant to anyone, especially at the initial stage." Thus, there is an attempt to avoid the responsibility for ongoing unpleasant reforms by stressing that it is not the local government's decision but the one of the EU. This also means the recognition (even if not properly realized) of the leading role of conditionality (Sedelmeier 2011, 12; Schimmelfennig 2012, 8) in pushing the current reforms. Another MP from the parliamentary majority acknowledges the EU's role in stimulating the present reforms with a complex rhetoric stressing the importance of both EU demands and the desire to catch up with the EU. As noted, "principles and standards such as defense of human rights and the like come from the Western civilization, are part of the Western development process, so we should adopt them from there. This is what we actually do. Approximation with the EU and the association agreement agenda require the implementation of certain standards. We follow some, try to catch up with others, and might even be ahead in certain instances, while the EU helps us to correctly identify and clearly see our priorities." This once again confirms that Georgian political elites view the adoption of EU standards in the light of DI, as even the implementation of basic democratic principles such as protection of human rights is believed to be embedded in the Western civilization. Accordingly, Georgia makes a major civilizational choice to ensure its democratic development. It is stated that the EU does not impose civilizational standards on the country but only assists it "to correctly identify and clearly see" its priorities, which rejects the recognition of conditionality but it still stresses the role of self-conditionality or what is called normative emulation (Börzel and Lebanidze 2015, 19), as Georgia is so motivated to pursue EU standards that it is even "ahead in certain instances," and hence overdoes EU conditionality. The role of conditionality, although openly rejected, is also reflected in the following observation: "Georgia implements the reforms not because someone dictates something from outside but because it is necessary for our wellbeing. This dictation can only have an encouraging effect" (government official). Thus, the respondent initially refuses to recognize the dictated character of EU reforms though later acknowledges the encouraging effect of such a dictation. The ambivalence is further reinforced by the discourse of forced socialization represented by one of the MP's abovementioned words that "the legislation will provide the framework for us to gradually learn how to respect others." Although the enforced learning of respect looks more like conditionality than socialization, the most important aspect is its pedagogical function. It seems the participants view socialization and conditionality as the mutually reinforcing processes believing that it is conditionality that should encourage the learning of certain norms and standards. This idea was also reflected in another government official's words discussed above, according to whom, "those who cannot learn tolerance themselves, will be taught it by force." Thus, the forced teaching of respect and tolerance is considered the only strategy for those who cannot learn them otherwise. Consequently, we get an impression that the Georgian model for enacting Europeanization is understood as a complex mixture of conditionality and socialization.

Whatever the driving force for implementing the reforms, the interviewed MPs and government officials' proudly underline the EU's recognition of Georgia's superiority over other EaP countries. Even the parliamentary minority representatives, who often criticize the ruling party for lacking pro-European sentiments and being reluctant to implement EU reforms, still emphasize that Georgia is far ahead of its EaP counterparts. Georgia is called an excellent student fulfilling its assignments so well that "the EU embarrassingly distinguishes it even from other EaP countries with association agreements such as Ukraine and Moldova" (government official). This is a particularly widespread discourse among the members of parliamentary majority, who might even stress that "whenever there are discussions at the parliamentary assembly, whether in regard to freedom of speech, human rights, political prisoners, etc., Georgia has nothing to discuss any more, as it faces more advanced issues, which are rather value-based, identity issues and represent a further step in the level of development (MP, parliamentary majority)." The presented discourse depicts Georgia as an advanced democracy, which has successfully solved and thus moved beyond the issues of defending various freedoms, including human rights. The author argues that as self-expression values (Inglehart and Welzel, 2005) are already effectively addressed, currently Georgia faces only more complex identity issues that mark a further step in its development. As Georgia is believed to be showing considerable achievements in terms of following the DI model, no wonder its political elites expect the EU not only to recognize such a progress but also to treat it differently from other EaP countries. One might often hear in the discourses of parliamentary majority that "the EaP's current format is already outdated as it has become too asymmetrical and the issues faced by particular countries do not overlap." Even the representatives of parliamentary minority, who are highly critical of the ruling party's performance in regard to implementing EU reforms, adopt a similar rhetoric of nesting orientalism (Bakić-Hayden 1995) and state that Georgia deserves more recognition and a differential treatment by the EU; therefore, "the EU should offer it a new format for collaboration, something in-between the association and candidacy." Thus, it seems Georgia's political elites think of inventing a new framework for the EU-Georgia partnership that has not been introduced before and would mark the EU's unique approach toward Georgia. Moreover, some officials underline that Georgia has higher ambitions and can even compete with the Western Balkans in terms of its scale of Europeanization. It is easy to guess the main motivation behind this competition. As the Western Balkan countries are the candidates for EU membership, competing with them would mean that Georgia also deserves to be considered a candidate for future membership.

No wonder such high expectations result in certain disappointment caused by the EU's lack of attention toward Georgia. Alongside stating that the EU "embarrassingly distinguishes" Georgia from other EaP countries, the same representatives of political and also intellectual elites regretfully note that Georgia's integration with the EU and especially its membership "is not really dependent on the implementation of reforms but is the EU's political decision" (government official), which is less related to the developments within Georgia but more to those within the EU (NGO representative, developmental sector). Moreover, it is argued that "only the implementation of required reforms is not sufficient because of Georgia's geographic location and problematic relations with Russia" (MP, parliamentary minority). The latter is considered the main obstacle on the way to not only Georgia's progress toward EU membership but also its acquisition of intermediary rewards. The respondents argue that the EU tries to avoid displeasing Russia, but it has to reward Georgia in order not to break its word and discredit itself. As noted by one of the MPs from parliamentary majority, "Georgia excellently performs its duties, while the EU, despite lacking the desire to do so, is forced to reward it, as otherwise it would mean it has broken its word." The granting of visa liberalization to Georgia is considered an example of such a forced reward. Another MP from the ruling party shares the same opinion arguing that the EU did not expect that Georgia would follow EU demands to such an extent and now it looks confused; as it cannot offer the main reward, that is EU membership, it does not know what intermediary rewards to offer after granting the country visa liberalization. Taking into consideration the abovementioned, no wonder it is stated that Georgia somehow "remains in the shade, which does not mean that the EU does not value it at all but at this point it is perceived as a less valuable partner" (NGO representative, developmental sector); therefore, the country should not really expect the EU's differential treatment and should not hope that even in the case of implementing reforms faster than the EU member states themselves, it will be offered its membership (NGO representative, foreign policy sector). In fact, the same vision has been revealed by the Q analysis that shows a fusion of optimistic and pessimistic views regarding the EU's treatment of Georgia. As illustrated by one of the leading factors consisting of a rather heterogeneous group of political and intellectual elites, despite the highest positive value of the statements on the EU's role in improving human rights' protection and safeguarding the country's security, there are also profound doubts that Georgia can really hope for the EU's help when it itself faces lots of internal issues; neither it is believed that Georgia will ever be granted EU membership. Thus, we encounter rather ambivalent perceptions of the EU's simultaneous attention and inattention, distinguished treatment and neglect of Georgia, which reveals that the study participants are concerned about the country's asymmetrical dependence on the EU.

This concern can be better understood in the light of Georgia's prospects of differentiation as the most visible sign of the EU-Georgia asymmetry. The EU's differentiation usually takes two forms: Exemptions and discrimination (Zhelyazkova et al. 2015). While the former unburdens the new member and accession countries from certain obligations that the old members have, the latter deprives them of the benefits of membership. No wonder, these countries attempt to obtain exemptions and avoid discrimination (Zhelyazkova et al. 2015, 21). We can say that such an attempt is even more manifest in the case of associated countries lacking a membership perspective. Evidence shows that smaller countries with stronger economies and better governance capacities that show more Eurosceptic attitudes are less likely to be discriminated and more likely to benefit from the EU's exemptions than larger countries with poor economies and weaker governance capacities expressing pro-European sentiments (Zhelyazkova et al. 2015, 29). Georgia's small size can hardly counterbalance its poor economy and weak governance capacity, and is less likely to help it obtain benefits and avoid discrimination, especially even if its EU-supportive attitudes (according to the CRRC's 2017 survey on Knowledge of and Attitudes toward the EU in Georgia, more than 70 percent of the population supported the country's European integration) cannot be considered an asset. Therefore, the country's asymmetrical dependence on the EU is expected to be quite prolonged feeding Georgians' respective concerns.

Such an asymmetrical dependence is most painfully perceived when it comes to Russian threats. To use Diez' typology of othering (2005, 628), Russia as Georgia's Other is represented in the Georgian political and popular discourses as its existential threat, as violating universal (democratic) principles, as different from and also inferior to Georgia in terms of its democratic aspirations and values. Russia's status as Other was and still remains sharp not only in Georgia and other EaP countries with association agreements, but also in the new, post-socialist EU member states. However, evidence shows that the same sentiments are not shared by the elites from the founding member states. Studies demonstrate that twice as high a portion of elites from the post-socialist countries (60 percent) perceives Russia as a big threat to Europe as that from the EU founding states (30 percent) (Matonyte and Morkevicius 2012, 103). This difference is explained by both territorial proximity and historical past of the post-socialist countries, "whose elites define the Russian threat . . . in harsh terms as an existential threat (securitization), adding that Russia transgresses the universal principles of human rights, democracy, etc." (Matonyte and Morkevicius 2012, 103). Thus, Georgians' concerns related to Russian threats are similar to those of the new EU Member States that, as noted above, are less shared by the founding and more powerful member states, who are perceived as the EU's key decision makers. That is why the representatives of Georgian political and intellectual elites regretfully note that Georgians do not have much choice but to cautiously wait for further developments when Russia progresses with its "creeping occupation," while the EU only formally expresses its displeasure and disappointment, and no action is followed (government official). Moreover, some officials even state that the EU perceives Georgia as Russia's backyard, as Russia itself does (government official). Therefore, Georgians should not hope too much for the EU's support. In addition, it is believed that the major powerful actors have already divided their areas of influence and no one is a good fellow, but then everyone attempts to consolidate and increase one's own power (government official). There is no hope, in the study participants' words, that in these power games the EU confronts Russia because of small and minor Georgia. Thus, based on such a vision, Georgia encounters a double power asymmetry with Russia and the EU, with the former representing an existential threat to the country and the latter being unwilling to defend it from this threat. In this context, the status insecurity becomes especially problematic, that is, an uncertainty caused by Georgia's geopolitical location as a contested space between the EU and Russia, its foreign policy aspirations that clash with the Russian plans to drag the post-Soviet countries into the Eurasian Economic Union as an alternative to the EU, and finally, its "detachment from international institutions" that makes Georgia's ambition of being a Europe quite uncertain, rather ensuring the status of "a 'Europe in between' located at the edge of competing spheres of influence" (Webber 2007, 5).

Georgia's status insecurity is also clearly reflected in the population's discourses on Russian threats and the EU's perceived role in safeguarding the country against them. The focus group participants from all the regions acknowledge that Georgia needs the EU to ensure its security that, based on the Q analysis, is considered one of the major pragmatic gains resulting from the country's European integration. However, concurrently they doubt that the EU can really safeguard Georgia against Russian threats, which is again voiced by citizens from each region and each age category. Their main concern is that "while Russia continues its terror, the EU representatives only condemn Russia's actions declaring that they are in dismay" (Female, 26–40, Batumi). Another participant questions the EU's ability to safeguard Georgia by asking: "Can the EU's disappointment with Russia's actions really save us? Before the EU decides how to act, Russia will just swallow us" (Male, 41–65, Kutaisi). In order to avoid "being swallowed" by Russia, the participants advise Georgian politicians to be diplomatic and not to irritate it, especially because they believe that Russia represents a threat to not only Georgia but also the EU itself, which usually unsuccessfully challenges Russia's soft and hard power (Female, 18–25, Kutaisi). Georgia can hardly count, therefore, on the EU, which will not further complicate its tense relations with Russia because of insignificant and powerless Georgia.

To summarize the participants' discourses on securitization, we encounter rather ambivalent views: They both believe and doubt that the EU can act as Georgia's safeguard against Russian threats. This ambivalence pushes the participants to argue that Georgia should use a thoughtful diplomatic approach toward both Russia and the EU: The former should not be shown Georgians' special hostility in order not to irritate it, while the latter should be often reminded of Georgians' special pro-European sentiments in order to invoke its motivation to truly safeguard the country against Russian threats. Thus, it seems Georgians try to overstate their pro-European sentiments in the light of Russian threats. This is how performative practices become intertwined with securitization: In order to avoid both existential and status insecurity, Georgians try to downplay their negative sentiments toward Russia and overplay their positive sentiments toward the EU.

National Identity Concerns

Alongside the elites and citizens' pragmatic perspectives on European integration viewed in the light of human rights' defense and Georgia's security against Russian threats, the impact of European integration on the national identity and traditions is one of the most actively discussed topics. Based on Q analysis, the statement that European integration threatens Georgian traditions represents the ultimate negative pole, which means that the study participants (both elites and population) evaluate it as the most significant statement to which they highly disagree. This is quite an unexpected result in the case of population as, according to the CRRC's representative surveys on Knowledge of and Attitudes toward the EU in Georgia (2009–2015) it used to be the main identity concern for Georgians. The CRRC's recent surveys showed a declining trend in this attitude: while the 2015 wave revealed that 45 percent of the population thought that European integration threatened Georgian traditions, the portion of those sharing this view fell to 25 percent in 2017. This might be related to the fact that in March 2017 Georgia was granted visa liberalization, the citizens directly felt the benefits of free movement, and the myth of Georgian identity and traditions being threatened by the EU was contested. As illustrated above, despite certain decline, a quarter of the population still feared the EU's negative impact on the Georgian identity. Therefore, the fact that the statement on European integration threatening Georgian traditions occupied an ultimate negative pole not only in the political and intellectual elites but also the population's Q grids was quite surprising. Despite this, as the subsequent discussion shows, the questions related to the national identity invoke rather ambivalent discourses among the study participants, likewise in the case of the above-mentioned pragmatic factors related to human rights and Russian threats.

There is a general agreement that the impact of European integration on national identity raises particular concerns among citizens, especially in the new member and aspirant states. However, it is also recognized that "with reference to identity, Europeanness sometimes appears in implausible and contradictory combinations" (Conti 2012, 198). While one might expect that Europeanness be considered in contradiction to national culture and sovereignty, evidence shows that the new member states of Central and Eastern Europe often refer to the European culture and values as a means of fostering their national identity and sovereignty (Best 2012a). The studies reveal "a strong convergence between emotive ties to the national and European focus of identity, indicating a mutual reinforcement of these ties" (Best 2012a, 232). Presumably, it is the reason why the discourse of returning to the European Family was so prominent in the Eastern enlargement countries attempting to get rid of the remnants of the socialist past (Kuus 2007; Melegh 2006). The discourse of returning to the European Family is also quite strong in the EaP countries with association agreements, even those with a rather questionable European status such as Georgia (Tsuladze et al. 2016). Thus, we might encounter a paradoxical reality when European integration is concurrently viewed in terms of threatening and promoting national culture and traditions. Attempting to explain rather ambiguous perceptions related to the relationship between national and European identities, especially in the new member states (we can also add here the EaP countries), it is argued that "a concurrent emphasis on European culture and national identity – particularly in the new member states – primarily represents an attempt to mark the distance of own country/nation from the out-group of non-Europeans, more than being a genuine devotion to the EU and to its attempts to build a European citizenship rooted in a set of EU-led values" (Conti 2012, 198). Indeed, gaining a European status might be a means of distancing oneself from what is believed to be non-Europe or Europe's Other as with Georgians' perceptions of Russia. It might also be a useful means to overcome a positional and status insecurity characteristic of in-between countries with a rather questionable European status and an asymmetrical dependence on the powerful EU players. In addition, it might be a means of stressing own progress on the modernization scale in terms of democratic and mental modernization. No doubt, all of these pragmatic considerations do matter in the course of Georgia's European integration. However, to refer to the above quote, the question is whether they signify a genuine devotion to the EU or the EU-led values (even if these values might represent "liberal humanitarian utopias" (Melegh 2006, 2)) and whether they imply a close interconnection between the European and Georgian identities.

According to the political and intellectual elites involved in our research, Georgian values and traditions are in compliance with those of Europe and Georgia naturally belongs to the European Family. Three main points are provided in support to this argument. Firstly, Georgia's belonging to the European Family is justified by its Christian heritage and it is argued that "European values are in fact Christian values and hence European integration cannot threaten Georgian Orthodox values" (MP, parliamentary majority). It is even stated that "the values promoted by Christianity are the closest to European values such as benevolence, solidarity, and humanism" (MP, parliamentary majority). As a Christian country Georgia is believed to inherently possess these virtues, "on which later European culture and the EU were based" (MP, parliamentary minority). Thus, it is delicately noted that as "European values are in fact Christian values," while Georgia adopted Christianity earlier than the European countries did, Georgia had even preceded Europe and the EU in following these values. Besides sharing a common Christian worldview, another argument for representing Georgia as a country with European values is stressing that "what is valued here is also valued there" (government official), usually supported by the argument on Georgians' inborn tolerance, which has been discussed in the context of human rights' defense. As noted above, it is recognized that this tolerance has been somehow forgotten as a result of Soviet rule but it is believed that it will be recollected in the process of Georgia's Europeanization. Despite the fact that the two discussed arguments seem closely related, they still have two diverse foci. The first one is based on what Thomas Risse (2010) considers a primordial identity discourse, while the second one on what he defines as a sacred identity discourse, which is not founded on religious considerations but on the locals' perception of EU norms and values as somewhat sacred. From this perspective, membership of the European family is not an outcome of the Christian culture but the internalization of liberal democratic values. Finally, Georgians' "historical aspiration to be European" that is considered an inseparable part of their existence or inner nature (MP, parliamentary majority) is believed to be one of the main reasons for their belonging to the European Family. Various examples from the history of Georgia are brought to support this argument stressing that "everyone who is familiar with the [Georgian] literature of the nineteenth century or the beginning of the twentieth century knows that Europe was that natural space where we were supposed to belong" (MP, parliamentary majority). Again, the Russian occupation and the Soviet rule are believed to hinder this aspiration.

It is these three aspects – Christian values, tolerance and historical aspiration toward Europeanness – that are believed to be the main reasons why the Georgian mentality is a European mentality and even the Russian domination could not change it. In fact, Russia's negative impact is recognized, especially in terms of causing "the slowdown of our democratic and liberal development, so now we have to regain these values," but it is stated that "our society bears European values so naturally that all the attempts to make it deviate from these values are futile, and hence it is a member of the European Family" (MP, parliamentary minority). Therefore, no danger of the European values' negative impact on Georgian traditions is envisaged, rather some kind of Europeanized nationalism gleams through the above lines, which is especially manifest in the argument of European integration being a means of preserving the Georgian identity and values: "Europe is a unity of the countries with rich traditions and when this Europe opens its doors to you, it means you preserve your identity, sovereignty, and common values" (NGO representative, developmental sector). Representing European values as a threat to the Georgian identity is believed to be part of anti-European propaganda mainly referred to as the Russian propaganda (MP, parliamentary minority) or the Russian fake news (NGO representative, foreign policy sector). Furthermore, there is even a viewpoint that in the course of Georgia's Europeanization its traditions should change and this is a highly positive process, as "the transformation of traditions is the only natural event that ensures a nation's survival and development, and safeguards it against the stagnation" (NGO representative, educational sector). Thus, European integration viewed as a process of returning to the European Family is perceived as a means of preserving the Georgian identity and traditions, as well as reviving the common (national and European) values. As an additional effect, it also implies the defeat of Russia's anti-European propaganda and the avoidance of the country's stagnation through "the increased opportunity of interacting with different cultures and getting familiar with diverse traditions" (NGO representative, foreign policy sector).

Despite the abovementioned positive outlook, the representatives of political elite still provide quite ambivalent discourses on European values, in which two main arguments can be identified: according to one discourse, there is nothing special about European values and such an excessive emphasis on them is "just invented" (MP, parliamentary majority). In this context, the participants again refer to Georgians' inborn tolerance and aspiration for freedom stressing that "European values imply nothing else but the appreciation of freedom and tolerance, which in fact represent two virtues that are most valued by Georgians" (government official). Thus, it is believed that Georgians naturally possess European values and hence such a buzz around them is redundant (which is indirectly reflected in the sacred identity discourse). Another argument refers to the country's history to prove that Georgia decided to follow European values and thus made its European choice even prior to the establishment of the EU (which is also indirectly reflected in the abovementioned primordial identity discourse); therefore, it does not need to be taught

European values: "When the first Georgian republic was established one hundred years ago and when the EU and NATO did not exist at all, the Georgian people already decided to create a European state" (MP, parliamentary minority). This argument is quite common to Georgian political elites and was even openly declared by the Head of Parliament Davit Usupashvili in 2015: "Georgia used to be Europe even before Europe knew it was Europe." It seems Georgian political elites use the same primordial and sacred identity discourses to both justify and resist the argument about the Georgians' need to be taught European values.

The population's assessment of the compliance of Georgian and European values is quite close to the views of political and intellectual elites. According to the study participants, Georgia and Europe share common values and one of the main arguments to justify it, like in the case of political and intellectual elites, is the emphasis on the shared Christian worldview. As Georgia has a long Christian tradition, the participants think that Georgians can even share "something authentic" with Europeans: "The EU is a union of Christian countries. Our old Christian culture has created something authentic we can share with Europeans" (Male, 26–40, Batumi). Another argument has to do with certain virtues characteristic to both Georgians and Europeans. Here again the main focus is on tolerance promoted by the EU and it is proudly announced that "Georgians are famous for their tolerance" (Male, 41–65, Kutaisi), thus emphasizing that tolerance is the value shared by Europeans and Georgians. The final argument has to do with Georgians' inborn Europeanness that can be traced back in the thirteenth century, the epoch of King Tamar, and naturally makes Georgia a member of the European Family (Female, 41–65, Zugdidi). It is argued that although "the Russian domination has caused certain stagnation, the people's motivation [to return to the European Family] is so strong that we are gradually catching up" (Male, 41–65, Tbilisi). Thus, it is obvious that the DI perspectives are incorporated even in the discourses of national identity and values. It is also noticeable that the citizens' arguments of Georgians' Europeanness directly echo the ones of political and intellectual elites. Likewise, they share certain reservations regarding European values resulting in rather ambivalent discourses. However, the citizens' perspectives differ from the elites' in that they do not state that Georgia used to follow European values even prior to Europe itself, rather the other way around – they are concerned that Georgians lack an authentic devotion to European values, which is expressed even in minor details such as throwing garbage in the streets or violating traffic rules (Female, 18–25, Gori). The representatives of each region and each age group state that unless Georgians learn how to follow the established rules and show a full compliance with "mental Europeanness" (Male, 26–40, Telavi), there will be only a performative pursuit of European values. One might get an impression that the study participants are highly self-critical and worry about Georgians' superficial compliance with European norms. However, the same participants express their concerns that the dissemination of European liberal values might be harmful to Georgian traditions.

It should be noted that while talking about European liberal values the representatives of all regions and age groups refer primarily to homosexual relations, which they consider detrimental to Georgian family traditions. The following passage is probably one of the best examples of the widespread discourse that Georgians "are fast in learning harmful things" and therefore, when it comes to lifestyle, they should be cautious of taking after Europeans: "I am not against anyone, but I do not agree . . . They [homosexuals] should not be provocative; it should not be infectious. New generations are raised with these ideas and everyone fears what might happen to a Georgian family" (Female, 26–40, Kutaisi). In the participant's view, homosexuality might be infectious and hence harmful to the new generation. However, in order to make sure that she does not leave an impression of discriminating against sexual minorities, the participant starts with a positive statement ("I am not against"), which is immediately followed by a disclaimer ("but"). It is a good example of how the discourse on national vis-à-vis European values is organized by both "underlying norms" (one should not discriminate against dissimilar groups) and "ambiguous attitudes" (though these groups might be harmful) (van Dijk 2013, 187). In fact, this duality is expressed in all the participants' discourses fearing a negative impact of liberal values (viewed in the light of promoting homosexual relations) on the Georgian society. Moreover, homosexual relations are considered so incompatible with the Georgian lifestyle and traditions, that it is believed that Georgians may only pretend they welcome homosexuals in order to perform their own tolerance: "Even if we declare we like homosexuals, deep in our heart we don't. They cannot fit our traditions" (Female, 26–40, Zugdidi). Even those who acknowledge that homosexual relations have certainly previously existed in Georgia stress that they "have not been on display," while alongside Georgia's Europeanization they become public. That such publicity is considered unacceptable is evident from the following rhetoric: "Do we arrange demonstrations that we are males and want females?" (Male, 26–40, Zugdidi) or "It was also happening before, but today it is extreme. If you want to take after Europe, why don't you adopt something normal?" (Female, 41–65, Telavi). Thus, the publicizing of homosexual relations is promptly ascribed to Europe and because the Georgians' attempt to take after Europe is considered natural, they are instructed to at least adopt something normal – the category that cannot accommodate homosexual relations. Considering such a vision it is not surprising that the target population has revealed negative perspectives on the anti-discrimination law viewed as being introduced solely for the protection of homosexuals' rights. It should be noted though that the youngest target group (18–25) has expressed far more permissive attitudes in this regard than the older participants. Moreover, the youngest participants even state that the generation raised in the Soviet period and characterized by the Soviet nostalgia is the main obstacle to the real enactment of European values in the Georgian society, which can only count on the younger generation with European education in terms of succeeding with mental modernization (Male, 18–25, Tbilisi).

Conclusion

To return to our initial question of what Georgian political and intellectual elites and population consider desirable and undesirable outcomes of Georgia's European integration, three main aspects have been revealed based on both quantitative and qualitative components of the research. Two of them represent pragmatic considerations related to the impact of European integration on the protection of human rights and the defense of Georgia against Russian threats; while the third one represents the identity concern related to the impact of European integration on the Georgian identity and values. The research has revealed that both pragmatic and identity considerations related to the country's European integration invoke rather ambivalent views among the population and elites in Georgia.

The findings show that the participants expect significant achievements resulting from Georgia's European integration in terms of both improved protection of human rights and increased security against Russian threats. Based on Q analysis, these are two statements with the highest positive correlation among the target elites and population. The ultimate negative pole is represented by the statement that European integration threatens Georgian traditions, which means that the participants do not envisage value-based, identity threats stemming from the country's Europeanization. However, a look behind the statement rankings and an in-depth analysis of both political and popular discourses reveal a rather complicated picture, which might represent an outbreak of little nationalism embedded in Europeanization; it is believed that Georgia has been historically tolerant, and hence does not need to be taught tolerance and respect to human rights by the EU. Furthermore, it is regretfully noted that the EU does not really express its readiness to safeguard Georgia against Russian threats, as it is unwilling to complicate its relations with Russia because of small and minor Georgia. The participants note that the EU's expression of merely displeasure or disappointment whenever Russia progresses with its occupation of Georgian territories points to the fact that the EU should not be expected to confront Russia. Finally, despite claiming that Georgians had been sharing European values long before they decided to integrate with the EU, and hence believing that they naturally belong to the European Family, the participants fear that the European liberal values endorsing homosexual relations might be harmful to Georgian family traditions.

Thus, the abovementioned discussions reveal Georgians' ambivalence regarding the European integration process. They both attempt to be instructed and reject the need to be taught by the EU; they both perceive the EU as Georgia's security guarantee and doubt that it can really safeguard the country against Russian threats; they both believe that Georgia shares European values and are concerned that European values might threaten Georgian traditions. Such an ambiguity related to both pragmatic and identity factors points to Georgia's status insecurity vis-à-vis the EU making its ambition of being a Europe quite uncertain, rather ensuring the status of "a Europe in between." Therefore, in the ongoing process of European integration

Georgia needs to find a way to obtain a European status, which can only be achieved via an effective implementation of the DI model with its accompanying mental modernization. Indeed, our participants argue that it is through the process of mental modernization that Georgia should reactivate its European mentality and return to its European Family abandoned as a result of the Russian occupation back in the nineteenth century. This is how Georgians reinvent Europe that accommodates Georgia as its member and invent their own Europeanness.

Funding

This work was supported by Shota Rustaveli National Science Foundation of Georgia (SRNSFG) (grant FR17_91).

References

Bakić-Hayden, Milica. 1995. "Nesting orientalisms: The case of former Yugoslavia." *Slavic Review* 54(4): 917–931.

Best, Henrich. 2012a. "Elite foundations of European integration: A causal analysis." In *The Europe of Elites: A Study into the Europeanness of Europe's Political and Economic Elites*, edited by Henrich Best, Gyorgy Lengyel, and Luca Verzichelli, 208–233. Oxford: Oxford University Press.

Best, Henrich. 2012b. "Elites of Europe and the Europe of elites: A conclusion." In *The Europe of Elites: A Study into the Europeanness of Europe's Political and Economic Elites*, edited by Henrich Best, Gyorgy Lengyel, and Luca Verzichelli, 234–241. Oxford: Oxford University Press.

Börzel, Tanja, and Bidzina Lebanidze. 2015. "European Neighbourhood Policy at the crossroads: Evaluating the past to shape the future." *MAXCAP Working Paper Series*, No. 12. www.maxcap-project.eu.

Brusis, Martin. 2001. "European and national identities in the accession countries: The role of the European Union." In *National and European Identities in the EU Enlargement: Views from Central and Eastern European Countries*, edited by Petr Drulak, 195–207. Prague: Institute of International Relations.

Carey, Sean. 2002. "Undivided loyalties: Is national identity an obstacle to European integration?" *European Union Politics* 3(4): 388–413.

Chakrabarty, Dipesh, ed. 2000. *Provincializing Europe, Postcolonial Thought and Historical Difference*. Princeton, NJ: Princeton University Press.

Conti, Nicolo. 2012. "Party elites and the domestic discourse on the EU." In *The Europe of Elites: A Study into the Europeanness of Europe's Political and Economic Elites*, edited by Henrich Best, Gyorgy Lengyel, and Luca Verzichelli, 192–207. Oxford: Oxford University Press.

CRRC Georgia. 2009–2017. "Knowledge of and attitudes toward the EU in Georgia." www.crrc.org.

Delanty, Gerard. 1995. *Inventing Europe: Idea, Identity, Reality*. London: Palgrave Macmillan.

della Porta, Donatella, and Manuela Caiani. 2009. *Social Movements and Europeanization*. Oxford: Oxford University Press.

Diez, Thomas. 2005. "Constructing the self and changing others: Reconsidering 'normative power Europe'." *Millennium: Journal of International Studies* 33(3): 613–636.

Dimitrova, Antoaneta. 2015. "The effectiveness and limitations of political integration in Central and Eastern European member states: Lessons from Bulgaria and Romania." *MAXCAP Working Paper Series*, No. 10. www.maxcap-project.eu.

Doyle, Orla, and Jan Fidrmuc. 2006. "Who favors enlargement?: Determinants of support for EU membership in the candidate countries' referenda." *European Journal of Political Economy* 22 (2): 520–543.

Hooghe, Liesbet, and Gary Marks. 2008. "A postfunctionalist theory of European integration: From permissive consensus to constraining dissensus." *British Journal of Political Science* 39(1): 1–23.

Inglehart, Ronald, and Christian Welzel. 2005. *Modernization, Cultural Change, and Democracy.* Cambridge: Cambridge University Press.

Kuus, Merje. 2007. *Geopolitics Reframed: Security and Identity in Europe's Eastern Enlargement.* New York: Palgrave Macmillan.

Manners, Ian. 2002. "Normative power Europe: A contradiction in terms?" *Journal of Common Market Studies* 40(2): 235–258.

Matonyte, Irmina, and Vaidas Morkevicius. 2012. "The other side of European identity: Elite perceptions of threats to a cohesive Europe." In *The Europe of Elites: A Study into the Europeanness of Europe's Political and Economic Elites*, edited by Henrich Best, Gyorgy Lengyel, and Luca Verzichelli, 94–121. Oxford: Oxford University Press.

Melegh, Attila. 2006. *On the East-West Slope: Globalization, Nationalism, Racism and Discourses on Central and Eastern Europe.* Budapest: Central European University Press.

Melegh, Attila, Anna Vancsó, Márton Hunyadi, and Dorottya Mendly. 2019. "Positional insecurity and the hegemony of radical nationalism: Migration and justice in the Hungarian media." *The International Spectator* 54(3): 54–71.

Nanz, Patrizia Isabelle. 2000. "In-between nations: Ambivalence and the making of a European identity." In *Europe and the Other, Europe as the Other*, edited by Bo Stråth, 279–309. Brussels: Peter Lang.

Neumann, Iver B. 1998. "Russia as Europe's other." *Journal of Contemporary European Studies* 6 (12): 26–73.

Risse, Thomas. 2010. *A Community of Europeans? Transnational Identities and Public Spheres.* Ithaca, NY: Cornell University Press.

Schimmelfennig, Frank. 2012. "Europeanization beyond Europe." *Living Reviews in European Governance* 7(1): 5–31.

Sedelmeier, Ulrich. 2011. "Europeanisation in new member and candidate states." *Living Reviews in European Governance* 6(1): 5–52.

Thornton, Arland, Shawn F. Dorius, and Jeffrey Swindle. 2015. "Developmental idealism: The cultural foundations of World Development Programs." *Sociology of Development* 1(2): 277–320.

Toshkov, Dimiter, Elitsa Kortenska, Antoaneta Dimitrova, and Adam Fagan. 2014. "The 'old' and the 'new' Europeans: Analyses of public opinion on EU enlargement in review." *MAXCAP Working Paper Series*, No. 2. www.maxcap-project.eu.

Tsuladze, Lia, Flora Esebua, Irakli Kakhidze, Ana Kvintradze, Irina Osepashvili, and Mariam Amashukeli. 2016. *Performing Europeanization: Political vis-à-vis Popular Discourses on Europeanization in Georgia.* Tbilisi: Nekeri.

Usupashvili, Davit. 2015. "Georgia used to be Europe even before Europe knew it was Europe." *Pirvelirnews*, 5 June, http://pirveliradio.ge/index.php?newsid=46926.

van Dijk, Teun A. 2013. "Ideology and discourse." In *The Oxford Handbook of Political Ideologies*, edited by Michael Freeden, Sargent, Lyman Tower, and Marc Stears, 175–196. Oxford: Oxford University Press.

Webber, Mark. 2007. *Inclusion, Exclusion and the Governance of European Security*. Manchester: Manchester University Press.

Wolff, Larry. 1994. *Inventing Eastern Europe*. Stanford, CA: Stanford University Press.

Zhelyazkova, Asya, Tanja Börzel, Frank Schimmelfennig, and Ulrich Sedelmeier. 2015. "Beyond uniform integration? Researching the effects of enlargement on the EU's legal system." *MAXCAP Working Paper Series*, No. 8. www.maxcap-project.eu.

Biljana Vankovska

8 Guiding Macedonia to the EU: Walking Over European Values

The vast theoretical literature concerning the European Union enlargement process has been remarkably politically correct for quite some time. The conventional wisdom is that the EU is a force of peace and good (something that was affirmed even with a Nobel Peace Prize in 2012), as well as a regional and global actor with normative power seeking to spread values and good governance principles in problematic societies and failed states (Whitman 2011). Scholars who dare to take a more critical approach, usually risking being black-listed and treated as reactionary and/or nationalistic, remain a minority; in this small circle, academic freedom and critical thinking are reserved almost exclusively for the Western authors (or authors affiliated with Western universities). The ones coming from democratically less developed countries, particularly those which are EU candidates, tend to stick to mainstream opinions and knowledge production so they will be welcome (or at least, not ostracized). Accordingly, the essential question coming to mind, alongside the ideas offered by Hamid Dabashi (2019) and Gayatri Chakravorty Spivak (1988) is: Are people from non-EU states allowed to speak their mind? Or better, are those who inhabit the periphery being heard? This is not to say that there are no academic studies that meticulously detect the shortcomings of the EU enlargement process or deficiencies of the EU per se (Chandler 2000, Gillingham 2016, Woodward 2017). However, the blame for the failures is usually attached to the locals and their incapacity or unwillingness to reform (Bieber 2020). Even if there are undeniable failures on the side of the EU and/or other internationals, they are met with benevolent interpretations of unintentional mistakes and objective obstacles to the well-intentioned plans. The scholars who expose the EU and the world system to a radical critique are a tiny minority (Böröcz and Kovács 2001; Fouskas and Gökay 2019; Lapavitsas 2018; Pugh 2017; Streeck 2016).

The methodological approach applied to this study is grounded in postcolonial theory. Building upon the work of Edward Said's notion of orientalism and Maria Todorova's understanding of the Balkans, the key idea is to point out that European integration is a continuation of the old colonial spirit transformed into a soft imperialism (economic, political, and administrative). In fact, the interlinkage between European integration and colonialism has been increasingly acknowledged in the scholarly literature (Ahmed 2000; Bhambra 2009; Kinnvall 2016). For example, Dabashi (2019) deals with Europe as an allegory and traces how the condition of coloniality persists even after the collapse of empires. Undeniably, almost all European nations had their own imperial experience whether they were the founders of empires or parts of larger imperial structures (Harris and Lévai 2008, xi). David Chandler (2006) argues that the modern Western empire (not necessarily limited to the EU) is

https://doi.org/10.1515/9783110684216-008

very different from any other in history. First of all, it is in denial, since it refutes any such allegation as something indecent and incorrect. Second, it does not have any territorial claims like it used to in the old times; it conquers in a soft manner, through state-building mechanisms and neoliberal or ordoliberal economic prescriptions. Furthermore, it does not even pretend to be governing the European space – this empire is allegedly made of equals who joined it voluntarily and contribute to the decision-making process on an equal footing. Instead, its representatives (mostly dubbed Euro-mandarins) use doublespeak, especially while talking to the others. The EU is prone to self-representing as Europe as a whole.

With the above in mind, it is necessary to critically deconstruct and re-evaluate the so praised EU enlargement as a narrative and politics of power. The postcolonial approach allows us to make hidden power hierarchies, exclusions, and biases more visible (Turunen 2019). Thomas Diez (2005) rightly stresses that through its normative power narrative, Brussels as the capital of the EU necessarily others those international actors that lack moral commitment. The process of being or becoming European is subject to monitoring and improvement, but rules and norms are often kept intentionally vague. For instance, the dispute over the name of the Republic of Macedonia could not be found anywhere among the Copenhagen criteria; yet, it served as an excuse for halting the European integration for years, and once it was allegedly resolved, it was done by violating the Copenhagen criteria. The potential member states are nevertheless stuck in "the waiting room of history" (Chakrabarty 2000), and in this state of constant liminality, Turkey comes first and Macedonia second. Dabashi (2019) goes a step further, arguing that the condition of coloniality, with the European West on one side and the colonized rest on the other, has now metastasized and entered a whole new phase, in which the colonized are no longer divided nationally, regionally, or continentally; the colonial has always been embedded in the capital and the capital in the colonial.

Discussing the history of international intervention in the Balkans since the 1880s, Susan Woodward, one of the few scholars who have properly understood the roots of the Balkan tragedy (as she referred to in her discussion of the dissolution of Yugoslavia), argues that the current Western regulatory regime is largely only the institutionalization of patterns of international practice in the Balkans since the late nineteenth century (2013, 1170). She argues that John Galbraith's (1960) analysis of a dynamic of unintended colonial expansion in the nineteenth century based on the concept of "a turbulent frontier" is particularly useful in the Balkan cases. According to this concept, the best defense is a good offense, which suggests that cumulative gains in the imperial periphery can be reaped through aggressive action, whereas passivity brings cumulative defeats. Therefore, as explained by Galbraith, the solution to security problems at the turbulent frontier of the empire is to conquer even more territory in order to punish or prevent harassment by contiguous barbarians. For example, alongside this understanding, while addressing the US Senate Foreign Relations Committee in early-2015, the US State

Secretary John Kerry assessed that "Serbia, Kosovo, Montenegro and Macedonia are the new front line between Russia and the West" (cited in Dérens and Geslin 2015).

Vassilis Fouskas and Bülent Gökay (2019, 2) stress another important aspect of today's globalized world: our post-Cold War era is defined by *intra*-imperialist and *inter*-imperial contradictions. Until recently one could say that the Balkans represent a microcosm of multipolarity or, more precisely, a region in which global fault lines clash. Ever since the COVID-19 pandemic struck, everything is in a process of change. While the EU has failed to provide not only a coordinated medical response but also basic solidarity with the most vulnerable countries, China and Russia were the first ones to offer humanitarian assistance. At first, Western Balkan governments received a cold shoulder when they asked for medical assistance, but because of the public pressure and geopolitical concerns (Bender, Cerimagic, and Knaus 2020), they ended up getting some symbolic financial assistance. Somewhat ironically, Albania and Macedonia finally got a vaguely formulated positive decision on the start of the EU negotiation process, on 24 March 2020. As the President of the European Commission, Ursula von der Leyen, put it, "[t]he European Union delivers on its promise. North Macedonia and Albania did what was asked of them and they have continued making progress in the reforms needed. Today marks the start of the journey to a bigger and stronger European Union. And this decision is in the European Union's geostrategic interest" (European Commission 2020). Commissioner for Neighborhood and Enlargement, Olivér Várhelyi, was even more explicit: "Today's decision confirms the geostrategic importance of the Western Balkans and demonstrates that Europe is willing and able to take geopolitical decisions even in these trying times of corona virus pandemic" (European Commission 2020). However, a more insightful analysis shows that the decision is supposed to pacify the worried citizens, while the EU may claim moral and geopolitical victory. In any case, Dimitar Bechev (2020) is right when saying that despite good news, the Western Balkans are in trouble due to long-lasting problems in political and socio-economic spheres. Accordingly, this study examines the Macedonian path toward EU membership in the context of unprecedented expectations to submit itself to both the West (the Brussels and Washington administrations) and its southern neighbor Greece (through the signature of the so-called Prespa Agreement in June 2018).[1]

---

1 For the full text of the Final Agreement for the Settlement of the Differences as Described in the United Nations Security Council Resolutions 817 (1993) and 845 (1993), the Termination of the Interim Accord of 1995, and the Establishment of a Strategic Partnership between the Parties, see https://vlada.mk/node/17422.

Macedonia's Tantalizing Path to the EU

During the turmoil in the 1990s, the Republic of Macedonia appeared as a small miracle; the most underdeveloped republic of socialist Yugoslavia not only avoided war and gained independence in a peaceful manner, but it also smoothly introduced a liberal democratic system. However, instead of the widely discussed end of history and new bright future, the country had to deal with an issue that had nothing to do with the promise of democracy, but rather with the long-forgotten historic context of the Balkans over its constitutional name. The period between 1991 and 1995 witnessed mass pauperization and creation of new bourgeoisie (in a rather criminal way), with everything being overshadowed by the struggle for international recognition. Due to Greece's objection to the name Macedonia and its allegations that the small neighbor possessed irredentist claims and thus represented a security threat, the young Macedonian state had a thorny path to the UN membership. In other words, the issues concerning the Macedonians' history, identity, and right to self-determination were securitized to the highest possible extent. Furthermore, for the sake of alleged regional security, the UN Security Council violated Article 4 of the UN Charter through the imposition of illegal conditions for the country's admission (Janev 1999). Since then the country had to use a provisional reference – the Former Yugoslav Republic of Macedonia (FYRoM) – that was *de facto* dragging it back to the past rather than leading it to the future. During one conference, held in the late 1990s and devoted to the future of the region, the renowned Croatian philosopher Žarko Puhovski (2019) wittily pointed out the absurdity of debating the future of a state that unwillingly bore an attribute related to something former.

In fact, the first communication of the newly independent Macedonian state with the outer world was through Brussels. Europe's ability to deal with problems in its own backyard was *inter alia* tested and found wanting precisely over the name dispute. Not only did the then European Community turn a deaf ear to the recommendation of its own arbitration body, known as Badinter Commission, which asserted that the new state fulfilled all requirements for international recognition and that its name did not imply any security threat or territorial aspirations but it also solidarized with Greece. The 1992 Lisbon Summit made the state's recognition conditional upon the choice of "a name which does not include the term Macedonia" (EU Council 1992). It was the zenith of the Greek success on the name front but there are a few possible scenarios with regard to the bargaining that happened in Brussels. Demetrius Floudas (2002) refers to an alleged deal: in exchange for the Brussels's support on the Macedonian issue, Greece promised to ratify the Maastricht treaty, participate in sanctions against its traditional ally Serbia, and ratify the European Community's financial protocol with Turkey. Håkan Wiberg (2009) describes a slightly different scenario: despite the fact that the Greek position on the name issue was an irritation to many EU members, Greece "was first given a promise by Germany as payment for recognizing Slovenia and Croatia; some years later Germany had found a legal loophole to cheat Greece, which wisely chose Macedonia rather than Germany for retaliation." Having been incapable of dealing with a range of intertwined and complex Balkan issues, the Brussels leadership tried to wash its hands of it and leave it to the UN mediation effort, carried out by the US diplomat Matthew Nimetz. The September 1995 Interim Accord between Athens and Skopje introduced a framework for a normalization of relations between Greece and Macedonia. Interestingly, the EU established diplomatic relations with Macedonia a couple of months later. Yet it seemed not to be aware of the risk of conflict within and around the country; one of the powder-kegs was the so-called Serbian – Albanian – Macedonian complex, with a clear spillover potential (Wiberg 1993, 100).

The EU's inept treatment of the predictably volatile situation in Macedonia was just one example among several of European conflict mismanagement in the former Yugoslavia (Oberg 2004). Some authors go as far as to claim that the disintegration of Yugoslavia and its aftermath could hardly be grasped without understanding the role of the Western powers, which had largely been overlooked, in helping to produce and channel the crisis. Indeed, few scholars and activists dared spell it out and deconstruct the hidden fight over the spheres of interest in the disintegrating federation. For Peter Gowan (1999), the Western states' operations in the Yugoslav theatre had not been governed by any universalist norms geared to improving the conditions of the peoples of the area, but by their own state political interests and state political goals. Furthermore, he believes that those operations had been a major cause of many of the barbarities that had confronted Yugoslav men and women in the past. The old rivalries and appetites of the European powers to get back what allegedly always belonged to them (as they saw Yugoslavia's spoils) pushed the country over the brink. Germany and Austria directly assisted separatist forces in Slovenia and Croatia, Hungary was interested in Serbia's northern province of Vojvodina, etc. Wiberg brilliantly analyzed third party intervention in Yugoslavia, including the incompetence and ulterior motives of the external parties involved. Referring to the European Council's unsuccessful attempt to put itself forward as a key mediator, he points out the following: "This EC 'monopoly' was retained throughout 1991 at least, after which it was increasingly shared with the UN, and then both of them were shoved aside by various *ad hoc* constellations of great powers acting collectively or unilaterally" (Wiberg 1996, 207).

The 1999 NATO intervention was a catalyst for the internal conflict potential in Macedonia; it was just a matter of time until the genie would be released from the bottle. Ten years of negative peace were wasted and no sustainable prospects for positive peace were ever present. Conflict prevention efforts overwhelmingly focused on the country's ethnic mix, which was frequently referred to as an explosive Macedonian fruit salad. For a period of ten years, Macedonia hosted an array of international organizations whose projects focused on conflict prevention and resolution, inter-ethnic dialogue and tolerance, and so on; yet these projects paid far more attention to the classic cliché of inter-ethnic relations and largely neglected factors more fundamental to the conflict, such as the political economy of the conflict (ESI 2002). The solution of the conflict was again a ready-made model of power sharing between the two major ethnic communities (Macedonian and Albanian). To paraphrase Mary Kaldor (1999), in its haste to fix the problem the international community (the EU and the US) fell into a trap set by the local parties in conflict, and rushed to embrace the thesis of ancient hatred between ethnic groups and the impossibility for them to live together. The simplest solution was to separate the hostile ethnic groups, to impose political power sharing and territorial arrangements that would guarantee a sort of negative peace (based on the ethnicization of politics and ghettoization of citizens from different ethnic backgrounds). Today there is almost nothing left of the idea of the civic approach articulated in the 2001 Ohrid Framework Agreement (OFA). Multi-ethnicity has been sacrificed and replaced by bi-nationality, while the power-sharing arrangement makes democracy seem like a pipe dream (Vankovska 2007).

Paradoxically, Macedonia's path to EU membership has achieved a more concrete form in the least favorable conditions possible. Amidst the ongoing military hostilities between the state security forces and the Albanian paramilitary formation Kosovo Liberation Army (UÇK), the EU decided to offer a carrot in the form of signing the Stabilization and Association Agreement (SAA) on 9 April 2001 in Luxembourg. Macedonia was the first to sign this new *sui generis* instrument designed for the countries of the Western Balkan region. It was ratified by the Macedonian parliament three days later and came into force on 1 April 2004. The application for EU membership was submitted in March 2004, in the year of another great challenge – the implementation of the OFA. Namely, the power-sharing model could hardly produce any positive results without the continuous and direct involvement of the so-called international community. According to Arend Lijphart (1977), for this model to be functional some criteria should have been met. Most importantly, there should have been at least three segments/communities in the respective problematic society, while Macedonia had only two (with disproportional size, too). In other words, in a similar way to the 1995 Dayton Agreement, which marked the end of the war in Bosnia and Herzegovina, the OFA was condemned to failure from the very start, but the international powers had to do something. Ever since, the EU and the US ambassadors, or other envoys and representatives, had to take the role of the third or balancing factor in order to sustain their widely praised success story. Macedonian politics became an empty shell, having been totally dependent on the mediatory role of the external factors. The first major test for the OFA came in 2004, when the EU directly intervened in the referendum process over the revision of the municipalities' territorial borders along ethnic lines (ethnic gerrymandering). The referendum failed due to the powerful propaganda and scaremongering by the government and the international actors. For instance, during his visit to Skopje, the United Kingdom Minister of State for Europe, Denis MacShane took off his wrist watch and started moving its pointers in front of the people of the press to further dramatize his statement: "It is a simple message; don't turn the clock back. I understand the fears and the concern, but on Sunday, 7 November – stay home" (cited in Karajkov 2004). European Commission President Romano Prodi addressed the Macedonian parliament, saying that the referendum decision depended on Macedonians themselves "as to whether they wanted Europe or not" (cited in ICG Europe 2005), as if they were not already Europeans and the indirect democracy was something non-European. No wonder, the government's anti-referendum campaign was carried out under the slogan Europe Now, while the citizens who were against the proposed law were quickly branded as hardliners and nationalists. In December 2005, Macedonia was rewarded again, this time with candidate status. Ironically, on the very same day of public celebrations and fireworks, a laid off-miner died of a heart attack during a press conference. The ruling coalition (between the social democrats and the Albanian party that was composed of former UÇK fighters) lost the elections in 2006; it would take more than a decade for the social democrats to recover and gain power, through a colorful revolution.

The country was the first one in the region to gain EU candidate status, but also the first one ever not to be automatically allowed to start negotiations upon being granted such a status. The limbo lasted until 2009 when the European Commission for the first time explicitly recommended the opening of the negotiation process, almost coinciding with the visa liberalization. Due to the Greek opposition, Macedonia's candidacy remained only an abstract reward with no effect on society but just an object of frustration in the coming years. Ever since, regardless of the real state of affairs in terms of democracy, development, and good governance, the European Commission and the European Parliament used to regularly recommend the negotiation process be open, with no fear that it would be accepted by the Council. This was just lip-service, and in order to bypass the obvious blockade and thus hide its embarrassment, in 2012 the EU invented one more *sui generis* mechanism – the High-Level Association Dialogue. Obviously, the dosage of carrots had to be increased, especially because of the negative effects of the 2008 NATO summit's great disappointment, which strengthened the rule of the semi-autocratic government of Nikola Gruevski. The 2016 Colorful Revolution, which was *de facto* a soft regime change supported by the West, introduced changes in the wording of the European Commission; the usual annual recommendations to open the association process became conditional, and as Simonida Kacarska (2019) rightly notes, Macedonia was also the first country to experience the term backsliding, used by the European Commission to freeze the recommendation with regard to accession negotiations between 2015 and 2018.

The new government led by Zoran Zaev took power in May 2017, and by mid-June 2019 the Prespa Agreement, which allegedly resolved the name issue, was signed. Ever since, instead of the promised quantum leap, the citizens witnessed the tale of the boy who cried wolf (Kacarska 2019), the only difference being that the boy was the government and the wolf was the good news from Brussels. Ever since, there have been three instances when the European Council failed to make any positive decision. Yet the Macedonian government took any opportunity to turn the inconvenient facts into a message that the accession process was just about to start. According to media reports, its opening was to prove that the EU remained operational in the face of rival powers such as China, Russia, and Turkey, altogether having a growing influence in the region (Barigazzi 2020). However, the alleged green light does not mean much without a clear date and set of conditions; moreover, as stressed by Bulgarian representatives, the blackmailing is still on the table, since they expect the negotiation framework to consider the Bulgarian identity demands, which corresponds to a denial of the Macedonian minority's existence and of a separate Macedonian language, among other things (Damovski 2020; EU Council 2020).

Debunking the Myth of European Values and the Prespa Agreement

The conventional wisdom is that European values represent a normative and moral compass for potential EU member states. With regard to the Balkan region, the widespread opinion is that "amid the usual bilateral disputes from the region, such as the Serbia-Kosovo relations or the constant ethnopolitical fragmentation in Bosnia and Herzegovina, North Macedonia and Greece demonstrated that core European values can prevail in the traditionally turbulent Balkans" (Armakolas and Petkovski 2019). Here, it is important to clarify what European values really mean, what makes certain values European (Union), especially if there is no European demos and there are many facets of the union as such. Consequently, what kind and how are the values embedded in the Prespa process, including the enactment and implementation of the Prespa Agreement? The definition of European values is instrumental in understanding why a small nation accepted something that no other European nation has ever been asked to do, or even dreamt of doing so.

Since 1993, EU membership candidates are expected to meet certain values and principles, known as the Copenhagen criteria. At the early stage, all reforms are about political criteria such as democracy, rule of law, human rights, and respect for and protection of minorities (the economic ones as well as ability to put into function EU acquis have hardly been strict criteria for any country that has joined the EU so far). No matter how flexible the interpretation of the political criteria is, the change of one's name and identity cannot be found elsewhere, but in the Macedonian case. The name dispute has always been interrelated with the notion of good neighbor relations (understood as a one-way street, or power relation), because the pressure and supervision has always been on the behavior, or even the very existence, of the potential member state, and never on the behavior of the member state. Macedonia was forced to see itself as a bad neighbor only because Greece had fears of alleged irredentism. Furthermore, Greece has never had a clear and positive record when it comes to respect for minority rights. The Greekness (imposed as artificial ethnic homogeneity in practice) has been imposed as a substantial value in the constitution's eternal clause. So, the Macedonian side, the one that had already accepted a concept of bi-ethnic division covered by the phrases of multi-ethnic democracy, was made to believe that one more concession, no matter how absurd and non-European it may look, should be made for the greater good.

The literature and practice have only vague ideas about the exact list of European values. In 2014, Jan Peter Balkenende, the former prime minister of the Netherlands, said that "European fundamental values are sacred," but then when asked to define those values, he admitted: "We have been discussing the idea of Europe for the last 1,200 years but we cannot grasp what it means" (cited in Harding 2012). Values matter because they are the glue that keeps communities and different peoples together; as such, they help define what society stands for and against. The EU is surrounded by myths, both internally and externally. According to Della Sala (2010), social organizations need to develop myths in order both to legitimize their functions externally and to provide purpose, direction, and identity for those who work in them. Myths do not need to be true to be successful, nor does the reality need to live up to the myth for a policy to succeed. In the case of the EU enlargement policy, myths have contributed at least in part to the successful accession of a number of former East-Central European countries. They have been successful to the extent to which they have become part of established political discourse. But there are limits to the path to success through the narrative of the EU as a promised land. Luisa Passerini (2012) rightly notes that the references to these values in official statements are not a particularly European phenomenon, but rather one that is repeated in the official narratives of almost all contemporary political entities. These abstract value mantras are "a constant characteristic of Eurocentrism" and "definitions of identity based on such conceptions run the risk of reproducing rhetorical formulae which are either empty or suspect" (Passerini 2012, 124). With all these ideas in mind, Gareth Harding (2012) is right to remind us that the European dream has become a nightmare for many, with the euro teetering on the brink of collapse and the EU that produced it mired in a triple crisis that will take years, if not decades, to resolve. The economic catastrophe has generated high unemployment, almost nonexistent growth, and indebted governments running out of money, with some facing the prospect of a generation of hardship. Deep political crises, border controls among the states, no visionary leadership, and populism also exist. However, all these inconvenient facts have been presented almost as fake-news or even as Russian anti-EU propaganda by the advocates of the Prespa Agreement. This became become especially visible during the September 2018 referendum campaign, when both European and local elites had to combine two myths in order to make people swallow the bitter pill. So, the first collateral victim of the Prespa operation was the truth (including the academic freedom to criticize it).

The myth of the Prespa Agreement is also a complex one. First, it had to be presented as the European way of resolving disputes between neighbors. Second, it was portrayed as a compromise: allegedly, both sides gained and lost equally. Third, it was said to be in accordance with international law, despite the fact that the agreement and its implementation under the auspices of both Greece and the Brussels administration are in breach of many international legal norms including UN *jus cogens*, principles of the right to self-determination and non-interference in a country's internal affairs, let alone the UN Covenant on Civil and Political Rights, the European Convention on Human Rights, and the Vienna Convention. Fourth, there is a false and imposed belief that the country has voluntarily changed its name. *De facto* the government undertook all the steps on the way both against the norms of the national law and against the popular will (clearly expressed in the 2018 referendum). In short, the Prespa Agreement violated the presumed European values, including democracy, rule of law, human rights, and internal peace (instead of induced further inter- and intra-ethnic divisions and raising conflict potential), and it eroded the enthusiasm for EU membership. Everything that was supposed to be embedded and promoted as Europeanness has become collateral damage of the Prespa process.

With regard to the notion of democracy – an issue going far beyond the scope of this analysis – what the EU usually refers to under its political criteria is functional democratic governance, which allows equal citizens' participation in the political decision making at every single governing level, from local municipalities up to the national level. It also assumes free and fair elections, free political organization without any hindrance from the state, separation of powers where the executive power is restricted by laws, political freedoms, and free media. The process of reaching the Prespa Agreement violated all those principles. Macedonia could have hardly been defined as a democracy even prior to 2018, given the proofs confirming its semi-protectorate status, since the early-2000s. Lacking a balancing element in the power-sharing system, the representatives of the so-called international community were the ones who made the system work more smoothly but not necessarily to Western standards. For instance, the 2016 Przino process concluded that the Colorful Revolution resulted in a crippled state unable to make any decision through democratic means (formal institutions). In fact, the work of the parliament has been marked by a few occasions of misuse of the European flag during the law-making process, including the ratification of the Prespa Agreement.

The most important instance exposing not only the democratic deficit of the Prespa process but also mockery of indirect democracy is related to the 2018 referendum. It was preceded by the overt intervention of a range of EU and US officials who informally campaigned for the positive response and helped demonize anyone who was against. In democracy not only is transparency important in the decision-making process, but also making all information available so that the voters can make informed decisions. The referendum process was marred not only with moves contrary to the laws but also with ones against common sense; for instance, the referendum question was a ridicule by any criteria, some of which are embedded in the Code of Good Referendum Practices of the Venice Commission as well as in the national legislation. The question read: "Are you in favor of EU and NATO membership by accepting the agreement between Macedonia and Greece?" It was both crassly tendentious and brazenly deceitful (Plavšić 2018). The promise of two memberships were intended to sugar coat what could be seen as a bitter pill, resolving the controversial name issue by the back door. To respond with a plain 'yes' or 'no' was impossible, due to the three variables and eight possible combinations in answering. The question lacked the formal, substantial, and hierarchical logic required by the Venice Commission's Code of Good Practice on Referendums.

Parliament was the formal proposer of the referendum, so the government was not entitled to run the campaign with budgetary means. According to the Law on the Referendum, the Venice Code, and the Przino Agreement, this was a clear breach of the rule of law. In bypassing the Electoral Code that regulates some aspects relevant for the referendum process, the government extended the length of the campaign for over twenty days. Under Macedonian law, it is illegal to finance a referendum with foreign funds or from the state budget, but state ministers were dominant in all media outlets that strongly favored the 'yes' side of the campaign. It was speculated that the government used the services of a British public relations firm Stratagem (funded by the UK Foreign Office), which prides itself on being "a resource for the referendum taskforce (Yes Campaign)" (Purkiss 2018). Moreover, from the very beginning (the day after the parliament had issued the notice), the basic line of the government campaign supported by a long list of foreign officials and dignitaries – including the visits of the NATO Secretary-General, the German and Austrian Chancellors, and EU Commissioners, altogether aimed at giving support and encouraging Euro-Atlantic integration of the Republic of Macedonia – was that the referendum had to be successful. For instance, Angela Merkel paid her first official visit to Macedonia just days before the launch of the official campaign and stressed that the referendum would open the doors to EU and NATO memberships: "The day 30 September is a historic opportunity and do not stay home, take the advantage of democratic possibility to express yourselves about the future of your country." In response, Prime Minister Zaev added: "I, the whole government, and our people are very happy about your visit, and in return we aim to reciprocate with a successful referendum" (Merkel and Zaev cited in Delimitov 2018).

Securing a successful referendum called for an action against the opponents who were demonized and intimidated. For instance, Vlado Kambovski, a professor of criminal law and member of the Macedonian Academy of Sciences and Arts, argued that organizing a boycott of the referendum would be subject to prosecution for engaging in criminal activity (*Nezavisen vesnik* 2018). Simultaneously, the government's propaganda was blatantly phony, not only because of false promises but also because of fake facts or news (for example, that the EU provides free schooling and healthcare to all). Occasionally, it looked as if the government was promising communism instead of prospects (although weak ones) in a neoliberal empire. Faced with such an undemocratic and often threatening atmosphere, with no equality of opportunity for all sides and the abuse of public funds for campaigning purposes, so that the freedom of voters to form an opinion was limited, citizens self-organized in the I'm Boycotting movement. Bearing in mind the national regulation and the current context, there was a widespread opinion that boycotting would be the most intelligent and most effective strategy to make the referendum fail. It did not imply an anti-European stance, but that some national values meant more than EU promises. As it turned out, the referendum result was a mixture of a very expensive public opinion poll and a reality show. With a turnout of only 36 percent, it showed that the citizens were largely aware that the government had no intention of acting on the vote, as it had already announced its determination to proceed with the implementation of the Prespa Agreement regardless of the outcome of the referendum. The overwhelming abstention from voting represents a very wide and conscious rejection of the agreement. The citizens' vote was intended to annul the result of the 1991 referendum on independence[2] and provide the ruling elite with a sort of political legitimacy for the upcoming constitution change, once and for all, as the Greek side demanded. Despite the government's endless efforts to translate the defeat into a victory by counting and comparing the number of votes with those achieved in various parliamentary, local, or presidential elections, bare legal logic meant that the referendum did not pass – an outcome that was confirmed in the formal report of the State Electoral Commission. The boycott movement delegitimized the government; in fact, the prime minister had already publicly admitted that he had been gambling 'all in' with his people (*Kurir* 2018).

Although the referendum failed, the international community continued its support using a political oxymoron, claiming that the Agreement had received popular and wide support, despite the fact that the turnout had been far below the constitutional requirement (less than 37 percent vis-à-vis the 50 percent required). In other words, meeting the constitutional requirements were to be ignored because a visible majority of those who voted were in favor of the agreement. The question "Does this not cross the line of infringement upon a nation's sovereignty and the

---

2 The turnout of the 1991 referendum when Macedonia decided to form a sovereign and independent state was over 75 percent (despite the boycott by ethnic Albanians who were still waiting and hoping for an integral solution of the Albanian question on a regional basis). Over 95 percent of the votes were in favor of independence. It was hoped that this second referendum would eventually substitute the expressed will of the people who voted for "an independent state of Macedonia" and instead decide on "the second independence" (to use Prime Minister's words) for the state of North Macedonia.

will of its people?" is nothing but a rhetorical question (Vasilevski 2019), and this was not the first instance of showing that people's will does not count unless it fits the interests of power circles. Two weeks later, the government initiated a constitutional revision, and in mid-October it managed to provide a two-thirds majority for the second stage of the process. So, the Prespa Agreement prompted a fast-track constitutional change. Still, the process was highly controversial, to say the least, as opposition MPs (who were under serious criminal charges) were bribed or blackmailed to join the parliamentary majority, as later confirmed by the Minister of Justice in a TV interview (*Kanal 5* 2019). The mockery took a bizarre form, as the eight votes needed for providing a two-thirds majority for the constitutional revision were secured by the initiation of a controversial and much-disputed amnesty law that would include the mob attack on the parliament in 2017 precisely by the opposition MPs under charges. Three of them were actually on trial or in custody. Yet, the EU turned a blind eye and greeted the law as a step "for reconciliation in society and for the need to overcome painful polarization," noting that the process was "crucial in helping build a national consensus on strategic issues for the interests of the country" (EEAS 2018). Somewhat paradoxically, the international media took more interest in the alleged Russian interference than in the way democracy was undermined *inter alia* through the involvement of the Western ambassadors. One of the rare objective observers, Panagiotis Lafazanis, the leader of the Greek party Popular Unity, compared the Western powers' treatment of people and referenda in both countries: "In a similar way as they did with the 2015 referendum in Greece, they managed to set one more 'night of the long knives', an orgy of blackmail and pressures in order to get 'yes' votes and to achieve the magic number of 80 parliamentarians" (cited in *Protothema* 2018). According to him, "the real masters of Greece and Macedonia – two countries that have become loose protectorates of the US and NATO – are the US ambassadors. Also, it is not possible to sustain agreements in the long run purely by relying on the signatures of the governments and parliaments susceptible to corruption, pressures, led by their selfish interests; agreements need the people."

Concerning the rule of law matter, such a principle is supposed to keep politics within the legal frontiers. In this sense, a number of members of the ruling elite have been working not only outside these boundaries but were even blessed while doing so. For example, according to the Macedonian constitution, within the bicephalic executive, a prime minister and president, the Minister of Foreign affairs (or better, the government) has a position of *secundus* when it comes to concluding international treaties. The president holds the position of *primus* in these matters, but President Gjorge Ivanov was bypassed due to his overt disagreement with the way the compromise was envisioned. In legal terms, the signature of the Prespa Agreement was an *ultra vires* act (Apasiev 2019; Nikodinovska Krstevska 2019; Siljanovska Davkova 2018); it was never ratified in accordance with the law, while its entering into force and announcement in the *Official Gazette* (signed by the speaker of the parliament only) represents a crime according to the Criminal Code. The flagrant breaches of the rule of law principle were committed with the blessing of the EU; as rightly pointed out by Angelos Chryssogelos (2019), the Brussels leadership "has chosen to ignore problematic aspects of a ratification process that has challenged constitutional norms and rule of law principles in both Macedonia and Greece." For the deal to be pushed through, both states had to push the limits of legality. The problem with the legality principle is that it rests upon the strictness of its implementation, and therefore, pushing the limits of legality suggests promotion of illegality as politically useful along with politicians' impunity for the breach of law. Unfortunately, the Constitutional Court remained loyal to its long-standing position of non-interference.

The ramming through of the agreement was possible due to the infamous encouragement of EU Commissioner Johannes Hahn to then Prime Minister Zaev to carry on with the Prespa Agreement regardless of the failure of the referendum, suggesting a "combination of the Balkan and rational approach" in securing the two-thirds majority, necessary for the constitutional change and ratification of the agreement (Marusic 2018). Apart from ignoring the scandalous breaches of the national constitution and the Venice Code of good referendum practices, the European partners pretended not to see or hear the biased propaganda, and even the calls for bribery and racketeering expressed by Zaev during the campaign (*Denešen vesnik* 2018). The process was completed in such a way that the whole idea of the rule of law was sacrificed on the altar of (geo)political effectiveness, by first intimidating and trialing opposition Members of the Parliament, and then changing the Criminal Code to provide them with guarantees that they would not be charged in the future. The government believed that due to the unreserved support from foreign administrations, it was untouchable and above the law; so, once the government itself started violating the principle it was supposed to protect, the message sent to the rest of the society was that as soon as there was enough power accumulated, everything was allowed.

In the field of human rights, the Prespa Agreement's introductory part promotes key international norms, but this is just sugar-coating for the blatant violation of collective and individual human rights. With all the claims made, the most starkly provocative is the claim that the agreement respects the Macedonian people's dignity and its right to self-determination. The agreement *de facto* and *de jure* does the opposite; it infringes the right to self-determination by ensuring that Macedonia's name will not be self-determined by its people, but by the more powerful neighbor (Plavšić 2018). The Macedonian citizens have been stripped of their right to decide on their political system through the means of popular sovereignty.

The implementation of the Prespa Agreement displays its authoritarian features, suggesting that North Macedonia is possible only as an authoritarian state (Korybko 2018). At the same time, any opposition to the agreement (primarily centered on the undemocratic way surrounding its adoption as well as the consequent diktat around its implementation) is immediately labeled as right-wing populism. The disillusionment with the Colorful Revolution took its toll, so the citizens continued to grumble from the margins. The silence or self-censorship of the academic community is far more difficult to justify, especially because the agreement not only imposes state control over academic work (especially in the field of history-related disciplines) but also that the control is supposed to be carried out by a bilateral body made of state officials from both countries. Academic freedom, as well as the freedom of the media, is greatly limited in terms of freedom of thought and speech. The risk is that such an approach could lead not only to historical revisionism and misinterpretation, but falsification of basic facts about individuals' personal records. For instance, the formal school documents show that children born prior to 2018/2019 were born in North Macedonia. Equally problematic is the case of birth certificates which, in the box of citizenship, show slash symbols. The politicians do not restrict themselves when euphorically claiming that the rebels during the former Ottoman times and even the later partisans fought for the freedom of North Macedonia. Furthermore, quite early in the process of implementation of the Prespa Agreement, the government issued formal Media Guidelines concerning the use of terms Macedonia(n) and North Macedonia(n).[3] Allegedly, one could call oneself a Macedonian and use the name / attribute Macedonia(n) but only for private purposes. All the state institutions have been renamed accordingly, but not consistently. With such a move, the Macedonian nation has been practically erased, and all institutions (with few exceptions)[4] became national with no further reference to which nation they actually belong.

Finally, with regard to minority rights, the Prespa Agreement and the consequent constitutional reform in Macedonia have led to absurdities. It is not an exaggeration to say that Macedonia's record in minority rights protection is far better than Greece's (*BBC* 2019). Yet the weaker side had to denounce the very existence of its minority in Greece – twice! The first time Macedonia made amendments to its constitution was back in 1992, expressly denying any claims on any country's territory, as well as any interference in the internal affairs of countries with a Macedonian minority. That concession was not enough, so the third amendment of 2019 specifies that the country will "protect, guarantee and cherish the characteristics, historical and cultural

---

3 As a form of disobedience, the domestic actors tend to avoid using official terminology and speak of 'our country' instead. All this takes the Macedonians back into the past when the praxis of 'nashism' (ourism) was the least painful way to avoid foreign repression and assimilation policies (Rossos 2008).

4 Exceptions (such as the Macedonian theatre) are allowed only in order to designate the ethnic character of an institution (in line with the existing Turkish or Albanian theatres). The term 'national' is supposed to refer to something that belongs to all citizens regardless of their ethnic origin. Yet, the political nation (demos) remains unidentified and unnamed. Bearing in mind the internal inter-ethnic divisions and the bi-national character of the power-sharing system, this move is in accordance with the state-builders' intention of creating a new nation from above.

heritage of the Macedonian people and the rights and interests of its citizens, including different ethnic groups that live abroad." The same amendment also stipulates that the country will not intervene in the sovereign rights of other states and in their internal affairs. In other words, the Macedonian state has done some horse-trading by exchanging minorities for the members of the Macedonian diaspora (as if they need any constitutional or other protection from the state that is weak and incapable of protecting the rights of its citizens). This was confirmed by then Greek Minister of Foreign Affairs Nikos Kotsias, who explicitly said that the agreement forbade the Macedonians in Greece and in Macedonia to ask for recognition of a national minority in Greece (*Expres.mk* 2018). In the already demonstrated cooperative spirit, both the Foreign Minister Nikola Dimitrov and Prime Minister Zaev have not dared speak out about the Macedonian minority (or their language) in public, and especially in media interviews, but insist that such questions represent an internal matter for Greece to decide.

Having been stuck between one external (Macedonian-Greek) and one internal (Macedonian-Albanian) ethnic security dilemma, the geopolitical goal of stabilizing the region is confronted with major challenges, if not impossible. The name change has always been strongly opposed by the majority of ethnic Macedonians (and simultaneously, supported by the vast majority of ethnic Albanians); no wonder Zaev had to compensate by gaining the support of the Albanian minority, offering a range of ethnic concessions in spite of the constitutional framework. His government has managed to survive only thanks to the Albanian coalition parties' support in the parliament, which makes him a hostage of a number of unprincipled concessions at the expense of the common good. As rightly explained by Chryssogelos (2019), the deal sets a coalition of minorities against a majority of the majority. Therefore, the agreement was bound to reignite ethnic tensions and increase political and intra-ethnic polarization in Macedonia, which is the exact opposite of the EU's intention. By closing one problem and allegedly opening the road to EU accession, the Prespa deal, along with all the other constellations, has become a self-fulfilling prophecy.

Dreams and Reality: The Painful Wake Up of North Macedonia

For almost two decades, while Macedonia kept struggling to open negotiations with the EU, the international system has experienced a range of dramatic challenges. On one hand, the 2008 global financial crisis (followed by the migrant crisis) forced the EU to gradually abandon its dreams about raising into a global power (although no EU institution has ever acknowledged it), while, on the other, multipolarity has come to penetrate the Balkan region (Vankovska 2020). Having been fundamentally incapable of delivering and meeting the citizens' expectations, every Macedonian government sought to offer unrealistic promises about forthcoming European integration, and any positive signal from different EU representatives was a useful chip in the internal political battle.

The EU (and NATO, due to the imposed false claim that joining the alliance was a *sine qua non* to join the EU) has gradually become an undisputable entity, characterizing both political and academic discourse. As one study has put it, "[s]ince the fall of communism in Eastern Europe, the Republic of Macedonia has shared a common dream with the overwhelming majority of Central and Eastern European countries – the dream of meeting the standards of the European Union and becoming a part of the united European family in the foreseeable future" (Milchevski 2013, 40). References to a common dream and a united European family have dominated the everyday life for too long. Even the political rhetoric surrounding the 2018 referendum campaign on the Prespa Agreement, portrayed an insightful understanding of the EU: on one hand, it was pictured as a benevolent entity and something worth any sacrifice (including one's constitutional sovereignty and identity), while, on the other, the EU represented an external moral and political vertical with power to discipline or make better the worthless people in the periphery. One of the most illustrative speeches in this tone was given by the then Prime Minister Zaev who referred to the EU (and NATO) as a master with a whip in their hands (*MakFax* 2018). It speaks for itself that the general reference was directed to describe the nation's ineptness, laziness, and need to be dominated by a morally, politically, and culturally superior entity. The paradox here is that there is neither a single idea of Europe, nor of the EU.

Accordingly, Macedonian citizens have been made to believe in a narrative of political and religious pseudo messianism; as summarized by Boško Karadjoski (2019): "The Macedonian idea of Europe is an idea of a not yet reached paradise ... This idea of Europe as a *master narrative* for the Second Coming of the so-called 'Welfare Parousia' that will start the process of an investment boom, donor cash assistance, financial injections, pre-accession funds is a fanatically naïve and unconditionally adopted propaganda for the arrival of the financial Kingdom of Heaven after EU accession. That is why the Macedonian idea of Europe is a sort of political and eschatological illusion. Therefore, any rational political philosophy of the idea of Europe in the Macedonian public and political discourse must begin with the deconstruction of this grand narrative." Consequently, Macedonia is substituting or exchanging its national identity and sovereignty for an illusion. The political discourse usually uses a phrase about going or moving to Europe, which by default means that the country is not (in) Europe yet and would not be able to be European without an EU membership card. Like everyone else in the Western Balkan region, Macedonia strives to divorce itself from the Balkan identity as something unworthy, primitive, and even dirty. On the other hand, public opinion polls in the EU show that Macedonia's desire and love for Europe is unreciprocated: the enlargement fatigue had been there for quite some time, and the majority of European citizens did not favor embracing their poor relatives from the Balkans. Actually, the stigmatization of the Bulgarian and Romanian citizens (especially, of Roma origin) has been visible for a long time after the two countries joined the EU. The French negative stance in October 2019 concerning both (North) Macedonia and Albania was only superficially an unpleasant surprise. In President Emmanuel Macron's view, "Europe is a big and beautiful house, which we live in together," but that house is not for everyone (cited in Momaz and Gray 2019). Indeed, he is not the first French president to use the same metaphor; Jacques Chirac used to warn the newcomers that the EU was truly a big and beautiful house, but not everyone could occupy the sunnier rooms and rooms with a view. Or, even Francois Mitterrand rightly brought back the recollection of France's tradition of conceiving Europe in terms of concentric circles that dates back to his presidency. In his vision ... "Eastern Europeans are welcome to do business and cooperate with the EU, but they do not belong to the 'truly European' inner sanctum" (Bechev 2019). One of the most ardent advocates of the Prespa Agreement, the Macedonian philosopher Katerina Kolozova (2019), just a year later placed the blame on the EU for Balkanizing the Balkans. Referring to Macron's argument that there are "thousands and thousands and thousands" of Albanians applying for an asylum in France, she said: "This fear of immigration from within Europe betrays a gaze that does not see all Europeans as equal – i.e. some Europeans are apparently more European than others ... Belonging to a single continent, sharing a similar cultural heritage and different yet intersecting histories apparently is not what 'Europeanness' is. Rather, the measure for being truly European appears to be from a rich, capitalist neoliberal state, especially a former colonial power which still enjoys some post-colonial perks. All former communist countries on the continent are expected to emulate this model through the process of so-called integration, by adopting 'measures,' 'instruments,' and 'reforms' dictated by Western technocrats."

In addition to the close circles around the leaders of two countries, Alexis Tsipras and Zoran Zaev, a good number of apparently left-wing intellectuals have uncritically supported both governments and the Prespa Agreement as something genuinely European and progressive. Robert Cox argued that "theory is always for someone and some purpose" and this seems to be the case more than ever. According to critical theory, knowledge cannot be objective and timeless in the sense that positivists would like to believe. Undeniably, researchers bring their values into the analyses they make. According to Cox, it is necessary to look closely at all theories and concepts that claim to be value-free and to pose the crucial question as to who or what it is intended for. Edward Said argued that the true intellectual had almost disappeared, leaving the landscape to be dominated by policy-oriented intellectuals who had internalized the norms of the state (to which we could add the norms of the so-called international community). Also, over time, intellectuals have been defanged and their task reduced to that of "the manufacturing of consent" (Jennings and Kemp-Welch 2003, 1). With regard to the Prespa case, even before the people's referendum, some international academic circles rushed to welcome the agreement as a miraculous achievement and final solution of the conflict between two Balkan states. In a matter of weeks after the ceremony in Prespa, over forty-five prominent scholars (including Étienne Balibar, Judith Batler, and Mary Kaldor) expressed their wholehearted support in an open letter entitled "Historic deal on shared Macedonian identity must be honoured" (*The Guardian* 2018). Its content is insightful for many reasons, with one aspect deserving special attention: the signatories (few of whom with legal knowledge or established expertise in the Balkans) far too easily took sides and pinpointed the potential enemies. According to them, "the agreement still faces big hurdles in both countries, where hardliners and extremists are mobilizing against it. North Macedonia's government, in particular, desperately needs all parties to fulfil their promises if it is to win the ratifying referendum in the autumn. In these critical times, when Europe faces the rise of extreme right-wing nationalism and racism, and dangerous revisionisms are resurfacing in the Balkans and Europe dividing people into 'traitors' and 'patriots,' it is more important than ever to support those who take risks for reconciliation. We support this fair agreement and call on all parties to fulfil their end of the bargain." The letter echoed a similar attitude offered by the political and media elites, meaning that it looked as if everyone agreed that it was high time to close the name issue regardless of the means and costs. The organic relationship between knowledge and power was displayed at its clearest, which was particularly true for the local scholars.

The Macedonian intellectuals have largely remained silent when it comes to role of the Prespa Agreement and its relation to the EU and NATO. In order to be welcomed and integrated in the international academic circles they have learned self-censorship and how to be politically correct. As pointed out by Spivak (1988), knowing the Other is not just epistemology – it is politics. In this very case, the Macedonians (and Macedonia as such) are the Other not only in the eyes of the Western observers who apply their (de)constructivist and postmodern discourses on the Macedonian nation-building. On the contrary, it has become a mantra of domestic authors too, who echo the indisputable truths of their international mentors (Armakolas and Petkovski 2019; FES 2019; Shkaric 2018). One of the rare Macedonian philosophers who deciphered coloniality long ago, Branko Sarkanjac (2004, 32), has argued that in the context of belonging and self-reflection, there are a number of aspects to consider, including the issue of language (and Bulgaria's reluctance to recognize the Macedonian language), the issue of name (due to Greece's insistence on the reference FYRoM in international organizations), the issue of history (as to the real history of the Macedonian people and its acknowledgment in relevant academic circles and institutions), the issue of ethnic origin (closely related to the notion of fatherland and the position vis-à-vis spatiality), and, finally, the issue of the geopolitical location of Macedonia (accompanied by the question of Macedonia's place on the core-periphery axis). He concludes that all these issues *de facto* form part of the postcolonial discourse, no matter which parts of the world the discourse comes from. The Prespa Agreement was quite honestly defined as an outcome of a postcolonial treatment by Stavros Mavroudeas (2018), for whom "the agreement . . . was forcefully imposed upon both countries by the EU and the US. The leaders and governments of both countries are very subservient, very weak, and they did not object to the agreement, which means that it is artificial, intended not to ensure stability, friendship, and peace in the area, but to secure the area in the Western sphere of interest and potentially against Russia. Such an agreement, on the other hand, aggravates tensions in the area and nationalist tendencies in both countries. The pressure from the West is extreme, and it reminds one of colonial-era involvement in internal politics."

The name change for the alleged EU membership is just one example of a wider phenomenon. The name issue has always been just a fig leaf that hid other deeper reasons for Europe's reluctance to fully integrate its less developed (less civilized) relatives from the periphery. According to Angelos Chryssogelos and Elena Stavrevska (2019, 429), "while the agreement theoretically removes one national objection to initiate accession negotiations with Skopje – that of Greece – it puts into starker relief the lacklustre or even outright negative attitudes of other member states – most notably France and the Netherlands – toward enlargement." Bogdan Stefanescu (2012) is right to insist that postcommunism and postcolonialism are siblings of subalternity. Although formally and legally Macedonian citizens did not legitimize the name change (the government was obedient to Brussels and disregarded the popular will), the lack of more powerful resistance confirms the relevance of the self-colonizing metaphor. Alexander Kiossev (1995) has clarified the very notion in the following way: "The concept of self-colonizing can be used for cultures having succumbed to the cultural power of Europe and the west without having been invaded and turned into colonies in actual fact. Historical circumstances transformed them into an extracolonial 'periphery' . . . the asymmetry between the European *métropoles* and the colonized rest of the world underlines the common oeuvre of shared knowledge, ideological representations and popular myths. Its purpose was to explain and justify European expansion from the 16th up until the mid-20th century, which is why these perceptions ranked peoples and geographic spaces as 'superior' and 'inferior,' delineated them not only geographically but in terms of value into 'Western,' 'Eastern,' and 'Southern,' defined them as 'big' and 'small,' historic and nonhistoric." The self-colonizing cultures do not resist, or rather they lovingly colonize their own authenticity through the imposed superior models that come from the core. Thus, they are doomed to an ineluctable sense of failure and a generative doubt: "We are Europeans, although not really!" Due to the ongoing battle of interpretations over the meaning of the Prespa Agreement the Macedonians are confronted with an even greater dilemma, the one as to whether they are allowed to call themselves Macedonians at all and what such a word actually means.

Conclusion

The political construction of the Western Balkans is an example of othering in the context of European integration, with this part of the continent being still treated as not fully European or as a potential Europe. In place is a modern *mission civilisatrice* applied through a vast range of state-building methods aimed at pacifying and carrying out national engineering in a way that would benefit the European core regardless of the price and effects on its respective societies. Following the Yugoslav chaos of the 1990s and once it became clear that the results of EU involvement were far worse than expected, stabilitocracy popped up on the surface. While coined by a historian of Montenegrin origin, many rushed to exploit the term seeking to developed theories as to why the Western Balkan region is hard or even impossible to democratize. In the words of Srdja Pavlović (2017), the inventor of the term, "the core value of *stabilitocracy* is a conviction that protecting and promoting Western interests is paramount . . . Regimes which understand that core conviction and are willing to protect and sustain western geopolitical, security, military, economic or energy-related interests in a given country are usually spared the wrath of the great powers such as the United States, the United Kingdom, or the European Union. Local autocrats, therefore, can do whatever suits their needs in their private domains. Any criticism directed toward them is usually dismissed as either sour grapes from a political loser or an attempt by retrograde undemocratic political forces to gain the upper hand."

With its war legacy from the 1990s, the biggest part of the former Yugoslav area is Europe's dark Other, burdened by ancient hatred and ineptitude. The point of neologism Western Balkans – inaugurated during the 2003 Summit in Thessaloniki to include post-Yugoslav states (without Slovenia, but with Albania) and assure them that they would become "an integral part of the EU, once they meet the established criteria" – has evolved over time (especially since Croatia's EU accession) to suggest a sanitary cordon or a dark place requiring special treatment. In the case of Macedonia, in order to pursue accession to NATO and the EU, the state was forced to change its name to North Macedonia. Even among scholars who supported the Prespa name deal, there are those who complain that "the persistence of the construct 'Western Balkans' has the exact opposite (and immediate) political effect: it has transformed a set of countries with their own (sometimes distinct) challenges into an artificially homogenous and politically charged mental box" (Fidanovski 2019). Moreover, the Prespa process exposed once again the existence of complex bargains between the EU and national elites that prefer stability to the detriment of democracy as well as the neoliberal and geopolitical considerations as the priority of their agenda, regardless of the price paid by the less worthy locals. With this in mind, the following statement seems rather pointless, even though it come from the Brussels administration: "For citizens to give their full support to European integration, greater emphasis should be placed on their common values, history and culture as key elements of their membership of a society founded on the principles of freedom, democracy, respect for human rights, cultural and linguistic diversity, tolerance and solidarity" (European Parliament 2006). However, for the sake of a bright future in an imagined EU, as Stefanescu (2012) would put it, Macedonia has ended up experiencing historical vacancy (void of historical action), significant silence (void of vocality), anonymous Macedonians (void of personality), and rigor mortis (void of vitality).

Hereby analysis provokes a range of rhetorical questions: Are the Macedonians (in the context of the presented arguments) actually Europeans? Will potential EU membership make them better Europeans? How can a formal political decision change self-perception on both sides of the EU border? Ironically enough, for the sake of (post)modernity, Macedonia surrendered to two continuity myths – Greekness and Europeanness. As Alexis Tsipras synthetized them in his statement on the eve of the October 2019 EU Summit: "The Prespa Agreement demonstrates the values that the EU is fighting for. Membership of the EU is also a part of it. The agreement reaffirms the EU's ambition to establish peace and stability in the region" (cited in *Nezavisen vesnik* 2019). For some other assessors, the Prespa deal is a product of Greek imperialism (Puhovski 2019). More importantly, the European Commission's Creative Europe Project supports the European Heritage Label, which not only promotes a greater continuity myth but also uses the Parthenon in Athens for cover purposes, accompanied by a slogan Europe Starts Here (EHL). The EHL website stipulates that the "European Heritage sites are milestones in the creation of today's Europe. Spanning from the dawn of civilization to the Europe we see today, these sites celebrate and symbolize European ideals, values, history and integration." Even from this basic definition, it is evident that through the EHL pages, the EU (by employing authorized heritage discourse) seeks to create a progressive, continuous narrative of Europe, spanning from the first steps of what is termed as European civilization to the contemporary European Union (Turunen 2019, 194).

The EU's indirect or soft imperial dominance could be explained by the Gramscian notion of cultural hegemony. Its normative power is still power, regardless of all the ways of its legitimation in the countries of its periphery or sub-periphery, and it relies on the following premises: (1) EU integration as an ideology (with any criticism being met with an arsenal of labeling and even geopolitical discrediting); (2) the EU as a proper religion (with rewards and punishment for (dis)obeying, whereas scaremongering goes hand in hand with (unrealistic) promises for heavenly, post-accession, life); (3) the mode of knowledge production which reflects the spirit of self-colonizing (with universities, academic writings, and numerous NGOs and think-tanks, dedicated to promoting the idea of Europe); and (4) the geopolitics of EU enlargement being based on Western capital that has penetrated the Balkans (with debtocracy in the (sub)periphery as an ordinary way of survival, keeping the lower strata of the society distant and unwelcome). Still, the story of the implementation of the Copenhagen criteria and acceptance of the so-called European values and conditionality is overshadowed by the proverbial double standards, which additionally question legitimacy and the credibility of the EU enlargement policy. The external imposition of constitutional revisions, interference in government coalition formations, debtocracy and growing economic dependency, financing of the media and NGO sector as means for spreading cultural hegemony, and the flexibility of the rule of law in the wake of conflict resolution, seem to suggest that the enlargement policy has become part of the EU's wider geopolitical considerations rather than a plan to expand the European family.

References

Ahmed, Sara. 2000. *Strange Encounters: Embodied Others in Post-coloniality*. London: Routledge.

Apasiev, Dimitar. 2019. "Pravnite aspekti na referendumot za t.n. Prespanski dogovor megju Republika Grcija i 'Vtorata strana'." *Yearbook of the Faculty of Law* 8, http://js.ugd.edu.mk/index.php/YFL/article/view/2987.

Armakolas, Ioannis, and Ljupcho Petkovski. 2019. *Blueprint Prespa? Lessons Learned from the Greece-North Macedonia Agreement*. Skopje: FES.

Barigazzi, Jacopo. 2020. "North Macedonia, Albania get green light for EU membership talks." *Politico*, 25 March, https://www.politico.eu/article/north-macedonia-albania-eu-membership-talks/.

BBC. 2019. "Greece's invisible minority: The Macedonian Slavs." 24 February, https://www.bbc.com/news/stories-47258809.

Bechev, Dimitar. 2019. "Did Macron kill the EU enlargement dream?" *Al Jazeera*, 23 October, https://www.aljazeera.com/indepth/opinion/macron-kill-eu-enlargement-dream-191023072639960.html.

Bechev, Dimitar. 2020. "Despite good news, the Western Balkans are in trouble." *Al Jazeera*, 1 April, https://www.aljazeera.com/indepth/opinion/good-news-western-balkans-trouble-200401155854613.html.

Bender, Kristof, Adnan Cerimagic, and Gerald Knaus. 2020. "EU has turned enlargement into a hamster wheel." *Balkan Insight*, 15 January, https://balkaninsight.com/2020/01/21/eu-has-turned-enlargement-into-a-hamster-wheel/.

Bhambra, Gurminder, K. 2009. "Postcolonial Europe or understanding Europe in times of the postcolonial." In *The SAGE Handbook of European Studies*, edited by Chris Rumford, 69–86. London: Sage.

Bieber, Florian. 2020. *The Rise of Authoritarianism in the Western Balkans*. Cham: Palgrave Macmillan.

Böröcz, Jozsef, and Melinda Kovács, eds. 2001. *Empire's New Clothes: Unveiling EU Enlargement*. Telford: Central Europe Review.

Chakrabarty, Dipesh. 2000. *Provincializing Europe: Postcolonial Thought and Historical Difference*. Princeton, NJ: Princeton University Press.

Chandler, David. 2000. *Bosnia: Faking Democracy After Dayton*. London: Pluto Press.

Chandler, David. 2006. *Empire in Denial: The Politics of State-building*. London: Pluto Press.

Chryssogelos, Angelos. 2019. "Macedonia's name change deal is a triumph for the EU, but worrying for democracy." *Time*, 22 January, https://time.com/5508640/prespes-macedonia-greece-eu-democracy/.

Chryssogelos, Angelos, and Elena B. Stavrevska. 2019. "The Prespa Agreement between Greece and North Macedonia and the discordancies of EU foreign policy." *European Foreign Affairs Review* 24(4): 427–446.

Cox, Robert. 1981. "Social forces, states and world orders: Beyond international relations theory." *Millennium* 10(2): 126–155.

Dabashi, Hamid. 2019. *Europe and its Shadows: Coloniality after Empire*. London: Pluto Press.

Damovski, Aleksandar. 2020. "Bugarija ni go uslovuva datumot so makedonskiot jazik I malcinstvo. 'Ova se kosi so evropskite vrednosti,' veli Dimitrov." *MKD*, 17 April, https://www.mkd.mk/makedonija/politika/bugarija-ni-go-uslovuva-datumot-so-makedonskiot-jazik-i-malcinstvo-ova-se-kosi.

Delimitov, Kostadin. 2018. "Merkel: Referendumot e istoriska shansa." *Deutsche Welle*, 8 September, https://www.dw.com/mk/меркел-референдумот-е-историска-шанса/a-45410061.

Della Sala, Vincent. 2010. "Political mythology, myth and the European Union." *Journal of Common Market Studies* 48(1): 1–19.

Denešen vesnik. 2018. "Zaev gi povika biznismenite da gi potkupuvaat rabotnicite za referendumot." 13 September, https://denesen.mk/zaev-gi-povika-biznismenite-da-gi-potkupuvaat-rabotnicite-za-referendumot/.

Dérens, Jean-Arnault, and Laurent Geslin. 2015. "Balkans are the new front line." *Le Monde diplomatique*, July, https://mondediplo.com/2015/07/04balkans.

Diez, Thomas. 2005. "Constructing the self and changing others: Reconsidering 'normative power Europe'." *Millennium* 33(3): 613–636.

Dizdarević, Zlatko. 2019. "Europe and the Western Balkans: Dull reality and unrealistic expectations." *Green European Journal*, 8 November, https://www.greeneuropeanjournal.eu/europe-and-the-western-balkans-dull-reality-and-unrealistic-expectations/.

EEAS. 2018. "Spokesperson statement on the adoption of the Law on Amnesty by the Assembly of the Former Yugoslav Republic of Macedonia." 19 December, https://eeas.europa.eu/topics/human-rights-democracy/55761/spokesperson-statement-adoption-law-amnesty-assembly-former-yugoslav-republic-macedonia_en.

ESI. 2002. "Ahmeti's village: Political economy of interethnic relations in Macedonia." 1 October, https://www.ecoi.net/en/document/1237624.html.

EU Council. 1992. "Lisbon European Council 8–9 June." http://aei.pitt.edu/1420/1/Lisbon_june_1992.pdf.

EU Council. 2020. "Communication." 25 March, https://www.parlament.gv.at/PAKT/EU/XXVII/EU/01/66/EU_16606/imfname_10969905.pdf.

European Commission. 2020. "Commission welcomes the green light to opening of accession talks with Albania and North Macedonia." *Press Release*, 25 March, https://ec.europa.eu/commission/presscorner/detail/en/IP_20_519.

European Parliament. 2006. "Decision No. 1855/2006/EC of the European Parliament and of the Council of 12 December 2006 establishing the Culture Programme (2007 to 2013)." 27 December, https://eur-lex.europa.eu/legal-content/EN/TXT/HTML/?uri=CELEX:32006D1855&rid=4.

Expres.mk. 2018. "Kocijas: Dogovorot zabrani makedonsko malcinstvo vo Grcija, 'Vinožito' e grupa prijateli." 22 June, https://expres.mk/kodzias-dogovorot-zabrani-makedonsko-malcinstvo-vo-grcija-vinozhito-e-grupa-prijateli/.

FES. 2019. "Post-prespanska Severna Makedonija i predizborna Evropa." *Predizvici* 1, https://www.fes-skopje.org/fileadmin/user_upload/documents/Predizvici.pdf.

Fidanovski, Kristijan. 2019. "Why I don't like the term 'Western Balkans'." *Vostokian*, 4 February, https://vostokian.com/why-i-dont-like-the-term-western-balkans/.

Floudas, Demetrius Andreas. 2002. "Pardon? A name for a conflict? FYROM's dispute with Greece revisited." In *The New Balkans: Disintegration and Reconstruction*, edited by George A. Kourvetaris et al., 85–117. New York: Columbia University Press.

Fouskas, Vassilis K., and Bülent Gökay. 2019. *The Disintegration of Euro-Atlanticism and New Authoritarianism: Global Power-Shift*. Cham: Palgrave Macmillan.

Galbraith S. John. 1960. "The 'turbulent frontier' as a factor in British expansion." *Comparative Studies in Society and History* 2(2): 150–168.

Gillingham, John. 2016. *The EU: An Obituary*. London: Verso.

Gowan, Peter. 1999. "The NATO powers and the Balkan tragedy." *New Left Review* 234: 83–105.

The Guardian. 2018. "Historic deal on shared Macedonian identity must be honoured." 20 July, https://www.theguardian.com/global/2018/jul/20/historic-deal-on-shared-macedonian-identity-must-be-honoured.

Harris, Mary N., and Csaba Lévai, eds. 2008. *Europe and Its Empires*. Pisa: Pisa University Press.

Harding, Gareth. 2012. "The myth of Europe." *Foreign Policy*, 3 January, https://foreignpolicy.com/2012/01/03/the-myth-of-europe/.

ICG Europe. 2005. "Macedonia: Not out of the woods yet." *ICG Europe Briefing*, 25 February, https://www.crisisgroup.org/europe-central-asia/balkans/macedonia/macedonia-not-out-woods-yet.

Janev, Igor. 1999. "Legal aspects of the use of a provisional name for Macedonia in the United Nations system." *American Journal of International Law* 93(1): 155–160.

Jennings, Jeremy, and Anthony Kemp-Welch, eds. 2003. *Intellectuals in Politics: From the Dreyfus Affair to Salman Rushdie*. London: Routledge.

Kacarska, Simonida. 2019. "Unfulfilled promises and missed opportunities in North Macedonia." *Green European Journal*, 28 November, https://www.greeneuropeanjournal.eu/unfulfilled-promises-and-missed-opportunities-in-north-macedonia/.

Kaldor, Mary. 1999. *New and Old Wars. Organized Violence in a Global Era*. Cambridge: Polity Press.

Kanal 5. 2019. "Samo intervju." 22 November, https://www.youtube.com/watch?v=5vjsZFAMMIs.

Karadjoski, Boško. 2019. "Cartography of one political eschatology: Macedonian idea of Europe and the problem of identity." Conference paper presented at the Fifth International Philosophical Dialogue East-West, 2 October, https://karadzovbosko.wordpress.com/2020/03/07/.

Karajkov, Risto. 2004. "Macedonian referendum: What's the time?" *OBCT Newsletter*, 3 November, https://www.balcanicaucaso.org/eng/Areas/North-Macedonia/Macedonian-Referendum.-What-s-the-Time-27105.

Kinnvall, Catarina. 2016. "The postcolonial has moved into Europe: Bordering, security and ethno-cultural belonging." *Journal of Common Market Studies* 54(1): 152–168.

Kiossev, Alexander. 1995. "The self-colonizing metaphor." *Atlas of Transformation*, http://monu menttotransformation.org/atlas-of-transformation/html/s/self-colonization/the-self-colonizing-metaphor-alexander-kiossev.html.

Kolozova, Katerina. 2019. "How the EU Balkanised the Balkans." *Al Jazeera*, 2 November, https://www.aljazeera.com/indepth/opinion/eu-balkanised-balkans-191029092720597.html.

Korybko, Andrew. 2018. "Macedonia's about to become the world's first 'politically correct' police state." *EurAsia Future*, 14 June, https://eurasiafuture.com/2018/06/14/macedonias-about-to-become-the-worlds-first-politically-correct-police-state/.

Kurir. 2018. "Zaev od Strumica so pokerski recnik: Nemam rezerven plan, igrav so mojot narod na se ili nisto." 24 September, https://kurir.mk/makedonija/vesti/video-zaev-od-strumica-so-pokerski-rechnik-nemam-rezerven-plan-igrav-so-mojot-narod-na-se-ili-nishto/.

Lapavitsas, Costas. 2018. *The Left Case against the EU*. London: Polity Press.

Lähdesmäki, Tuuli, et al., eds. 2019. *Dissonant Heritages and Memories in Contemporary Europe*. Cham: Palgrave Macmillan.

Lijphard, Arend. 1977. *Democracy in Plural Societies: A Comparative Exploration*. New Haven, CT: Yale University Press.

MakFax. 2018. "Zaev: Ni treba kamsikar, ni treba nekoj od NATO i EU da dojde i da ne potsredi." 12 September, https://makfax.com.mk/makedonija/видео-заев-ни-треба-камшикар-ни-треба/.

Marusic Sinisa Jakov. 2018. "Macedonia starts procedure on changing country's name." *Balkan Insight*, 8 October, https://balkaninsight.com/2018/10/08/macedonia-starts-procedure-for-name-change-10-08-2018/.

Mavroudeas, Stavros. 2018. "Interview for *Press TV*." 30 September, https://www.youtube.com/watch?time_continue=6&v=LWZ3VAri_g4.

Merlingen, Michael. 2007. "Everything is dangerous: A critique of 'normative power Europe'." *Security Dialogue* 38(4): 435–453.

Milchevski, Ilcho. 2013. "A requiem for a dream: The name issue and the accession of Macedonia to the EU." *International Issues & Slovak Foreign Policy Affairs* 22(4): 40–59.

Momaz, Rym, and Andrew Gray. 2019. "Macron urges reform of 'bizarre' system for EU hopefuls." *Politico*, 16 October, https://www.politico.eu/article/macron-urges-reform-of-bizarre-system-for-eu-hopefuls/.

Nezavisen vesnik. 2018. "Academics are in favor of the 'yes' vote in the referendum." 29 August, https://nezavisen.mk/academics-are-in-favour-of-the-yes-vote-in-the-referendum/?lang=en.

Nezavisen vesnik. 2019. "The Economist Western Balkans Summit sends a strong message: We expect the EU to materialize its promises." 1 October, https://nezavisen.mk/the-economist-western-balkans-summit-sends-a-strong-message-we-expect-the-eu-to-materialize-its-promises/?lang=en.

Nikodinovska Krstevska, Ana. 2019. "Prespa Agreement between the Republic of Macedonia and the Republic of Greece through the prism of international law." *Yearbook of the Faculty of Law* 8: 125–135.

Oberg, Jan. 2004. "Peace-prevention: Western conflict management as the continuation of power politics by other means." *Yugoslavia: What Should Have Been Done*, 30 June, https://yugoslavia-what-should-have-been-done.org/2004/06/30/.

Passerini, Luisa. 2012. "Europe and its others: Is there a European identity?" In *The Oxford Handbook of Postwar European History*, edited by Dan Stone, 120–138. Oxford: Oxford University Press.

Pavlović, Srdja. 2017. "West is best: How 'stabilitocracy' undermines democracy building in the Balkans." *LSE Blog*, 5 May, https://blogs.lse.ac.uk/europpblog/2017/05/05/west-is-best-how-stabilitocracy-undermines-democracy-building-in-the-balkans/.

Plavšić, Dragan. 2018. "Macedonia, without additions: Why we must oppose the Tsipras-Zaev agreement." *Lefteast*, 21 September, http://www.criticatac.ro/lefteast/macedonia-tsipras-zaev/.

Protothema. 2018. "Lafazanis: A ban on blackmail, pressure and redemption to pass the deal to FYROM." 20 October, https://www.protothema.gr/politics/article/831437/lafazanis.

Pugh, Michael. 2017. "Oligarchy and economic legacy in Bosnia and Herzegovina." *Peacebuilding* 5 (3): 223–238.

Puhovski, Žarko. 2019. "Dogmatica: Politički analitičar Žarko Puhovski." *Z1 Televizija*, 28 May, https://www.youtube.com/watch?v=0zn17q36q1E.

Purkiss, Jessica. 2018. "Macedonia name referendum: Russian warriors and British PR firms fight it out for the country's soul." *Independent*, 28 September, https://www.independent.co.uk/

news/world/europe/macedonia-name-referendum-vote-russia-uk-pr-firms-europe-nato-kremlin-a8559556.html.

Rossos, Andrew. 2008. *Macedonia and the Macedonians (a History)*. Stanford, CA: Hoover Institution Press.

Said, Edward. 1994. *Culture and Imperialism*. New York: Vintage Books.

Sarkanjac, Branko. 2004. *Makedonski katahresis: Kako da se zboruva za Makedonija*. Skopje: Forum.

Shkaric, Svetomir. 2018. "Dogovorot so Grcija i ustavnite promeni." *Res Publica*, 14 September, https://respublica.edu.mk/blog/2018-09-14-08-02-16.

Siljanovska Davkova, Gordana. 2018. "On the Prespa Agreement and beyond." *UMD*, 28 January, http://umdiaspora.org/tag/gordana-siljanovska-davkova/.

Spivak, Gayatri Chakravorty. 1988. "Can the subaltern speak?" In *Marxism and the Interpretation of Culture*, edited by Cary Nelson and Lawrence Grossberg, 271–313. Urbana, IL: University of Illinois Press.

Stefanescu, Bogdan. 2012. *Postcommunism / Postcolonialism: Siblings of Subalternity*. Bucharest: Editura universitatii din Bucharesti.

Streeck, Wolfgang. 2016. *How Will Capitalism End: Essays on Failing System*. London: Verso.

Todorova, Maria. 2009. *Imagining the Balkans*. Oxford: Oxford University Press.

Turunen, Johanna. 2019. "A geography of coloniality: Re-narrating European integration." In *Dissonant Heritages and Memories in Contemporary Europe*, edited by Tuuli Lähdesmäki et al., 185–214. Cham: Palgrave Macmillan.

Vankovska, Biljana. 2007. "The role of the Ohrid Framework Agreement and the Peace Process in Macedonia." In *Regional Cooperation, Peace Enforcement, and the Role of the Treaties in the Balkans*, edited by Stefano Bianchini et al., 41–61, Ravenna: Longo Editore.

Vankovska, Biljana. 2020. "Geopolitics of the Prespa Agreement: Background and after-effects." *Journal of Balkan and Near Eastern Studies* 12(2): 343–371.

Vasilevski, Alek. 2019. "The Prespa Agreement unwrapped." *UMD Generation M*, 23 May, http://www.umdgenm.org/2019/05/23/the-prespa-agreement-unwrapped/.

Whitman, Richard G. 2011. *Normative Power Europe: Empirical and Theoretical Perspectives*. Basingstoke: Palgrave Macmillan.

Wiberg, Håkan. 1993. "Societal security and the explosion of Yugoslavia." In *Identity, Migration and the New Security Agenda in Europe*, edited by Ole Wæver et al., 93–109. London: Pinter.

Wiberg, Håkan. 1996. "Third Party Intervention in Yugoslavia." In *Organized Anarchy in Europe: The Role of Intergovernmental Organizations*, edited by Jaap de Wilde and Håkan Wiberg, 203–225. London: I.B. Tauris.

Wiberg, Håkan. 2009. "What's in a name?" *TFF*, 27 November, http://www.oldsite.transnational.org/Area_YU/2009/Wiberg_MacName.html.

Woodward, Susan L. 2013. "The long intervention: Continuity in the Balkan theatre." *Review of International Studies* 39(5): 1169–1187.

Woodward, Susan L. 2017. *Ideology of Failed States. Why Interventions Fail?* Cambridge: Cambridge University Press.

Leandrit I. Mehmeti

9 Kosovo's EU Perspective: Pushing it Forward or Pulling it Away?

Kosovo's unique position, largely due to its contested political status in international relations, makes it unclear as to whether the country will ever join the EU. The key cornerstone is normalization of relations with Serbia, the outcome of which should provide for further consolidation of Kosovo's statehood, including a membership in different international organizations. The EU integration of Kosovo and Serbia, as well as the entire Western Balkan region, is expected to strengthen security, ease the ongoing political tensions, and ideally accommodate different ethnic communities' demands (living in respective countries) for equal political and social rights. In fact, scholars of the region are in agreement that the integration of the entire Western Balkans into the supranational structures of the EU does have the potential to ensure long-lasting peace (Belloni 2009; Elbasani 2013; Noutcheva 2009; Savic 2007).

For quite some time, Europe has been defined in terms of the EU, while Europeanization and Europeanness are increasingly measured by the aspiring countries' institutional consolidation and their adoption of EU norms and rules (Katzenstein 1997, 261–262; Schimmelfennig and Sedelmeier 2002, 501). Here, both rationalism and constructivism – social metatheories defined by a set of assumptions about the social world rather than by specific hypothesis – help explain political developments in the Western Balkans and thus Kosovo's perspective to join the EU. In this sense, in rationalist institutionalism, the casual status of institutions generally remains secondary to the individual and material interest (Schimmelfennig and Sedelmeier 2002, 509). Institutions are, therefore, treated only as variables between material interest and collective outcomes, providing constraints and incentives, not reasons for actions and altering cost/benefit calculations, not identities. In contrast, the constructivist perspective is interested more on how the institutions shape actors' identities and interest and how institutions provide meaning to the rights and obligations entailed in their social roles (Schimmelfennig and Sedelmeier 2002, 509). In the case of Kosovo, both of these theories are helpful to explain the dynamics of political developments and the relation between Kosovo and the EU but also of Kosovo and Serbia.

With the above in mind and for the purpose of this study, I adopt Brian Fay's insistence on objectivism and fallibilism. Fay points out that objectivism is a complex of ideas, which may be defined as the "thesis that reality exists 'in itself' independently of the mind and that this reality is knowable as such" (1996, 200). In order to achieve a considerable degree of objectivity, it is important to go through a process of elimination and ridding ourselves of deceptive mental elements of subjective factors, which may cloud our mental perception (Fay 1996, 202). This epistemic orientation is broadly

https://doi.org/10.1515/9783110684216-009

positivist in nature; however, Fay points out that positivism asserts that "empirical observation and testing freed from preconceptions are the means by which facts are ascertained and explained" (Fay 1996, 72). Such claims are completely unfeasible because all human perceptions are affected by preconceptions, ranging from common sense ones to theoretical ones of varying degrees of sophistication; in fact, positivists' "facts" are inherently "theory impregnated" (Fay 1996, 72–74). Furthermore, Fay sees that objectivism presupposes a realist ontology and interprets that "the structure of reality exists separately from mind and thus that the objective truth exists whether cognizers know about it or not, or value it or not or wish it were the way it is or prefer some alternative" (Fay 1996, 202). This understanding and interpretation of objectivity is useful for the analysis in this chapter especially when describing or assessing a political reality on a given context and situation. However, the analysis here also takes into consideration that objectivist lines of analysis often have fallacies and may create incoherence. According to fallibilism, as Fay puts it, "nothing about the world can be known for certain; certainty is not something which science can provide us" (Fay 1996, 208). As further clarified, this is not to say that the science is flawed, but simply that this is an inherent feature of the epistemology of science and reasoning and that no amount or quality of empirical confirmation or disconfirmation is sufficient to guarantee ascertainable truth or falsity.

The analysis here takes the above elements seriously, especially in relation to the political dynamics and developments concerning Kosovo as such and its EU integration perspective. More precisely, I examine how different players such as governments in Kosovo and Serbia (and individual actors within these structures) as well as different EU institutions perceive and discursively construct the EU integration and enlargement tendencies. Altogether they are ontologically real social and political forces whose constructed discourse can drive forward or stall and delay the Balkans' integration perspective and the accompanying EU's transformative initiatives. Here, I focus on the case of Kosovo and three dimensions in particular. I start by looking at corruption and state capture phenomena as factors that hinder democratization, which is considered as the backbone of the EU integration. The analysis proceeds with an examination of the normalization process, both its understanding and expected outcomes. Finally, the paper assesses how the previously mentioned processes are influenced by geopolitical rationales and how such dimensions impact the EU conditionality policy.

Post-independence Democratization

Before its proclamation of independence in 2008, Kosovo did not have a very vocal and active political opposition. While all political parties were part of the government (both local and national) during the UN Mission in Kosovo (UNMIK) administration, they performed rather poorly in terms of good governance. In the aftermath of the 1999 NATO intervention, with too much focus being placed on security and stability and not enough on institutional and state-building capacities, corruption was not combatted; on the contrary, it properly developed and continued to flourish, regardless of the context. For example, Katarina Tadić and Arolda Elbasani (2018, 185) analyzed recruitment practices and identified different inconsistencies embedded in the UNMIK's promulgated legislation, enabling formal and informal strategies of recruitment of political cronies in the newly created civil service. Thus, the local actors' malpractices were of secondary relevance for as long as the external players were in charge, acting as the ultimate authority to decide on the rules and monitor their implementation (Tadić and Elbasani 2018, 188–192). The loose legislation and procedural irregularities accompanying UNMIK involvement enabled the establishment of a patronage network of clientelist based appointments, impossible to get rid of later on. In fact, as concluded by one comparative study, the post-2008 legislation regulating the civil service has witnessed increased levels of partisan control and influence (Doli, Korenica, and Rogova 2012).

Some early studies about corruption viewed it more in political terms, in the sense of corrupt political leaders who focused on creating environments that would maximize their chances to be reelected (Schumpeter 1950; Welch 1974). Subsequently, authors have considered corruption of both administration and policymakers, united around power maximization and wealth accumulation, which necessitated a careful selection of members in key positions (Breton 1974; Fenno 1977; Mayhew 1974; Rose-Ackerman 1978). More recently, and also referring to the Balkans, analyses have investigated the impact of corruption on transition, suggesting that it actually represents a major roadblock in the establishment of consolidated democracies (Andreas 2004; Grødeland 2013; Phillips 2010; UNODC 2011). Accordingly, they have looked into the EU role in combatting corruption, trying to identify the most appropriate mechanisms that can assist with the democratization process (Balfour and Stratulat 2011; Kurtouglu-Eskisar and Komsouglu 2015; Moravcsik and Vachudova 2003; Pond 2006; Staal 2014). In all this, state capture, largely understood as a process of manipulation of the state for individual needs, is the most acute form of corruption. In her analysis of state capture in Serbia, Vesna Pešić points out that political party leaderships are the primary agents that have seized state property including public companies and institutions for their own interest, financially backed up by wealthy tycoons (Pešić 2007, 6). Some newer studies about state capture insinuate that the situation in Serbia has actually worsened, with the democratic system being seriously endangered by an authoritarian one (Keil 2018; Radeljić 2019). Despite this, however, Serbia has progressed relatively well on its path toward the EU integration also strengthening the perception that reporting about the progress of a country toward the EU integration may be influenced by other geopolitical issues rather than the reality on the ground.

In the case of Kosovo, state capture is vital due to its capacity to endanger the state's EU perspective and consolidation of its political status in international relations. Despite some progress in relation to democratic development having been made, high levels of corruption demonstrate that the Prishtina leadership has developed mechanisms which actually pull Kosovo away rather than closer to the EU integration perspective. The civic spectrum of the society, including different NGOs and think tanks (the FOL Movement, GAP Institute, Democracy for Development, Kosovo Center for Investigative Journalism (KCIJ), Kosovar Institute for Policy Research and Development (KIPRED)) as well as the local media are crucial in raising concerns and awareness about the malpractice. For example, the FOL Movement produced a report exposing the involvement of international staff working for the UNMIK, NATO-led Kosovo Force (KFOR), and the EU Rule of Law Mission (EULEX), in corrupt and criminal affairs in cooperation with local politicians through the abuse of hundreds of millions of euros from both the Kosovo budget and the EU financial packages; in addition to discussing the abuse of official positions and major monetary allocations, the report also offers insights into the smuggling activities and corruption at high positions, including the Special Representative of the Secretary General's involvement in securing a monopoly of Monaco's mobile telephone services despite better offers from other networks (Symonds 2010, 6–9).

Some other reports investigate how the local political actors abuse their power to recruit party loyalists and establish solid grounds for political patronage and clientelism, which altogether facilitates the capture of state institutions. According to a study conducted by Democracy for Development, it is unlikely that an individual may join public service based on merit (Gashi and Emerson 2013). As clarified, positions and career progress are mostly conditioned by political affiliation or personal connections, which consequently provide political parties with an opportunity to strengthen their influence over state institutions. During the UNMIK administration, the existence of clientelism and political patronage was reflected in the recruitment practices to high ranking public positions through the Senior Public Appointment Committee, many of whom accommodated members of the dominant political parties, the Democratic League of Kosovo (LDK) and the Democratic Party of Kosovo (PDK). Back then, "[t]he international community did everything to prevent violence among Kosovar Albanian political groupings" (Gashi and Emerson 2013, 32). The internationals' decision to prioritize stability alone, while ignoring other aspects of the state building process, has proved detrimental for Kosovo's democratization and Europeanization. Such conclusions are complemented by the KCIJ's research, which reveals that the volume of clientelism and political patronage gradually increased in the period from 1999 to 2014, with direct links between public administration and political parties' officials having reached some very high and thus seriously concerning levels (Boletini and Kalaja 2014). The extension of malpractice and the need to accommodate loyal party clients in the public sector has also resulted in the establishment of additional ministries and institutions. For example, the coalition government led by Ramush Haradinaj (also the founder and president of the Alliance for the Future of Kosovo), had five deputy prime ministers, twenty-one ministers, seventy-five deputy ministers, and four national coordinators (a position created for the first time). Referring to the additional, either fictitious or unnecessary appointments, a study from the GAP Institute suggested reduction of the overall number of ministries and staff employed in public administration (GAP Institute 2015). However, the attractiveness of high public positions is best understood when considering financial aspects. As found out by the KIPRED, the MPs' declaration of wealth in the period between 2008 and 2012 showed an unprecedented increase without any proof of its origins; for example, in two years, a PDK member managed to increase wealth by 428 percent, and another MP, from the LDK, by 258 percent (Qosaj-Mustafa 2013, 10).

With regard to the key role played by the media, the online outlet *Insajderi* (2020) has published a big number of investigative reports, exposing the widespread abuse of power, ranging from the placement of party loyalists in high positions (including the judiciary), to the manipulation of privatization processes and budget allocation, so that procurement agencies would favor companies and businesses where specific groups and individuals have shares and interests. With the exception of the Vetëvendosje (Self-determination) Movement (VV), the numerous analyses show that very few cases of wrongdoing have ended up in courts or were under investigation. In fact, in only one instance, the accused – Azem Syla, also nicknamed the Uncle, was arrested and taken into custody by the Kosovo Police in 2016 (Morina 2018). Syla, a former commander of the Kosovo Liberation Army (UÇK) and an MP representing the PDK, was accused by a EULEX prosecutor of having illegally appropriated land near Prishtina by falsifying the ownership documents, but then was released in 2018, a few months after the case was transferred from EULEX (which had labelled Syla and his group of two dozen individuals as one of the most significant criminal groups that ever existed in Kosovo) to the local courts (Gashi 2016; Morina 2018). Another scandal included the so-called 2013 Pronto Affair, which involved a conversation between Adem Grabovci, the leader of PDK parliamentary group, and Hashim Thaçi, the then prime minister, Vlora Çitaku, then minister of EU integration, and Sami Lushtaku, the former mayor of Skenderaj municipality. The affair got its name because of Thaçi's use of the Italian word *pronto* to answer Grabovci's phone calls, largely resembling the Italian mafia-like style. The conversations were about appointing party loyalists in certain positions such as company boards, courts, prosecution, state agencies, police and intelligence, national public media, etc. Grabovci was dismissed from his position after public pressure and the publication of the 2016 Pronto Two affair (*Te Sheshi* 2016), involving again Thaçi and Kadri Veseli, the Chairman of the Assembly (and formerly, head of the shadow Kosovo intelligence service, controlled by the PDK). The case was brought in front of the courts, but all of the accused were acquitted in January 2020 by the local court, ruling that there was not enough evidence to indict them (Ramaj 2020). Yet another example is the resignation of Elez Blakaj, one of the prosecutors of the Special Prosecution of Kosovo, due to the threats he received while investigating sensitive cases, including those of international terrorism and the manipulation of the veterans lists involving the names of high-level politicians implicated in the 1999 war (Isufi 2018). Once escaped to the United States, Blakaj posted a letter on his social media confessing the reasons behind his resignation, including the pressures from political figures as well as from the Chief State Prosecutor, Aleksander Lumezi (Bllaca 2018). The whole drama resulted in protests calling for Lumezi's resignation; in return, he kept calling Blakaj "a failed prosecutor" (*Koha* 2018), and for Prime Minister Haradinaj, Blakaj was "a thief and a joker" (Sertolli 2018). What characterizes all the above scandals, recorded conversations, and exposing investigative reports, is the lack of reaction from members of Kosovo's political circles, with the exception of the VV. As proved by Naser Miftari (2015, 68), "[n]o one was fired, no official resigned, no one called for extraordinary elections, and nothing unusual happened after all." However, following the 2017 general election, the voting pattern has changed. The published stories and live conversations concerning the degree of state capture in Kosovo seemed to have generated a reaction among the public, consequently deciding to support the opposition force, the Vetëvendosje Movement.

The emergence of the VV in 2005 signifies a crucial development in the process of Kosovo's democratization. Its leader Albin Kurti and other founding members had already been active before, when resisting Serbian oppression. Moreover, while in favor of dialogue and peaceful solutions, they often found themselves caught up between different violent actions when confronting the international administration before and after independence. The VV has consistently depicted the UNMIK as "colonialist" and "anti-democratic," and thus found it paradoxical that such controversial administration was tasked with promoting democracy (Cocozzelli 2013; Vetëvendosje 2010). Apart from offering a fresh understanding of Kosovo's political and economic perspective, the VV was actually the first social movement in the post-1999 context to adopt a position that was more civic- than service-based, as was the case with other civic organizations. The VV organized protests against the UNMIK and Kosovo government because of their corrupt affairs and decisions, and opposed different political developments such as the negotiation of the final political status, the 2013 agreement between Serbia and Kosovo, decentralization proposals, etc. Because of the protests and their political articulation, the VV was qualified as nationalist and even extremist by the local parties and international community. Robert Austin observes that "the internationals who still rule over Kosovo have marginalized it as much as possible" (Austin 2019, 180). For Stephanie Schwandner-Sievers, a careful examination of various UN reports suggests that the VV was widely perceived as radical and dangerous, capable of endangering a peaceful political process, while some other sources went as far as to label the movement as terrorist in nature; overall, the international attitude toward the

VV was "ambiguous and contradictory, if not outright helpless or even defamatory" (Schwandner-Sievers 2013, 106). In any case, the VV promoted consolidation of civil society, seeing it as crucial part of democratization process. As Juan Linz and Alfred Stepan argue, a vibrant civil society must exist side by side with a healthy political society not just for the transition to democracy but also for the consolidation process to take place and primarily when civil society exists autonomously from political society (Linz and Stepan 1996, 9–10).

The VV modified its approach when it decided to run in the late 2010 parliamentary election, eventually succeeding to become a significant political force. Since then, it has progressed to become the dominant player in the 2017 and 2019 elections. In an interview with *Chicago Policy Review*, Kurti stated that even though the VV had decided to join the parliament, they did not abandon their old methods and thus would continue with demonstrations (Wallin 2014). For example, their protest mentality was evident in the parliament when throwing water or gas canisters in order to top the ratification of border demarcation with Montenegro. Apart from transforming the parliament into a more vibrant place, the VV's presence implied fresh antagonism and polarization among political actors, especially when the discussions about corruption, institutional accountability, and the EU integration process started to take place.

Understanding the Normalization Process

The process of the normalization of relations between Kosovo and Serbia commenced in 2011 and almost a decade later, it still remains unclear in terms of the expected outcomes. While ranking high on both Belgrade and Prishtina's policy agendas – indicated by an advocacy of reconciliation and better living conditions, as well as by a number of technical agreements already signed, with some of them being implemented – the ongoing normalization process lacks clarity and as such represents a major challenge (Mehmeti 2016, 221–228). With regard to Serbia's aspirations, it is keen to progress with EU accession, to see the Serbian community in Kosovo achieve higher levels of autonomy, and to preserve the *status quo* concerning the Kosovo status. Keeping its status contested for as long as possible is largely due to the hope that some future geopolitical shifts may cause major disagreements among the dominant supporters of Kosovo's independence in the West and possibly where some of them change their mind. Even though such an approach is neither attractive nor tenable because of the complex relations between the two sides (Economides, Ker-Lindsay, and Papadimitriou 2010), the Serbian leadership has nevertheless managed to obstruct Kosovo's consolidation of statehood and presence in international relations, as well as to remain a key player within Kosovo's internal affairs and thus affect its political stability. On the other hand, apart from being keen on its own solidification, Kosovo is also interested in EU integration and incorporating the Serb-dominated northern part of Kosovo under Prishtina's legislative framework, rather than Belgrade's.

Thus, it is only the EU integration perspective that Kosovo and Serbia share in terms of their interests and policy considerations. In other areas, the two sides are diametrically distant, since each of them has sought to stick with its original plan A – to validate or prevent independence – without showing any incentive to compromise. According to the Brussels administration, the aim of the normalization process is "to promote cooperation between the two sides, help them achieve progress on the path to Europe and improve the lives of the people" (European Union External Action 2020). However, since 2016, the process has been in trouble, with political issues and the implementation of technical agreements (with unavoidable political implications) brought to a standstill position. The prospect of coming up with a plan B is a matter of what each party deems a good- or bad-case scenario, which always requires consideration of current and future geopolitical climate. With this in mind, other options including that of partitioning or, as presented to the public by Kosovo's president since August 2018, of border adjustments have come to occupy more space in the official discourse. Here, we should stress that the idea of Kosovo's partition is not new; the first one to bring it publicly was the Serbian writer and politician Dobrica Ćosić, following the 1968 clashes between Albanian demonstrators and Serbian police (Brown 1999). Later, during the NATO intervention and settlement efforts, Ćosić restated his idea, insisting that "partition of Kosovo and Metohija and demarcation between Serbia and Albania would lastingly settle the Kosmet question" (cited in Biserko 2011).

Looking more broadly, the question of partition as a solution to conflicts of ethnic nature has been analyzed widely. While considered as a viable solution by some academics (Chapman and Roeder 2007; Dawnes 2004, 2006; Johnson 2008; Kaufmann 1996, 1998, 2007), others are more critical because of the costs of population transfers and, even more drastically, loss of life (Schaeffer 1990), as well as because of the argument maintaining that termination of wars by partition may not necessarily prevent reemergence of conflict (Sambanis 2000). Back in the 1990s, John Mearsheimer and Stephen Van Evera discussed the case of Bosnia and Herzegovina and proposed a partition along ethnic lines, which would allow establishment of a state for Bosnian Muslims whereas other parts would be allowed to join either Croatia or Serbia, altogether with the idea to create better functioning states rather than force the three communities to stay together as prescribed by the highly problematic Dayton Peace Accord (Mearsheimer and Van Evera 1995). Similarly, Mearsheimer proposed a partition of Kosovo alongside ethnic lines, according to which northern Kosovo would join Serbia whereas the remaining part of Kosovo would be allowed to become independent or join the neighboring Albania (Mearsheimer 2000, 133–134). In his view, such an approach was something sustainable given that the Kosovo Albanian population would never accept living under Serbia after the long-lasting struggles, even with the guarantee of an extended autonomy. Moreover, he suggested that the Serbian authorities could be inclined to accept partition if granted a portion of Bosnia and Herzegovina (in case its division ever materialized), as he previously proposed (Mearsheimer 2000, 135–137). Some more recent analyses of prospects for Kosovo's settlement have also concluded that a partition, accompanied by a very precise agreement between the concerned parties, may be a viable option and as such may not constitute a precedent (Economides, Ker-Lindsay, and Papadimitriou 2010, 107–108), while some assessments going as far as to claim that a *de facto* partition did actually happen under the UNMIK administration (Jenne 2009, 282).

In terms of political discourse, the Serbian Foreign Minister Ivica Dačić has been the most vocal official to promote partitioning but has continuously been rejected by the Kosovo authorities (*Radio Free Europe* 2017). However, this rhetoric was revitalized when Kosovo's president Thaçi started to talk about border adjustments with Serbia as a new way to solve the dispute (Kostreci 2018). This was the first time that a high-level Kosovo Albanian politician openly considered such an option; as clarified, it would include a land swap between parts of northern Kosovo with those of the Preševo Valley (an Albanian-dominated region in Serbia). Even though the accompanying statements triggered harsh opposition within the Kosovo Albanian political establishment, as well as international experts, academics, and commentators, the impact of such an idea was noticeable. With regard to scholarly input, in his *New York Times* opinion piece, Charles Kupchan from Georgetown University and a former fellow in the National Security Council, supported the idea, including a population transfer, to which he referred as "a peaceful ethnic cleansing" (Kupchan 2018). For David Phillips, director of the Institute for the Study of Human Rights at Columbia University and a former senior advisor to the UN Secretariat and US State Department, the changing of borders would only reward Serbia's bullying practices (Phillips 2018).

With regard to experts and policymakers, the US National Security Advisor John Bolton stated that "the US would not stand in the way . . . if two parties to the dispute reached a mutually satisfactory settlement" (*Radio Free Europe* 2018a). Similarly, Federica Mogherini, the EU High Representative for Foreign Affairs and Security Policy, said that "the EU is ready to accept any deal between Kosovo and Serbia that is in accordance with international law and the EU acquis" (*The Economist* 2018). This particular statement was assessed as rather ambiguous (as the EU's overall approach toward the normalization process), as there is no acquis or international law that prevents two states from agreeing to change their border (*The Economist* 2018). In the same line with Mogherini, the EU Commissioner for Enlargement, Johannes Hahn, assessed that the EU was ready to support any agreement between Kosovo and Serbia, but with a note that a bilateral agreement of this kind should not be seen as a blueprint for other cases (Rettman 2018). Finally, Austrian Chancellor Sebastian Kurz, during his visit in Prishtina, also supported the idea of a land swap as a solution (*EUobserver* 2018). On the other hand, German Chancellor Angela Merkel strongly rejected the idea (Gray 2018) and her standpoint was also embraced by different regional leaders, including the prime ministers of Croatia, North Macedonia, and Bosnia and Herzegovina (*The Economist* 2018). The position of Albania's Prime Minister Edi Rama seemed ambiguous; in an interview for an Albanian national television station, he stated that it was up to the Kosovo authorities to decide what was best for them and proceed accordingly (*Ora News TV* 2018).

In Kosovo, the opposition to the above proposal was sound, including both local politicians and representatives of the Serbian Orthodox Church (MacDowal 2018). However, the partitioning idea was put on hold and the normalization process additionally eroded following the failure of yet another Kosovan another attempt to secure place in Interpol. In response to Serbia's lobbying of other Interpol members not to support Kosovo's membership, the Haradinaj government decided to apply a ten percent customs tariffs on imported goods from Serbia and Bosnia and Herzegovina, which was soon after increased to a hundred percent, the lifting of which was conditioned by Serbia's recognition of Kosovo's independence (Morina 2019; *Radio Free Europe* 2018b). Understandably, the tariffs were strongly opposed by the Serbian authorities, but also the Brussels administration. The EU High Representative Mogherini issued a statement requesting Kosovo to immediately revoke the tariffs as it was in clear violation of the Central European Free Trade Agreement (CEFTA) and the spirit of the Stabilization and Association Agreement between the EU and Kosovo (European Union External Action 2018). The initial reaction coming from Washington seemed milder and limited to only advising the Prishtina authorities to revoke the tariffs, but then became tougher and a proper requirement (*Associated Press* 2019). In any case, the tariffs blocked the normalization process entirely, since the Belgrade authorities refused to continue with it while the tariffs were in place. Moreover, and somewhat paradoxically, the tariffs imposition showed that the political establishment in Kosovo was not united around the normalization process, with obvious discrepancies between Prime Minister Haradinaj, who stood at the forefront of it, and President Thaçi, who advocated for its unconditional lifting. In addition to exposing the polarization of the local political scene, the tariffs issue also displayed Kosovo's fragility to withstand international pressures, having eventually had to lift all tariffs (*Deutsche Welle* 2020).

Despite the enlargement prospects, in the above set of circumstances, the EU was often paralyzed, incapable of finding alternatives in order to resume the dialogue. While difficulties closely related to the normalization process were to be expected (Mehmeti 2013), the more it has progressed, the more reformatting it has necessitated. More than an observer, the EU should perform the role of a mediator rather than leave the initiative to the conflicting parties, both incapable of compromising. With its advocacy of future inclusion of the Western Balkans in its structures, the EU has sought to present itself as an answer to the region's political disputes and, with this in mind, the EU conditionality is supposed to transform the societies. Still, as rightly warned elsewhere, the fact that the conditionality approach has had limited success in the case of the Western Balkans' democratization and Europeanization, especially when compared to the countries of the Central and Eastern Europe (Freyburg and Richter 2010; Noutcheva 2009; Pridham 2005), the EU's role in the Kosovo-Serbia normalization process should be complemented with soft power mechanisms as well as freedom to put any perspective (including the provision of EU funds) on hold,[1] until both parties make progress. The less the EU remains engaged in this process the more it opens up the area to other international players to exert their influence in the region.

External Actors and Geopolitical Considerations

The relationship between the EU and the Western Balkans is complex, dominated by mixed signals with regard to the integration process and accompanying policies, altogether largely due to the continuous experimenting with its transformative powers rather than having an established set of policies to be followed. More often than not, the EU seems to apply forms of inductive reasoning when adopting mechanisms to foster relations with individual countries in the region (Vickers 2014), allowing for false conclusions even if all premises suggest otherwise. For example, the implementation of a number of agreements that were signed between Kosovo and Serbia as part of the normalization process has been stalled by the Serbian authorities, but the Brussels administration has not considered this troubling; quite the contrary, it has continued to praise Serbia's progress toward the EU integration by opening further accession chapters.

Here, we should stress that the EU has to deal with political figures in the Western Balkans, many of whom were in one way or another implicated in the previous conflicts and abused their access to state structures to strengthen their own political influence. While empowering them to pursue reforms and bring their countries closer to the EU accession point, the Brussels administration is actually shielding problematic members of the elite from future criminal indictment. At the same

---

1 Legal provisions are already in place for such actions. The EU can recall Chapter 35 in negotiations with Serbia, according to which "the advancement of Serbia's EU accession negotiations will be guided by Serbia's progress in preparing for accession, which will be measured in particular against Serbia's continued engagement toward a visible and sustainable improvement in relations with Kosovo," and that "the European Commission will on its own initiative or on the request of one third of the member states . . . propose to withhold its recommendations to open and/or close other negotiating chapters, and adapt the associated preparatory work, as appropriate, until this imbalance is addressed" (Conference on Accession to the European Union 2015).

time, aware of the implications of a proper pursuit of reforms, even though they would advance their countries' path toward EU membership, the local figures are reluctant to take any major steps, since they do not feel comfortable threatening their own standing. The international community's decision to back up politicians with criminal or highly controversial past, while showing a degree of hesitation to support other, genuinely clear, political actors, leaves voters with limited options. As a consequence, the voting process is a tool to maintain the *status quo* rather than a tool to promote change and political alternatives. The groups wanted and supported by the West are presented as pro-EU and, therefore, voting for them is desirable in order to progress toward EU membership.

While in charge, the Brussels and Washington administrations have played a key role in numerous electoral rounds in the Western Balkans due to their capacity to either promote their preferred candidate or withdraw their support, once that candidate has not been a good fit any longer. Such an approach is found in Croatia (in the case of Franjo Tudjman), Serbia (in the case of Slobodan Milošević), and more recently, in Kosovo (in the case of Hashim Thaçi). Looking back, Croatia is one example where the support for political groups who were keen on reforms enabled the transformative powers of the EU to have more positive effects. By openly supporting reformists and also moderates, altogether committed to domestic change, over nationalists, the Brussels authorities contributed to the implementation of necessary reforms. An excellent example to illustrate this is the point at which the EU decided to withdraw support for the Tudjman nationalist regime, which in turn strengthened the opposition and also encouraged an internal democratization of Tudjman's Croatian Democratic Union (Börzel 2011, 7). In the same way, the EU's strong stance against the Milošević regime ensured the strengthening of the opposition in Serbia and their victory in 2000. However, such support has shifted away in more recent years, with members of the former nationalist and radical forces, with Aleksandar Vučić (the Minister of Information under the Milošević regime) at the forefront, now playing the role of reformists and moderates.

The external support for Vučić, formerly a prime minister and now president of Serbia, is evident by looking at the EU's decision not to criticize the Belgrade leadership's obstruction of different agreements as part of the normalization process. Similarly, the EU has never clearly condemned Serbia's denial and need to avoid responsibility for crimes committed during the 1990s conflicts. For example, during his visit to Kosovo in September 2018, Vučić was blocked from going to a village in Drenica region, with the local Albanians displaying the slogans "Vučić will not pass!" and "You must apologize for crimes!" (Luci 2018). However, in the Serb-dominated Mitrovica, he delivered a speech, during which he stated that "Milošević was a great Serbian leader whose intentions were certainly the best, but our results were very poor. Not because he wanted that but because our wishes were unrealistic, while we neglected and underestimated the interests and aspirations of other nations" (Gotev 2018). In the view of the Prishtina leadership as well as the Croatian government, this was a provocation (*Radio Free Europe* 2018c). In her statement, the EU's High Representative spokesperson, Maja Kocijančič expressed regret that President Vučić did not fulfil his itinerary (*European Western Balkans* 2018), and only commented about his praise of Milošević after being confronted by a journalist. She read from a paper, prepared in advance, that "[r]econciliation, normalization, and good neighborly relations will only be possible if the policies of the past, which brought a decade of misery and suffering to the Western Balkans region and the people there, are rejected and overcome. We must not leave any room or praise for those who upheld these policies or actions" (Gotev 2018). She did not mention Vučić whatsoever and the language used, on closer reading, is contradictory at best. Such an episode may sound trivial, but for the people in Kosovo it is a sign that the Serbian authorities have remained the same as in Milošević's time. Writing about Vučić's remarks in Kosovo, the Belgrade-based journalist Miloš Ćirić, said: "His speech could have been a moment to divorce himself from the policies that Milošević implemented during 1990s and that Vučić supported at that time. Sadly, but not surprisingly, he remained who he always was, the disciple of and successor to Serbian Radical Party leader Vojislav Šešelj and to Milošević himself; a man who never took back anything he did or said" (Ćirić 2018).

Similarly, the Brussels administration has offered remarkable support to Kosovo's President Thaçi, despite his alleged criminal past, as exposed by Dick Marty, a Swiss human rights investigator.[2] In late 2018, following Thaçi's endorsement of the narrative of border adjustment between Kosovo and Serbia, the Kosovo government passed a resolution establishing a negotiating team, which also included members of the opposition.[3] However, following the parliament's approval of the resolution, the government received a letter from EU officials, including Federica Mogherini, Johannes Hahn, and Cecilia Malmström, European Commissioner for Trade; while acknowledging the relevance of the negotiating team, they pointed out that in its role, the team should only provide information to the president of Kosovo since his office was

---

2 In his December 2010 report, prepared for the Council of Europe (2010), Dick Marty identified directly Thaçi, formerly a prime minister and later president of Kosovo, as the head of a criminal network in charge of heroin trade and detention centers on Albania's border with Kosovo, where civilian captives, including Serbs, were killed and their organs sold in the black market. The report also included other figures, such as commanders of the former Kosovo Liberation Army, close to Thaçi's inner circle. Thaçi has denied the allegations and said that he was ready to cooperate with any investigation into the claims. He also claimed that he would be suing Dick Marty for false allegations, but that has not happened so far. Both the UN and EULEX have pursued investigations into the alleged organ harvesting but failed to yield any evidence. In any case, Marty's report remains a report based on allegations, until further investigation is conducted.

3 Here, the opposition was the Social Democratic Party of Kosovo (PSD), a group that had split from the VV, as the other two opposition parties (VV and LDK) were not supportive of such a team because of their request that the format of the negotiations for the normalization process be fully revisited and the implementation of the already reached agreements be reassessed. Consequently, the VV and the LDK did not vote for the resolution in the parliament.

recognized as "the only institution in charge of the normalization of relations between Prishtina and Belgrade" (Ibrahimi 2018). The letter attracted a lot of attention, from both the government and two prominent opposition parties, the VV and the LDK. The government clarified that it supported the team's input to the president but only for as long as his actions stayed within his constitutional competencies (Shehu 2018). In fact, Prime Minister Haradinaj accused Mogherini personally of "deviating the dialogue and putting the EU's role in the normalization process at risk, while ignoring the fact that since its inauguration, Kosovo has been the biggest loser." Moreover, the leaders of the opposition parties insisted that Thaçi was not credible, and, therefore should not lead the negotiations in the normalization process (Ibrahimi 2018). Still, the EU's insistence on Thaçi as their key negotiator in front of Kosovo, despite a clear legal framework as to which institution is competent to lead on the negotiations as part of the normalization process, manifests the EU's readiness to prioritize particular individuals rather than competence.

A new round of external pressures came with the Kurti government, following the October 2019 election. As part of his campaign, Kurti committed himself to lifting the previously imposed tariffs and replacing them with full reciprocity measures, not only with regard to trade, but also the implementation of the already agreed, yet stalled, agreements. Once the government was inaugurated and this became its official stance, Richard Grenell, US ambassador to Germany and US envoy for the Kosovo-Serbia talks, made it clear that such an approach was not acceptable since it threatened the normalization process and would not be beneficial for Kosovo's economy. The dynamic developments of March 2020 and a vote of confidence in the parliament, brought the Kurti government down. In an interview to *Foreign Policy*, Kurti sought to explain his position by saying that "the international motor behind the motion of no confidence was definitely Ambassador Grenell" and that Grenell was keen on a speedy agreement that would help the Trump administration to consolidate its standing on the international scene (Mackinnon 2020). From a different perspective, the LDK saw the reason for the parliament's vote of no confidence in the government's behavior toward the Covid-19 pandemic outbreak and its reluctance to declare the state of emergency, as supported by the president. The declaration of a state of emergency in Kosovo would have given additional constitutional rights to the president, including some executive powers, which in Kurti's view, could mean taking ownership of the normalization process and bringing the issue of partition or border adjustment back to the table (Mackinnon 2020). In any case, the Kurti government, which lasted for less than two months, was truly against corruption and state capture. Within three weeks, many individuals serving on different boards or working for the police and government agencies were dismissed. Such an approach mobilized political parties whose members had contributed to state capture to organize against the government in order to bring it down.

Looking more closely at geopolitical interferences apart from those of the Brussels and Washington administrations, the tense political situation between Kosovo and Serbia has provided space for an involvement of other players, such as Russia, to exert influence and in some ways represent an alternative to the West. The Russian influence is more evident in Serbia and the Serbian part of Bosnia and Herzegovina, and to some extent attempted in North Macedonia when Nikola Gruevski was in charge, rather than elsewhere in the region (Bechev 2015). The Russian influence started as political in nature, but it has increasingly become characterized by economic and military aspects, as demonstrated with the 2013 agreements between Belgrade and Moscow to share strategic information and organize joint military exercises (*Radio Free Europe* 2013), and the 2016 Serbia's decision to purchase military equipment, including tanks, warplanes, and armored vehicles (*B92* 2016). Somewhat paradoxically but expectedly, the Russian influence has enabled the Serbian authorities to use it as a leverage and strengthen their negotiating position vis-à-vis the EU. Such a positioning has generated concerns that Serbia's submission to the Russian sphere of influence would jeopardize EU enlargement by complicating the relations with the Brussels administration during the pre-enlargement phase, which in reality means that the EU has had to be one step ahead and bring Serbia closer to its structures. For example, Serbia refused to align its foreign policy with that of the EU with regard to the EU sanctions against Russia following Moscow's decision to annex Crimea (European Commission 2019a). However, Belgrade's approach has not jeopardized Serbia's progress toward EU membership in any way; it has actually marked further progress by opening new chapters as part of the accession process.

On the other hand, European Commission reports about Kosovo, including the 2019 one (European Commission 2019b), do not acknowledge Kosovo's position toward Russia, despite Kosovo government's clear stance on this matter as early as of September 2014, when it supported the EU's adoption of sanctions against the Russian Federation (Qeveria e Kosovës 2014). One of the possible reasons here is that Kosovo has not opened any accession chapters and, therefore, reporting about its performance in the field of Chapter 31, covering foreign, security, and defense policy, is left out. According to the Stabilization and Association Agreement, signed between the EU and Kosovo, the Prishtina leadership is required to align its policy with the EU's. As specified by Article 11(c), Kosovo is expected to show "increasing convergence with certain Common Foreign and Security Policy measures, in particular restrictive measures taken by the EU against third countries, natural or legal persons or non-state entities also through the exchange of information as appropriate, and, in particular, on those issues likely to have substantial effects on the parties" (EUR-Lex 2016). Still, despite Kosovo's apparent position on the matters of relations between the EU and Russia, there is no official assessment in either periodical reports or press statements of the Stabilization and Association Council about Kosovo's foreign policy, let alone its alignment with that of the EU (Visoka 2019).

In fact, ambiguities and inconclusive evaluations which accompany official reporting are further stressed when comparing the 2018 and 2019 progress reports about both Kosovo and Serbia. Talking about the normalization process, four different reports offer exactly the same, copy-paste, comment: "As regards the Technical Dialogue Agreements (2011–2012), some are not or only partially being implemented. Both sides need to remain committed to the continued implementation of the agreement on representation and participation of Kosovo in regional forums. The issues of cadaster and university diplomas recognition are yet to be solved, as are the license plate related elements of the agreement on freedom of movement" (European Commission 2018a; 2018b; 2019a; 2019b). Here, it is also important to note that the instructions are vague, without specifying who needs to implement what. The reality is that since 2011, when first of the agreements was reached, the implementation of some agreements has been stalled by the Serbian leadership and there is no sign of any change of such a practice without major pressure from the Brussels administration. The fact that the same wording is used for both parties could be interpreted as an EU warning that both were equally responsible for obstructing the implementation of the agreements. Should the reporting be more specific and reflect the reality on the ground, it would reveal that Serbia's own progress toward EU accession is much more challenging. However, the opposite has happened, and one may associate this to geopolitical considerations rather than the very scope of EU conditionality.

Conclusion

As pointed out, the relationship between Kosovo and the European Union is complex. With Kosovo's political status being contested, the direction of its accession to the EU is insecure. While the EU conditionality remains the main policy mechanism to push forward the Western Balkan region toward the EU, many elements of the EU's approach are in need of adjustments, largely due to geopolitical challenges penetrating the region. Too often, the EU has been unclear about its expectations and what kind of support it is ready to offer. As witnessed in the case of Kosovo with the VV at the forefront, issues such as corruption and state capture can be combatted. However, the fact that the VV is the only sizable political party that is genuinely interested in it, makes the whole process much more challenging. The discreditation of the VV shortly after its hold of power, mainly because of other geopolitical priorities, sent a clear message that the state-building process and its main accompanying features – democracy and rule of law – are of secondary relevance. Whether this political party will take the fight against corruption and the liberation of Kosovo from state capture seriously and whether this party will be able to form the government in the future alone, remains to be seen.

As it stands, the normalization process between Kosovo and Serbia requires a resetting and a far better defining of the expected outcomes, since in its current format the process is stuck in a vicious cycle. Here, the EU's role is crucial and thus the integration perspective remains the main leverage capable of driving the process forward and simultaneously reforming it through soft power mechanisms. So far, the ambiguities characterizing the EU's approach have not helped; a much-needed change of its role and improvement of its standing (to become a proper mediator) might assist the continuation of the normalization process and thus strengthening of Kosovo's EU perspective. The more the EU proceeds with the current format of normalization of relations between Belgrade and Prishtina, the more it risks opening up the region to alternative geopolitical penetration with potentially destabilizing consequences. In fact, with regard to security, the region is rather fragile and this is why different political establishments throughout have tended to argue that a well-grounded EU perspective would ensure stability, including the protection of ethnic minorities. Considering that the accession to the EU has regularly been advertised as a common interest of the Western Balkan region, the Brussels authorities should take the lead in pursuing it as the EU's geopolitical interest and treat the issue of inclusion of the Western Balkans more seriously in order to ensure a long-lasting stability and security across the European continent.

References

Andreas, Peter. 2004. "Criminalized legacies of war: The clandestine political economy of the Western Balkans." *Problems of Post-Communism* 51(3): 3–9.

Associated Press. 2019. "US says Kosovo tax on Serb goods hurting its interests." 25 Janaury, https://apnews.com/a283882cc64b4651aed16acde334e4c2.

Austin, Robert C. 2019. *Making and Remaking the Balkans: Nations and States since 1878*. Toronto, ON: University of Toronto Press.

B92. 2016. "Serbia to get Russian warplanes, tanks, armoured vehicles." 21 December, https://www.b92.net/eng/news/politics.php?yyyy=2016&mm=12&dd=21&nav_id=100019.

Balfour, Rosa, and Corina Stratulat. 2011. "The democratic transformation of the Balkans." *European Policy Centre Issue Paper 66*, http://cms.horus.be/files/99931/Newsletter/The%20democratic%20transformation%20of%20the%20Balkans.pdf.

Bechev, Dimitar. 2015. "Russia in the Balkans: How should the EU respond?" *Policy Brief*, 12 October, https://www.ceas-serbia.org/images/2015-i-pre/pub_6018_russia_in_the_balkans.pdf.

Belloni, Roberto. 2009. "European integration and the Western Balkans: Lessons, prospects, and limits." *Journal of Balkans and Near Eastern Studies* 11(3): 313–331.

Biserko, Sonja. 2011. "The end of the myth of Kosovo." *Helsinki Charter* 155–156, https://www.helsinki.org.rs/hcharter_t38a01.html.

Bllaca, Eldira. "Prokurori Elez Blakaj nxit shumë reagime në Kosovë." *Zëri i Amerikës*, 20 August, https://www.zeriamerikes.com/a/kosovo-procecutor/4536174.html.

Boletini, Besnik, and Besa Kalaja. 2014. "Employment Party: Physiognomy of political patronage in Kosovo." *Preportr* 10, http://preportr.cohu.org/repository/docs/Employment_10_Party_541680_963129.pdf.

Börzel, Tanja A. 2011. "When Europeanization hits limited statehood: The Western Balkans as a test case for the transformative power of Europe." *KFG Working Paper* 30, http://userpage.fu-berlin.de/kfgeu/kfgwp/wpseries/WorkingPaperKFG_30.pdf.

Breton, Albert. 1974. *The Economic Theory of Representative Government*. Chicago, IL: Aldine.

Brown, Justin. 1999. "The dispute over splitting Kosovo." *Christian Science Monitor*, 17 May, https://reliefweb.int/report/serbia/dispute-over-splitting-kosovo.

Chapman, Thomas, and Philip G. Roeder. 2007. "Partition as a solution to wars of nationalism?" *American Political Science Review* 101(4): 677–691.

Ciric, Milos. 2018. "Vucic's Kosovo speech promoted a dangerous fantasy." *Balkan Insight*, 10 September, https://balkaninsight.com/2018/09/10/vucic-s-kosovo-speech-promoted-a-dangerous-fantasy-09-10-2018-1/.

Cocozzelli, Fred. 2013. "Between democratization and democratic consolidation: The long path to democracy in Kosovo." *Perspectives on European Politics and Society* 14(1): 1–19.

Conference on Accession to the European Union. 2015. "European Union common position, Chapter 35: Normalization of relations between Serbia and Kosovo*." 30 November, http://data.consilium.europa.eu/doc/document/AD-12-2015-INIT/en/pdf.

Council of Europe. 2010. "Inhuman treatment of people and illicit trafficking in human organs in Kosovo." 12 December, http://assembly.coe.int/committeedocs/2010/20101218_aj doc462010provamended.pdf.

Dawnes, Alexander B. 2004. "The problem with negotiated settlements to ethnic civil wars." *Security Studies* 13(4): 230–279.

Dawnes, Alexander B. 2006. "More borders, less conflict: Partition as a solution to ethnic civil wars." *SAIS Review* 26(1): 49–61.

Deutsche Welle. 2020. "Kosovo lifts all tariffs on Serbian, Bosnian goods." 1 April, https://www.dw.com/en/kosovo-lifts-all-tariffs-on-serbian-bosnian-goods/a-52975561.

Doli, Dren, Fisnik Korenica, and Artan Rogova. 2012. "The post-independence civil service in Kosovo: A message of politicization." *International Review of Administrative Sciences* 78(4): 665–691.

Economides, Spyros, James Key-Lindsay, and Dimitris Papadimitriou. 2010. "Kosovo: Four futures." *Survival* 52(5): 99–116.

The Economist. 2018. "Serbia-Kosovo border change unlikely." 18 September, http://country.eiu.com/article.aspx?articleid=777151461&Country=Serbia&topic=Politics.

Elbasani, Arolda. 2013. "European integration in the Western Balkans: Revising the transformative power of the EU." *E-International Relations*, 30 May, https://www.e-ir.info/2013/05/30/european-integration-travels-to-the-western-balkans-revising-the-transformative-power-of-the-eu/.

EUobserver. 2018. "Austria: EU would back Kosovo-Serbia land swap." 7 November, https://euobserver.com/tickers/143313.

EUR-Lex. 2016. "Stabilisation and Association Agreement between the European Union and the European Atomic Energy Community, of the one part, and Kosovo*, of the other part." *Official Journal of the European Union*, 16 March, https://eur-lex.europa.eu/legal-content/EN/TXT/?qid=1476698477996&uri=CELEX%3A22016A0316%2801%29.

European Commission. 2018a. "Serbia 2018 report." 17 April, https://ec.europa.eu/neighbourhood-enlargement/sites/near/files/20180417-serbia-report.pdf.

European Commission. 2018b. "Kosovo* 2018 report." 17 April, https://ec.europa.eu/neighbourhood-enlargement/sites/near/files/20180417-kosovo-report.pdf.

European Commission. 2019a. "Serbia 2019 report." 29 May, https://ec.europa.eu/neighbourhood-enlargement/sites/near/files/20190529-serbia-report.pdf.

European Commission. 2019b. "Kosovo* 2019 report." 29 May, https://ec.europa.eu/neighbourhood-enlargement/sites/near/files/20190529-kosovo-report.pdf.

European Union External Action. 2018. "Statement by Federica Mogherini on the Kosovo Government decision on taxing goods from Serbia and Bosnia and Herzegovina." 21 November, https://eeas.europa.eu/headquarters/headquarters-homepage/54242/statement-federica-mogherini-kosovo-government-decision-taxing-goods-serbia-and-bosnia-and_en.

European Union External Action. 2020. "Dialogue between Belgrade and Prishtina." 29 January, https://eeas.europa.eu/diplomatic-network/eu-facilitated-dialogue-belgrade-pristina-relations/349/dialogue-between-belgrade-and-pristina_en.

European Western Balkans. 2018. "EU expresses regret over cancellation of Vučić's visit to village in Kosovo." 9 September, https://europeanwesternbalkans.com/2018/09/09/eu-expresses-regret-cancellation-vucics-visit-village-kosovo/.

Fay, Brian. 1996. *Contemporary Philosophy of Social Science*. Oxford: Blackwell.

Fenno, Richard T. 1977. "US House Members in their constituencies: An exploration." *American Political Science Review* 71(3): 883–917.

Freyburg, Tina, and Solveig Richter. 2010. "National identity matters: The limited impact of EU political conditionality in the Western Balkans." *Journal of European Public Policy* 17(2): 263–281.

GAP Institute. 2015. "Reforming public administration in Kosovo: A proposal to decrease the number of employees in the public administration." *Policy Brief*, https://www.institutigap.org/documents/99892_Reforming%20%20Public%20Administration%20in%20Kosovo.pdf.

Gashi, Drilon, and Shoghi Emerson. 2013. "A class of its own: Patronage and its impact on social mobility in Kosovo." *Public Interest* 2, https://d4d-ks.org/wp-content/uploads/2013/05/D4D_PI_2_ENG_WEB.pdf.

Gashi, Kreshnik. 2016. "Ekskluzive: Aktakuza voluminoze ndaj grupit të Azem Sylës." *Kallxo*, 30 October, https://kallxo.com/gjnk/ekskluzive-aktakuza-voluminoze-ndaj-grupit-te-azem-syles/.

Gotev, Georgi. 2018. "Commission frowns at Serbian president's praise of Milošević." *Euractiv*, 10 September, https://www.euractiv.com/section/enlargement/news/commission-frowns-at-serbian-presidents-praise-of-milosevic/.

Gray, Andrew. 2018. "Angela Merkel: No Balkan border changes." *Politico*, 13 August, https://www.politico.eu/article/angela-merkel-no-balkan-border-changes-kosovo-serbia-vucic-thaci/.

Grødeland, Åse B. 2013. "Public perceptions of corruption and anti-corruption reform in the Western Balkans." *The Slavonic and East European Review* 91(3): 535–598.

Ibrahimi, Arbesa. 2018. "BE-ja e do Thaçin negociator të Kosovës." *Zëri*, 19 December, https://zeri.info/aktuale/230570/be-ja-e-do-thacin-negociator-te-kosoves/.

Insajderi. 2020. "Hulumtime." https://insajderi.com/hulumtime/.

Isufi, Përparim. 2018. "Kosovo Prosecutor resigns after alleged threats." *Balkan Transnational Justice*, 15 August, https://balkaninsight.com/2018/08/15/kosovo-prosecutor-quits-amid-alleged-threats-08-15-2018/.

Jenne, Erin K. 2009. "The paradox of ethnic partition: Lessons from de facto partition in Bosnia and Kosovo." *Regional & Federal Studies* 19(2): 273–289.

Johnson, Carter. 2008. "Partitioning to peace: Sovereignty, demography, and ethnic civil wars." *International Security* 32(4): 140–170.

Katzenstein, Peter J. 1997. "United Germany in an integrating Europe." In *Tamed Power: Germany in Europe*, edited by Peter J. Katzenstein, 1–48. Ithaca, NY: Cornell University Press.

Kaufmann, Chaim. 1996. "Possible and impossible solutions to ethnic civil wars." *International Security* 20(4): 136–175.

Kaufmann, Chaim. 1998. "When all else fails: Ethnic population transfers and partitions in the twentieth century." *International Security* 23(2): 120–156.

Kaufmann, Chaim. 2007. "An assessment of the partition of Cyprus." *International Studies Perspective* 8(2): 206–223.

Keil, Soeren. 2018. "The business of state capture and the rise of authoritarianism in Kosovo, Macedonia, Montenegro, and Serbia." *Southeastern Europe* 42(1): 59–82.

Koha. 2018. "Lumezi: Elez Blakaj, prokuror i dështuar, mori 72 mijë euro pa asnjë sukses." 20 August, https://www.koha.net/arberi/112343/lumezi-elez-blakaj-prokuror-i-deshtuar-mori-72-mije-euro-pa-asnje-sukses/.

Kostreci, Keida. 2018. "Kosovo president: Defining borders will help solve disputes with Serbia." *Voice of America*, 28 November, https://www.voanews.com/europe/kosovo-president-defining-borders-will-help-solve-disputes-serbia.

Kupchan, Charles A. 2018. "An offensive plan for the Balkans that the US should get behind." *The New York Times*, 13 September, https://www.nytimes.com/2018/09/13/opinion/kosovo-serbia-land-swap.html.

Kurtoglu Eskisar, Gul M., and Aysegul Komsouglu. 2015. "A critical assessment of the transformative power of EU reforms on reducing corruption in the Balkans." *Southeast European and Black Sea Studies* 15(3): 301–326.

Linz, Juan J., and Alfred Stepan. 1996. *Problems of Democratic Transition and Consolidation: Southern Europe, South America, and Post-Communist Europe.* Baltimore, MD: The Johns Hopkins University Press.

Luci, Besa. 2018. "Vučić's Milošević reference is not a mere side-note: It's the whole problem." *Kosovo 2.0*, 11 September, http://kosovotwopointzero.com/en/vucics-milos%D0%B5vic-reference-is-not-a-mere-side-note-its-the-whole-problem/.

MacDowal, Andrew. 2018. "Could land swap between Serbia and Kosovo lead to conflict?" *The Guardian*, 22 August, https://www.theguardian.com/world/2018/aug/22/serbia-kosovo-could-land-swap-between-lead-conflict.

Mackinnon, Amy. 2020. "In the Balkans, if you neglect history, it will backfire." *Foreign Policy*, 23 April, https://foreignpolicy.com/2020/04/23/balkans-kosovo-serbia-albin-kurti-richard-grenell/.

Mayhew, David. 1974. *Congress: The Electoral Connection.* New Haven, CT: Yale University Press.

Mearsheimer, John J. 2000. "The Case for partitioning Kosovo." In *NATO's Empty Victory: A Postmortem on the Balkan War*, edited by Ted Galen Carpenter, 133–138. Washington, DC: CATO Institute.

Mearsheimer, John J., and Stephen Van Evera. 1995. "When peace means war: The partition that dare not speak its name." *The New Republic*, 18 December, https://mearsheimer.uchicago.edu/pdfs/A0023.pdf.

Mehmeti, Leandrit I. 2013. "Kosovo-Serbia: Normalization of relations or just diplomatic theatre? An analysis of the April 2013 EU brokered agreement between Kosovo and Serbia." https://www.auspsa.org.au/sites/default/files/kosovo_serbia_leandrit_mehmeti.pdf.

Mehmeti, Leandrit I. 2016. "Perspectives of the normalization of relations between Kosovo and Serbia." In *Kosovo and Serbia: Contested Options and Shared Consequences*, edited by Leandrit I. Mehmeti and Branislav Radeljić, 216–242. Pittsburgh, PA: University of Pittsburgh Press.

Miftari, Naser. 2015. "The in-between states: Enduring catastrophes as sources of democracy's deadlocks in Kosovo." In *Culture, Catastrophe, and Rhetoric: The Texture of Political Action*, edited by Robert Hariman and Ralph Cintron, 68–86. New York: Berghahn Books.

Moravcsik, Andrew, and Milada Anna Vachudova. 2003. "National interests, state power, and EU enlargement." *East European Politics & Societies* 17(1): 42–57.

Morina, Die. 2018. "Kosovo Court releases Azem Syla from custody." *Balkan Insight*, 12 March, https://balkaninsight.com/2018/03/12/kosovo-court-releases-again-the-accused-politician-azem-syla-03-12-2018/.

Morina, Die. 2019. "Kosovo PM rejects US ultimatum over import taxes." *Balkan Insight*, 13 February, https://balkaninsight.com/2019/02/13/kosovo-pm-rejects-us-ultimatum-over-import-taxes/.

Noutcheva, Gergana. 2009. "Fake, partial and imposed compliance: The limits of the EU's normative power in the Western Balkans." *Journal of European Public Policy* 16(7): 1065–1084.

Ora News TV. 2018. "Rama thyen heshjen për kufijtë e Kosovës: Shqiptarët duhet të diskutojnë si burra të Kuvendit, jo hidh e prit në TV." 13 September, http://www.oranews.tv/article/rama-thyen-heshjen-kufijte-e-kosoves-shqiptaret-duhet-te-diskutojne-si-burra-te-kuvendit-jo-hidh-e-prit-ne-tv.

Pešić, Vesna. 2007. "State capture and widespread corruption in Serbia." *CEPS Working Document* 262, https://www.ceps.eu/wp-content/uploads/2013/02/1478.pdf.

Phillips, David L. 2010. "The Balkans' underbelly." *World Policy Journal* 27(3): 93–98.

Phillips, David L. 2018. "Changing Kosovo's borders will merely reward Serbia's bullying." *Balkan Insight*, 6 September, https://balkaninsight.com/2018/09/06/changing-kosovo-s-borders-will-merely-reward-serbia-s-bullying-09-04-2018/.

Pond, Elizabeth. 2006. *Endgame in the Balkans: Regime Change, European Style*. Washington, DC: The Brookings Institution Press.

Pridham, Geoffrey. 2005. *Designing Democracy: EU Enlargement and Regime Change in Post-Communist Europe*. Basingstoke: Palgrave Macmillan.

Qeveria e Kosovës. 2014. "Vendimet e mbledhjes së 196-të të Qeverisë 2014." 17 September, https://kryeministri-ks.net/wp-content/uploads/docs/Vendimiet_e_Mbledhjes_se_196te_te_Qeverise_se_Republikes_se_Kosoves_2014(1).pdf.

Qosaj-Mustafa, Ariana. 2013. "The impunity in Kosovo: Inexplicable wealth." *KIPRED Policy Paper* 5, http://www.kipred.org/repository/docs/THE_IMPUNITY_IN_KOSOVO_INEXPLICABLE_WEALTH_632453.pdf.

Radeljić, Branislav. 2019. "What Europeanization? Getting away with corruption in the Progressivists-dominated Serbia." In *Balkanizing Europeanization: Fight against Corruption and Regional Relations in the Western Balkans*, edited by Vladimir Djordjević and Vladimir Vučković, 129–150. Berlin: Peter Lang.

Radio Free Europe. 2013. "Russia, Serbia sign military pact." 13 November, https://www.rferl.org/a/russia-serbia-military-pact-/25167365.html.

Radio Free Europe. 2017. "Kosovo rejects Serbian partition plan for ending territorial dispute." 14 August, https://www.rferl.org/a/serbia-kosovo-dacic-partition-could-end-dispute/28676209.html.

Radio Free Europe. 2018a. "Bolton says US won't oppose Kosovo-Serbia land swap deal." 24 August, https://www.rferl.org/a/bolton-says-u-s-won-t-oppose-kosovo-serbia-land-swap-deal/29451395.html.

Radio Free Europe. 2018b. "Kosovo slaps 100 percent tariffs on Serbia, Bosnia to 'defend vital interest'." 21 November, https://www.rferl.org/a/kosovo-slaps-100-percent-tariffs-on-serbia-bosnia-to-defend-vital-interest-/29613285.html.

Radio Free Europe. 2018c. "Serbian President's praise of Milošević a 'provocation,' neighbors say." 10 September, https://www.rferl.org/a/serbian-president-vucic-praise-milosevic-provocation-kosovo-croatia-mogherini/29482484.html.

Ramaj, Saranda. 2020. "Shpallet aktgjykimi në rastin 'Pronto,' lirohen nga akuzat të gjithë të përfshirët." *Koha Ditore*, 3 January, https://www.koha.net/arberi/201961/mungojne-te-akuzuarit-e-aferes-pronto-vetem-dy-nga-ta-te-pranishem-ne-seance/.

Rettman, Andrew. 2018. "EU Commissioner goes against Merkel on Balkan borders." *EUobserver*, 27 August, https://euobserver.com/enlargement/142655.

Rose-Ackerman, Susan. 1978. *Corruption: A Study in Political Economy*. New York: Academic Press.

Sambanis, Nicholas. 2000. "Partition as a solution to ethnic wars: An empirical critique of the theoretical literature." *World Politics* 52(4): 437–483.

Savić, Obrad. 2007. "Balkans and Europe to come." In *Identiteti Evropian i Kosovës*, edited by Forum 15, 55–71. Prishtina: Forum 2015.

Schaeffer, Robert. 1990. *Warpaths: The Politics of Partition*. New York: Hill and Wang.

Schimmelfennig, Frank, and Ulrich Sedelmeier. 2002. "Theorizing EU enlargement: Research focus, hypothesis, and the state of research." *Journal of European Public Policy* 9(4): 500–528.

Schumpeter, Joseph A. 1950. *Capitalism, Socialism and Democracy*. New York: Harper and Brothers.

Schwandner-Sievers, Stephanie. 2013. "Democratization through defiance? The Albanian civil organization 'self-determination' and international supervision in Kosovo." In *Civil Society and Transitions in the Western Balkans*, edited by Vesna Bojičić-Dželilović, James Ker-Lindsay, and Denisa Kostovicova, 95–116. London: Palgrave Macmillan.

Sertolli, Naser. 2018. "Haradinaj e quan 'pishpirik' prokurorin e dorëhequr Elez Blakaj." *Kallxo*, 20 August, https://kallxo.com/haradinaj-e-quan-pishpirik-prokurorin-e-dorehequr-elez-blakaj/.

Shehu, Bekim. 2018. "Prishtina reagon ndaj letrës së BE lidhur me dialogun me Serbinë." *Deutche Welle*, 18 December, https://www.dw.com/sq/prishtina-reagon-ndaj-letr%C3%ABs-s%C3%AB-be-lidhur-me-dialogun-me-serbin%C3%AB/a-46792620.

Te Sheshi. 2016. "Shpërthen afera e përgjimeve 'Pronto 2' në Kosovë: Protagonist Kadri Veseli, Hashim Thaçi e Adem Grabovci; ja si e kontrollon PDK shtetin." 1August, http://tesheshi.com/shperthen-afera-e-pergjimeve-pronto-2-ne-kosove-protagonist-kadri-veseli-hashim-thaci-e-adem-grabovci-ja-si-e-kontrollon-pdk-shtetin-video/.

Staal, Lieke. 2014. "EU Western Balkans candidate countries and the adoption of EU anti-corruption measures: A comparative research." University of Twente, http://essay.utwente.nl/65585/1/Staal_BA_MB.pdf.

Symonds, George. 2010. "Trust me I'm an international: On the relationship between civil society and the international community in Kosovo." Prishtina: FOL Levizja.

Tadić, Katarina, and Arolda Elbasani. 2018. "State building and patronage networks: How political parties embezzled the bureaucracy in post-war Kosovo." *Southeast European and Black Sea Studies* 18(2): 185–202.

UNMIK. 2001. "Regulation No. 2001/36 on the Kosovo Civil Service." http://www.unmikonline.org/regulations/2001/RE%202001-36.pdf.

UNODC. 2011. "Corruption in the Western Balkans: Bribery as experienced by the population." https://www.unodc.org/documents/data-and-analysis/statistics/corruption/Western_balkans_corruption_report_2011_web.pdf.

Vetëvendosje. 2010. "Historik i Lëvizjes Vetëvendosje." http://www.vetevendosje.org/wp-content/uploads/2013/09/Historik_i_Levizjes_VETEVENDOSJE.pdf.

Vickers, John. 2014. "The problem of induction." *Stanford Encyclopedia of Philosophy*, https://plato.stanford.edu/entries/induction-problem/.

Visoka, Gezim. 2019. "Monologu politik mes BE-së dhe Kosovës." *Sbunker*, 8 January, https://sbunker.net/osf-alumni/89833/monologu-politik-mes-be-se-dhe-kosoves/?fbclid=IwAR1fHa_kB8Rx3orAwNelUpbaP8EFtVAhGoqRZpXSDE15E_6_KPmPV6bOblU.

Wallin, Natalya. 2014. "Albin Kurti, leader of 'Self-Determination' Party, on the future of Kosovo." *Chicago Policy Review*, 30 September, http://chicagopolicyreview.org/2014/09/30/albin-kurti-leader-of-self-determination-party-on-the-future-of-kosovo/.

Welch, William P. 1974. "The economics of campaign funds." *Public Choice* 20(1): 83–97.

Migena Pengili

10 Can Albania Europeanize? Actors and Factors

The EU's decision to block membership negotiations with Albania and North Macedonia in October 2019 was accompanied by both self-criticism and finger-pointing. On the one hand, key leaders, including Jean-Claude Juncker and Federica Mogherini in front of the European Commission, Donald Tusk in front of the European Council, and German Chancellor Angela Merkel, considered it "a historic mistake" with consequences for the stability of the region and the resilience of the union (*AP News* 2019, Nielsen 2019, Rankin 2019). On the other, representatives of the Albanian Socialist Party (ASP), such as Prime Minister Edi Rama and the former Minister of Foreign Affairs Ditmir Bushati (2019), pointed the finger toward the EU retaining that Albania could become "a collateral damage," while also calling into question the EU's reliability in the Western Balkans (Hopkins 2019). Meanwhile, the leader of the Albanian Democratic Party (ADP), Lulzim Basha blamed Prime Minister Rama, declaring that the EU had, in fact, closed its door to the Rama government, but not to the Albanian state (Basha 2019). Given the political balagan (in Modern Hebrew בלגן, untidy situation), which has slowed down the country's progress over the past three decades, the words of the Albanian politicians, regardless of their orientation, sound like the fox's sulk for the sour grape; rather than admitting faults and taking responsibility, they have used fairytale-like explanations to cover up Albania's inability to join membership talks.

In order to understand Albania's EU fatigue, this paper refers to the Europeanization – the process of complying with the EU accession requirements – as an indicator to measure the country's ability and suitability for membership. Europeanization is based on a continuous interaction and interdependence caused by the diffusion of the supranational dimension into the national. For Claudio Radaelli (2000), Europeanization refers to a process of political penetration of the EU system of rules and norms on domestic level, financial costs of the deep impact the EU exercises, and identity formation. In Maarten Vink's (2003) view, to Europeanize signifies to impact domestic level from the EU level, and Othon Anastasakis (2005, 78) seeks to be even more specific: "Europeanization acquires different meaning for different countries . . . [F]or the less advanced it means modernization and structural transformation." For other scholars, Europeanization also denotes a metamorphosis in the institutions and the identity of the state (Hix and Goetz 2000). Understandably, the process implies a continuous policy dialogue between seekers and receivers, where decision-making and problem-solving issues are benefits that both sides enjoy (Müller and de Flers 2009). Such a development reflects "national adaptation, national projection, and identity reconstruction" (Wong 2011).

https://doi.org/10.1515/9783110684216-010

In Albania, while indispensable for the state and the survival of democracy, Europeanization has required adjustments within domestic structures so that they would come closer to EU models and meet conditions for membership. With this in mind, the postponement of negotiations can be interpreted as either motivating or dispiriting. In the case of Albania, the process of Europeanization in the past decade has been characterized by a range of problems, beginning with the denial of candidate status in 2011 and again in 2013, and ending with the refusal of opening of membership negotiations in 2019. The political struggle between the ASP and the ADP in January 2011, followed by the juxtaposition of the executive and legislative powers with the president and general prosecutor's office, the noncompliance with the EU standards of the local elections in May, and the failure to reach consensus in the 2012 presidential election, were some of the reasons leading to the rejection of the candidate status (*Top Channel* 2011). In December 2013, the Dutch parliament's decision with a majority vote of the People's Party for Freedom and Democracy (VVD) obliged the Dutch government to prevent the Brussels administration from voting in favor of Albania's candidate status (*Euractiv* 2013). A year later, as per the European Commission's assessment, candidacy was finally granted. The membership talks were expected to commence in June 2019, but they were postponed in October until further notice; for Denmark, France, and the Netherlands, "Tirana still remains a no-go" (*Euractiv* 2019). As pointed out, the lack of political dialogue, the failure to pursue internal reforms, and the irregularities dominating local elections, altogether contributed to the decision.

But, can Albania Europeanize? And, does Albania's degree of Europeanization reflect (un)wanted Europeanness? In the case of Albania, the EU has established what should be transposed into the domestic system, how it should be done, and based on what conditions. Teodor Moga (2010) categorizes the Europeanization of a candidate country to be "enlargement-led and conditionality-driven." This means that the course of actions moves downwards and is associated with a continuous fusion of the supranational and national interests. A sort of local (here country) response follows by activating specific targets, EU mechanisms, and national mediators, with targets relying on the dimensions of "scope and depth," as already suggested by scholarship on international institutions and state power (Keohane 1989, 4). Whereas scope is concerned with the domains linked to institutions, depth refers to the degree of institutionalization under which Europeanization is measured by the Copenhagen criteria. In order to meet them, certain qualitative and quantitative conditions prevail, such as stability of state institutions, a functioning market economy, and the capacity to cope with obligations set by the union (Mayhew 1998). EU mechanisms are country-specific, and involve dialogue and partnership, EU coherence and mainstreaming, and visibility and international cooperation. Lastly, mediators are rational state and non-state actors. In the case of Albania, the incapability of the mediators to cope with mechanisms results in deficiency to reach the preset targets; as a result, the local response is a national

Europeanization style standing on the difference between the country's absorption capacity of and the copying capacity or "goodness of fit" (Miskimmon 2007), with the EU requirements.

Every time Albania knocks on the EU's door, something happens preventing it from progressing further. Accordingly, this paper seeks to identify and analyze actors and factors that condition and determine the process of Albania's Europeanization. The discussion starts by offering some proper background about its bid for EU membership, in the period between 2010 and 2019. It then moves on to explore enlargement benefits which are enjoyed by both the EU and Albania, as well as to tackle some of the key push factors responsible for the country's gridlock. The conclusion will argue that Albania's Europeanization might be an example of Parrondo's paradox, where a combination of losing strategies eventually becomes a winning strategy. In other words, European stakeholders have to consider the disadvantages of the Albanian state and social culture, and thus seek to accomplish its Europeanization process by revisiting the Copenhagen criteria and setting up alternative scenarios for a multi-speed Europe applicable to the country. In any case, any candidate country has to prove its fitness for coping with and absorbing the European dimension, and also the capability to evolve into a cooperative institutional interdependence with the supranational structures.

State of the Affairs

Albania became a NATO member in April 2009 and in the same period it applied for EU membership. Although there is no official link between the two enlargements (NATO and EU), the reality has shown that most EU members become NATO members first, as EU enlargement foresees the stability and security of the union's neighborhood area. Albania, like the rest of the other Europe, looks toward the West for the state survival and the model of a democratic society based on freedom, pluralism progress, and self-determination. Both memberships, therefore, are perceived as a national priority (Pridham 2005).

The process of Albania's Europeanization has been accompanied by a range of rather negative implications. In early 2011, the political struggle between the ASP and the ADP, originally stemming from the parliamentary boycott of 2009, transformed the pacific protest of the ASP into a violent one; as a result, the government forces killed a number of protesters, and journalists were blackmailed, while the bugged political elite sought to exploit extra-institutional means to achieve its own objectives. Consequently, the government and parliament juxtaposed with the president and the general prosecutor's office. Later, in May, the noncompliance of the local elections with the EU standards highlighted the absence of political dialogue and deadlock in the country, and the European Commission refused to grant candidate status to Albania (*Top Channel* 2011). The 2012 presidential election represented another test, which the Brussels administration expected Albania to pass; instead, the country failed. Although conducted in line with the constitution, the election of President Bujar Nishani was not done through consensus; he was voted only by the ruling majority, the ADP. The election did not "represent the unity of the people," as prescribed by the constitution (Parliament of Albania 2019), and it preceded a slow reform process in the areas that require political agreement (Stern and Wohlfeld 2012). However, in 2013, the European Commission's progress report recommended the candidate status for Albania. By saying that "Albania has delivered, and so should the EU," Commissioner Štefan Füle meant that "the enlargement policy is only credible when both sides live up to their side of the bargain" (European Commission 2013b). A few days later, the Brussels December Summit did not deliver what the Albanians had hoped for. The Dutch parliament adopted a resolution with a majority of votes of the VVD, requesting the government to prevent the Brussels leadership from granting EU candidacy to Albania (*Euractiv* 2013). In spite of all this, in June 2014, the country was awarded the candidate status, with June 2019 marked as the beginning of membership negotiations. In the meantime, the country dedicated itself to the fulfillment of its obligations, with the restructuring of the judiciary and the alignment of its foreign policy with EU foreign policy being regarded as a top priority (Keshilli i Ministrave 2019a). While for Prime Minister Rama the EU's signals suggested that its authorities undoubtedly recognized Albania's achievements, in the view of Sali Berisha, the founder of the ADP, Albania did not fulfill its obligations and thus it was not ready yet for major steps in terms of EU membership (Ruci 2019).

The beginning of 2019 was characterized by a student protest demanding abolition of the Law on Higher Education and more investments in the education sector (Salaj 2019). The opposition parties, led by Basha, used this situation to embark on anti-government protests; they boycotted the parliament, burned their parliamentary mandates, and refused to participate in the local elections, scheduled for June. The political crisis was associated with the constitutional one, with Prime Minister Rama ignoring the decree of President Ilir Meta to postpone the elections to October (Browne 2019). The opposition's disapproval toward Rama's decision escalated in uncivilized acts, which included attacking (and in some cases damaging) of voting centers in different towns (Erebara 2019a). Nonetheless, the local elections were held in a tense climate, without the participation of the opposition parties; as reported by the Central Electoral Commission (KQZ 2019b), only 22.96 percent of the population voted, and the ASP-led coalition Alliance for a European Albania (AEA) won in sixty municipalities out of sixty-one – a victory which left the ADP out of any local power (KQZ 2019a). Basha's boycott strategy was criticized by the international actors, as well as senior members of his own party; for the Americans, such a move was obstructive (Erebara 2019b) and for EU officials, it "seriously undermines the country's path to potential membership of the bloc" (Emerging Europe 2019).

Likewise, both ahead and after the elections, some senior democrats, also serving as Members of the Parliament, accused Basha of imprudent intentions and of adopting a dangerous political approach in light of EU integration (*Tirana Echo* 2017; *Top Channel* 2019). In modular terms this altogether suggested that Albania should be a qualitative member for the EU, first of all. In Albania, what the chaotic political developments had clearly revealed by the end of the decade was the following: what actually mattered to every single administration was not a timely completion of negotiations and membership in the EU, but rather who would be in charge of the process and eventually receive praise. This kind of egoism has encouraged delays, additionally burdened by the issues of migration and the UK's divorce from the EU, altogether impacting on some sound external support for Albania's EU membership (Albanian Embassy in Turkey 2019; Emmott 2019).

In terms of international actors, neither the Washington administration nor the Russian Duma wish to see a larger and admittedly stronger EU. While President Donald Trump has supported Brexit, President Vladimir Putin's attention is on EU members such as Finland and Sweden (Saakashvili 2019). When it comes to the Western Balkans, Russia together with Turkey and China have no interests to see the region in the EU. Their foreign policy goals in the region exemplify this; China focuses on economic relations, while Russia and Turkey focus on politics, security, and societal issues. For instance, the security initiatives as the Slavic Military Brotherhood demonstrate a sort of Russian military presence in Serbia and opposition to NATO membership, although Serbia is already a NATO's Partnership for Peace member (ECFR 2019). Also, the revival of Ottoman ties with Southeastern Europe is largely supported by the increasing Turkish commercial and cultural investments; the trade flow between the Western Balkans and Turkey reached three billion US dollars in 2016, with the exchanges with Serbia alone, as the main partner, having reached one billion in 2018 (Harper 2018). Moreover, as argued elsewhere, the economic aid provided by Turkey to Serbia, Bosnia and Herzegovina, and North Macedonia, is an expression of Turkization intentions, which are in competition with and diverge from Europeanization aspirations (Demirtaş 2015).

The EU's Benefits of Enlargement

The 2019 G7 meeting in Biarritz made it obvious that the EU had to reinvent itself in front of imminent critical issues such as the rise of populism, Brexit and its implications, American trade war with China, Turkey turning its head to China and Russia for new alliances, etc. (Hinnant et al. 2019; *Hürriyet Daily News* 2016; Rapoza 2019). In terms of the Western Balkan region, having it inside rather than outside would contribute to the uniformity and consolidation of the EU, including the strengthening of its boundaries especially in the southern and eastern flanks – one of the five key priorities of the EU Global Strategy 2016 (EEAS 2016). To this end, teamworking with multilateralist instruments (transboundary cooperation platforms) is a strategic trick for the EU to live up to its global commitments and existential challenges. For instance, the initiatives Cross-Border Cooperation (CBC) and Regional Development (RD) engage countries in working together to promote growth and social development beyond their borders (European Commission 2007). Here, borders are not a limit, but rather an opportunity for the further harmonization of the EU territory, and this explains the joint participation of members and candidate countries in a variety of projects. For example, one of the Instrument for Pre-Accession Assistance's (IPA) projects – the Cross-Border Cooperation among Italy, Albania, and Montenegro – with an EU contribution of €78 million, fosters interconnectedness between members and non-members to meet together the respective 2020 national targets in the areas of the environment, sustainable tourism, and connectivity and competitiveness of small and medium enterprises (SMEs) (European Commission 2014a). Other initiatives, facilitated by the Regional Cooperation Council (RCC), the Central European Initiative (CEI), the Adrian Ionian Initiative (AII), and the Black Sea Economic Cooperation Organization (BSECO), have focused on increasing human and digital connectivity, as well as socioeconomic capacity building through regional cooperation in the areas of common relevance for the EU and the aspiring countries (free movement of people, fight against organized crime, establishment of free trade zones in the region; sustainable regional strategies in relation to energy and transport, etc.) (AII n.d.). Economic growth comes from market expansion and the growth of direct investment, and, therefore, enlargement increases the attractiveness of the EU market. A growth of trade stimulates development, offers commercial potential, and brings in new technologies for the production of goods and services with gains of €600/consumer per year (European Commission 2020). Also, a growing presence of EU and non-EU businesses would minimize the risk of doing business and maximize profits, due to the use of a single currency (Nuroğlu and Kurtagić 2012).

The 2018 European Commission roadmap concerning the European future of the Western Balkans centers on the policy of connectivity, the agenda of which was launched in 2015. Connectivity is directed toward new markets-building and generation of fresh business opportunities for the EU in the region, including competitive production and reliable cross-border infrastructure (European Commission 2018a). In addition, connected markets establish sustainable relations among EU and non-EU members, making the concept of national less relevant. For the period between 2015 and 2020, the allocated fund amounted to five billion euros, to be invested in thirty-nine connectivity projects (thirty-two of which deal with transport) (European Commission 2019e). In terms of investments, as per the 2019 Communication on Enlargement Policy, EU businesses provide 73 percent of foreign direct investment (FDI), which has amounted to over ten billion euros for the previous five years (European Council 2018). Recently, a growing trend is the green field investment, a type of FDI where a company creates a subsidiary in a different country; accordingly, the Central European Financial Observer reported the largest inflow of greenfield investments in 2018 with the value of almost ten billion dollars and 147 projects, with Albania alone having attracted $809.9million of inbound (Harper 2019). Investments reflect the degree of understanding of EU members of the advantage of doing business in the Western Balkans; for example, Dutch businesses' interests in sectors of agriculture, energy, textile, water, and IT industry, are directed toward development of products with trade opportunities to expand the Dutch trade economy (Netherlands Worldwide n.d.).

Europe should develop resilience through understanding and acting upon the ebb and flow of its own wellbeing; as stressed by President Juncker in his 2017 State of the Union address, "a Europe that protects, empowers, and defends" (European Commission 2017). For an autonomous Europe, in order to be able to master its responsibilities and adapt to crises unitedly, it needs to generate self-efficacy, which comes from within. In his study, Melvyn Leffler considers ideology to be linked to the threat of opportunity and power (Leffler 1999). Resilience came up with the EU Global Strategy; nonetheless, it is widely understood as the ability to resist and adapt to crises, and in fact it is becoming a survival doctrine for the EU should the latter continue to be what it is and preserve its values and norms. In Leffler's terms, the union's resilience is generated as a consequence of decomposition (threat opportunity) and strategic partnerships (power). The decomposition of the EU is marked by the euro and the Schengen crises, as well as Brexit and the internal insecurity. The management of the euro and migrant crises showed that concerns in efficiency and input/output legitimacy originate from the way the financial and migration policies were operated, and that credible integration projects need, first of all, a strong public support and information sharing. The outcome of the crises impacted on the EU institutional architecture; while in the case of the euro crisis, new institutions were established to redistribute power among the EU institutions and, the case of the migrant crisis witnessed "an intergovernmental distributional conflict" which had to prioritize the less costly options among problem-solving instruments (Schimmelfennig 2018, 977). As a consequence, maximization of the national interest seemed to prevail in decision-making processes. The 2016 Bratislava Summit, for instance, was one of the tangible indicators of EU fragmentation; even though the member states managed to agree on common security concerns, they did not agree on common solutions. A year later, the Višegrad leaders threatened the disintegration of the EU (Marković 2016; Zalan 2017). Meanwhile, the elections in Germany and Austria in 2017, and Italy and Sweden in 2018, confirmed the existence of diffidence in the European integrationist project, with the populists coming to power. In the case of Brexit, the evocation of Article 50 questioned the overall unity and preservation of the EU, since the UK's departure is likely to result in the weakening of the EU's voice in the international arena. Considering Russia, China, and Turkey's interests in the European geopolitical area, small states such as those in the Western Balkans could come to serve as big allies in the context of borders and neighborhoods. The guarantee of internal security is a pertinent issue; accordingly, the EU Internal Security Strategy (2015–2020) identified the joint engagement of EU institutions, member states, and partners and neighbors, to work together to fight cybercrime, terrorism, illegal migration, Islamic radicalization, and other major issues (Council 2015a, 8). In order words, enlargement comes across as an investment in the union's durability.

While the EU seeks support in strategic partnerships within the Western Balkan region, it simultaneously works to cement its own peace and security. Under the Common Security and Defence Policy (CSDP) umbrella, the EU has used civilian and military means to respond to crises, stabilize fragile environments, and build institutional capacities of its partners – in other words, to prevent a new crisis at home. The CSDP's first military operation, Concordia, was deployed in 2003 in North Macedonia; in the same year, the first civilian mission, the European Union Police Mission, arrived in Bosnia and Herzegovina, followed by the military deployment Althea in 2004. In 2014, the European Union Rule of Law Mission reached Kosovo (EUISS 2017). Throughout these years, Albania, Montenegro, Serbia, and North Macedonia turned into active security providers, by participating in CSDP operations, signing Framework Partnership Agreements (FPA) with EU, and engaging in the management of the migrant crisis from 2015 onwards. In terms of individual commitments, Albania contributed with 1,473 troops to Althea and 189 troops in the EU's Tchad/RCA mission, between 2008 and 2010; its contribution was more operational than financial or decision-making (Council 2015b; Tardy 2014; Visoka 2014). Whereas considering the Western Balkan engagement with the Middle-Eastern migration, the European Commission's 2018 strategy proposed the finalization of the European Border and Coast Guards agreements in order to enact operations on migration and border management – as a new Balkan route emerged through Albania, Montenegro, and Bosnia and Herzegovina (European Commission 2018a; Lee 2018). The EU-Western Balkans Summits in Sofia (2018) and Poznań (2019) as part of the Berlin Process emphasized the importance of collaboration with the region in the field of security and migration (Council 2018; European Commission 2019d). Strategic partnerships with the Western Balkans are seen as a vehicle to transport European strategic culture beyond the EU's borders, which in return contributes to the process of Europeanization of national foreign policies in the region, with a hope that the region will eventually be admitted to the EU. The close link between NATO and EU memberships point out to the complementarity of their agendas; membership and participation in the activities of the former (in planning, cooperation, and information sharing), complements the 2016 EU Global Strategy (EEAS 2016).

Albania's Benefits of Enlargement

Ronald Asmus (2008), responsible for NATO enlargement during the Clinton administration, maintained that painful institutional reforms at domestic level are indispensable to qualify for a membership in the alliance or the EU. The quality of institutions and progress of institutional reforms are discussed in the European Commission's reports, supported financially by the Instrument for Pre-Accession Assistance, and promoted through projects within the Horizon 2020 framework. Looking at Albania more closely, the 2018 European Commission report particularly recognized the progress in the field of rule of law (European Commission 2019b). Positive results were achieved in the establishment of the self-governing institutions of the judiciary and the run of the vetting process under the International Monitoring Operation (IMO), an EU-funded project that provides for alignment of the judiciary system with the EU acquis by involving public and private sector (Center for International Legal Cooperation 2019). Moreover, under IPA I and II components – Transition Assistance and Institutions Building (I) and Cross-Border Cooperation (II), Albania was awarded over one billion euros in the period between 2007 and 2020, in support of key reforms and state-building (European Commission 2013a; European Commission 2014b; European Commission 2019f; Jonuzaj 2019). Reforms in public administration, particularly in enhancing transparency and professionalism and strengthening policymaking in regulatory issues continued to mark improvements (European Commission 2019a). Finally, Albania participates in INFORM, a Horizon 2020 project bringing together Western Balkan countries and four EU members (Croatia, Latvia, Slovenia, and the United Kingdom). The project is set to monitor the impact of formal and informal stakeholders on the implementation of EU regulations by coupling research and innovation. Eleven out of top thirty-five research projects funded under the Horizon 2020 scheme are Albania's (UCL 2019; Euraxess Researches in Motion 2017), altogether placing an emphasis on consolidation of national institutional framework and increased networking and cooperation with the EU structures.

The conduct an independent foreign policy enables Albania to put forward its strategic choices and provide institutionalized solutions to security concerns by uplifting its national interest to the EU level. Due to its size, culture, and material resources, Albania's behavior is constructive and opportunistic. By participating in various arrangements in the region and beyond, Albania has established diplomatic relations with 115 countries. As already pointed out elsewhere, "[c]ooperative security arrangements emerge around security communities" (Mölder 2006, 17), and, therefore, Albania has sought to acquire capacity to respond to crises and protect its citizens by sharing common beliefs with other European countries. It contributed to international peace operations with 6,000 troops in the period between 1996 and 2013, and in June 2012, it signed an FPA with the EU to participate in crisis management operations – an involvement steering the shape of a national security policy, the development of technical security aspects, and the production and standardiza-tion of military capabilities (*New Europe* 2012; Visoka 2014). Also, considering the country's current engagement in NATO and EU-led operations, it is predictable to include Albania, as a third country, in projects of common defense initiatives, such as the Permanent Structured Cooperation's Military Mobility, which aims to im-prove the movement of troops and equipment in Europe (PESCO 2018). In addition, as a NATO member and CSDP contributor, Albania is bounded with other countries in the region by NATO-SOFA and EU-SOFA bilateral agreements. Unifying legal frameworks on cross-border transit of troops and equipment facilitates cooperation with NATO and quick deployment in the field, but also streamlines Albania's activi-ties with those of EU members and increases investments in infrastructure to meet operational needs.

Being outside the EU, Albania is neither a full participant in the union's market area, nor in the fiscal and monetary policies, which makes evaluation of the coun-try's economic benefits impossible. However, in order to gain a better picture of Albania's economic performance, it is necessary to use alternative data and indica-tors of a functioning free market economy and an effective economic governance. For example, the 2018 Doing Business Report, ranked Albania 63rd out of 190 econo-mies worldwide for providing measures of business regulations. The enforcement of business law has improved along the years due to the successful implementation of reforms concerning contract enforcement, transboundary trade, protection of mi-nority investors, and simplification of procedures to resolve conflicts. In fact, Albania's overall score in terms of business climate is not far from the regional aver-age (World Bank 2018; World Bank 2020). Furthermore, in 2019, Albania came to chair the Central European Free Trade Agreement (CEFTA), a pre-membership trade platform which introduces the economies of the aspiring countries to EU standards (European Commission 2019b). Following the CEFTA protocol and different sum-mits on the Western Balkans, the government of Albania together with other partic-ipants endorsed the Multi-annual Action Plan (MAP) for the Regional Economic Area (REA) concentrating its efforts on the areas of trade, mobility, investment, and digital integration. The implementation of MAP objectives is coordinated by the Regional Cooperation Council (RCC) with the support of European Commission (Regional Cooperation Council 2017). As such, REA is considered an instrument to meet the economic criteria for integration and also as a mini-Schengen area among the Western Balkan countries in order to increase its investment attractiveness.

The EU is the main trading partner for Albania, dominating 72.2 percent of all trade volume, with main players being Italy (38.6), Greece (8.1), and Germany (6.9). Since 2000, exports to the EU increased ten times and imports nearly four times (INSTAT 2018; 2019). The growth in trade with the EU gives Albania the opportunity to enter the Single Market, contribute to the intra-EU trade, and take advantage of bilateral trade agreements with EU members. Also, Albania marks a positive trend in terms of foreign direct investments, the inflow of which from the EU grew by 22 percent in 2016 and 44 percent in 2017. In goods, Albania runs a large trade deficit because of manufacturing services and revenues from foreign tourism; the number of foreign businesses in tourism and agriculture increased by 12 percent from 2016 to 2017 (European Commission 2019b). The engine of the national economy is the small and medium enterprises, and in 2016, the SME sector employed 81 percent of all active work forces with a turnover of 77.8 percent and 74.9 percent of total investments. In order to assist SMEs in expanding their business, the EU introduced the Western Balkans Enterprise Development and Innovation Facility initiative (WB EDIF) in 2013, currently operating in seven countries with nearly €650 million in support. Albania started to benefit from the initiative in 2017 through the Guarantee Facility Instrument (WB EDIF 2020). Within the Single Market arrangements, Albania is allowed to benefit from EU autonomous trade preferences until end of 2020, permitting nearly all exports to enter the EU without customs tax. The country, as per the 2019 European Commission's report (2019b), is moderately equipped for the free movement of goods, services, workers, and capital. In addition, some progress was achieved in the sectoral alignment with the requirements on product legislation and the 2018 law on transfer of military equipment and dual-use goods. However, as recommended, more had to be done in terms of harmonization of national legislation as per the acquis and in terms of enforcement measures enhancing the accountability and administrative capacity of the respective structures (European Commission 2019c; 2019b). Overall, the alignment with EU standards has positively affected the development of the national economy; the economic growth increased from 3.8 percent in 2017 to 4.2 percent in 2018, and unemployment and budget deficit decreased (European Commission 2019a). With everything taken into account, as remarked by the Brussels authorities, Albania has progressed toward establishing a functioning market economy.

The Unnavigable Path to the European Union

The 2018 Democracy Index depicted Albania as a hybrid regime, ranked 76th in the overall classification (The Economist 2019). Despite the self-destructive internal politics caused by competition between the dominant political parties, the process of Europeanization is also linked to issues closely related to statehood, nationalism, religious occurrences, and Europeanization and Euroscepticism, which altogether complicate Albania's road toward the EU membership.

Looking at statehood problems, back in 2013, the European Commission (2013a) urged Albania to implement public administration reform, reinforce the autonomy and transparency of judicial institutions, fight against corruption and organized crime, and reinforce the protection of human rights. Some years after, although some progress was made, expressions such as "moderately prepared" and "has some level of preparation" often occurred in the European Commission's findings (2019b). In the view of the Brussels authorities, delays in the electoral reform and the adoption of amendments to the Law on the Status of Judges and Prosecutors were due to the boycott by the opposition of the parliament, which began in September 2018. In addition, the Nations in Transit report communicated the existence of political pressure and interfering in the judiciary, and the Transparency International ranked Albania 99 among 180 countries (Kajsiu 2018; OSCE 2019). For example, according to the opinion poll "Trust in Governance 2017," 21 percent of the participants viewed courts as the most corrupt of all institutions and for 72 percent believed that courts were the most influenced of all institutions, by the political administrations (Institute for Democracy and Mediation 2018). Some of the unanswered corruption cases include the 2008 Gerdeci affair (Chivers 2008), the 2010 video Meta-Prifti uncovering a corrupt deal (Anon. 2010; ERCAS 2011), the 2013 accusations of the former Minister of Defense, Arben Imami, of abuse of power and tender rules (Likmeta 2013), the 2017 ties between the former Minister of the Interior, Saimir Tahiri, and an Albanian-Italian drug trafficking cartel (Kajsiu 2018), the 2018 accusation of two ministers of the Rama government, Arben Ahmetaj and Damian Gjiknuri, of corrupt activities by the opposition (Ruci 2018), and so on. Moreover, as per the 2019 Narcotics Control Strategy Report, Albania "made no significant progress toward thwarting money laundering and financial crimes in 2018," with the country being listed as one of the main stations from which organized crime evolves and penetrates other regions in the world (US State Department 2019). On the other hand, the country did claim to have pursued steps in addressing the above issues and some success in the establishment of the Task Force, the implementation of the Intra-sectorial Strategy, and the institutionalization of the specialized Special Anticorruption Structures and National Investigation Bureau (Keshilli i Ministrave 2019b). However, with everything taken into consideration, the 2019 report of the Albanian Council of Ministers prepared for the parliament noted that there was no progress in fulfillment of the Copenhagen criteria and, for example, when compared to North Macedonia, Albania was behind with reforms in public administration and freedom of press and information (Keshilli i Ministrave 2019b).

As a fundamental human right (Article 19, Universal Declaration of Human Rights), respect for freedom of expression and the media should be considered an indicator of a candidate's suitability to join the EU. According to Freedom House, Albania is a partly free country, scoring below the EU average, and in the view of the 2019 World Press Freedom Index, the overall situation deteriorated when compared to the previous year. Albania's score is one of the worst in the Western Balkans and comparable to that of Kyrgyzstan and East Timor (Reporters Without Borders 2019; Taylor 2019). Like in the case of its neighbors, the correct and professional functioning of the Albanian media is impaired with legal, political, and censorship issues, with members of the ruling elite trying to silence critical reporting. As one analysis has put it, problems in the media sphere derive from a tired institutional framework unable to regulate, protect, and hold media structures accountable (Durham 2014). For example, in December 2019, the Italian channel Rai 3 dedicated an entire documentary to the (lack of) freedom of the press in Albania. Entitled *Bocche cucite* [Sewn Mouths], the broadcast illustrated the worrying situation by looking at the recent earthquake and the media coverage of it. In many instances people were threatened, brought under arrest, and prevented from publishing information via social networks. As it happened, Albanian journalists accused the government of not collaborating with the media and in the majority of the cases, the media had to feature material prepared by the government officials (*Albania News* 2019). In fact, concerned about the media environment in Albanian, in June 2019 representatives of seven press freedom organizations, including the Committee to Protect Journalists (CPJ), the European Federation of Journalists (EFJ), and the European Centre for Press and Media Freedom (ECPMF), conducted an investigation in Albania. The subsequent report meant not only to illustrate the reality experienced and observed by the experts, but also to collect information which would serve as input to national decision-makers and broadcasters and tell them that the world cannot be turned off. While reading the report, the first message is that the right to be informed and provide information is a human right and it is unreasonable and disrespectful to influence the journalism narrative, especially for a country that aspires to EU membership as Albania (European Federation of Journalists 2019).

Starting from 2014, the Albanian economy has marked an upturn due to increases in consumption and investments which resulted in better annual output and economic growth (in 2017, the output increased by 3.5 percent, being the highest level in a number of years). Although the unemployment rate decreased to 13.6 percent, the result was not satisfactory because of anomalies in the labor market caused by informal employment, many untrained employees, and sectoral composition of employment, etc. (Hysa et al. 2018). The economic transition, despite its efforts to harmonize with the free market standards, is associated with risks and challenges, including the weak judicial system, SMEs' limited access to finance, decline of the construction and manufacturing sectors, corruption and informality in the infrastructural sector, etc. (EBRD 2016). Moreover, since the end of the Cold War, the Albanian state – while trying to cope with market liberalization, national boundary dispute, and threat of ethnic conflicts – has also experienced the emergence of new agents that were not bound to any state whose presence led to privatization of state power. For example, the investigation of the 2008 explosion of an ammunition deposit in Gerdec, near Tirana, when three hundred people were injured and twenty-six killed, exposed a questionable deal between the private contractor AEY (a licensed defense contractor to the US government who moved ammunition to Afghanistan through Albania, but without applying adequate storage standards) and the corrupt Albanian governmental structures (Chivers 2008). Following the investigation, as per the local media, the accused (civil servants and military personnel) went to either political asylum or served the sentence in Albania. However, as per media reporting, none of the high-ranking members of the establishment who had been accused of being implicated in the case have served any sentence, and even some of the High Court members who have dealt with the trial and legal proceedings have been accused of dishonesty (Baze 2015; Doci 2018; *Lajme* 2017; Mero 2013; *Top Channel* 2018).

In terms of nationalism, the advocacy of the union of Albanians and their territories is increasingly present in the Albanian public discourse, embodying both progressive and regressive elements, such as patriotism and expansive nationalism. Patriotism has focused for the political and cultural autonomy and is driven by the idea that unification of the Albanian territories could be reached by suppressing religious diversities. The standpoint according to which "the Albanians' religion is Albanianism" has served as the foundation of the state and contributed to the development of a particular ethnic tradition during history. Events such as the 1878 League of Prizren and League of Tosks, which advocated for the rights of the Albanian community; the language used by diaspora associations like Rilindja (Italy) and Bashkimi (Romania) to identify Albanians with a state and with an ethnic identity, and the attitude of the Albanian government and people during the 1999 Kosovo crisis, represent some of the many forms of expression of patriotism (Vickers 2009). Moreover, the so-called besa code (given word or pledge of honor) was vividly present, among many cases in the Albanian history, in the salvation of Jewish residents in Albania during the Nazi occupation. Albania, a European country with a predominantly Muslim population, succeeded where other countries failed; in its 1934 notes, US Ambassador to Albania, Herman Bernstein, wrote that Albania was one of few countries in the world where racist and religious prejudices did not exist (Izraeli Sot 2018; Sinani 2014). More recently, the existence of a strong relationship between Albania and Israel was confirmed through the latter's immediate offer to provide expertise and financial support to the SAR operations and reconstruction of damaged houses after the 2019 earthquake (Eichner 2019; *Lajmi* 2019).

Expansive nationalism gained ground with the activity of populist movements such as the Red and Black Alliance, and with the joint unions of the governments of Albania and Kosovo, held in the name of national unification. The Red and Black Alliance, a political movement that turned into a political party in 2012, with its outbursts – including attacks against the Patriarch of the Orthodox Church of Albania (*Koha Net* 2014), the proposal to Albanize toponyms and promote marriages among Albanians rather than with other nationalities (*KosovAlb* 2012), and the call for a referendum for Albania's unification (Aleanca Kuq e Zi-Maqedoni 2012) – reflect extremism and immature political behavior, with consequences for ethnic relations in Serbia and North Macedonia where Albanian minorities live. Furthermore, the idea of a Greater Albania would have every potential to inspire a Greater Greece and Greater Serbia given the case of their own scenarios concerning minorities and territories. Nonetheless, the joint unions of the governments of Albania and Kosovo might result in a positive sentiment in Albania to support and seek an even greater connection with its neighbor. In January 2014, Prime Minister Rama travelled with this cabinet members to Prizren to meet their Kosovar homologues. A year later, during a similar occasion, Rama delivered the message that national unification could actually happen through the mediation of the EU (Erebara 2015). If not unification, the nationalistic rhetoric might also suggest a symbolic annexation of the smaller state by its mother state. While Rama suggests "a Single President for Albania and Kosovo and a single national security policy" and threatens that if the two fail to integrate into the EU, they would unite in a single state, other Western Balkan countries and international partners consider his declarations problematic and capable of destabilizing the region (Janjević 2018; *Notizie Geopolitiche* 2017). As a NATO member, Albania should prioritize positive nationalism to ensure coexistence with its partners in the region; in fact, Kosovo is a partner, an independent republic, and per its constitution, adopted following its proclamation of independence in 2008, "[Kosovo] shall seek no union with, any State or part of any State" (Office of the Prime Minister 2008).

With regard to religion, almost 58 percent of the Albanian population is Muslim, 17 percent is Christian, 200 Albanians are Jews, and the rest either belongs to another religion or has no religion (World Population Review 2019). On the one hand, Albanian society is religiously tolerant, which is also evident from the fact that there are more interfaith marriages than intrafaith, and there is a harmonious coexistence of all monotheistic religions. Pope John Paul II and Pope Francis have prized these values in times of the abuse of religion, with obvious consequence for the entire humanity (*Il Messaggero* 2014). On the other hand, the return of the extreme Islam and so-called Turkization of the Balkan region – largely pursued through investments and cultural initiatives – might change the context and the religious perspective of the country (Pedrazzi 2019). In 1992, Albania joined the Conference of Islamic Countries because of potential economic advantages even though such a move seemed to be at odds with its own multi-religious identity (*Osservatorio Balcani e Caucaso Transeuropa* 2002). Until 1994, Arab foundations promoted Islamization of the country by providing financial assistance and advertising Islamic values, altogether aimed at the establishment of an Albanian Islamic State (Elbasani and Puto 2017). These foundations sponsored building of mosques and education of young Muslim Albanians, usually led by instructors with experience in Islamic theological training from the Arab and Asian countries (Shtuni 2015). Until 2018, there were eight madrassas located in different cities of Albanian culture (Elbasan, Shkodra, and Tirana) and one institution of higher education, Hena e Plote (Full Moon) Beder University (Komuniteti Mysliman i Shqipërisë 2019).

In the view of Albanian intellectuals, religion is in need of state supervision, so that the country's aspiration toward EU membership can freely continue (Babuna 2012). In his interview to the Italian weekly Tempi, Prime Minister Rama accentuated the fact that religion should not be the reason for not granting EU membership to

Albania; in his view, religion is not a barrier for the Albanians, and it should not represent a barrier for the EU. He went as far as to claim that "Albanian Muslims are more europeist than the non-Muslim European voters" (cited in Amicone 2014). However, the issue of foreign fighters coming from Albania, Bosnia and Herzegovina, Kosovo, North Macedonia, and Serbia, and being arrested for having links and planning attacks in the name of the Islamic State (ISIS), has been viewed as a major security concern, as per the Counter Extremism Project's report (2017). It is estimated that in the period between 2012 and 2014, some 100–150 Albanian citizens joined extremists in Syria, including ISIS and the Nusra Front, whereas almost five hundred fighters were of ethnic Albanian origin, all from the Western Balkan region. For example, the August 2016 and January 2017 terrorist acts in Albania and Austria respectively, involved ethnic Albanians from Kosovo (Shtuni 2015). According to Besfort Lamallari (2016), the different counterterrorism operations in Albania and Kosovo have revealed the modus operandi of extremist networks and their affiliation with foreign-funded Islamic organizations. In any case, the returning foreign fighters are seen as a threat to the Albanian society, particularly due to a weak judiciary system and lack of proper rehabilitation programs. Knowing that cultural tolerance is a key element of a well-functioning European society, it is unclear and therefore, open to speculation what kind of Islam Albanian society will construct and to what degree Albanian Islamism will comply with the European democratic and humanistic values.

As widely maintained, Europeanization is determined by the national culture, which matters in terms of common norms and values; as demonstrated by Emanuel Adler and Michael Barnett (1998), community members are tied and interacted thanks to social relations and a common identity. With this in mind, Torsten Selck and Renke Deckarm (2013) are right when arguing that culture influences the speed of EU accession and that the Copenhagen criteria alone cannot determine a country's EU membership (for example, in the case of Turkey). Thus, in Albania, Europeanization is about the society's capacity to adapt to the EU regime of rules and principles. On the one hand, corruption, political polarization, clutching market economy, fragmented and incomplete judicial system, and the political culture of statism and authoritarianism, all prevent the EU from pursuing substantial changes in the country. On the other hand, the same deficiencies seem to be the means the Albanian political elite seeks to exploit and rely upon in order to speed up the process of EU accession; instead of creating the just conditions to foster Europeanization, the elite is employing extra-institutional means to power and manipulation (Korski 2011). As Dorian Jano (2008, 57) has pointed out, the passage from "a violent disintegration (the 'last' Balkanization)" to "institutional and policy adaptation (the 'pre-'Europeanization)" goes through the so-called delayed transition, which is characterized by "governance incapacity." Apart from the impression that members of the Albanian political elite lack vision for the state and would like to escape from their responsibilities, there is an ongoing requirement for external mediators to enable communication between the government and the opposition so crises are avoided, especially in the case of parliamentary boycotts and in the eve of either parliamentary or local elections (Deloy 2013; Freedom House 2019; Redei 2017). Also, this sort of dependence on international actors leads to a pathetic sovereignty of the state, which is at odds with the personality of an EU member state. Since communitarian policies are about supranational and intergovernmental dimension, political executives are expected to demonstrate that they possess the will and capacity to adopt public policies that are in the interest of their people by taking on moral and institutional responsibilities.

The October 2019 rejection of the opening of EU's membership negotiations with Albania sounded as if the Brussels authorities were worried about the stability of new members and their potential to erode the security of the union. For example, some older members of the EU, with France and Finland at the forefront, feel strongly against further expansion, and for many the enlargement policy of the EU is the single policy enjoying minor support (European Commission 2018b; *European Views* 2018; Tcherneva 2019). Moreover, the 2008 financial crisis marked the rise of populism and revival of identity politics, and in such a climate, economic concerns coupled with social concerns have enhanced Eurosceptic views, resulting in populist policies. While attractive for the public and political classes across the EU, largely because of their capacity to promote a sense of national belonging in order to address national concerns, such an approach has come to represent a threat to supranational negotiations and the rhetoric inspired by common interests.

Conclusion

If Albania's NATO membership was a kind of present, the EU membership will have to be earned. The status quo and country's ongoing challenges suggest that there is a need for new narratives, tailored to Albania's needs and citizens. So far, Albania's style of Europeanization followed a path dependency approach, clearly confirming that one-size-does-not-fit-all when it comes to the fulfillment of previously prescribed criteria and requirements (the Copenhagen and Maastricht criteria). During the 2017 Malta Summit, German Chancellor Merkel stated that a multi-speed Europe is indispensable with regard to further integration and development (Durden 2017). In fact, aware of the complexities, European Commission President Juncker proposed a revision of the existing criteria; if applied to the case of Albania, three set-ups – differentiated integration, type of conditionality, and proximity accession – could serve to transform the country's weaknesses into a winning strategy. Differentiated integration is interest-driven (Economides 2010). Thinking about Albania, the speed of Europeanization (followed by EU membership) depends on the EU's policy preferences of EU, but then the EU itself is short of applicable instruments. Moreover, the whole conditionality agenda implies a cooperation model that is based on motives and restrictions. The Copenhagen criteria imposed double conditionality – positive and negative (Puente 2014) – which suggests a choice between an Albanian Europeanization style and a long reform fatigue. With this in mind, many policy-makers have come to believe that the EU has to adapt itself to the innovative type of conditionality for future newcomers. Finally, the proximity accession criteria, introduced by Romano Prodi (2002), is about equilibrium of the two sides of the conditionality. When applied to the Western Balkans, the reform fatigue is associated with political instability; however, the exercise of differentiated power at all layers domestically and horizontal cooperation between the EU and prospective members would reduce direct interference of the leadership and would actually generate quicker progress and stability.

Albania's membership in the EU, like that of the rest of the Western Balkan region, is motivated by strategic challenges that the EU itself has faced. Albania is already in Europe and, therefore, it does not have to go to Europe. However, while different Albanian governments have, to a greater or lesser extent, failed to absorb the EU standards, the Brussels authorities have been incapable of adopting custom-made strategies and understanding their implementation as necessary. If the region is imagined as part of the Single Market, a proximity policy seems the right way forward, similarly to the very launch of the European integrationist project. In fact, the Parrondo's Paradox made sense in the early 1950s, with the creation of the European Coal and Steel Committee when truly divergent political views (or weaknesses) transformed into a success story – why should it not work for Albania?

References

Adler, Emanuel, and Michael Barnett, eds. 1998. *Security Communities*. Cambridge: Cambridge University Press.

All. n.d. *Regional Cooperation*. http://www.aii-ps.org/component/content/article/10-about-the-aii/92-links.

Albania News. 2019. "Rai3, Fuori Tg: Albania, bocche cucite." 11 December, https://www.albania news.it/rassegna/rai3-albania-bocche-cucite.

Albanian Embassy in Turkey. 2019. "In their meetings with Cakaj, Austria, Spain, and Sweden support the opening of negotiations." http://www.ambasadat.gov.al/turkey/en/their-meet ings-cakaj-austria-spain-and-sweden-support-opening-negotiations.

Aleanca Kuq e Zi- Maqedoni. 2012. "AK: Referendum për bashkimin." *Facebook*, 26 November, https://www.facebook.com/pg/Aleanca-Kuq-E-Zi-Maqedoni-222664847760496/posts/.

Amicone, Luigi. 2014. "Edi Rama. Intervista al premier dell'Albania, il paese che sogna l'Italia e l'Europa dopo cinquant'anni di comunismo." *Tempi*, 18 October, https://www.tempi.it/edi-rama-intervista-premier-albania.

Anastasakis, Othon. 2005. "The Europeanization of the Balkans." *The Brown Journal of World Affairs* 12(1): 77–88.

Anon. 2010. "Video Prifti-Meta (Me cilesi te larte)." *YouTube*, https://www.youtube.com/watch?v= Uo5QNBtV37M.

AP News. 2019. "Mogherini rues 'historic mistake' over EU membership talks." 20 October, https://apnews.com/0bfc70b6143d4328aac18851439be8fd.

Asmus, Ronald D. 2008. "A strategy for integrating Ukraine into the West." *Central & Eastern Europe Series* 04/06: 1–12.

Babuna, Aydin. 2012. "Albanian national identity and islam in the post-communist era." http://www.sam.gov.tr/wp-content/uploads/2012/02/AydinBabuna.pdf.

Basha, Lulzim. 2019. *Lulzim Basha @lulzimbasha_al*. 22 October, https://twitter.com/lulzimbasha_al/status/1186659639347298304.

Baze, Mero. 2015. "Te gjithe ata qe nuk u ndeshkuan per Gerdecin." *Tema*, 14 March, http://www.gazetatema.net/2015/03/14/te-gjithe-ata-qe-nuk-u-ndeshkuan-per-gerdecin-2/.

Browne, Gareth. 2019. "Tirana mayor warns against Albania being 'the Pyongyang of Europe'." *Euronews*, 28 June, https://www.euronews.com/2019/06/28/tirana-mayor-warns-against-albania-being-the-pyongyang-of-europe.

Bushati, Ditmir, 2019. "EU accused of betraying promises on Albanian accession." *Euronews*, 21 June, https://www.euronews.com/2019/06/20/eu-accused-of-betraying-promises-on-albanian-accession.

Chivers, C. J. 2008. "Supplier under scrutiny on arms for Afghans." *The New York Times*, 27 March, https://www.nytimes.com/2008/03/27/world/asia/27ammo.html?.

Center for International Legal Cooperation. 2019. "Project: International monitoring operation – support to the process of temporary re-evaluation of judges and prosecutors in Albania." https://www.cilc.nl/project/international-monitoring-operation/.

Council. 2015a. "Draft Council Conclusions on the Renewed European Union Internal Security Strategy 2015–2020." 10 June, http://data.consilium.europa.eu/doc/document/ST-9798-2015-INIT/en/pdf.

Council. 2015b. "Council Decision (CFSP) 2015/528 of 27 March 2015." *Official Journal of the European Union*, 28 March, https://eur-lex.europa.eu/legal-content/en/TXT/?uri=CELEX%3A32015D0528.

Council. 2018. "Vertice UE-Balcani occidentali a Sofia, 17 maggio 2018." https://www.consilium.europa.eu/it/meetings/international-summit/2018/05/17/.

Counter Extremism Project. 2017. "Albania: Extremism & counter-extremism." https://www.counterextremism.com/countries/albania.

Deloy, Corinne. 2013. "European elections monitor: What kind of majority will emerge after the Albanian general elections?" *Fondation Robert Schuman*, 23 June, https://www.robert-schuman.eu/en/doc/oee/oee-1443c-en.pdf.

Demirtaş, Birgül. 2015. "Turkish foreign policy towards the Balkans: A Europeanized foreign policy in a de-Europeanized national context? *Journal of Balkan and Near Eastern Studies* 17(2): 123–140.

Doci, Adriatik. 2018. "Pastrimi i drejtësisë / Si u rrëzuan gjyqtarët e Gërdecit dhe 21 Janarit." *Shqiptarja*, 21 August, https://shqiptarja.com/lajm/pastrimi-i-drejtesise-si-u-rrezuan-gjyqtaret-e-gerdecit-dhe-21-janarit.

Durden, Tyler. 2017. "Goodbye old EU, hello new multi-speed Europe." *Zero Hedge*, 15 March, https://www.zerohedge.com/news/2017-03-14/goodbye-old-eu-hello-new-multi-speed-europe.

Durham, Jennifer. 2014. "The EU should set explicit press freedom requirements for candidate countries." *LSE Blog*, 2 September, https://blogs.lse.ac.uk/lsee/2014/09/02/the-eu-should-set-explicit-press-freedom-requirements-for-candidate-countries/.

EBRD. 2016. "Strategy for Albania as approved by the Board of Directors at the meeting on 13 January 2016." https://www.ebrd.com/documents/strategy-and-policy-coordination/strategy-for-albania.pdf.

ECFR. 2019. "Europe's new agenda in the Western Balkans." 7 August, https://www.ecfr.eu/arti cle/commentary_europes_new_agenda_in_the_western_balkans.

Economides, Spyros. 2010. "Balkan Europe." In *Which Europe? The Politics of Differentiated Integration*, edited by Kenneth Dyson and Angelos Sepos, 112–125. Basingstoke: Palgrave Macmillan.

The Economist. 2019. "The retreat of global democracy stopped in 2018: Or has it just passed?" 8 January, https://www.economist.com/graphic-detail/2019/01/08/the-retreat-of-global-democ racy-stopped-in-2018.

EEAS. 2016. "Shared vision, common action: A stronger Europe – a global strategy for the European Union's Foreign and Security Policy." June, http://eeas.europa.eu/archives/docs/ top_stories/pdf/eugs_review_web.pdf.

Eichner, Itamar. 2019. "Israel Rescue and Service Team assisting emergency operations in Albania." *YNetNews*, 27 November, https://www.ynetnews.com/article/H11Eu433r.

Elbasani, Arolda, and Artan Puto. 2017. "Albanian-style *laïcité:* A model for multi-religious European home? *Journal of Balkan and Near Eastern Studies* 19(1): 53–69.

Emerging Europe. 2019. "EU official tells Albania's opposition its protests are counter-productive." 8 March, https://emerging-europe.com/news/eu-official-tells-albanias-opposition-its-pro tests-are-counter-productive/.

Emmott, Robin. 2019. "Mission impossible: Next EU foreign policy chief warns of EU irrelevance." *Reuters*, 7 October, https://uk.reuters.com/article/uk-eu-commission-borrell/mission-impossi ble-next-eu-foreign-policy-chief-warns-of-eu-irrelevance-idUKKBN1WM1QK.

ERCAS. 2011. "Corruption caught on tape sets Albania on fire once more." https://www.againstcor ruption.eu/articles/corruption-caught-on-tape/.

Erebara, Gjergj. 2015. "Albania's nationalist show: All bark and no bite." *Balkan Insight*, 25 March, https://balkaninsight.com/2015/03/25/albania-s-nationalist-show-all-bark-and-no-bite/.

Erebara, Gjergj. 2019a. "Tensions rise in Albania ahead of disputed elections." *Balkan Insight*, 19 June, https://balkaninsight.com/2019/06/19/tensions-on-rise-in-albania-as-elections-day-ap proaches/.

Erebara, Gjergj. 2019b. "Albania avoids violence in contested local elections." *Balkan Insight*, 30 June, https://balkaninsight.com/2019/06/30/albania-avoids-violence-in-contested-local-elec tions/.

EUISS. 2017. "European security and defence: The basics." 20 November, https://www.iss.europa. eu/content/european-security-and-defence--basics.

Euractiv. 2013. "The Netherlands vetoes Albania's EU candidate status." 13 December, https:// www.euractiv.com/section/enlargement/news/the-netherlands-vetoes-albania-s-eu-candi date-status/.

Euractiv. 2019. "North Macedonia nears accession talks, Albania falling behind." 17 June, https:// www.euractiv.com/section/enlargement/news/north-macedonia-nears-accession-talks-alba nia-falling-behind/.

Euraxess Researches in Motion. 2017. "Euraxess country in focus: Albania." *Euraxess India Quarterly Newsletter Issue* 4: 2–12.

European Commission. 2007. "Commission Regulation (EC) No 718/2007 of 12 June 2007." *Official Journal of the European Union*, 29 June, https://eur-lex.europa.eu/legal-content/EN/TXT/PDF/ ?uri=CELEX:02007R0718-20130526&from=EN.

European Commission. 2013a. "Albania 2013 progress report." 16 October, https://ec.europa.eu/ neighbourhood-enlargement/sites/near/files/pdf/key_documents/2013/package/al_rap port_2013.pdf.

European Commission. 2013b. "Albania has delivered and so should the EU." 10 December, https://ec.europa.eu/commission/presscorner/detail/en/SPEECH_13_1057.

European Commission. 2014a. "IPA CBC Italy – Albania – Montenegro." https://ec.europa.eu/re
gional_policy/en/atlas/programmes/2014-2020/italy/2014tc16i5cb008.

European Commission. 2014b. *2013 Annual Report on Financial Assistance for Enlargement (IPA,
PHARE, CARDS, Turkey Pre-Accession Instrument, Transition Facility)*. Brussels: European
Commission.

European Commission. 2017. "President Jean-Claude Juncker's State of the Union Address 2017*."
13 September, https://ec.europa.eu/commission/presscorner/detail/en/SPEECH_17_3165.

European Commission, 2018a. "A credible enlargement perspective for and enhanced EU
engagement with the Western Balkans." 6 February, https://eur-lex.europa.eu/resource.html?
uri=cellar:d284b8de-0c15-11e8-966a-01aa75ed71a1.0001.02/DOC_1&format=PDF.

European Commission. 2018b. *Standard Eurobarometer 90*. Brussels: European Union.

European Commission. 2019a. "2019 communication on EU Enlargement Policy." 29 May,

European Commission. 2019b. "Commission staff working document: Albania 2019 report." 29
May, https://ec.europa.eu/neighbourhood-enlargement/sites/near/files/20190529-albania-
report.pdf.

European Commission. 2019c. "Trade preferences: Western Balkans." 14 June, https://ec.europa.
eu/trade/policy/countries-and-regions/regions/western-balkans/.

European Commission. 2019d. "Western Balkans Summit in Poznań: Strengthening links within the
region and with the EU." 5 July, https://ec.europa.eu/commission/presscorner/detail/en/IP_
19_3669.

European Commission. 2019e. "EU connectivity agenda for the Western Balkans."

European Commission. 2019f. "Albania: Financial assistance under IPA II." https://ec.europa.eu/
neighbourhood-enlargement/instruments/funding-by-country/albania_en.

European Commission. 2020. "10 benefits of trade." https://trade.ec.europa.eu/doclib/docs/
2010/november/tradoc_146935.pdf.

European Council. 2018. "Infographic: EU and Western Balkans intertwined." https://www.consi
lium.europa.eu/en/infographics/western-balkans-economy/.

European Federation of Journalists. 2019. "Mission preliminary findings: Press freedom is
deteriorating in Albania." 21 June, https://europeanjournalists.org/blog/2019/06/21/albania-
preliminary-findings-of-joint-freedom-of-expression-mission/.

European Views. 2018. "Albania overwhelmingly wants EU membership, Serbia not so much." 27
December, https://www.european-views.com/2018/12/albania-overwhelmingly-wants-eu-
membership-serbia-not-so-much/.

Freedom House. 2019. "Freedom in the world 2019: Albania." https://freedomhouse.org/report/
freedom-world/2019/albania.

Harper, Jo. 2018. "Will Turkey cut investment to the Balkans?" *Observator Finansowy*, 6 October,
https://financialobserver.eu/cse-and-cis/will-turkey-cut-investment-to-the-balkans/.

Harper, Jo. 2019. "Western Balkans with the largest inflow of greenfield investment." *Observator
Finansowy*, 7 October, https://financialobserver.eu/cse-and-cis/western-balkans-with-the-
largest-inflow-of-greenfield-direct-investment/.

Hinnant, Lori, David McHugh, and Sylvie Corbet. 2019. "Leaders at the G7 Summit made power
moves, traded barbs, and threatened tariffs in a 'difficult test of the unity and solidarity of the
free world'." *Business Insider*, 25 August, https://www.businessinsider.com/g7-summit-
world-leaders-clash-2019-8?IR=T.

Hix, Simon, and Klaus H. Goetz, 2000. "Introduction: European integration and national political
systems." *West European Politics* 23(4): 1–26.

Hopkins, Valerie. 2019. "Balkan leaders warn that EU accession delay risks stoking tensions."
Financial Times, 4 November, https://www.ft.com/content/9d0f4f6a-fbdf-11e9-a354-
36acbbb0d9b6.

Hürriyet Daily News. 2016. "President Erdoğan: EU not everything, Turkey may join Shanghai five." 20 November, http://www.hurriyetdailynews.com/president-erdogan-eu-not-everything-tur key-may-join-shanghai-five-106321.

Hysa, Eglantina, Güngör Turan, and Timothy P. Hagen. 2018. *Albanian Economic Performance: 2017 Annual Report.* Tirana: Epoka University.

Il Messaggero. 2014. "Papa Francesco a Tirana: Albania è esempio di pacifica convivenza tra le religioni." 21 September, https://www.ilmessaggero.it/video/speciale_papa/papa_fran cesco_a_tirana_albania_e_esempio_di_pacifica_convivenza_tra_le_religioni-149561.html.

INSTAT. 2018. "Eksporti dhe Importi sipas vendeve 2014–2018." http://www.instat.gov.al/al/ temat/tregtia-e-jashtme/tregtia-e-jashtme-e-mallrave/.

INSTAT. 2019. "Tregtia e Jashtme e Mallrave." http://instat.gov.al/media/6172/tj-korrik-2019.pdf.

Institute for Democracy and Mediation. 2018. *Opinion Poll 2017: Trust in Governance.* Tirana: Institute for Democracy and Mediation.

Izraeli Sot. 2018. "The Jews of Albania and their salvation during the Holocaust." 27 March, https://www.izraelisot.com/2018/03/27/the-jews-of-albania-and-their-salvation-during-the-holocaust/.

Janjević, Dorian. 2018. "Albania's Edi Rama floats joint president idea in Kosovo." 19 February, https://www.dw.com/en/albanias-edi-rama-floats-joint-president-idea-in-kosovo/a-42642058.

Jano, Dorian. 2008. "From 'Balkanization' to 'Europeanization': The stages of Western Balkans complex transformations." *L'Europe en Formation* 3-4(349-350): 55–69.

Jonuzaj, Klaudjo. 2019. "EU, Albania sign 94 mln euro agreement in support of key reforms." *SeeNews*, 13 September, https://seenews.com/news/eu-albania-sign-94-mln-euro-agree ment-in-support-of-key-reforms-669013.

Kajsiu, Blendi. 2018. "Nations in transit: Albania." Freedom House, https://freedomhouse.org/re port/nations-transit/2018/albania.

Keohane, Robert. 1989. *International Institutions and State Power: Essays in International Relations.* Boulder, CO: Westview Press.

Keshilli i Ministrave. 2019a. Raportim per Vitin 2018 mbi Ecurine e Procesit te Integrimit te Shqiperise ne Bashkimin Evropian. Tirana: Keshilli i Ministrave.

Keshilli i Ministrave. 2019b. Mbi gjetjet dhe rekomandimet e Raportit te Komisionit Evropian per Shqiperine 2019. Tirane: Keshilli i Ministrave.

Koha Net. 2014. "AK kundër kryepeshkopit serb Irinej, vendos parulla në Kishën Ortodokse." 1 June, https://archive.koha.net/?id=27&l=12273.

Komuniteti Mysliman i Shqipërisë. 2019. "Medresete." https://www.kmsh.al/al/komuniteti-mysli man-i-shqiperise/medresete/.

Korski, Daniel. 2011. "Stop Albania's self-destruction." *Atlantic Council*, 27 January, https://atlantic council.org/blogs/natosource/stop-albanias-selfdestruction/.

KosovAlb. 2012. "Aleanca KuqeZi e shqetësuar nga martesat me sllavët." 24 August, https://koso valb.com/2012/08/24/aleanca-kuqezi-e-shqetesuar-nga-martesat-me-sllavet/.

KQZ. 2019a. *Zgjedhje Vendore 2019: Tabela Permbledhese.* Tirana: KQZ.

KQZ. 2019b. *Zgjedhjet Vendore 2019: Pjesëmarrja në votime për Bashki.* Tirana: KQZ.

Lajme. 2017. "Sot, 9 vite nga vrasjet shtetërore në Gërdec." 15 March, https://www.lajme.al/sot-9-vite-nga-vrasjet-shteterore-ne-gerdec/.

Lajmi. 2019. "Izraeli do të vijojë kontributin në rindërtimin e banesave në Shqipëri." 11 December, https://lajmi.net/izraeli-do-te-vijoje-kontributin-ne-rindertimin-e-banesave-ne-shqiperi/.

Lamallari, Besfort. 2016. *Dealing with Returning Foreign Fighters.* Tirana: Open Society Foundation.

Lee, Laurence. 2018. "Balkan countries pressured by EU over refugee migration route." *Al Jazeera*, 27 June, https://www.aljazeera.com/news/2018/06/balkan-countries-pressured-eu-refugee-migration-route-180627190722447.html.

Leffler, Melvyn P. 1999. "The Cold War: What do 'we now know'?" *The American Historical Review* 104(2): 501–524.

Likmeta, Besar. 2013. "Albania charges former defence minister." *Balkan Insight*, 10 December, https://balkaninsight.com/2013/12/10/albania-ex-defense-minister-accused-of-corruption/.

Marković, Frank. 2016. "Bratislava Summit: Beginning of the end for the EU?" *European Public Affairs*, 26 September, http://www.europeanpublicaffairs.eu/bratislava-summit-beginning-of-the-end-for-the-eu/.

Mayhew, Alan. 1998. *Recreating Europe: The European Union's Policy towards Central and Eastern Europe*. Cambridge: Cambridge University Press.

Mero, Armand. 2013. "Viktimat e Gërdecit kërkojnë hapjen e procesit ndaj Fatmir Mediut." *VoA*, 22 February, https://www.zeriamerikes.com/a/gerdec-viktima-prokurori-fatmir-mediu-voa-ditari-shqip/1609033.html.

Miskimmon, Alister. 2007. *Germany and the Common Foreign and Security Policy of the European Union: Between Europeanisation and national Adaptation*. London: Palgrave Macmillan.

Moga, Teodor. 2010. "Connecting the enlargement process with the Europeanization theory: The case of Turkey." *CES Working Papers* II(1): 5–20.

Mölder, Holger. 2006. "NATO's role in the post-modern European security environment, cooperative security and the experience of the Baltic Sea region." *Baltic Security & Defence Review* 8, 7–33.

Müller, Patrick, and Nicole Alecu de Flers. 2009. "Applying the concept of Europeanization to the study of foreign policy: Dimensions and mechanisms." *EIF Working Papers* 5: 1–32.

Netherlands Worldwide. n.d. "Doing business in the Western Balkans." https://www.netherlandsworldwide.nl/doing-business-in-the-west-balkan.

New Europe. 2012. "EU and Albania sign a military cooperation agreement." 5 June, https://www.neweurope.eu/article/eu-and-albania-sign-a-military-cooperation-agreement/.

Nielsen, Nikolaj. 2019. "Juncker: 'Historic mistake' against Balkan EU hopefuls." *EUobserver*, 18 October, https://euobserver.com/enlargement/146340.

Notizie Geopolitiche. 2017. "Edi Rama e la 'Grande Albania' minacciano la pace nei Balcani." 2 May, https://www.notiziegeopolitiche.net/edi-rama-e-la-grande-albania-minacciano-la-pace-nei-balcani/.

Nuroğlu, Elif, and Haris Kurtagić. 2012. "Costs and benefits of the EU enlargement: The impact on the EU and SEE countries." *Journal of Economic and Social Studies* 2(2): 41–64.

Office of the Prime Minister. 2008. "Constitution of the Republic of Kosovo." http://www.kryeministri-ks.net/repository/docs/Constitution1Kosovo.pdf.

OSCE. 2019. "Corruption perceptions index for Albania concerning and indicates that ongoing reforms have to continue, says OSCE Head of Presence Bernd Borchardt." 31 January, https://www.osce.org/presence-in-albania/410531.

Osservatorio Balcani e Caucaso Transeuropa. 2002. "L'Albania e l'islamismo: una minaccia per l'Occidente?" 24 January, https://www.balcanicaucaso.org/aree/Albania/L-Albania-e-l-islamismo-una-minaccia-per-l-Occidente-19710.

Parliament of Albania. 2019. "Kushtetuta e Republikës së Shqipërisë." https://www.parlament.al/Kuvendi/Kushtetuta.

Pedrazzi, Nicola. 2019. "Albania: candidata all'Europa o provincia ottomana?" *Osservatorio Balcani e Caucaso Transeuropa*, 19 June, https://www.balcanicaucaso.org/aree/Albania/Albania-candidata-all-Europa-o-provincia-ottomana-195112.

PESCO. 2018. "Military mobility." https://pesco.europa.eu/project/military-mobility/.

Pridham, Geoffrey. 2005. *Designing Democracy: EU Enlargement and Regime Change in Post-Communist Europe*. Basingstoke: Palgrave Macmillan.

Prodi, Romano. 2002. "A wider Europe: A proximity policy as the key to stability." 5-6 December, https://ec.europa.eu/commission/presscorner/detail/en/SPEECH_02_619.

Puente, Carlos. 2014. "Historical evolution of conditionality criteria in external relations of the EU with CEEC from Cold War to the accession: An insider's perspective." *Romanian Journal of European Affairs* 14(4): 56–77.

Radaelli, Claudio. 2000. "Wither Europeanization? Concept stretching and substantive change." *European Integration online Papers* 4(8): 1–25.

Rankin, Jennifer. 2019. "EU failure to open membership talks with Albania and North Macedonia condemned." *The Guardian*, 18 October, https://www.theguardian.com/world/2019/oct/18/eu-refusal-to-open-talks-with-albania-and-north-macedonia-condemned-as-historic-mistake.

Rapoza, Kenneth. 2019. "Trump the trade tyrant targets the WTO." 29 July, https://www.forbes.com/sites/kenrapoza/2019/07/29/trump-the-trade-tyrant-targets-the-wto/#363c61b165f8.

Redei, Lorinc. 2017. "MEPs as mediators: An emerging trend of parliamentary diplomacy?" Paper presented at the European Union Studies Association Biennial Conference.

Regional Cooperation Council. 2017. "Multi-annual action plan for a regional economic area in the Western Balkans – MAP." 12 July, https://www.rcc.int/priority_areas/39/multi-annual-action-plan-for-a-regional-economic-area-in-the-western-balkans–map.

Reporters Without Borders. 2019. "2019 world press freedom index." https://rsf.org/en/ranking.

Ruci, Ani. 2018. "Shqipëri: Kryeministri Rama shpall ndryshimet në qeveri." *Deutsche Welle*, 28 December, https://www.dw.com/sq/shqipëri-kryeministri-rama-shpall-ndryshimet-në-qeveri/a-46888137.

Ruci, Ani. 2019. "Shqipëri: Kundërthëniet pozitë dhe opozitë për raportin e KE." *Deutsche Welle*, 30 May, https://www.dw.com/sq/shqipëri-kundërthëniet-pozitë-dhe-opozitë-për-raportin-e-ke/a-48974960.

Saakashvili, Mikheil. 2019. "Russia's next land grab won't be in an ex-Soviet state: It will be in Europe." *Foreign Policy*, 15 March, https://foreignpolicy.com/2019/03/15/russias-next-land-grab-wont-be-in-an-ex-soviet-state-it-will-be-in-europe-putin-saakashvili-sweden-finland-arctic-northern-sea-route-baltics-nato/.

Salaj, Ron. 2019. "Albanian students waited 28 years for this moment." *Political Critique*, 30 January, http://politicalcritique.org/cee/2019/albanian-students-moment/.

Schimmelfennig, Frank. 2018. "European integration (theory) in times of crisis: A comparison of the euro and Schengen crises. *Journal of European Public Policy* 25(7): 969–989.

Selck, Torsten J., and Renke Deckarm. 2013. "A cultured club: Explaining EU membership." *Turkish Journal of Politics* 4(2): 127–132.

Shtuni, Adrian. 2015. "Ethnic Albanian foreign fighters in Iraq and Syria." *CTC Sentinel* 8(4): 11–14.

Sinani, Shaban. 2014. *Albanians and Jews: The Protection and Salvation*. Tirana: Naimi.

Stern, Ulrike, and Sarah Wohlfeld. 2012. "Albania's long road into the European Union." *DGAP Analyze* 11: 1–21.

Tardy, Thierry. 2014. "CSDP: Getting third states on board." *EU Institute for Security Studies*, March, https://www.iss.europa.eu/sites/default/files/EUISSFiles/Brief_6_CSDP_and_third_states.pdf.

Taylor, Alice Elizabeth. 2019. "Albania drops seven places in internationally respected media freedom report." *Exit News*, 18 April, https://exit.al/en/2019/04/18/albania-drops-seven-places-in-internationally-respected-media-freedom-report/.

Tcherneva, Vessela. 2019. "Europe's new agenda in the Western Balkans." *ECFR*, 7 August, https://www.ecfr.eu/article/commentary_europes_new_agenda_in_the_western_balkans.

Tirana Echo. 2017. "Albania opposition party risks major internal rift ahead of June elections." 1
   May, http://www.tiranaecho.com/latest-news/albania-opposition-party-risks-major-internal-
   rift-ahead-of-june-elections/.
Top Channel. 2011. "Sequi on top story: Why EU rejected Albania." 13 October, http://top-channel.
   tv/english/sequi-on-top-story-why-eu-rejected-albania/.
Top Channel. 2018. "Gjyqtari i "Gërdecit," në makinën e të pandehurit." 26 June, http://top-chan
   nel.tv/2018/06/26/gjyqtari-i-gerdecit-ne-makinen-e-te-pandehurit/.
Top Channel. 2019. "Topalli-Bashës: Tradhëtove dhe fyeve demokratët, je fajtor që Partia
   Demokratike humbi pushtetin." 30 June, http://top-channel.tv/2019/06/30/topalli-bashes-
   tradhetove-dhe-fyeve-demokratet-je-fajtor-qe-partia-demokratike-humbi-pushtetin/.
UCL. 2019. "INFORM: Closing the gap between formal and informal institutions in the Balkans."
   https://www.ucl.ac.uk/ssees/research/funded-research-projects/inform.
US State Department. 2019. *International Narcotics Control Strategy Report*. Washington, DC:
   Bureau of International Narcotics and Law Enforcement Affairs.
Vickers, Miranda. 2009. *The Albanians: A Modern History*. London: I.B. Tauris.
Vink, Maarten P. 2003. "What is Europeanization? And other questions on a new research agenda."
   European Political Science 3(1): 63–74.
Visoka, Gëzim. 2014. "Peacekeeping contributor profile: Albania." 12 June, http://www.providing
   forpeacekeeping.org/2015/03/30/peacekeeping-contributor-profile-albania/.
WB EDIF. 2020. *Albania*. http://www.wbedif.eu/wbedif-in-your-country/albania/.
Wong, Reuben. 2011. "The Europeanization of foreign policy." In *International Relations and the
   European Union*, edited by Christopher Hill and Michael Smith, 150–170. Oxford: Oxford
   University Press.
World Bank. 2018. *Doing Business 2018*. Washington, DC: World Bank.
World Bank. 2020. "Business reforms in Albania." https://www.doingbusiness.org/en/reforms/
   overview/economy/albania.
World Population Review. 2019. "Albania population 2020." http://worldpopulationreview.com/
   countries/albania-population/.
Zalan, Esther. 2017. "Eastern Europe warns against EU 'disintegration'." *EUobserver*, 2 March,
   https://euobserver.com/news/137089.

Elif Uzgören

11 Studying Trajectory of Turkey's EU Membership: Criticisms and Contributions of Critical Political Economy

The historical trajectory of Turkey's integration to European structures is puzzling and distinctive from other cases of enlargement. The relations between Turkey and the European Union is often described as "wavering" and "cyclical with many ups and downs" (Eralp and Eralp 2012, 164) or "rollercoaster ride" (Yeşilada 2013, 6). A glance on history uncovers why; in 1963, Turkey entered into an association partnership with the then European Economic Community and applied for membership in 1987, but since then has been repeatedly excluded from successive enlargement waves. It is the first country to form Customs Union prior to membership. Although accession negotiations opened in 2005, it is only the chapter covering science and research that has been provisionally closed. The Justice and Development Party (AKP) governments endorsed reforms in the period between 2002 and 2007 without necessarily the end goal of attaining membership status. In fact, the process of carrying out the reforms without the end goal of membership status was codified under the motto of turning Copenhagen criteria into Ankara criteria – an approach well-received by the Turkish society. Still, there is a general agreement that the reform process has slowed down since 2007, with rising criticisms on Turkey's problems related to fundamental freedoms and judicial independence. Negotiations concerning a visa/re-admission agreement in relation to the Syrian refugee crisis have failed to revitalize Turkey-EU relations. Overall, the political and economic developments in both Europe and Turkey have made prospects of Turkish accession to the EU highly questionable; indeed, enlargement is off the agenda both in Ankara and Brussels. The EU has been preoccupied with internal concerns due to Brexit, the crisis of liberalism, the rise of populism and right-wing politics, as well as the Syrian refugee crisis. The European Parliament called the EU leadership to freeze the relations and accession talks in March 2019, which has provided an additional incentive for Turkish President Recep Erdoğan to advocate for Turkey to join the Shanghai Cooperation Organization.

Within such a historical context, this study aspires to compare reflections of theories and conceptual frameworks in the literature on Turkey-EU relations under two historical periods: the 2000s, when the reform process received praise, with the Turkish economy growing and Turkey being largely presented as a bridge between the East and the West; and the 2010s, which was a conjuncture determined by economic crises and populist politics, alongside stagnation in Turkey's membership trajectory. Accordingly, this paper has two aims. First, it will uncover how Turkey's trajectory is scrutinized in the European studies

https://doi.org/10.1515/9783110684216-011

literature, by looking at mainstream and critical approaches to Turkey's integration into the EU. Second, it will examine how the Turkish membership question is studied in the context of crises and rising populism, by considering different theoretical and conceptual frameworks in relation to Turkey's integration with the European structures under the current conjuncture. So far, Turkey's enlargement trajectory has been dominated by mainstream approaches, which constrain the debate to the end state of negotiations and future form of integration. Their reflections are equally problematic to debate structural factors such as globalization and ongoing power relations behind the current state of integration of Turkey with European structures. Yet, critical political economy approaches contribute to the debate to read Europe within structural dynamics, to question power relations behind ongoing integration, and to invite alternative socio-economic orders into the debate. Integration and enlargement decisions are not outcomes of economic or market necessity but are determined by class struggle. Accordingly, the literature in this area uncovers agency behind integration and disintegration by incorporating class politics. Under the current conjuncture of crises, mainstream literature often focuses on discussing terms and conditions of a probable future differentiated integration, and as such, it constrains the debate. For critical political economy scholarship, the future trajectory is uncertain, and it will be determined by an open-ended struggle. The paper starts by analyzing mainstream integration theories and their reflections on the Turkish enlargement case, followed by a critique of their future projections. It then proceeds with an examination of how critical political economy represents an alternative reading by identifying its contribution to the debates concerning Turkey's European trajectory.

Mainstream Studies within European Studies Literature and the Trajectory of Turkey-EU Relations

While the literature on Turkey's EU membership bid is extensive, the bulk of this scholarship focuses on the historical development of relations. As such, there are few studies which are informed from any theoretical framework (Müftüler-Bac and McLaren 2003: 19). Here, they will be analyzed under three categories: functionalism–intergovernmentalism debate, Europeanization, and constructivism. With regard to the first category, neofunctionalism assumes that integration that starts in a decisive economic sector would spill-over to other interdependent sectors which would ultimately cultivate institutionalism, loyalty shift and political community (Haas 1958, 11–19). In *The Uniting of Europe*, Ernst Haas describes the means and ways to transcend the nation-state while discussing construction of European integration (Haas 1958). Contrarily, intergovernmentalists argue that integration is an outcome of inter-state bargaining often acquired at the lowest common denominator after negotiations among nation states, suggesting that integration has not worked to the disadvantage of nation states. Nation states are in charge of integration (Hoffmann 1966, 889). Indeed, supranationalism and nationalism are not opposites; the European integration project has rescued the nation-state which determines main coordinates of integration (Milward 1992, 12, 44). Andrew Moravcsik further developed intergovernmentalism through incorporating interest group politics and rational institutionalism to realism. In liberal intergovernmentalism, Moravcsik conceives of integration as an outcome of inter-state bargaining among national leaders who act rationally taking economic interests, macro-economic preferences and conditions of asymmetrical interdependence in the anarchical international system into consideration (Moravcsik 1998, 5–18). In her study, Catherine Macmillan employs neo-functionalism arguing that intergovernmentalism fails to explicate how integration with Turkey endures despite opposition from various member states; rather, the relations between Turkey and the EU can be explained by functional spill-over (Macmillan 2009, 789). Writing in the context of the 2000s, Macmillan refers to the progress contending that "there is . . . room for cautious optimism that Turkey will eventually accede to the EU" (2009, 806). Çınar Özen (1998) draws on intergovernmentalist studies while arguing that Turkey-EU relations started with concerns over foreign and security policy during the Cold War rather than economic functional links contrary to neofunctionalist assumptions. For Metem Müftüler-Bac and Lauren McLaren, intergovernmentalism helps us to explicate member states' preferences toward enlargement and thus explains how member states changed their policy from not incorporating Turkey as a candidate in 1997 Luxemburg European Council to declaring it a candidate country in 1999 Helsinki Council. They argue that as political and economic conditions have not been altered between 1997 and 1999, it is only intergovernmental decision-making and its reference to member states' preferences that can explain this dramatic change (Müftüler-Bac and McLaren 2003, 19).

The reflections of the debate between functional logic and intergovernmentalism can be criticized on various grounds. First, neofunctionalism cannot explain the timing of enlargement. It assumes that countries with more functional economic links would first become members. Here, although Turkey starts to form economic links through becoming an associate member with the 1963 Ankara Treaty, it has been excluded repeatedly from following enlargement waves. Second, although economic links are consolidated through completion of the Customs Union with Turkey, this has not engendered political integration as neofunctionalism would anticipate. Third, intergovernmentalism treats states as monolithic entities overlooking state-society relations (Risse-Kappen 1996: 57). As a result, intergovernmentalist reflections on the Turkish case discuss membership decisions with a sole focus on political decisions, overlooking economic actors and interests. Fourth, intergovernmentalism approaches the question of membership as a foreign relations matter, rather than integration per se. More importantly, although neofunctionalism and intergovernmentalism take opposite positions with regard to the relationship be-tween national and supranational spheres, they can be posited in the same para-digm; with this in mind, their reflections concerning Turkey's EU trajectory can be criticized on the same ground. The neofunctionalism versus intergovernmentalism di-chotomy restrains the debate to the end state of negotiations – the form of integration with the pioneering concern on the question of whether Turkey will become a mem-ber or not. In addition, their sole focus is on transfer of sovereignty from national to supranational; hence, they ignore the social purpose and social content behind the current form of ongoing integration. Indeed, current state of integration is pre-eminently relying on negative integration – market liberalization – without the nec-essary socio-economic precautions for a sustainable integration with instruments of positive integration. In parallel with their failure to problematize structuration of power relations in the social sphere (van Apeldoorn et al. 2003, 18), their reflections on the Turkish case overlooks ongoing power relations behind the current state of integration of Turkey with European structures. Furthermore, reflections of neo-functionalism to the Turkish case are silent in reading integration within structural factors such as globalization and neo-liberal restructuring. Although studies follow-ing liberal intergovernmentalism conceive structural change, they largely focus on re-evaluating Turkey's place in the post-Cold War context (Müftüler-Baç 1997). They thus conceive structural change as transition from bipolar to multipolar international system, ignoring changes globalization has engendered for the EU and Turkey.

In terms of the second category of research, the examination of Turkey-EU rela-tions within the Europeanization framework dominated the 2000s. This was largely due to the historical developments between Turkey and the EU and general scholarly trends of European studies literature. On the one hand, Turkey became as a candidate country in 1999, which was followed by a pro-European mood through the opening of European divisions within the ministries, founding of European studies graduate pro-grams in universities, and the beginning of screenings in relation to EU acquis. On the other hand, the ever-expanding research within comparative politics has provided more space for the Turkey-EU case in the European studies literature. For instance, Simon Hix argues that the EU has transformed into an "internal political arena" which renders comparative politics as a field of study better to explain European politics rather than International Relations which treats integration as inter-state bargaining (Hix 1994, 22–23). Research in European studies has witnessed the rise of research drawing from Europeanization, multi-level governance, rational choice, historical and sociological institutionalism (Checkel 2001; Hall and Taylor 1996; Pollack 2005). As far as enlargement is concerned, this literature focuses on the effects of Europeanization on candidate countries as well as changes in the EU governance including its institu-tions, administrative capacities, decision-making, party systems, voting patterns, and political ideas (Jachtenfuchs and Kohler-Koch 2005, 112). Frank Schimmelfennig and Ulrich Sedelmeier (2004; 2005) focus on how Europeanization and conditionality af-fected the domestic politics of the Central and Eastern European countries, and the main emphasis was explicating how and to what extent candidate countries adopt rules and institutions of the EU. As far as Turkish case is concerned, the expectation after 1999 Helsinki European Council was that candidacy would stimulate credibility of the EU through political conditionality which would in return trigger the reform process and help Turkey to consolidate its democracy. Various studies measure domestic change in Turkey through a focus on Europeanization of a number of diverse but related issues including civil-military relations, the rule of law, human rights, political parties, and foreign policy (Aydın and Açıkmeşe 2007; Derviş et al. 2004; Diez et al. 2005; Heper 2005; Müftüler-Baç 2005; Öniş 2003; Schimmelfennig et al. 2006).

It is possible to criticize reflections of Europeanization on the Turkish case on four grounds. First, Europeanization literature overemphasizes the role of Europe in stimulating domestic change in the candidate countries. Its adherents turn a blind eye to the role of structural factors in stimulating change in Turkish politics; thus, they fail to differentiate whether so-called policy changes in the 2000s in Turkey are stimulated by European or global induced factors. Second, Europeanization literature takes state-society relations as autonomous and externally related spheres. Accordingly, they repeat the main assumption of the strong state tradition, the dominant approach in political science literature on Turkey (Buğra 1994; Heper 1985; Keyder 1987). The strong state tradition conceives the main struggle in Turkish society as one of strong state versus weak civil society or strong center of bureaucratic and military elites versus a weak periphery of political elites. Accordingly, Europeanization scholarship expects that reform process would constrain the role of military and a strong state apparatus in Turkish politics, opening space for civil society, and consolidating democracy. Third, this literature denies any role for class struggle in understanding Turkish politics and contributes to further neoliberalization. Indeed, it is argued that a "traditional left/right axis" or pros and cons of socio-economic policies is unsatisfactory in the Turkish political context (Öniş 2007, 249). Fourth, there is a veiled Orientalism and Eurocentrism in the Europeanization accounts in assuming that candidate countries have to catch up with European standards that are presented as superior and progressive for non-Europeans to adopt.

Finally, the third category of research in Turkey-EU relations falls within constructivism. Such an approach is concerned with the role of norms and rules in the construction of identities, including national and European identities. It equally examines the EU as a normative power, a civilian form of international actorness in setting norms and rules as standards in world politics (Checkel 2001; Manners 2002). In debating enlargement, membership is explained in relation to ideational factors. For instance, Schimmelfennig and Sedelmeier argue that as the costs of membership of Central and Eastern European countries outweigh the benefits, the decision of EU member states to support enlargement can only be explained by ideational factors such as commitment to EU norms and collective identity (Schimmelfennig 2001, 47; Sedelmeier 2005, 120–126). As far as Turkey's enlargement is concerned, Turkey's status of long candidacy is explained as a result of inability of Turkey to adopt European norms and standards (Schimmelfennig et al. 2006). Some other scholars, while drawing on constructivism, end up arguing that Turkish and European identities are constructed in relation to each other (Rumelili 2008, 97–99, 108). In the 2000s, it was argued that Turkey's integration can contribute to the formation of a more "inclusive, multicultural, tolerant, and universalistic" European identity, while Turkey can act as a bridge among civilizations (Grigoriadis 2009, 4; Rumelili 2008). Nevertheless, the critique of constructivism is also notable. For example, constructivism depicts the EU as a civilian power veiling the imperialist nature of the expansionist policies of the EU especially through its market mechanism; this reading abstracts imperialism from capitalist accumulation, reducing imperialism to military intervention. In addition, it ignores socio-economic imbalances and unequal power relations established as a result of Turkey opening its market to the EU through the Customs Union prior to getting welfare benefits of membership. Lastly, there is also an embedded Eurocentrism in constructivism as Europe is presented as an ideal case in terms of its record on human rights and democracy.

Considering critical political economy approaches to Turkey's European trajectory, the existing European studies literature has largely turned a blind eye in front of those. As Ian Manners and Richard Whitman (2016, 3) warn us, "dissenting voices that attempt to theorize Europe differently and advocate another European trajectory have been largely excluded and left unheard in mainstream discussions." A similar understanding is also offered by Hellen Wallace (2017, 11) that "the field of EU studies has been inhabited by researchers who are mostly sympathetic to the integration process." The rationale behind this exclusion, for Manners and Whitman (2016, 10), is the tendency of approaching critical studies as "a Eurosceptic threat." Yet, there is literature explaining European integration from a critical political economy perspective[1] and few studies employ them in approaching Turkey-EU relations (Uzgören 2018; 2020; Yalman and Göksel 2017). The reflections of critical political economy perspectives to the

---

1 It is possible to refer to three approaches: Gramscian historical materialism, regulation school, and open Marxism. Needless to say, these three schools of thought share a critical historical materialist perspective, but they also have disagreements. Research within Gramscian historical materialism studies European integration within structural dynamics of globalization and neoliberal restructuring as a market-oriented hegemonic project (van Apeldoorn 2002; Bieler and Morton 2001; Cafruny and Ryner 2003), and enlargement as expansion of this socio-economic order (Bieler 2000; Shields 2004). Regulation theory aims to unravel multiple economic, social, ideological, and political dynamics behind a particular capitalist accumulation and growth regime, how this regulation falls into crisis and how it is reproduced as a new mode of regulation at different historical specificity of the capitalist development (Bieling et al. 2016; Boyer and Saillard 1995). Scholars within open Marxism aim to study political economy from Marxist texts at a time when studying Marxism was seen as unfashionable and/ or outdated following the rise of the New Right alongside the collapse of communist regimes (Bonefeld and Psychopedis 1992, ix). They read the EU as a supranational entity for "domestic pursuit of market freedom" stressing that the EU is an economic and monetary union without a political union (Bonefeld 2015, 869).

European integration scholarship contribute to the debate especially on a number of grounds. To begin with, the first contribution of critical approaches is the emphasis on the socio-economic content of current state of Turkey's integration with European structures. Critical theory problematizes structuration of power and the asymmetrical and uneven nature of power relations embedded within integration, and as such, critical scholarship within Turkey-EU relations also questions power relations behind Turkey's current state of integration. The bulk of literature on Turkey-EU relations focuses on the form of enlargement (the question of whether Turkey will become a member or not). This is a non-debate as there has always been relations between Turkey and Europe throughout history though it takes different forms in each historical period. In contrast to the Ottoman Empire, which had been treated as a semi-colonial country in its declining period, Turkey became an associate member with the signature of the 1963 Ankara agreement with the European Economic Community, resulting to in the candidacy for EU membership in 1999. Turkey became a party of the Customs Union before full membership; as such, it has liberalized its trade and opened its market to European competition without any social dimension for the disadvantaged groups such as structural funds or free movement of labor. The socio-economic content of its integration relies on negative integration (based on market liberalization) without the necessary instruments of positive integration that would contribute to eliminate inequalities through a social dimension.

Moving on, critical studies criticize the mainstream for conceiving of integration as determined by necessities behind an economic rationale. Rather, integration decisions are determined by a struggle among social forces, which in return unravels agency behind integration and integrates class struggle into analysis. For instance, enlargement decisions are determined by open-ended struggle among capital and labor in candidate countries (Bieler 2000; Bohle 2006). Class, here, is not conceived simply as "a static, descriptive term applied to groups of individuals sharing common experiences of life-chances or consumption patterns," but it describes "a class society which rests on the shifting sands of the contradictory labor/capital relationship" (Burnham 1994, 225). As far as the reflections of critical political economy on Turkish enlargement is concerned, this body of scholarship problematizes the structural power of capital behind ongoing integration of Turkey with European structures through the Customs Union short of membership. The current state of integration between Turkey and the EU helps Turkish capital groups to take advantages of the Single Market without bearing the burden of adjusting to the European Social Model or European environmental standards. Furthermore, critical political economy approaches situate European integration within structural dynamics of world capitalist system. Here, European integration is analyzed within globalization and neoliberal restructuring (Bieler 2000, 36), and critical political economy especially contributes to examine transnational dynamics of production and finance (Bieling et al. 2016, 53). Finally, critical approaches question alternatives. They highlight the need to question disadvantaged groups from liberalization and integrate labor and trade unions into analysis (Becker et al. 2014; Bieler 2000; 2005). Turkey-EU relations literature turns a blind eye to labor and trade unions, and alternative socio-economic orders are overlooked. Indeed, mainstream literature debates alternatives either as opposition to membership among conservative and nationalist groups (Öniş 2007; Yılmaz 2011) or in relation to alternative foreign policy alignments such as strengthening relations with Turkic states (Yeşilada 2013, 143), or alternative forms other than membership such as privileged partnership (Karakas 2013). As such, alternative socio-economic orders as a result of uneven market integration of Turkey with the European structures is considerably neglected (with the exception of Uzgören 2018). Yet, there is more space in Turkey for opposition on socio-economic grounds as Turkey is the only country which liberalized its regime through the Customs Union without welfare benefits for disadvantaged groups from liberalization such as free movement of workers or structural funds.

European Integration Theory and Turkey's European Trajectory within the Context of Eurozone Crisis and Disintegration

The past decade has witnessed stagnation of European integration with disintegration being on the agenda. The 2008 crisis has engendered a serious challenge to integration questioning to what extent the Internal Market has generated economic convergence among member states especially given the socio-economic disparities among the Northern and Southern European member states. The EU is preoccupied with internal problems evolving around economic crisis, the rise of populism and far-right politics, and the Syrian refugee crisis, and it is due to the complexity of a new context of the European integrationist project that theoretical assumptions have had to be revisited. Although European integration theories have been considerably developed to explicate integration, they were tested to explain disintegration or spillback with member states taking diverse responses. In her opening speech to the *Journal of Common Market Studies* Annual Lecture, Wallace described this period as "testing times for the academic and research communities" (Wallace 2017, 8). For Ben Rosamond, there has been no theory of disintegration especially for two reasons. While on the one hand, European integration scholarship was mostly preoccupied with the question of "how political unification takes place," on the other, there is an institutionalist bias as both neofunctionalism and intergovernmentalism take the EU as institutionally resilient (Rosamond 2016, 865–866). As far as the first debate in integration scholarship is concerned, scholars argue that both neofunctionalism and intergovernmentalism continue to have explanatory power.

Scholars contend that neofunctionalism is still highly relevant particularly in explaining driving forces for integration (Niemann and Ioannou 2015, 212). For instance, functional logic is able to account for further integrative measures taken during the reform process to complete the "incomplete EMU (Economic and Monetary Union) architecture" such as banking union as well as discourses of functional dissonances among particular interest groups and policy makers to lobby for pro-reform policies (Niemann and Ioannou 2015, 196, 213). Schimmelfennig argues that former integration practices have generated transnational interdependencies, supranational capacities as well as interests for further integration which shaped "institutional and material path-dependencies;" these in return are successful to defeat domestic politicization and intergovernmental distributional conflict around economic crisis (Schimmelfennig 2018, 971). For instance, neofunctionalism defends that functional logic is more able to explain how economic interdependencies have sustained a formula to keep the United Kingdom integrated to the Single Market through free trade of goods and services (Hooghe and Marks, 2019: 1123). Similarly, Philippe Schmitter and Zoe Lefkofridi (2016) take different economic and political policies of integration and examine the level of integration with the help of various available data sources and scholarly research. They argue that as neofunctionalism anticipated integration and interdependence have incrementally accelerated among member states; however, they add, neofunctionalism cannot anticipate how distribution of benefits are uneven among member states with Germany being the key beneficiary from trade for instance (Schmitter and Lefkofridi 2016, 26). According to them, the benefits are not distributed evenly neither among member states (for example, Southern European countries' youth unemployment rates are higher than Northern European member states) nor inside the member states (for example, German workers could not experience these benefits of trade due to declining wages).

In contrast, intergovernmentalism, which explains integration as an outcome of competition and cooperation among nation states, asserts that its conceptual tools are better to explicate policy at times of crisis. For instance, intergovernmentalism can shed light on divergent responses of the EU and member states to Syrian refugee crisis or debates around distributional effects of economic crisis. Intergovernmentalism claims to explain the United Kingdom's Brexit decision better as it argues that "integration depends on the benefits of cooperation mediated by intergovernmental bargaining" (Hooghe and Marks 2019, 1123). Schimmelfennig uses liberal intergovernmentalism and its tools of national preferences, international bargaining and institutions to explicate crisis; he argues that institutional choices and bargains related to reforms were mostly preferences of German-led coalition (Schimefennig 2015). Indeed, it is argued that liberal intergovernmentalism is better equipped to explain how and why reforms for institutional arrangements mostly reflect German preferences (Ioannou et al. 2015, 168). Yet, in the view of Tanja Börzel and Thomas Risse (2018, 101) neither neofunctionalism nor liberal intergovernmentalism can account for why the Schengen crisis is in a stalemate with the collapse of common asylum and migration policy. Despite the welfare loss of reintroducing internal border controls, member states' responses to the refugee crisis favor either the status quo or disintegration (Börzel and Risse 2018, 84). They propose that constructivism and its conceptual framework regarding identity politics is better equipped to explain the Schengen crisis as populist politicians discuss with references to "us" versus "them" while calling for "a fortress Europe" (Börzel and Risse 2018, 102). For the institutionalist approach, a comparison of past and present institutional design uncovers that although crisis constitutes a critical conjuncture, there are important institutional continuities (Verdun 2015). Here, it is possible to observe path dependent institutional structures whereby previous institutions condition solutions to current problems.

Under the current conjuncture, enlargement is not a privileged path of inquiry, because of the challenges with which the European integrationist project has been confronted. Yet, there are some studies uncovering coordinates of Turkey-EU relations in this conjuncture, notably, an important number of studies have again approached this relationship through a focus on the end state of relations. The focus is shifting toward debating terms and conditions of a probable future differentiated integration (external model of differentiated integration, deepened functional cooperation, a model closer to United Kingdom-EU deal, gradual membership, and so on), with an effort to embed the debate around future of Europe discussions such as concentric circles, spaghetti bowls, Europe a-la-carte, etc. (Cianciara and Szymanski 2019; Müftüler-Baç 2017; Tocci and Bechev 2013). For Rosamond, these different forms of differentiated or flexible integration are suggested as a technique to prevent disintegration through "a patchwork quality of integration, characterized as it is by multiple national derogations and opt-outs from core treaty goals or common policy areas" (Rosamond 2016, 866). Still, this body of literature again debates the future form of Turkey's integration without being informed by a particular conceptual framework. Yet, some studies approach Turkey-EU relations from a particular theoretical scholarship within the current conjuncture, and here, they can be considered under two categories: mainstream approaches and critical political economy. Scholars within mainstream continue to draw especially from functionalism, Europeanization, and constructivism. As far as the functional logic is concerned, scholars argue that although there has been democratic backsliding from EU norms and rules in Turkey, there has not been a rupture. Thus, functionalist logic is creating joint interdependencies which are influential in regulating Turkey-EU relations at times of crises; for instance, Beken Saatçioğlu argues, the March 2016 refugee deal reveals that functionalism increasingly characterizes Turkey-EU relations which continues to develop in essential and strategic sectors of joint interests such as migration and/or energy policy, deepening the functional cooperation (Saatçioğlu 2020, 169–172). Macmillan refers to Arne Niemann contending that spillback[2] or a halt in integration is possible as a result of countervailing forces such as leaders who do not want to hand

---

2 Schmitter and Lefkofridi (2016, 2–3) define spillback as a scenario when "member states no longer wish to deal with a policy at the supranational level, e.g., the collapse of the Euro or Member States (MSs)' exits from the eurozone or even the EU – be they coerced (e.g., Grexit) or voluntary (e.g., Brexit)."

sovereignty to supranational institutions, negative attitude of domestic groups such as lobby groups, opposition parties, media or public opinion, and diversity among member states (Macmillan 2009, 804). As Eurobarometer polls reveal, negative public opinion among EU countries is the main countervailing force for Turkish enlargement. With regard to the future projection from a neofunctional perspective, for Macmillan, three possible scenarios are possible: "spillback in the form of a failed accession process, encapsulation in the form of a 'privileged partnership' or similar arrangement, or spillover in the form of a successful and complete integration of Turkey into the EU" (Macmillan 2009, 806).

Another cluster of research within mainstream scholarship focuses on de-Europeanization (Aydın-Düzgit 2016; Saatçioğlu 2020; Yılmaz 2016). This body of research argues that the EU conditionality was very influential to stimulate domestic change through reforms following the 1999 Helsinki European Council. However, the reforms started to stall in 2007 with blocked chapters in the negotiations, loss of interest of the AKP governments for reform and calls for a privileged partnership. The credibility of EU's conditionality to create an impact in Turkey's domestic and foreign policy is deteriorated in the absence of the carrot of membership, a process depicted as de-Europeanization. In their analysis, Gergana Noutcheva and Senem Aydın-Düzgit (2012, 68) compare the EU's impact on the rule of law for Croatia, Albania, and Turkey, and highlight that Turkey approved more than half of the amendments related to judiciary since its adaption of the 1982 constitution between 1999 and 2005, when the credibility of EU conditionality was high. After 2005, the EU's credibility started to decline with debates on the union's absorption capacity, Turkey's size, population, and culture and religion, and the overall unpopularity among EU citizens. Besides, discourses on probability of permanent safeguard clauses such as free movement of workers or agricultural and structural funds coupled with the decision of the EU Council not to open new chapters for negotiations unless Turkey would decide to open its seaports and airspaces to Greek Cyprus negatively impacted the relations (Noutcheva and Aydın-Düzgit 2012, 68). All of these historical developments created the impression that Turkey is treated unfairly and would not accede to the EU even though it would comply with the formal criteria.

Studies from the constructivist perspective focus on the effect of Turkey as the Other in defining the European identity (Morozov and Rumelili 2012). According to Bahar Rumelili, Turkey has been a part of European state system since 1856, when it was admitted to the Concert of Europe with a status of "being in but not of Europe" (Rumelili 2011, 235–236). She highlights the need to consider Turkey's place beyond the member/non-member dichotomy and argues that although prospects of Turkey's probable membership decline, a post-enlargement situation is highly unlikely. Instead, Turkey will continue to constitute European identity as the Other and, even more recently, Turkish identity is presented as a hybrid one from both Western and Middle East (Rumelili 2011, 241). Critical constructivism is also used to uncover how particular discursive articulations have engendered Turkey's distancing from the EU (Aydın-Düzgit 2016). Here, it is argued that negative discourses in representing the EU such as "an unwanted intruder in Turkish politics, . . . an essentially discriminatory entity . . . [and] inferior to Turkey on political and economic (and sometimes normative) grounds" have constructed the Turkish self-dissociated from the European/EU Other (Aydın-Düzgit 2016, 55). As pointed out, it is difficult to expect cooperation given these negative discursive articulations.

Critical political economy literature criticizes how mainstream studies interpret the period and develops an alternative reading. Mainstream reads the crisis as an outcome of "'usual suspects' of low productivity, high wage costs, administrative inefficiency and rapidly declining competitiveness" with reference to especially south Mediterranean countries (Nousios et al. 2012, 6). Critical political economy reads crisis as structural rather than a systemic fault or a result of malfunction of the market (Burnham 2011, 499). Crisis is endemic to capitalism, and as scholars would put it, "the current economic turmoil is structurally conditioned by global social and geo-economic imbalances" (Nousios et al. 2012, 6). Since the 1980s, European integration has been shaped by neoliberal policies by monetarist monetary policy, financial market liberalization, and flexibilization of labor markets (Becker and Jäger 2012, 174). In the last four decades, economy is depoliticized, labor union movement is curtailed, and welfare state is transformed alongside liberalization of economy (Bonefeld 2017, 755). Accordingly, European integration has strengthened liberal policies and cut mass democratic systems and parliamentary rule-making at the national level (Bonefeld 2015: 880), and euro is "the world's only stateless currency" as its governance is outside the democratic control of territorial national regimes (Bonefeld 2017, 749). As clarified further, the "European integration institutionalizes the rule of money and law at a denationalized level of policy-making," which not only makes the liberal state stronger but undermines mass democratic regimes of national parliaments (Bonefeld 2015: 869). Hence, the democratic deficit in the EU is not simply a design fault; rather, democracy is an impediment for the free market and liberal restructuring of European governance Besides, the EMU has intensified class exploitation of neoliberal restructuring and further depoliticized labor movement (Bonefeld 1998, 56).

These processes engender two asymmetries which structurally forms the basis of the eurozone crisis. On the one hand, economic integration develops unevenly between financialized economies of peripheral member states and export-oriented core economies (Becker and Jäger 2012, 183–184). Whereas this preeminent uneven accumulation provides surpluses for export-oriented core European countries, it creates further dependencies for peripheral countries (for example, the Mediterranean member states), which have to resort to credits furthering dependencies and unevenness. On the other hand, whereas monetary policy is regulated at the European level, policies impacted from distribution such as social policy, fiscal policy, collective bargaining are regulated at the national level (Bieling et al. 2016, 64). Besides, the reform process radicalizes neoliberalism through further cutting the welfare state and weakening labor movement, which would deepen the crisis (Becker and Jäger 2012,

181–184). Crisis equally helps capitalists to further subordinate labor in its accumulation regime, as insisted by mass demonstrations and sit-in protests against social cuts and rising capitalist control over labor movements in France, Greece, and the United Kingdom (Burnham 2011, 501–505). In his study, Peter Burnham interprets these protests as "politicization of large sections of the European working class" and a crisis of capitalist state as the state fails to take mass loyalty in the absence of a clear depoliticization strategy (Burnham 2011, 506). According to Bastiaan van Apeldoorn, the eurozone crisis is also a crisis of hegemony of the transnationally oriented capital to take consent from the masses at the European level (van Apeldoorn 2009, 21). For the author, European integration of the 1990s developed as an embedded neoliberal hegemonic project which integrates social cohesion through the European social model to neoliberal market integration at the European transnational level (van Apeldoorn 2002). Yet, this hegemonic project has reached its limits due to the gap between governing competitiveness of the European market at the transnational level while regulating social policies at national level (van Apeldoorn 2009, 22). Mass protests against social cuts as well as rising far right politics, populism and xenophobia unveil the crisis of hegemony as ruling classes cannot take consent from masses for its hegemonic project. This not only weakens democracy but also evolves into authoritarian neoliberalism (van Apeldoorn 2014, 199). In this period, ruling classes are not intended to rule through moral and intellectual leadership by taking consent from masses or neutralizing opposition through giving concessions; rather, they are willing to exclude or marginalize opposition (Bruff 2014, 116).

There are few studies from a critical political economy perspective approaching Turkey's European trajectory in the current conjuncture. Galip Yalman and Asuman Göksel read Turkey's trajectory of integration within structural dynamics of neoliberal restructuring, and end up arguing that accession negotiations of the 2000s were instrumental for neoliberal restructuring of Turkey's economy, while the EU's function was complementary to international financial institutions (Yalman and Göksel 2017, 24). Yet, since the 2008 crisis, the authors argue, "the fate of the protracted saga of Turkey's quest for the EU membership is back to square one" considering that the relations will likely proceed with modernizing the Customs Union which would be an alternative to membership without the fulfilment of political criteria (Yalman and Göksel 2017, 37). Others read Turkey's membership trajectory as an open-ended struggle among social classes and its fractions, while the overall pro-membership project is still hegemonic despite rising anti-European sentiments and the critical tone of the AKP governments (Uzgören 2020). Here, membership is seen key to attract foreign direct investment, to sustain a functioning market economy and liberal democracy, and moreover, while capital groups have already been integrated with the European market and continue to benefit from free trade without the burden of social or environmental acquis (Uzgören 2020). The question to ask is whether there is an alternative to neoliberal socio-economic content of membership. As demonstrated elsewhere, labor groups contest neoliberal membership perspective in two rival class strategies: ha-vet and neomercantilism. Whilst the former is against capitalist Europe, they still support membership for social Europe arguing that the economic aspect of the struggle has already been lost as a result of completion of the Customs Union and membership can allow Turkey to align with the European social model. The latter is critical of the EU's policies regarding the political aspect of the reforms; yet, they end up defending membership "on equal terms and conditions" (Uzgören 2018, 8). None, however, stands as an alternative. The future trajectory is uncertain as it is more difficult for capital groups to take consent from labor to sustain negative integration (market liberalization) without any future prospects of positive integration (social dimension) (Uzgören 2020).

Conclusion

In the last decade, one of the buzz words describing European politics is disintegration. With the EU being preoccupied with all sorts of internal issues, the question of future enlargement is off the agenda. Enlargement is increasingly not a priority area for the Turkish government either. Although Turkey's European trajectory was defined with reforms and accession talks in the 2000s, terms such as backsliding, train crash, and special partnership model are often used to describe the relations in the 2010s, especially following the collapse of Arab Spring and the Gezi Park protests. Relations have further deteriorated after the attempted July 2016 coup attempt in Turkey and in the subsequent period when Turkey was ruled under the state of emergency for two consecutive years. Officials have hoped that admission agreement for the Syrian refugee crisis would revitalize Turkey-EU relations. This was a short-sighted assumption. In its 2018 report, the European Commission assessed that Turkey's membership trajectory was "backsliding" and "moving away from the EU" on a number of issues such as freedom of assembly, freedom of association, independence of judiciary, freedom of expression, and public administration reforms (European Commission 2018).

As demonstrated through this chapter, although the volume of literature discussing Turkey-EU is truly abundant, most of these studies have not embarked on a specific theoretical perspective. Scholars focusing on Turkey-EU relations tend to draw assumptions from mainstream theories, including functionalism, Europeanization and constructivism. Functionalism lays the emphasis on the slow progress of Turkey's integration through economic functional links especially thanks to the Customs Union. The 2000s were dominated by scholarship falling within Europeanization, which measures the effect of the EU conditionality in stimulating change in domestic politics. Constructivist studies emphasize the role of ideational and study how Turkish and European identities are defined in relation to each other. Yet, mainstream scholarship expected that accession negotiations of the 2000s would consolidate democracy and a functioning market economy in Turkey whereas Turkish accession would contribute to the creation of a multicultural Europe. As also argued, critical approaches criticize mainstream studies to constrain the debate to the form of integration (the end state of negotiations), to turn a blind eye to the socio-economic content of ongoing integration and to fail to situate integration and enlargement to structural dynamics of globalization and neoliberal restructuring. Europeanization literature fails to differentiate whether the stimulus for domestic change is structural or regional, while ignoring class politics and treating state-society relations as externally related spheres. Constructivism presents the EU as a civilian and a normative power. This not only unveils the imperialist socio-economic content of market expansionary policies of the EU but uncovers a hidden Orientalism or Eurocentrism in which the EU is presented as an ideal case for human rights and democracy for candidates to catch up. Given all these shortcomings, critical political economy approaches contribute to European scholarship on a number of solid grounds, by questioning power relations, by embedding European integration within structural dynamics of globalization and neoliberal restructuring, by integrating class politics and unravelling agency behind integration and disintegration, and by posing questions about alternatives. As far as Turkey-EU relations are concerned, critical approaches contribute to question power relations behind ongoing integration through the Customs Union, to integrate the position of Turkish labor into debate and to open alternative socio-economic orders into debate. In the current conjuncture of crisis, enlargement is off the agenda. Yet, there are few studies drawing on mainstream and critical approaches which shed some light on future coordinates. Whereas functionalism expects to further develop functional integration among Turkey and the EU on key strategic sectors such as migration or energy on a differentiated model of integration, scholars within de-Europeanization and constructivism illustrate how Turkey is distancing from the EU in domestic and foreign policy as well as at a more ideational level. There is equally an emphasis to think in a flexible way to open the debate on terms and conditions of a probable future form around differentiated integration. Conceptual tools of critical political economy envisage that the future of Turkey-EU relations will be determined by ongoing struggle among social classes. Still, in the absence of any mechanism of positive integration (social dimension and welfare benefits of membership), it will be more difficult for capital groups to sustain ongoing integration through modernization of the Customs Union by taking consent and leading society around the membership perspective.

References

Aydın, Mustafa, and Sinem A. Açıkmeşe. 2007. "Europeanization through EU conditionality: Understanding the new era in Turkish foreign policy." *Journal of Southern Europe and the Balkans* 9(3): 263–274.

Aydın-Düzgit, Senem. 2016. "De-Europeanisation through discourse: A critical discourse analysis of AKP's election speeches." *South European Society and Politics* 21(1): 45–58.

Becker, Joachim, and Johannes Jäger. 2012. "Integration in crisis: A regulationist perspective on the interaction of European varieties of capitalism." *Competition & Change* 16(3): 169–187.

Becker, Joachim, Oktar Türel, and Mustafa Türkeş. 2014. "Introduction: Financialisation, crisis, social protests and development alternatives in Southeast Europe." *METU Studies in Development* 41(3): i–iv.

Bieler, Andreas. 2000. *Globalisation and Enlargement of the European Union, Austrian and Swedish Social Forces in the Struggle over Membership*, London: Routledge.

Bieler, Andreas. 2005. "European integration and the transnational restructuring of social relations: The emergence of labour as a regional actor?" *Journal of Common Market Studies* 43(3): 461–484.

Bieler, Andreas, and Adam David Morton, eds. 2001. *Social Forces in the Making of the New Europe: The Restructuring of European Social Relations in the Global Political Economy*, London: Palgrave.

Bieling, Hans-Jürgen, Johannes Jager and Magnus Ryner. 2016. "Regulation theory and the political economy of the European Union." *Journal of Common Market Studies* 54(1): 53–69.

Bohle, Dorothee. 2006. "Neoliberal hegemony, transnational capital and the terms of the EU's eastward expansion." *Capital & Class* 88: 57–86.

Bonefeld, Werner. 1998. "Politics of European Monetary Union: Class, ideology and critique." *Economic and Political Weekly* 33(35): 55–69.

Bonefeld, Werner. 2015. "European economic constitution and the transformation of democracy: On class and the state of law." *European Journal of International Relations* 21(4): 867–886.

Bonefeld, Werner. 2017. "Authoritarian liberalism: From Schmitt via ordoliberalism to the euro." *Critical Sociology* 43(4–5): 747–761.

Bonefeld, Werner, Richard Gunn and Kosmas Psychopedis. 1992. "Introduction." In *Open Marxism, Volume I Dialectics and History*, edited by Werner Bonefeld, Richard Gunn and Kosmas Psychopedis, ix–xx. London: Pluto Press.

Boyer, Robert, and Yves Saillard. 1995. "A summary of regulation theory." In *Regulation Theory, The State of the Art*, edited by Robert Boyer and Yves Saillard, 36–44. London: Routledge.

Börzel, Tanja A., and Thomas Risse. 2018. "From the euro to the Schengen crises: European integration theories, politicization, and identity politics." *Journal of European Public Policy* 25(1): 83–108.

Bruff, Ian. 2014. "The rise of authoritarian neoliberalism." *Rethinking Marxism: A Journal of Economics, Culture and Society* 26(1): 113–129.

Buğra, Ayşe. 1994. *State and Business in Modern Turkey: A Comparative Study*. Albany, NY: State University of New York Press.

Burnham, Peter. 1994. "Open Marxism and vulgar international political economy." *Review of International Political Economy* 1(2): 221–231.

Burnham, Peter. 2011. "Towards a political theory of crisis: Policy and resistance across Europe." *New Political Science* 33(4): 493–507.

Cafruny, Alan W., and Magnus Ryner, eds. 2003. *A Ruined Fortress? Neoliberal Hegemony and Transformation in Europe*. Lanham, MD: Rowman and Littlefield.

Checkel, Jeffrey T. 2001. "Social construction and European integration." In *The Social Construction of Europe*, edited by Thomas Christiansen, Knud Erik Jorgensen and Antje Wiener, 50–64. London: Sage.

Cianciara, Agnieszka K., and Adam Szymanski. 2019. "Differentiated integration: Towards a new model of European Union-Turkey relations?" *Turkish Studies* 21(2): 1–20.

Derviş, Kemal, Michael Emerson, Daniel Gros, and Sinan Ülgen. 2004. *The European Transformation of Modern Turkey*. Brussels: Centre for European Policy Studies.

Diez, Thomas, Apostolos Agnantopoulos, Alper Kaliber. 2005. "File: Turkey, Europeanization and civil society." *South European Society and Politics* 10(1): 1–15.

Eralp, Nilgün Arısan, and Atila Eralp. 2012. "What went wrong in the Turkey-EU relationship?" In *Another Empire? A Decade of Turkey's Foreign Policy under the Justice and Development Party*, edited by Kerem Öktem, Ayşe Kadıoğlu, and Mehmet Karlı, 163–183. İstanbul: Bilgi University Press.

European Commission. 2018. "Turkey 2018 report." 17 April, https://ec.europa.eu/neighbourhood-enlargement/sites/near/files/20180417-turkey-report.pdf.

Grigoriadis, Ioannis N. 2009. *Trials of Europeanization, Turkish Political Culture and European Union*. New York: Palgrave Macmillan.

Haas, Ernst B. 1958. *The Uniting of Europe: Political, Social and Economic Forces, 1950–1957*. Stanford, CA: Stanford University Press.

Hall, Peter A., and Rosemary C. R. Taylor. 1996 "Political science and three new institutionalisms." *Political Studies* XLIV: 936–957.

Heper, Metin. 1985. *The State Tradition in Turkey*. Walkington: The Eothen Press.

Heper, Metin. 2005. "The European Union, the Turkish military and democracy." *South European Society and Politics* 10(1): 33–44.

Hix, Simon. 1994. "The study of the European Community: The challenge to comparative politics." *West European Politics* 17(1): 1–30.

Hoffman, Stanley. 1966. "Obstinate or obsolete: The fate of the nation state and the case of Western Europe." *Daedalus* 95(3): 862–915.

Hooghe, Liesbet, and Gary Marks. 2019. "Grand theories of European integration in the twenty-first century." *Journal of European Public Policy* 26(8): 1113–1133.

Ioannou, Demosthenes, Patrick Leblond, and Arne Niemann. 2015. "European integration and the crisis: Practice and theory." *Journal of European Public Policy* 22(2): 155–176.

Jachtenfuchs, Markus, and Beate Kohler-Koch. 2005. "Governance and institutional development." In *European Integration Theory*, edited by Antje Wiener and Thomas Diez, 97–135. Oxford: Oxford University Press.

Karakas, Cemal. 2013. "EU-Turkey: Integration without full membership or membership without full Integration? A conceptual framework for accession alternatives." *Journal of Common Market Studies* 51(6): 1057–1073.

Keyder, Çağlar. 1987. *State and Class in Turkey: A Study in Capitalist Development*. London: Verso Books.

Macmillan, Catherine. 2009. "The application of neofunctionalism to the enlargement process: The case of Turkey." *Journal of Common Market Studies* 47(4): 789–809.

Manners, Ian. 2002. "Normative power Europe: A contradiction in terms?" *Journal of Common Market Studies* 40(2): 235–258.

Manners, Ian, and Richard Whitman. 2016. "Another theory is possible: Dissident voices in theorising Europe." *Journal of Common Market Studies* 54 (1): 3–18.

Milward, Alan S. 1992. *The European Rescue of the Nation State*. London: Routledge.

Moravcsik, Andrew. 1998. *The Choice for Europe, Social Purpose and State Power from Messina to Maastricht*. Ithaca, NY: Cornell University Press.

Morozov, Viatcheslav, and Bahar Rumelili. 2012. "The external constitution of European identity: Russia and Turkey as Europe-makers." *Cooperation and Conflict* 47(1): 28–48.

Müftüler-Baç, Meltem. 1997. *Turkey's Relations with a Changing Europe*. Manchester: Manchester University Press.

Müftüler-Baç, Meltem. 2005. "Turkey's political reforms and the impact of the European Union." *South European Society and Politics* 10(1): 17–31.

Müftüler-Baç, Meltem. 2017. "Turkey's future with the European Union: An alternative model of differentiated integration." *Turkish Studies* 18(3): 416–438.

Müftüler Baç, Meltem, and Lauren McLaren. 2003. "Enlargement preferences and policy-making in the European Union: Impacts on Turkey." *Journal of European Integration* 25(1): 17–30.

Niemann, Arne, and Demosthenes Ioannou. 2015. "European economic integration in times of crisis: A case of neofunctionalism?" *Journal of European Public Policy* 22(2): 196–218.

Nousios, Petros, Henk Overbeek, and Andreas Tsolakis. 2012. "Globalisation and European integration: The nature of the beast." In *Globalisation and European Integration: Critical Approaches to Regional Order and International Relations*, edited by Petros Nousios, Henk Overbeek, and Andreas Tsolakis, 3–32. London: Routledge.

Noutcheva, Gergana, and Senem Aydın-Düzgit. 2012. "Lost in Europeanisation: The Western Balkans and Turkey." *West European Politics* 35(1): 59–78.

Öniş, Ziya. 2003. "Domestic politics, international norms and challenges to the state: Turkey-EU relations in the post-Helsinki era." *Turkish Studies* 4(1): 9–34.

Öniş, Ziya. 2007. "Conservative globalists versus defensive nationalists: Political parties and paradoxes of Europeanization in Turkey." *Journal of Southern Europe and the Balkans* 9(3): 247–261.

Özen, Çinar. 1998. "Neo-functionalism and the change in the dynamics of Turkey-EU relations." *Perceptions: Journal of International Affairs* 3(3): 34–57.

Pollack, Mark A. 2005. "Theorizing the European Union: International organization, domestic polity, or experiment in new governance?" *Annual Review of Political Science* 8: 357–398.

Risse-Kappen, Thomas. 1996. "Exploring the nature of the beast: International relations theory and comparative policy analysis meet the European integration." *Journal of Common Market Studies* 34(1): 53–80.

Rosamond, Ben. 2016. "Brexit and the problem of European disintegration." *Journal of Contemporary European Research* 12(4): 864–871.

Rumelili, Bahar. 2008. "Negotiating Europe: EU-Turkey relations from an identity perspective." *Insight Turkey* 10(1): 97–110.

Rumelili, Bahar. 2011. "Turkey: Identity, foreign policy, and socialization in a post-enlargement Europe." *Journal of European Integration* 33(2): 235–249.

Saatçioğlu, Beken. 2020. "The European Union's refugee crisis and rising functionalism in EU-Turkey relations." *Turkish Studies* 21(2): 169–187.

Schimmelfennig, Frank. 2001. "The community trap: Liberal norms, rhetorical action, and the eastern enlargement of the European Union." *International Organization* 55(1): 47–80.

Schimmelfennig, Frank. 2015. "Liberal intergovernmentalism and the euro area crisis." *Journal of European Public Policy* 22(2): 177–195.

Schimmelfennig, Frank. 2018. "European integration (theory) in times of crisis: A comparison of the euro and Schengen crises." *Journal of European Public Policy* 25(7): 969–989.

Schimmelfennig, Frank, and Ulrich Sedelmeier. 2004. "Governance by conditionality: EU rule transfer to the candidate countries of Central and Eastern Europe." *Journal of European Public Policy* 11(4): 661–679.

Schimmelfennig, Frank, and Ulrich Sedelmeier. 2005. "Introduction: Conceptualizing the Europeanization of Central and Eastern Europe." In *The Europeanization of Central and Eastern Europe*, edited by Frank Schimmelfennig and Ulrich Sedelmeier, 1–28. Ithaca, NY: Cornell University Press.

Schimmelfennig, Frank, Stefan Engert, and Heiko Knobel. 2006. *International Socialization in Europe, European Organizations, Political Conditionality and Democratic Change.* Houndmills: Palgrave Macmillan.

Schmitter, Philippe C., and Zoe Lefkofridi. 2016. "Neo-functionalism as a theory of disintegration." *Chinese Political Science Review* 1: 1–29.

Sedelmeier, Ulrich. 2005. "Eastern enlargement, risk, rationality and role-compliance." In *The Politics of European Union Enlargement Theoretical Approaches*, edited by Frank Schimmelfennig and Ulrich Sedelmeier, 120–141. London: Routledge.

Shields, Stuart. 2004. "Global restructuring and the Polish state: Transition, transformation, or transnationalization?" *Review of International Political Economy* 11(1): 132–154.

Tocci, Nathalie, and Dimitar Bechev. 2013. "Will Turkey find its place in post-crisis Europe?" In *Global Turkey in Europe, Political, Economic, and Foreign Policy Dimensions of Turkey's Evolving Relationship with the EU*, edited by Senem Aydın-Düzgit, Anne Duncker, Daniela Huber, Fuat Keyman, and Nathalie Tocci, 31–45. Rome: IAI.

Uzgören, Elif. 2018. "Countering globalization and regionalization: Is there a united front within Turkish Labour and Disadvantaged Groups?" *Globalizations* 15(3): 347–361.

Uzgören, Elif. 2020. "Globalisation and the struggle over hegemony in a peripheral context: Turkey's membership bid to the European Union." *Journal of Balkans and Near Eastern Studies* (forthcoming).

van Apeldoorn, Bastiaan. 2002. *Transnational Capitalism and the Struggle over European Integration*, London: Routledge.

van Apeldoorn, Bastiaan. 2009. "The contradictions of 'embedded neoliberalism' and Europe's multi-level legitimacy crisis: The European project and its limits." In *Contradictions and Limits of Neoliberal European Governance: From Lisbon to Lisbon*, edited by Bastiaan van Apeldoorn, Jan Drahokoupil, and Laura Horn, 21–43. Houndmills: Palgrave Macmillan.

van Apeldoorn, Bastiaan. 2014. "The European capitalist class and the crisis of its hegemonic project." *Socialist Register* 50: 189–206.

van Apeldoorn, Bastiaan, Henk Overbeek, and Magnus Ryner. 2003. "Theories of European integration: A critique." In *A Ruined Fortress? Neoliberal Hegemony and Transformation in Europe*, edited by Alan W. Cafruny and Magnus Ryner, 17–45. Lanham, MD: Rowman and Littlefield.

Verdun, Amy. 2015. "A historical institutionalist explanation of the EU's responses to the euro area financial crisis." *Journal of European Public Policy* 25(2): 219–237.

Wallace, Helen. 2017. "The JCMS annual review lecture: In the name of Europe." *Journal of Common Market Studies* 55: 8–18.

Yalman, Galip L., and Asuman Göksel. 2017. "Transforming Turkey? Putting the Turkey-European Union relations into a historical perspective." *Uluslararası İlişkiler* 14(56): 23–37.

Yeşilada, Birol. 2013. *EU-Turkey Relations in the 21st Century.* London: Routledge.

Yılmaz, Gözde. 2016. "Europeanisation or De-europeanisation? Media freedom in Turkey (1999–2015)." *South European Society and Politics* 21(1): 147–161.

Yılmaz, Hakan. 2011. "Euroscepticism in Turkey: Parties, elites, and public opinion." *South European Society and Politics* 16(1): 185–208.

Zuzana Lučkay Mihalčinová

12 In Lieu of a Conclusion: Regaining Dignity in Europe

The existence of the European Union is threatened. This sentence has continuously been gaining and losing its dramatic impact since the inception of the geopolitical European project. Whereas on the one hand there are various political forces that would be glad to see the EU vanish, on the other, there are powerful initiatives that would not let it go just as yet or at all. Periodically, some speculations reach extreme levels; still, extremes are what rational thought needs least, but how often has rational thought governed sociopolitical issues? While democracy rejects extremism, the ultra-right and the ultra-left have nevertheless managed to secure their presence through legitimate means, such as elections and public support. Many people think that they pose a threat to the existence of the EU. However, prevention of their representation is also a form of repression and Europe has had its share of repressive regimes. One of the aims of the EU project is to uproot repression but also extremism, idealistically hoping to convert extremists to goodwill and open-mindedness. The EU is criticized for being too benevolent with extremism and this way signing its own death certificate but doing otherwise would be against the ideal of humanism the EU aims to represents. Political slogans are capable of provoking strong emotions as well as encourage questions about our worth. Our idea and sense of worth, our dignity, is so crucial to us that it makes us vulnerable. In turbulent times, real or induced by propaganda, our decision-making abilities impair, and the more vulnerable we feel, the more likely we are to jump into conclusions based on prejudices and stereotypes, which offer fertile soil for extreme thinking.

Cooperation is beneficial. It is not only sensible because it reduces vulnerability and the risk of extremism, but it also helps emotional equilibrium which consequently reduces the risk of violence and enhances our chances of survival. The increase of population and ever-challenging environmental concerns are at the core of the age of anxiety and ecological (and also epidemiological) urgencies. With some scientists claiming that we may not destroy the planet but make it unlivable for humans, we perhaps ought to reconsider the place of humans in the pecking order of sentient beings, and rethink our options of active participation in favor of the eco-system, thus increasing the chances of survival of the human species. Accordingly, this piece focuses on the regaining of dignity in Europe. Strictly speaking, regaining dignity is an impossible undertaking because in the legal framework (including that of the EU) human dignity cannot be lost because, it is inviolable. Still, people may feel their dignity being violated or taken away. This paradox is because the very notion is rather elusive and as such either too complex to grasp or

https://doi.org/10.1515/9783110684216-012

too abstract to have practical impact. But, when feeling threatened, it becomes recognized as something proper, capable of inducing action (possibly destructive). With this in mind, we can neither ridicule someone's interpretation of dignity nor dismiss it as incorrect. In a personal sphere, therefore, regaining dignity makes a lot of sense and can even be a life goal (even to the extreme). For this reason, there must be a qualitative, descriptive (psychological) level of dignity, which is non-abstract. I make a distinction between human dignity and the personal perception of dignity (sense and idea of worth): while the former makes sense on the species level, the latter makes sense on the individual descriptive level and it gains a different vehemence (for example, in a national frame of reference). Here, I discuss aspects of human dignity and the applicable, descriptive, dignity in relation to the geopolitical entity of the European Union as an institution and Europe as a space. As it will be argued, Europeanness is a conflicting state to long for; wanted or unwanted, belonging is geographically, historically, politically, psychologically, and socially conditioned.

The Problematic Concepts of Dignity and Human Dignity

When projected onto Europe, the old phrase "It all depends on the point of view" can help us shed light on sociopolitical turbulences. If we zoom out a geographical map, we see the western Eurasian landmass with its mountains, rivers, and lakes, and from this distance human disagreements appear miniscule, if not pathetic. Such a vantage point can be a useful mind exercise in resetting priorities since it is a well-known fact that different angles of examination make challenges approachable and much clearer. Also, in this case, critical analysis benefits from distinction between the abstract and the applicable, between the metaphysical and the tangible, without downgrading the role of either. Accordingly, understanding of the raison d'être of the EU project and our place in it depends on an expansion of our personal and limited point of view. In order to effectively comprehend everyday realities, consequent human behavior, and prevention of suffering, it is sufficient to look at human challenges from different vantage points. In case of the correlation of dignity and human dignity in the European context, a humanistic and humane approach is best; an economic or political perspective does not necessarily contain the critical-analytical tools required. More precisely, the political map of Europe shows boundaries between governmental units but not necessarily people. The national borders, often agreed or imposed after major conflicts, have come to serve nothing else but an administrative purpose in the EU context; and while from a geographical and anthropological point of view, national borders make no sense, from a psychosocial point of view, they can be divisive and coercive.

The concepts of nation and nationality are outdated. Still, they are being used as tools in identity politics to awaken strong emotions. The emotional pressure may induce an active search for arguments favoring the romanticized view of nationality, with nationalism being justified by value assignment. People can build their identity on national values, by spinning the abstract nation into a very real emotion of pride (national pride). Yet, imagining away abstractions, although possible, can be difficult or even traumatic for those who feel and think that it is part of their core. Therefore, however abstract and distant identification with a nation seems for some people, for others it constitutes an important part of self-worth, which can be easily flared up by identity politics. Still, given that conceptualizations of identity have been challenged, we no longer have to subscribe to a specific identity nor let ourselves be coerced into identity patterns and held onto values which are assigned to them. We can no longer be governed by the values and behavior a certain national identity requires of us. As a cause and effect the concept of nation is devoid of meaningful substance. Consequently, looking at Europe as a collection of nations is fruitless. The concept of nation has become devoid of real content. Urging to leave it behind altogether is neither an ethical claim nor a normative position, but a pledge to open and transparent thinking about the past and the present, which can eventually lead to sustainable cooperation, which is in contrast with separatory thinking, dominated by nationalistic idea(l)s that feed people with (super)heroes, ongoing nostalgia, and sense of false superiority. In searching for a common ground, the single most obvious characteristic we share is being human (biologically) and thinking of having worth (as a result of centuries of ontology). It is the very measuring of worth against fixed dogmatic ideologies that causes discrepancies.

Looking more closely at the complex concept of human dignity – for some, just a lofty rhetoric, for others, a self-explanatory idea or even something to die for – for the time I have dealt with it, it has rarely happened that someone had no view on the subject. Misunderstandings, however, are due to the linguistic carelessness and thus interchangeable use of words such as honor, pride, and human nature. In metaphysical and ontological debates, human dignity encourages questions about ethics, even though it is predominantly found in the legal framework and human rights. Sometimes it is dismissed as too broad to be useful or, as in philosophical debates, viewed as elliptic, since it is seen as synonymous with autonomy. In any case, the fact is that the concept of dignity is capable of touching us at, what we vaguely call, our core, and given that most of us claim to have a core, we rightfully feel that we have a say in what dignity implies. Philosopher Kurt Bayertz identified three elements constituting human dignity in modern philosophy – rationality, perfect-ability, and autonomy (1996, 77) – and since then, the same elements have continued to characterize the debate (Rosen 2012). However, when it comes to some other disciplines, the behavioral psychologist B. F. Skinner had dismissed the value of human dignity almost half a century ago (1971, 44), and more recently, Ruth Macklin, has disqualified it in medical ethics (2003, 327). Religious frameworks, especially theological debates in Abrahamic religions, explicate human dignity as intrinsic (and sacred) resultant from the concept of *imago dei*.

As intangible as it is, human dignity is the cornerstone of many declarations, national constitutions, and international treaties; to cite the Charter of Fundamental Rights of the European Union (2000), "[h]uman dignity is inviolable. It must be respected and protected." While simultaneously elusive and cornerstone, since it is expected to unite the best of human potential, human dignity could be interpreted as an ideal. Hence, the EU was built on an ideal picture of the best humans are capable of, thus on a belief (or potential) and not on knowledge or a factual reality. In this frame of reference only belief in the ideal can will it into reality. Unfortunately, this is not a strong argument. If that belief falters, so does the (f)actualization of it. In this sense, the Kantian categorical imperative could serve as an ethical guideline to behavior, with a presumption that it would be appealing enough to strive for. A capacity to make and follow moral judgement, or Bayertz's "moral self-legislation," could serve as a driving force (Bayertz 1996, 77). The Kantian "an end and not means argument" is sound in this respect, with Allen Wood referring to it as "a formula of humanity as end in itself" (Wood 1998, 169; Wood 1999). Kant's work has been challenged many on occasion yet in the human dignity argument deliberately selecting supportive arguments e.g. categorical imperative and not a holistic view of his work. Despite its philosophical instability, as a cornerstone, human dignity has a unifying potential when interpreted as equality for the whole human species. Yet this is only applicable if we take declarative statements seriously; otherwise, forcing people to subscribe to a particular interpretation of human dignity is like forcing them to believe in a particular god. In addition, drawing normatives from declaratives is a crucial mistake in the argumentation; for example, if organizations such as the EU, base their normatives on a declarative claim, then from a philosophical and ethical point of view it is problematic. This, however, does not prevent us from using and potentially benefiting from the concept of human dignity in political, socioeconomic, and interpersonal framework.

For as long as law is an accepted form of social contract, human dignity can be framed inasmuch, and the law can declare it to be equally belonging to all. Human dignity is the basis of constitutional law in many countries and has also served for many supranational initiatives and agreements. As stipulated by the Universal Declaration of Human Rights, "recognition of the inherent dignity and of the equal and inalienable rights of all members of the human family is the foundation of freedom, justice, and peace in the world." Alongside this, in an extended way, we attribute power to the concept of human dignity, that is the power to bring freedom, justice, and peace. We could argue that we are at a pivotal point when we are trying to implement the notion of inherence of human dignity. While the EU is far from sustainable justice, we have not had a major conflict in the EU's Europe for over half a century, even if such an achievement cannot be claimed a direct result of declarations promoting human dignity. Here, we should make it clear that human dignity is not a right per se but the basis of human rights, an explication that assigns it a moral or legal authority. For example, in the Slovak legal system, human dignity is used on three levels: in the constitution, legislation, and case law. The so-called dignity of man operates as an objective value, as well as an individual and subjective right, whereas at constitutional level, its meaning is still being developed (L'alík 2019). It is the combination of value and right that makes explication of human dignity most effective. Focusing on human dignity as a right alone is counterproductive because rights as such are tightly connected with entitlement and they demote responsibility.

In the course of European history, various communities have been denied human value for varying reasons. Although human dignity continues to be denied to some people, such conduct has been criminalized and is actively discouraged in the EU on different levels. Indeed, EU documents designate human dignity a value, which ought not be decontextualized from other complementing values (freedom, equality, democracy, rule of law and human rights); as such, it is considered inviolable: "It must be respected, protected, and constitutes the real basis of fundamental rights" (European Commission 2020). The aim of the EU is to create and maintain sociopolitical circumstances in which these values are upheld, resulting in living conditions where the capacity of moral judgement can be exercised. While administratively and legally secured, this ambitious project requires active citizen participation, which means taking responsibility in the shared project. No human being is independent from others and cooperation conditions survival and well-being. Without the acknowledgement of interdependence, no recognition of worth occurs, and neither can we talk about implementation of human dignity as right and value.

Populism and Human Vulnerability

Some recent political developments seem to benefit from human vulnerability. Perhaps the incorrect and superficial interpretation of the evolutionary theory as favoring the survival of the fittest has been found useful by some political forces for the propagation of their coercive leadership and self-elevation. Survival of the fittest proved not to be the most important factor in evolutionary biology and certainly not a survival strategy for the human species. Yet romanticized ideas of power politics still thrive. If we consider overpopulation, ecological catastrophes, extinction of flora and fauna, is it not farfetched to blame it on power ideologies of non-cooperation and threats. Yet we are told that if we dismiss leaders, we are also dismissing the people who had voted for them in a democratic election. However, elections these days are based on shallow knowledge and resulting false beliefs; with the shortening attention span of digital humans and busy lifestyles voters may more easily fall for populist slogans. Politicians often pose in the best light or con-tradict themselves without getting reprimanded. It is the fragile sense of worth and the urge to belong that is used and abused by presenting a limited view as the only valid one.

Dignity as experience can be fed by the groups we belong to. Group psychology talks about the immense power of wanting to belong and how the false pride which springs from mere identification with a group can shape our sense of worth. Yet groups can fall into their own trap of groupthink, a phenomenon that can lead to intergroup conflict (Janis 1982; Fisher 2006). Thus, dignity is violable, since it is not sustained by merely being a member of the human species and is not imparted to us by a god or declaration but a result of an active life of enquiry and mutual inter-subjective ongoing negation of worth. Since we all have a sense of worth – even if it is false, vague, or based on a belief rather than knowledge – we do get upset if our idea of worth or the one we present to the world is not recognized. In such cases, we do not necessarily start conflict immediately although the sensation can be trau-matic so much so that it can make us vulnerable to populist or even radical ideas. Unrecognized worth can be experienced as mere discomfort but also as shame or even humiliation; as Evelin Lindner has written, humiliation is "a nuclear bomb of emotion," which fuels hatred and cycles of revenge (Lindner 2006, 32).

Worth is framed around what we think is valuable. We hold flexible practical values as well as underlying principal values, although we may not ponder on them daily. We may not adhere to them and then experience various kinds of guilt or different levels or pride when we do. Interestingly enough, according to Skinner's controversial ideas, we rarely protest against aggrandizement. The much-criticized spirit of meritocracy has aided celebration of achievement but fueled false and potentially harmful self-aggrandizement. Perhaps we could replace meritocracy with symbiocracy. It would encompass what the EU sets out as a value system: a life where freedom and different rights are respected, and humans are primarily val-ued for what they are – humans, but not decontextualized or lifted out of the living environment. Europe does not have a shared language, and from a linguistic point of view, languages spoken in EU member states are fundamentally different. Still, Europe is attempting to establish a meta-language of values the adherence to which could serve as common ground for Europeanness in the aforementioned simbioc-racy. From a geopolitical, economic, and security perspective such an ambition makes sense; it does not require big systemic change but more cooperation, and it would help to replace nationalism with greater unification among people. But peo-ple do not always seem to want to be unified, cooperate or live in symbiosis with their environment, and with this in mind, talking about a unified European identity represents a major challenge. Political scientist Ivan Krastev talks about a resurfac-ing difference in western and eastern identities (in what is now central Europe) <IBM3>based on the reaction to migration, which he explains by different historical backgrounds, post-iron curtain cynicism, the distrust in national institutions, and disappointment in not being on the same economic level as the western states (Krastev 2018). Moreover, distrust is generalized to all European institutions and the economic benefits are expected regardless of the economic growth and without taking responsibility for migrants.

In Europe, immigration is a result of wanted Europeanness. Migration has not escaped crises mongering, which is a popular political tool and has strongly contributed to the current political discourse worldwide. Migration is about movement; we move when we want, or reluctantly when we are chased, persecuted, unwanted, or when our home becomes inhabitable. Recently, migration has acquired a negative connotation and has been turned into a security issue (and less a subject of social sciences analyses), which triggered a whole different migration narrative. The securitization of migration has led to seeing migrants as threats (Huysmans 2000). According to Zrinka Bralo, CEO of the UK-based Migrants Organize, the term migrant has become highly derogatory, associated with illegal people, with the press and politicians, not only giving migrants a bad name but going as far as to dehumanize them (Bralo 2016). Immigration requires more political attention, which results in frequent change of migration policies; as explained by the development economist Rachel Sabates-Wheeler and social scientist Rayah Feldman (2011, 24), "[m]igration policies are a response to contradictory political and economic pressures, with governments attempting to reconcile demand for cheap and flexible and/or highly skilled labor, or to meet Refugee Convention obligations, while pacifying xenophobic hostility from some sections of the public and media and demonstrating that governments are in control."

Migrants are easy targets of blame for all sorts of societal ills. They find it difficult to defend themselves. From a legal stance, they may have a pending status, they are in transition, or they are irregular. Regardless of the administrative labels, migrants are often avowed as a burden and as such they may feel alienated; a sense of being without roots and existing in a third space as hybrids may result in feeling anxious or having negative self-worth. In fact, acceptance in the new community is crucial in the mental migration experience; in migration terms this is what is called integration. Those who oppose migration, but are in agreement with saving lives, would grant asylum or residency only to those who are willing to integrate because a so-called good migrant integrates and ceases to be a migrant. On the other hand, Europeans themselves have had to integrate by embracing the identity of being European. If successful integration in the EU means adherence to the common values dictated by the so-called European way of life, then it is a requirement for all in all member states, not only for the migrants originating from outside Europe. Yet, from a sociopolitical point of view, integration is problematic because it assumes a whole into which one is to be integrated, thus assuming the existence of monoculture. Here, the concept of a particular way of life begs for a revision of the definition of culture as such. While being a common word that is being taken for granted, the understanding of culture remains vague (Williams 1976), and while it is often equated with shared values, it simultaneously provokes tension, self-defeat and un-wanted Europeanness.

Philosopher Wolfgang Welsch identifies three tenets of the traditional concept of culture (drawing on the eighteenth-century philosopher Johann Gottfried Herder): social homogenization, ethnic consolidation, and intercultural delimita-tion. Welsch sees the concept as unificatory, folk-bound, and separatory, but factu-ally inadequate because modern societies are not uniform (1999). While the classical model of culture is "not only descriptively unserviceable, but also norma-tively dangerous and untenable" (Welsch 1999, 194), interculturality and multicul-turality fail to advocate mutual understanding of different cultures because they presuppose the traditional conceptualization of cultures as island or spheres. Even if labelled as a way of life, the traditional view of (mono)culture, may lead to preju-dices and xenophobia. Transculturality, as coined by Welsch, on the other hand, encompasses ways of life which also "interpenetrate or emerge from one another" because they are "interconnected and entangled," resulting in "cultural hybrids" (2009). On macro level, transculturality refers to permeations: "In a nutshell: as a result of the increasing interpenetration of cultures there is no longer anything ab-solutely foreign. Accordingly, there is no longer anything exclusively one's own, ei-ther. Authenticity has become folklore . . . The delimitation of one's own culture and foreign culture has become invalid" (Welsch 2009, 7–8). On micro level, "for most of us, multiple cultural connections are decisive in terms of our cultural for-mation. We are cultural hybrids" (Welsch 2009, 8).

Transculturality is a reality of life which the EU has institutionalized. Cultural diversity of a new type means that "differences no longer emerge between different kinds of monolithic identities, but between identity configurations that have some elements in common while differing in other elements, in their arrangements as a whole, and often in their complexity" (Welsch 2009, 9). Hence, mutual influences of people in Europe constitute a European way of life, while defining a European identity is neither necessary nor desirable (because political forces which demar-cate European culture or identity may paradoxically turn it into a monoculture). As a result, integration seems problematic because it means squeezing into an unreal-istic interpretation of culture as monoculture, which further sustains binary opposi-tion and fuels separation in a vicious circle. Administratively regular citizens are not necessarily integrated themselves into a European way of life and they do not subscribe to the common European values. Yet, they expect migrants to embrace these same values. With all this in mind, it is fair to argue that culture as a concept has become too opaque and monocultural thinking is outdated. The alternate ex-pression way of life is to be welcomed in replacing it in the sociopolitical frame-work. Monocultures are fake authenticities yet often erroneously thought of as existing in reality, which create affective attachment by imaginary nostalgias of temporal displacement, invoking pride and governing lives and decisions. Folk-bound framing of identity and monocultural separatory rhetoric are politically dangerous precisely because of their power to awaken strong emotions. They can easily produce a sense of false pride, which for some people may constitute a sense of worth with minimal effort. Populist politicians harvest on the plasticity of the concept of culture.

Temporal migrants are chrono-displaced people. They live in one place but in another time and they forever long for an epoch that is gone or never really existed in the format they choose to remember. Consequently, consciously or not, they adhere to ideas which have been overturned either scientifically or ethically and logically. While spatial immigrants move physically and may feel rejected, temporal immigrants feel usurped; in James Meek's words, "for spatial immigrants, the old country is thousands of miles away in another place, whereas for temporal immigrants, the old country is right there, buried under the new one, and they have no way of digging it out, except through revolution, or the ballot box, or, if the right guy should come along, a revolution and an election at the same time" (Meek 2017). Here, the parallels with the political changes that have happened in the United Kingdom and the United States over the past couple of years are ghastly. Moreover, chrono-displacement may affect all age groups. People who were born in the EU may still feel alienated from it. Imaginary epochs are kept alive via stories and quasi traditional folk-based identity presented by the media and echoed by populist propaganda. An image of the past, which is not more than a selection of suitable moments glued into a subjective portrait is what Meek calls fake nostalgia or temporal patriotism. Temporal migrants are more vulnerable to political identity traps then those living in the reality of the present. Spatial migration involves relocation and change of physical space, and it includes diasporas, displacement processes, refugees and asylum seekers, whereas temporal migration is the one happening on a mental level (such as nostalgia for communism or east Germany). Temporal migrants live in a different time frame, which overtakes their present; of course, there is no harm in this, as everyone is free to choose to live by the illusions we choose, but when such an option fuels fear, racism, xenophobia, and eventually results in election of similar thinkers into power, than it does matter.

Conclusion

There are many ways of losing and regaining dignity as it is emotionally loaded and potent. Perhaps we forget that transculturality, like migration, is a fluid and ongoing process. We may come to the realization that we are all transcultural beings if we cannot let go of the word 'culture'. It could arguably be a source of relief, not having to choose a nationality, an ethnicity or a gender, not having to fit ourselves into a box into which we do not fit anyway or will never fit, or not having to make another box for ourselves and be restricted by it. Transculturality is a way of being, including the embracing of hybridity and ambivalence. Welsch's idea of permeations feeds into the EU model where human dignity can be maintained, which we can then expand to a symbiocratic model by installing humans back to our rightful place in the living environment in between all the other living organisms and learn to live together.

Human dignity cannot be regained in the European context because it cannot be lost – it is declared inherent. But just as humans can be dehumanized, people can be made to feel as if they had no worth or no dignity; the subjective notion of dignity may be experienced as lost due to circumstances beyond control. Still, a volatile sense of worth can be regained, and it is through other humans that we can strive to maintain our own. It is not a one-off event but an ongoing process. In times of idealization of strength, the innate fragility of the human being is denied. However, we, humans as social creatures are weak, vulnerable, and dependent on our environment, which means that interdependency is not an opinion but a fact, applicable to all sentient beings. Unions, just like the EU, are administrative geopolitical projects that humans can make functional, the success of which will be the realization of it, and in return help us maintain circumstances in which we can preserve our dignity in an ongoing mutual recognition and negotiation of worth.

References

Bayertz, Kurt. 1996. "Human dignity: Philosophical origin and scientific erosion of an idea." In *Sanctity of Life and Human Dignity*, edited by Kurtz Bayertz, 73–90. London: Kluwer Academic Publishers.

Bralo, Zrinka. 2016. "Moral imagination and migration." *BBC Radio 4*, 26 October, https://www.bbc.co.uk/programmes/b07zzspl.

Charter of Fundamental Rights of the European Union. 2000. *Official Journal of the European Communities*, 18 December, https://www.europarl.europa.eu/charter/pdf/text_en.pdf.

European Commission. 2020. "The EU values." https://ec.europa.eu/component-library/eu/about/eu-values/.

Deutsch, Morton. 2006. "Cooperation and competition." In *The Handbook of Conflict Resolution: Theory and Practice*, edited by Morton Deutsch, Peter T. Coleman, and Eric C. Marcus, 23–42. San Francisco, CA: Jossey-Bass.

Huysmans, Jeff. 2000. "The European Union and the securitization of migration." *Journal of Common Market Studies* 38(5): 751–777.

Fisher, J. Ronald. 2006. "Intergroup conflict." In *The Handbook of Conflict Resolution: Theory and Practice*, edited by Morton Deutsch, Peter T. Coleman, and Eric C. Marcus, 176–196. San Francisco, CA: Jossey-Bass.

Janis, Irving L. 1982. *Groupthink*. Boston, MA: Houghton Mifflin.

Krastev, Ivan. 2018. *Zanikne Európska únia podobným spôsobom ako habsburská monarchia*. Bartislava: Kalligram.

Ľalík, Tomáš. 2019. "Human dignity in Slovakia." In *Handbook of Human Dignity in Europe*, edited by Paolo Becchi and Klaus Mathis, 799–815. Cham: Springer.

Lindner, Evelin G. 2006. *Making Enemies: Humiliation and International Conflict*. Westport, CT: Praeger.

Macklin, Ruth. 2003. "Dignity is a useless concept." *British Medical Journal* 327, 10.1136/bmj.327.7429.1419.

Meek, James. 2017. "Refugees from the past." *London Review of Books*. 5 January.

Rosen, Michael. 2012. *Dignity: Its History and Meaning*. Cambridge, MA: Harvard University Press.

Skinner, B. F. 1971. *Beyond Freedom and Dignity*. New York: Hackett Publishing.

Sabates-Wheeler, Rachel, and Rayah Feldman. 2011. *Migration and Social Protection: Claiming Social Rights Beyond Borders*. Basingstoke: Palgrave Macmillan.

Welsch, Wolfgang. 1999. "Transculturality and the puzzling forms of culture today." In *Spaces of Culture: City, Nation, World*, edited by Mike Featherstone and Scott Lash, 194–213. London: Sage.

Welsch, Wolfgang. 2009. "On the acquisition and possession of commonalities." In *Transcultural English Studies: Theories, Fictions, Realities*, edited by Frank Schulze Engler and Sissy Helff, 3–36. Amsterdam: Rodopi.

Williams, Raymond. 1976. *Keywords*. New York: Oxford University Press.

Wood, Allen. 1998. "Humanity as end in itself." In *Kant's Groundwork for the Metaphysics of Morals: Critical Essays*, edited by Paul Guyer, 165–187. Lanham, MD: Rowman and Littlefield.

Wood, Allen. 1999. *Kant's Ethical Thought*. Cambridge: Cambridge University Press.

Notes on Contributors

Kürşad Ertuğrul is an associate professor at the Department of Political Science and Public Administration at Middle East Technical University in Ankara.

Jasmin Hasanović is a senior teaching assistant at the Department of Political Science, University of Sarajevo.

Jan Květina works as a historian of ideas and political scientist at the Institute of History of the Czech Academy of Sciences and at the Metropolitan University in Prague.

Zuzana Lučkay Mihalčinová is a linguist and literary theorist, with research interests in dignity and human dignity, at the Technical University of Košice.

Leandrit I. Mehmeti is a discipline lead at South Australian Institute of Business and Technology at the University of South Australia.

Marius-Mircea Mitrache is an independent researcher with interests in French political thought, Franco-German relations, and European integration and diplomacy.

Migena Pengili is a scholar specializing in politics and European and international studies, United Kingdom.

Branislav Radeljić is a professor of international relations at Necmettin Erbakan University, Konya.

William Jay Risch is a professor of history at Georgia College in Milledgeville.

Lia Tsuladze is an associate professor of sociology at the Faculty of Social and Political Sciences, Tbilisi State University.

Elif Uzgören is a lecturer at the Department of International Relations, Dokuz Eylul University.

Biljana Vankovska is a professor of international relations and peace studies at Ss. Cyril and Methodius University, North Macedonia.

https://doi.org/10.1515/9783110684216-013

Index

https://doi.org/10.1515/9783110684216-014